A Cross Section of Educational Research

Journal Articles for Discussion and Evaluation

Second Edition

Lawrence S. Lyne

Editor

Pyrczak Publishing
P.O. Box 39731 • Los Angeles, CA 90039

This edition was prepared in collaboration with Randall R. Bruce.

Although the editor and publisher have made every effort to ensure the accuracy and completeness of information contained in this book, we assume no responsibility for errors, inaccuracies, omissions, or any inconsistency herein. Any slights of people, places, or organizations are unintentional.

Project Director: Monica Lopez.

Editorial assistance provided by Sharon Young, Brenda Koplin, Cheryl Alcorn, Erica Simmons, and Kenneth Ornburn.

Printed in the United States of America.

Pyrczak Publishing is an imprint of Fred Pyrczak, Publisher, A California Corporation.

ISBN 1-884585-29-9

Contents

Continued ➔

Combined Qualitative/Quantitative Program Evaluation

Appendices

Notes

Introduction to the Second Edition

This book is designed for students who are learning how to evaluate published educational research. The 30 research articles in this collection provide the stimulus material for such a course.

Selection of the Articles

Several criteria were used in the selection of the articles. The first criterion was that the articles needed to be comprehensible to students taking their first research methods course. Thus, to be selected, an article needed to illustrate straightforward designs and the use of basic statistics.

Second, since most education majors become teachers, the articles needed to deal with topics of interest to classroom teachers. To apply this criterion, students taking an educational research methods course were given the titles and abstracts (i.e., summaries) of a large number of articles to rate for interest. Only those that received moderate to high average ratings survived the screening of the initial pool of potential articles.

Third, the articles, as a whole, needed to illustrate a wide variety of approaches to research. You will notice in the table of contents that the articles represent 13 types of research such as Qualitative Research, Content Analysis, Survey Research, Correlational Research, and so on.

Finally, the articles, as a whole, needed to be drawn from a large number of different journals. Since each journal has its own genre as well as criteria for the selection of submissions for publication, students can get a taste of the wide variations in educational research only by reading articles from a wide variety of journals. Application of this criterion resulted in 30 articles drawn from 21 different journals.

How to Use This Book

In the field tests, one or two articles were assigned for homework at each class meeting. Students were required to read the article(s) and answer the questions at the end of each one. At the next class meeting, the article(s) were discussed with the instructor leading the discussion. Other arrangements are, of course, possible. For example, each student might be responsible for leading the discussion of one of the articles after all members of the class have read the article.

About the Questions at the End of Each Article

There are three types of questions at the end of each article. First, there are *Factual Questions*. The answers for these are explicitly stated in the articles. In addition to writing down the answers, students should record the line numbers where they found the answers. The line numbers will facilitate discussions if there are disagreements as to what constitutes a correct answer to a question.

Second, there are *Questions for Discussion*. Since these are designed to stimulate classroom discussions, most of them ask for students' opinions on various decisions made by the researchers in conducting and writing up their research. In the field tests, these questions led to lively classroom discussions. Since professional researchers often debate such issues with each other, students should not be surprised by such debates in their own classrooms.

Third, students are asked to make *Quality Ratings* for each article. This is done by applying 11 fundamental criteria for evaluating research. These criteria may be supplemented by the more extensive list presented in Appendix A or with lists of criteria that are found in some research methods textbooks.

Reading the Statistics in this Book

Students who have taken a statistics class as a prerequisite to their research methods class should feel quite comfortable with the overwhelming majority of statistics found in this collection since articles that contained large numbers of obscure or highly advanced statistics were excluded from this book.

Students who are learning about statistics for the first time in the course in which they are using this book may need some additional help from their instructors. Keep in mind that it is not realistic to expect instructors of a methods class to also teach a full-fledged course in statistical methods. Thus, there may be times when an instructor asks students to concentrate on the researcher's *interpretation* of statistics without getting bogged down in discussions of the theory underlying specific statistics. It is possible to focus on the interpretation instead of specific statistics because almost all researchers describe their results in words as well as numbers.

The Classification of the Articles

If you examine five different educational research methods textbooks, you will probably find that they all differ to some extent in their system for classifying various types or approaches to research. While some labels such as "true experiment," "qualitative research," and "survey" are common to almost all textbooks, others that you find in your textbook may be more idiosyncratic. In addition, some categories of research overlap each other. For example, when analyzing the results of a survey, a researcher may compute correlation coefficients, making it unclear whether it should be classified as a survey or as correlational research. An interesting classroom discussion topic is whether a given article can be classified as more than one type of research.

About the Second Edition

Many of the articles from the First Edition were retained in this edition. New to this edition are articles 2, 3, 4, 5, 10, 12, 13, 14, 15, 16, 17, 18, 20, 24, 25, 27, and 30. In addition, Appendix B, which provides guidance on the evaluation of qualitative research, has been added.

Acknowledgments

I am grateful to Mildred L. Patten, who is the author of a similar collection titled *Educational and Psychological Research: A Cross Section of Journal Articles for Analysis and Evaluation*. Her collection emphasizes broad issues of interest to psychologists and educators, while this book emphasizes topics of interest to classroom teachers. Nevertheless, some structural elements of her book were employed in this one such as the inclusion of three types of questions at the end of each article. She also provided me with advice on the criteria for selecting articles and numerous technical matters while I was preparing this book.

I also am indebted to the publishers who hold the copyrights to the articles in this book. Without their cooperation, it would not be possible to amass a collection such as you find here.

Lawrence S. Lyne

Article 1

Whole Language Teaching as Practiced by Kindergarten Teachers

JOYCE L. KOSTELNIK
Arizona State University West

FRANK S. BLACK
University of Tennessee at Martin

JOHNNA TAYLOR
Greenfield Elementary School

ABSTRACT. This research focused on the teaching behavior of a small sample of rural self-described whole language kindergarten teachers to determine the level of consistency between their perceptions of whole language teaching and the extent to which whole language concepts were applied in their classroom instruction. Locally constructed and pilot-tested forms, "Whole Language Checklist Observation Form" and "Focus Group Interview Schedule," were used to gather evidence of teaching behaviors. Results indicate that although these teachers were able to articulate the components of whole language teaching, they were unable or unwilling to incorporate many of its most central features into their classroom instruction. Implications for further research are discussed.

From *Reading Research and Instruction*, 37, 207–216. Copyright © 1998 by The College Reading Association. Reprinted with permission. All rights reserved.

Seldom has an education theory been identified with the level of confusion and conflict which surrounds the implementation of the whole language philosophy. Advocates of this approach to teaching acknowledge the potential for misinterpretation and misapplication of the central premises on which whole language is based (Church, 1994; Engle, 1993; Goodman, 1992; Hoffman, 1992; Pryor, 1990; Reid, 1993; Tidwell & Stele, 1992; Waterman, 1991). Primarily, whole language represents a set of beliefs about learning which includes the following: (1) learning occurs through these modes of communication: listening, speaking, reading, and writing, (2) learning takes place in social contexts, (3) teachers are mediators and facilitators rather than dispensers of knowledge, (4) students are participants in decision making and take responsibility for their own learning, (5) classrooms are safe, supportive and learner-centered rather than teacher-centered environments, (6) phonics is not taught separately but is blended holistically into the overall reading instruction, (7) constructing meaning is the central issue in literacy development, and (8) instruction for reading is predominantly literature based (Altwerger, Edelsky, & Flores, 1987; Flynn, 1994; Johnson & Stone, 1991; Newman, 1991; Pearson, 1989; Rich, 1985; Ruddell, 1992). Moreover, the application of whole language philosophy tenets, by their very nature, are individually organized and separately implemented by teachers in the field based on their recognition of the needs of their students (Mancus & Hill, 1992; Richards & Gipe, 1990; Willinsky, 1994). Since whole language theory is most often applied in elementary classrooms where a main focus is guiding children's literacy development, activities frequently involve authentic reading, writing, listening, and speaking (Black, 1993; Cecil, 1993; Burns, Roe, & Ross, 1996; Sherwood, 1993; Swan, 1992. Vassalto, 1992).

Research about the efficacy of whole language instruction has often focused on measuring success in reading (Pressley & Rankin, 1994; Richards & Gipe, 1990). Other research has compared whole language with other teaching methodology, particularly in reading instruction (Bright, 1989; Smith & Wham, 1993; Stice, 1991). Even though teacher beliefs have been discussed (Combs, 1994; Groff, 1991; Hatch, 1991; Smith, 1992; Targovnik, 1993; Tidwell & Stele, 1992; Wakefield, 1992), less is known about how teacher beliefs impact the implementation of whole language instruction (Bruneau, 1992; Gross, 1992; Pace, 1992; Shepperson & Nistler, 1992).

The purpose of this research was to contribute to the whole language research knowledge base by attempting to further clarify the relationship between teachers' understanding of whole language and the extent to which they practiced it in their instruction. It focused on the teaching behaviors of a small sample of rural kindergarten teachers with regard to their perceptions of what whole language is, the extent to which they applied its concepts in their teaching, and their primary concerns about whole language instruction.

Method

Subjects

Eleven kindergarten teachers in a small rural southeastern school district were selected to participate in this study. The district consisted of six schools with kindergarten programs and a total population of 22 female kindergarten teachers. To ensure representation from each school, two teachers were randomly selected from each school where there were three or more kindergarten teachers. Where there were less than three teachers per building, all were automatically included in the study. One teacher was included in the sample from a school with only one kindergarten class. The majority of the teachers had baccalaureate degrees and 10 to 20 years of teaching experience. Class sizes ranged from 18–20 students.

The subjects were divided into two groups. Focus Group A (FGA) consisted of five randomly assigned teachers plus the teacher from the single kindergarten class school. The remaining teachers composed Focus Group B (FGB).

Instrumentation

75   The Whole Language Checklist Observation Form (Appendix A) and the Focus Group Interview Schedule (Appendix B) were used to collect data for this study. Both of these instruments were locally constructed and pilot tested. The 15-item Observation Form was designed to identify the teachers' understanding of whole language and its most common components such as print-rich environments, integration of language instruction, holistic instruction and child-centered classroom orientations (Altwerger, Edelsky, & Flores, 1987; Flynn, 1994; Johnson & Stone, 1991; Newman, 1991; Pearson, 1989; Rich, 1985; Ruddell, 1992). The Interview Schedule consisted of 10 items and was designed to identify teacher perceptions, needs, concerns, and characteristics of their current practice as they relate to whole language instruction.

Procedures

Each group, FGA and FGB, was interviewed separately by the same researcher using the Focus Group Interview Schedule. The interviews were recorded using notes and audio tape. Transcribed tape and notes were then analyzed to identify themes and categories among subject responses. These were clustered as to the similarity of viewpoints that emerged regarding the three research questions: perceptions of what whole language is, application of whole language concepts, and concerns about whole language instruction.

To observe the extent of consistency between what subjects said they do regarding whole language and what they "actually" do in the classroom, FGA teachers were observed teaching. Specifically, following the interviews, unannounced classroom observations using the Whole Language Checklist Observation Form were conducted. Each of the six teachers was observed for one three-hour period. Because these schools serve as clinical sites for early field experience for preservice students, teachers and students were accustomed to having observers present in the classroom.

Results

Interviews

How do teachers define whole language? Interview responses in FGA and FGB were consistent. No formal definition was given. Instead, teachers expressed their understanding of whole language in general terms. They most commonly referred to it as an integration of learning into thematic wholes. They associated it with using big books, teaching subjects-themed units, including language arts with content-area subjects, and student-centered classroom orientations. Examples of their definitions of whole language were:

Incorporating the language experience into all academic areas using theme-based units throughout all subject areas.

Teaching through the involvement of multiple subjects around one appealing topic.

To what extent do teachers apply whole language con-

cepts in their teaching? Both focus groups reported the use of big books and phonic teaching within subjects as the whole language activities they most frequently engaged in with students. Interestingly, while they taught phonics in a separate structured program they also attempted to integrate it into other lessons. A heavy reliance on print material accompanying basal readers supplemented by newspapers, charts, and labeling were noted by both groups of teachers. These whole language characteristics which were reported to be major components of the teachers' instruction—thematic units, learning centers, and shared reading teaching strategies—are all strongly emphasized within the school district.

What concerns teachers most about using whole language concepts in their teaching? Overwhelmingly, teachers in both groups cited a need for more whole language training.

I kind of know what whole language is, but I'm not very clear about it.

I wish I had more information about whole language. I haven't had the opportunity since I've been out of school to learn much about it.

In my college classes we didn't even talk about whole language much. Maybe my college instructors weren't very informed or comfortable with it.

They also expressed concerns regarding preparation time.

I don't have enough time to create child-centered activities.

It really takes lots more time to make a class child-centered. I don't have that kind of time.

They identified their teaching orientation as teacher-centered and expressed a great deal of concern about their ability to maintain classroom control in child-centered environments.

I don't want to give up control to students.

I don't want to look unorganized or have a class get rowdy or out of control.

It really takes lots more time to make a class child-centered. It's difficult to prepare for instruction if students choose things differently than what I was planning for.

It requires too much spontaneous change in instruction, if I'm not sure what direction the students' interests are going to go.

How can I adequately prepare for a good class, if I don't know the direction things are going to go?

With regard to what would help them develop a better whole language program, the following were typical responses:

A better understanding of how to run (manage) learning centers.

Having readily available materials and a smaller class.

Also, when asked to identify limitations to whole language program implementation, teachers most commonly responded:

Too many children per teacher to keep activities flowing.

The difference in student ability and learning styles.

Observations

Results from the observation of the FGA teachers (Table 1) tended to support the interview results of both groups. All six teachers observed emphasized the use of print-rich material. Five of them utilized instructional integration. Only two were observed practicing holistic language instructional orientations. Child-centered and holistic learning instructional orientations were not characteristic of these teachers' instruction. On the other hand, thematic unit presentations, learning centers, and shared reading instructional strategies were practiced by all of these teachers.

Table 1
Observation Results by Teaching Characteristics

Characteristics	Practiced*
Print-rich environment	6
Integration	5
Holistic learning	2
Child-centered	2
Thematic units	5
Learning centers	6
Shared reading	5

*Number of teachers in Focus Group A (FGA) found practicing this characteristic.

Discussion

Teacher behavior is obviously key to the success of any teaching approach. The findings of this study suggest that these teachers have a clear perception and understanding of the general thinking about what whole language is and are consciously practicing some of its characteristics especially as evidenced by the emphasis on print-rich milieus and integration of subject-matter, both of which are consistent with the work of Pearson (1989), and Altwerger, Edelsky, and Flores (1987), respectively.

Interestingly, holistic and child-centered instruction were among the least practiced by the teachers. The child-centered finding was particularly surprising since it is considered to be one of the central and most common components of whole language instruction (Rich, 1985) and the teachers identified it in their definition of whole language. Only in two instances were teachers observed engaging in instructional behaviors that allowed students some choice about the activities in which they participated. In one of these two instances, the teacher was observed sitting quietly with one group of students involved in deciding on a topic to write a group story about, while the rest of the class was engaged in individual or group work concerning topics they had already selected.

Classroom management is clearly a matter of concern to these teachers. It is not likely that they will feel comfortable moving beyond the "safest" aspects of whole language until they develop management skills that enable them to maintain the level of classroom control they feel they must have. For these teachers student-centered instruction and teacher control must occur simultaneously.

Equally of interest was the apparent comfort these teachers feel with integration of subjects as compared to holistic instruction. All of them integrated the instruction of language arts such as reading and spelling. Many did so through the use of thematic unit instruction and learning centers. But the integration and holistic orientation tended to stop when it came to social studies, mathematics, and science subjects. These subjects were taught as distinct topics by the majority of these teachers. This was also the case with holistic phonics instruction, which was infrequently observed. It appears that the more skill-oriented the topic the less likely teachers are to engage in holistic teaching. Could this be a control factor again? Could it be that teachers feel pressured to control student time on tasks in these areas in an attempt to maximize student learning and/or performance on standardize tests for accountability reasons? Do they have the time to explore alternative instructional approaches such as holistic science, mathematics, or social science teaching given the increasing demands for more and more material to be covered in a school year?

Implications

The restricted sample and qualitative nature of this study prohibit any broad generalizations based on its findings. However, its results do suggest issues that should be considered by whole language advocates.

Implications for Meeting Teachers' Whole Language Education Needs

Few would argue that the whole language philosophy is not well known in education today. One has only to look at the raging debates over the level of definition specificity—whether one calls it a philosophy or strategy—to appreciate the on-going awareness of this educational movement. However, as is noted in this study and suggested in others, a more hands-on approach to concept implementation appears sorely needed. Whole language supporters should consider shifting their emphasis more rapidly beyond advocacy to concept demonstration. This approach with a special emphasis on classroom management is likely to better meet the needs of practicing teachers. Further, it seems that whole language demonstration projects that are provided in a way that capitalize on teachers' competence, commitment to and familiarity with existing teaching strategies such as thematic units and learning centers are likely to be the most successful.

Additionally, since the teachers involved in this study were individuals who had been teaching from 10 to 20 years, any university courses they may have had in their preservice preparation for teaching were unlikely to have a whole language orientation. Their understanding of whole language, therefore, would be limited to information presented through in-service activities, or their own efforts to read about and implement whole language strategies as described in the professional literature. Their obvious interest in whole language, evidenced by their self-identifications as whole language teachers, could be supported by school districts collaborating with each other and with universities to share current theory and methodology developments with these teachers.

Implications for Research

Future studies should include larger samples but remain qualitative oriented so as to continue efforts to clarify the definition of whole language, particularly in operational terms. At this stage in the development of the whole language movement, these efforts perhaps best lend themselves to context-specific situations as noted by Willinsky (1994). Therefore, specific attention should be paid to investigating what aspects of the whole language philosophy tend to be effective and under what conditions. For example, we have seen in this study that print-rich and integration orientations tend to work well with thematic unit, learning center, and shared reading instructional strategies in kindergarten learning environments. This context specific research approach is further underscored by Goodman (1990) who also observed that "some fundamental questions can be studied in whole-language classrooms in ways that were not possible before because of the authenticity of the language transactions and the integration around themes and problem solving" (p. 216).

In sum, it is hoped that this exploration of the whole language concept as perceived and practiced by kindergarten teachers contributes to an acceleration in reports that serve to enlighten our understanding of what works as well as what does not work with regard to whole language. It is only with this kind of direction will we realize the full potential of whole language in our classrooms.

References

Altwerger, B., Edelsky, C., & Flores, B. M. (1987). Whole language: What's new? *The Reading Teacher, 2*(41), 144-155.

Black, S. (1993). From whole to part. *Executive Educator, 15*(10), 35-38.

Bruneau, B. J. (1992). A case study of kindergarten teachers in the process of initiating a whole language literacy program. *Teaching and Learning, 6*(2), 33-41.

Church, S. M. (1994). Is whole language really warm and fuzzy? *Reading Teacher, 47*(5), 362-370.

Combs, M. (1994). Implementing a holistic reading series in first grade: Experiences with a conversation group. *Reading Horizons, 34*(3), 196-207.

Engle, B. S. (1993, November). *Valuing children: Authentic assessment based on observation, reflection and documentation.* Paper presented at the meeting of the New England Kindergarten Conference, Cambridge, MA.

Goodman, K. S. (1986). *What's whole in whole language?* Portsmouth, NH: Heinmann.

Goodman, K. S. (1989). Whole-language research: Foundations and development. *The Elementary School Journal, 90*(2), 207-221.

Goodman, K. S. (1992). I didn't found whole language (Distinguished educator series). *Reading Teacher, 46*(3), 188-199.

Groff, P. (1991). Teachers' opinions of the whole language approach to reading instruction. *Annals of Dyslexia, 41*, 83-95.

Hatch, J. A. (1991, May). *Out from between a rock and a hard place: Whole language in Tennessee.* Paper presented at the meeting of the International Reading Association, Las Vegas, NV.

Johnson, B., & Stone, E. (1991). Is whole language restructuring our classroom? *Contemporary Education, 62*(2), 102-104.

Mancus, D. S., & Hill, A. (1992). Teacher's transition to whole language: Learning to let the child lead. *National Association of Laboratory Schools Journal, 17*(1), 1-23.

McKenna, M., Robinson, R., & Miller, J. (1990). Whole language: A research agenda for the nineties. *Educational Researcher, 19*, 3-6.

Newman, J. M. (1991). Whole language: A changed universe. *Contemporary Education, 62*(2), 70-75.

Norman, G., Blanton, W., & McLaughlin, T. (1994). The rhetoric of whole language. *Reading Research Quarterly, 29*(4), 308-329.

Pace, G. (1992). Stories of teacher-initiated change from traditional to whole-language literacy instruction. *Elementary School Journal, 92*(4), 461-476.

Pearson, R. D. (1989). Reading the whole language movement. *The Elementary School Journal, 90*, 231-241.

Pressley, M., & Rankin, J. (1994). More about whole language methods of reading instruction for students at risk for early reading failure. *Learning Disabilities Research and Practice, 9*(3), 157-168.

Pryor, E. G. (1990). Whole language rhetoric: Clarifying misconceptions. *Ohio Reading Teacher, 25*(1), 15-22.

Reid, D. K. (1993). First invited response: Another vision of "Visions and Revisions," *Remedial and Special Education (RASE), 14*(4), 14-16.

Rich, S. (1985). Restoring power to teachers: The impact of whole language. *Language Arts, 2*(62), 717-723.

Ruddell, R. B. (1992). A whole language and literature perspective: Creating a meaning-making instructional environment. *Language Arts, 69*(8), 612-620.

Shepperson, G., & Nistler, R. I. (1992). Whole language collaboration project: Implementing change in one elementary school. *Reading Horizons, 33*(1), 55-66.

Smith, M. C., & Wham, M. A. (1993). The dialects of the whole language versus traditional instruction debate. *Reading Psychology, 14*(3), 205-227.

Tidwell, D. L., & Stele, J. L. (1992, December). *I teach what I know: An examination of teachers' beliefs about whole language.* Paper presented at the meeting of the National Reading Conference, San Antonio, TX.

Wakefield, A. P. (1992). An investigation of teaching style and orientation to reading instruction. *Reading Improvement, 29*(3), 183-187.

Waterman, D. C. (1991). Whole language: Why not? *Contemporary Education, 62*(2), 115-119.

Willinsky, J. (1994). Theory and meaning in whole language: Enjoying Norman, Blanton, and McLaughlin. *Reading Research Quarterly, 29*(4), 334-339.

Appendix A
Whole Language Checklist Observation Form

A. Classroom is a print-rich environment including books, magazines, newspapers, directories, posters, signs, packages, etc.

B. Teacher uses thematic units. List:

C. Teacher uses holistic learning.

D. Learning centers in the classroom. List:

E. The classroom characteristics are child-centered rather than teacher-centered. Students' work displayed on bulletin boards, in student-made books, etc. List:

F. Teacher is viewed as a facilitator—guides the students' learning, not dictates it. List instances occurring:

G. Use student-selected texts in place of basal reading texts. List:

H. All language arts are related and taught together. Language, spelling, and reading taught as integrated lessons.

I. Classroom uses shared reading. List stories read:

J. Teacher blends phonics into a holistic approach rather than teaching separately. Phonics is not taught as a separate lesson.

K. Lacks direct instruction of specific skills, integrates skills such as phonics into other lessons. List:

L. Uses mathematics, language, art, music, drama, and other communication systems as vehicles for exploration. List:

M. Uses cooperative activities. List:

N. Students are allowed to publish their work. Student libraries, etc. List:

O. Students use invented spelling.

Appendix B
Whole Language Focus Group Interview Schedule

1. What is whole language?
2. What are some characteristics of whole language?
3. Which of these do you use in your classroom?
4. Do you use phonics in a structured program or integrate it within other lessons?
5. What would better assist you in creating a better whole language program if you chose to implement one?
6. What are limitations that may keep you from fully implementing a whole language program?
7. What type of textbooks do you use in your classroom?
8. What is the best teaching method you currently use that enables your students to have a good understanding of print awareness?
9. Is your classroom more child-centered or teacher-centered?
10. What type of assessment do you use?

Exercise for Article 1

Factual Questions

1. In which lines do the researchers first explicitly state their research purpose?

2. Two teachers were selected from schools where there were three or more teachers. How were they selected?

3. What was the basis for assigning teachers to FGA and FGB?

4. The letters FGB stand for what words?

5. To collect data, what was done with FGA teachers that was not done with FGB teachers?

6. What "overwhelmingly" concerned the teachers most about using whole language concepts in their teaching?

7. The researchers characterized what finding as "particularly surprising"?

8. According to the researchers, what two things prohibit any broad generalizations based on this study?

9. Do the researchers recommend that future studies be quantitative or qualitative?

Questions for Discussion

10. In lines 3–8, the researchers mention the misinterpretation and misapplication of the central premises of whole language teaching. Would it be desirable for the researchers to explain these more fully? Explain.

11. The researchers state that they "pilot tested" the two instruments used in this study. Do you think that pilot testing was a good idea? Would you like to know more about the pilot tests? Explain.

12. The researchers state that "teachers and students were accustomed to having observers present in the classroom." From the viewpoint of research methodology, is this an important point? Explain.

13. Six teachers were each observed for a period of three hours—for a total of 18 hours of observation. In your opinion, is this sufficient for the purposes of this study? Explain.

14. The researchers mention "holistic learning" and "holistic instruction" in various places in the article. Would you be interested in knowing their definitions? Explain.

15. Consider Appendix A on the previous page. Would you be comfortable using this checklist if you were making observations in kindergarten classrooms? Are all the items clear to you? Explain.

16. If you were planning a study on the same topic, would you make any changes in the research methodology? Explain.

Quality Ratings

Directions: Indicate your level of agreement with each of the following statements by circling a number from 5 for strongly agree (SA) to 1 for strongly disagree (SD). If you believe an item is not applicable to this research article, leave it blank. Be prepared to explain your ratings.

A. The introduction establishes the importance of the study.

SA   5   4   3   2   1   SD

B. The literature review establishes the context for the study.

SA   5   4   3   2   1   SD

C. The research purpose, question, or hypothesis is clearly stated.

SA   5   4   3   2   1   SD

D. The method of sampling is sound.

SA   5   4   3   2   1   SD

E. Relevant demographics (for example, age, gender, and ethnicity) are described.

SA   5   4   3   2   1   SD

F. Measurement procedures are adequate.

SA   5   4   3   2   1   SD

G. All procedures have been described in sufficient detail to permit a replication of the study.

SA   5   4   3   2   1   SD

H. The participants have been adequately protected from potential harm.

SA   5   4   3   2   1   SD

I. The results are clearly described.

SA   5   4   3   2   1   SD

J. The discussion/conclusion is appropriate.

SA   5   4   3   2   1   SD

K. Despite any flaws, the report is worthy of publication.

SA   5   4   3   2   1   SD

Article 2

How Parents Influence African American Students' Decisions to Prepare for Vocational Teaching Careers

JEWEL EVANS HAIRSTON
Bowling Green State University

ABSTRACT. The purpose of this study is to determine how parents influence African American students' decisions to prepare for vocational teaching careers. Qualitative methodology addresses the research objectives. Twelve African American college students were interviewed to determine how parents influenced them to prepare for vocational teaching careers and specific vocational concentrations. The following five influences emerged: (a) desire to imitate parents' altruistic behavior and role as community contributors; (b) high academic and career expectations by parents; (c) parental support for academic and occupational endeavors; (d) parents providing early exposure to vocational subject matter and/or the teaching field, and (e) parents aiding in the discovery of aptitudes and interests in vocational subject matter. Implications for recruiting African American students are discussed.

From *Journal of Career and Technical Education*, *16*. Copyright © 2000 by JCTE. Reprinted with permission.

The career choice process of young people can easily be compared to rocks in a rock polisher. "All kinds of people grind away at them...but, parents are the big rocks in the tumbler" (Otto, 1989, pp. 2–3). Indeed, parents serve as major influences in the lives of their children (Otto, 1989). Of the factors that influence career choice processes, family members, particularly parents, are the most influential determinant of career plans, occupational aspirations, and occupational expectations (Hines, 1997; Lee, 1984; Leong, 1995; Parham & Austin, 1994). "Even if schools had the resources with which to meet young people's career guidance needs, neither teachers nor counselors can replace the influence parents have on their sons' and daughters' career plans" (Otto, 1989, pp. 1–3).

Although the literature is replete with factors influencing the career choice processes of individuals from various races and nationalities, research highlighted the influence and support of significant others as foremost factors in the career choices of African Americans (Kimbrough & Salomone, 1993; Parham & Austin, 1994). African American parents, specifically, serve as major influences that define the career choices of African American youngsters (Leong, 1995; Parham & Austin, 1994).

Teaching is a career that is widely available for African Americans today. Extreme shortages, however, exist within many teaching concentrations. A specific need for vocational teachers exists where there is an overrepresentation of African American students and an underrepresentation of African American teachers (Irvine, 1988; Newby, Newby, Smith & Miller, 1995; Riviera-Batiz, 1995). The shortage of African American vocational teachers becomes more evident when one considers that only 2% of African Americans in the United States is preparing to become vocational teachers. Additionally, African American vocational educators constitute a mere 7% of secondary faculty members and 5% of post-secondary faculty members (American Association of Colleges for Teacher Education, 1994). Discerning the influence of African American parents over their children's career choices may be useful for addressing this long-standing shortage.

The vocational teacher shortage is extensive; thus, finding solutions that will lead to solving the problem is imperative. Identifying adequate solutions may derive from identifying the influences of African Americans who enter teaching careers. If parents serve as major influences in the career choice processes of African American children, their influence may provide key determinants behind motivations to enter the specific field of vocational teaching. Thus, the focus of this study is to determine how parents or parental caretakers influence African American students to prepare for vocational teaching careers.

Review of Relevant Literature

Career choice theory provides roadmaps for interpreting career choice processes. Many well-known career choice theories, however, fail to directly address the career behavior of ethnic minority groups, particularly African Americans (Leong, 1995; Osipow, 1983; Roe, 1956). The major criticism of many influential theories that focus on parental influences and career choice processes embody a lack of concept focus relevant to African American career choice processes (Leong, 1995). Very often, African Americans are treated as a homogeneous group with little consideration being made for intra-group differences. This practice typically confounds the effects of race, gender, culture, and class. Additionally, racial differences in African American cultures are often compared with the characteristics of Whites, who are typically considered the norm in American

society. In this comparison, the racial differences of African Americans are frequently treated as deficiencies, with little caution exercised to positively elucidate the observed differ-
70 ence (Ponterotto, 1988; Simpson, 1996).

Because most traditional career-choice theories lack emphasis for African Americans, a review of relevant literature may provide a meaningful knowledge base for interpreting this phenomenon. To date, much of the research addressing
75 African American parental influence focused on career aspirations. Generally, parents' career aspirations aid children in selecting occupational goals, influence their knowledge of occupations, and familiarize them with occupational roles and requirements. Whether the child internalizes those aspi-
80 rations is greatly determined by numerous values found within the home. The occupational orientations of parents familiarize children with occupational roles, while the value orientations of parents provide the learning environment that motivates the aspirations of children (Lee, 1984). The aspi-
85 rations of African American parents specifically provide powerful influences over their children's career choices (Dawkins, 1989). This influence may be due to the close social networks found within African American families (Riley, 1995). Furthermore, the perceptions of African
90 American parental expectations exert greater influences on the career aspirations of their children than do individuals of other cultures (Evans, 1976; Fields, 1981).

Upon analyzing the specific roles of parents in this process, the literature clearly identified mothers as the most in-
95 fluential parent (Bracey, 1992; Dawkins, 1989; Fields, 1981; Simpson, 1996). In early adulthood, many African American children, particularly African American females (Bracey, 1992; King, 1993; Simpson, 1996), are influenced by the aspirations of their mothers. The employment status of
100 mothers as well as the mother–child relationship influence the vocational outcomes of African American children (Bracey, 1992). African American mothers influence their children by establishing middle-class values of hard work and responsibility, placing emphasis on education, maintain-
105 ing high expectations, and introducing cultural values (Simpson, 1996). As opposed to mothers, fathers play more of a complementary role in career decision-making (Schulenberg, Vondracek, & Crouter, 1984).

A study by King (1993) specifically linked parental be-
110 havior to the career choice of teaching. In King's study, 53% of the participants identified mothers as very encouraging in their choice of teaching. Additionally, mothers in the study created a desire in their children to work with individuals of diverse family backgrounds, to be creative, and to feel that
115 their abilities were well suited for teaching.

Purpose and Objectives

Because the shortage of vocational teachers is a prominent issue, the National Center for Research in Vocational Education (NCRVE) is assessing the state of the current vocational teacher shortage (Farrell, 1998). A search of the
120 literature did not reveal current studies that focus on increasing the number of African American vocational teachers—a group that has much to contribute to the career preparation

of a culturally diverse workforce of the 21st century. African American teachers serve as cultural translators that help all
125 children understand diversity. Additionally, because they provide a teaching perspective needed to produce an education for all students that contributes to achieving pride, equity, power, wealth and cultural continuity, as well as character development within the African American culture,
130 their presence is needed in the vocational classroom (King, 1993).

If parents are identified as the number one influence on African American children's educational and career planning decisions (Orfield & Paul, 1995), further research may
135 be useful in determining how African American parents influence the specific career choices of their youngsters (Leong, 1995). Therefore, studying the singular influence of parents or parental caretakers on vocational teaching career goals will make a contribution to career development litera-
140 ture while simultaneously seeking solutions to the African American vocational teacher shortage.

The following served as research objectives of the study:

1. Identify how parents or parental caretakers influence African American students to prepare for vocational
145 teaching careers.

2. Identify how parents or parental caretakers influence African American students to select specific vocational teaching concentrations.

Method

Participants in the study were enrolled in vocational li-
150 censure programs at six universities in two southeastern states. All programs were accredited by the National Council for Accreditation of Teacher Education (NCATE). The six universities included in the study maintained enrollments of 6,000 to 25,000 students; three were Historically Black Col-
155 leges and Universities (HBCUs) and three were Traditionally White Institutions (TWIs).

The qualitative nature of the study necessitated the selection of respondents who could provide useful data for addressing the research objectives. To purposefully select a
160 small homogeneous group that would provide rich responses to the interview questions, initial selection criteria were established. I sought African American respondents who showed promise for graduating from a vocational teacher licensure program and who were most likely to enter a voca-
165 tional teaching career after graduation. Thus, respondents were selected based on the following criteria: (a) junior- or senior-year status in an accredited vocational licensure program; (b) nomination by the department chair who observed the student's interest in a vocational teaching career and was
170 confident of the student's program completion; and (c) acceptable academic standing determined by grade reports held by department chairs. Respondents were preparing to teach in the vocational program areas of agricultural education, business education, marketing education, technology educa-
175 tion, trade and industrial education, and work and family studies education.

Fifty-one African American respondents met the initial criteria for the study. Another criteria for the study, indi-

viduals who attributed their vocational teaching career
180 choice to parental or parental caretaker influence, also
needed to be determined. A questionnaire was developed for
this purpose. A panel of professional peers reviewed each
questionnaire item to determine that all questions facilitated
identification of participants who met this second criterion.
185 The questionnaire also included demographic questions that
would allow me to contact individuals for follow-up interviews. Using this questionnaire, the 51 participants were
asked to identify the greatest personal influence that led to
vocational teacher preparation. This question helped deter-
190 mine who had been mostly influenced by parents or parental
caretakers to prepare for vocational teaching careers. Of the
51 participants selected for the study, 41 returned the questionnaire. Those who did not mention parents as their single
greatest influence were not retained for the study. Eighteen
195 participants identified parents as their greatest influence for
preparing for vocational teaching careers. Of the 18 respondents, 12 were willing to participate in the study. Seven respondents from the pool were male, five respondents were
female. Ages ranged from 20 to 29 years. Six of the respon-
200 dents attended HBCUs and six attended TWIs. Two respondents were interviewed from each of the six vocational program areas.

To allow a holistic view of the phenomenon under study,
I used qualitative research methodology (Patton, 1990) to
205 collect data from the 12 remaining respondents. Patton noted
that qualitative data consists of detailed descriptions of
events, situations, interactions, and observed behaviors, as
well as direct quotes from individuals about their beliefs,
experiences, attitudes, and thoughts. One-on-one interviews
210 with open-ended interview questions allowed me to ascertain
personal perceptions and interpretations of how parents influenced African American students to prepare for vocational teaching careers.

During the interviews, respondents were asked to re-
215 spond to the following questions: (a) How did your parents
influence your decision to prepare for a career as a vocational teacher? and (b) How did your parents influence your
decision to select your specific vocational concentration?
Probing questions were included but are not specifically
220 stated because they differed slightly depending upon how
respondents addressed the two main questions of the study.
Probing questions focused on the parent–child interactions
and the experiences parents provided during childhood,
which potentially influenced respondents to choose voca-
225 tional teaching careers and specific vocational teaching concentrations. For example, several respondents were asked to
elaborate on a specific item purchased by a parent or a
memorable activity or experience shared with parents that
influenced their vocational teaching career choice.

230 Respondents were interviewed at predetermined campus
locations. Each respondent was assured confidentiality verbally and in writing. The one-on-one audio and videotaped
interviews lasted approximately 60 to 90 minutes. Respondents validated transcribed interview data by verifying that
235 their thoughts and actions were accurately represented. To
develop a trustworthy study, it was necessary to establish

credibility, transferability, and confirmability of the data, the
data interpretations, and the conclusions (Lincoln & Guba,
1985). To ensure credibility, data collection methods were
240 triangulated because "no single method ever adequately
solves the problem of rival cause factors. Because each
method reveals different aspects of empirical reality, multiple methods of observation must be employed" (Denzin,
1978, p. 28). Triangulation was accomplished using audio-
245 taped interviews, videotaped observations, and respondent
verification of transcribed data. Transferability was established by providing "thick descriptions" (p. 279) of findings
for determination of their appropriateness in other settings.
Confirmability was ensured by clearly outlining the data
250 collection methods and withholding interview tapes, records
of data analysis, and transcripts for any necessary reanalysis
(Miles & Huberman, 1994).

The transcribed data were initially analyzed using NUD-
IST software. The NUDIST software program facilitated the
255 division of transcribed text into smaller units of information.
This allowed me to attach codes to the units and then locate
those units that were commonly coded. The transcribed data
were fractured and reassembled in different combinations.
Data were further analyzed and refined according to the con-
260 stant comparative method (Silverman, 1993). As units of
data were analyzed, they were continuously compared to and
against other units, including the unit itself. This process
allowed me to ascertain the meaning of data, generate additional questions, and develop new categories in the study.
265 Ultimately, it allowed me to confidently identify the five
parental influences presented as results.

Results

Five parental influences emerged from the data: (a) desire to imitate parents' altruistic behavior and role as com-
270 munity contributors; (b) high academic and career expectations by parents; (c) parental support in academic and occupational endeavors; (d) parents providing early exposure to
vocational subject matter and/or the teaching field; and (e)
parents aiding in the discovery of aptitudes and interests in
275 vocational subject matter. The first three influences led
respondents to prepare for vocational teaching careers and
address the first research question of the study. Respondents
discussed the parental influences that led them to prepare for
the career of teaching in general, as well as vocational teach-
280 ing specifically. The remaining two influences led respondents to enter specific vocational teaching concentrations
and address the second research question of the study. Respondents discussed how those influences affected their decision to prepare for specific vocational concentrations. Re-
285 sults pertaining to the five influences are presented in the
following sections.

Desire to Imitate Parents' Altruistic Behavior and Role As Community Contributors

Respondents shaped this theme by discussing how their
parents' roles as community contributors influenced their
desires to give to others through the general career of teaching, as well as through the specific teaching concentration of
290 vocational education. Feelings of pride were evident as re-

spondents referred to the numerous contributions of their parents within local communities. Consistent references to parents' community contributions through work, church, social, and civic organizations highlighted the impact of these contributions. Like their parents, respondents were eager to make notable contributions to the community. More than one-third of respondents expressed they could contribute to the community by becoming vocational teachers. For example, after discussing the contributions of a mother to a local elementary school, a work and family studies student indicated that vocational education was a way to make direct community contributions: "My mother was always doing something in our local community…I feel being in work and family studies allows me to indirectly work in a capacity where I can make contributions to local areas around the school."

As students acknowledged the altruistic nature of parents, they appeared to tap into their personal desires of benevolence. Respondents acknowledged their parents' roles as helpers, then cited their personal desires to help children through teaching. Approximately one-fourth of respondents indicated that vocational education, more than other subject areas, would provide opportunities to help others because of the natural tie between vocational subject areas and community involvement. Furthermore, giving back to other African American students was identified as a very attractive quality of vocational teaching.

High Academic and Career Expectations by Parents

This theme derived from parental expectations regarding educational endeavors, academic achievement, and career goal success. Respondents consistently recalled parents pushing them to earn outstanding grades as opposed to being content with average grades. Expectations of academic achievement affected respondents' perceptions of their vocational teaching career goals. Furthermore, expectations of outstanding grades made respondents set high personal expectations during the teacher preparation process. Because parents expected them to excel during vocational teacher preparation, they diligently worked to achieve the career goal of vocational teaching. An agricultural education student recalled how his father pushed him to achieve academic success and discussed how it affected his attitude to achieve as he prepared for a vocational teaching career:

I got my first "C" when I was in the sixth grade. I was like, "Well Dad, all the rest of the kids have 'Cs'." He said, "Yeah, well you see, you're not going to be a dumb black child. You're gonna strive. We don't have any dumb people in our family, and we're not going to start now." I won't forget that. From that day, I've been striving ever since.

According to Sanders (1997) many African American parents engage in positive racial socialization with their children and emphasize the importance of hard work, a good education, and racial pride for survival in society. Because of high academic expectations, respondents displayed determination to excel during the vocational teacher preparation process. Respondents believed that their parents viewed academic success as key to occupational success and per-

ceived academic success as increasing their chances of successfully becoming vocational teachers.

Parental Support in Academic and Occupational Endeavors

All respondents in the study indicated a sense of parental support for their vocational teaching career choice—support that strongly encouraged them to seek and complete pursuits in the field of vocational teaching. Respondents indicated that career-choice apprehensions were eased when parents approved of their decisions to prepare for vocational teaching careers. Furthermore, parental support indicated career choice approval and elicited expressions of pride among respondents as they witnessed their parents' esteem for vocational teaching. Parental support was additionally motivating when parents showed interest, support, and involvement in respondents' vocational student organization activities.

Mothers were cited as particularly influential because they provided support that eased respondents' apprehensions about vocational teacher preparation. This finding adds to a myriad of literature citing the strong influence of mothers on the career choice of children (Bracey, 1992; Dawkins, 1989; Fields, 1981; Simpson, 1996). Many respondents shared the feeling of one work and family studies education student who indicated, "My mother encouraged me when school was hard and told me to hang in there because I would do just fine; I really couldn't have done it without her."

Parents Providing Early Exposure to Vocational Subject Matter and/or the Teaching Field

It became initially evident that exposure to the field of teaching in general often related to preparing for vocational teaching specifically. Thus, this theme was based on teaching-related and/or vocationally related experiences gained during childhood. Vocationally related experiences are those that can be associated with specific vocational concentrations.

Respondents with parent educators were strongly influenced to enter teaching. Their parents helped them gain an understanding of the field through direct, frequent, and early exposure to the profession. At a young age, respondents developed an understanding of the duties, responsibilities, and lifestyles of a teacher and eventually began to consider teaching. One respondent preparing to become a marketing teacher explained, "…just hanging out around my mother's school, just getting a feel for what teachers do, I liked it….That whole background and involvement made me kind of interested in teaching."

Respondents were introduced to vocationally related experiences during early ages. All respondents entered the specific vocational concentration they associated with the experiences they shared with parents during childhood. They remembered the first childhood experience with a parent, the first childhood responsibility obtained from a parent, or the first toy purchased by a parent that created initial interests in vocational subject areas.

The simultaneous introduction by parents to vocationally related activities and to the general career of teaching was extremely influential. Herein lies the link between the choice of the general field of teaching and the choice of vocational teaching specifically. The notion of being surrounded by the teaching profession, intermingled with exposure to vocational activities, led respondents to an understanding of teaching as well as to an understanding of vocational content. An agricultural education student recalled experiences with his parent educator, which influenced him to prepare for a vocational teaching career in agricultural education:

> Dad, he always surrounded me with some kind of farming activity. At two or three I would ride out with my dad and feed cattle, play with the little baby calves, just do different things. He [dad] always had me traveling around with his students to different Future Farmers of America (FFA) contests. He would take me up to the meeting at the [state] Department of Agriculture when I was 12 years old, I was always surrounded by it [agriculture] in some shape or form.

King (1993) found that early discussion about teaching as a career choice was one of the most influential factors affecting a career choice of teaching. King indicated, "The more familiar an individual is with the requirements and rewards of the work world, the better equipped they are to make a career choice" (p. 204).

Parents Aiding in Discovery of Aptitudes and Interests Related to Vocational Subject Matter

Respondents were strongly influenced to teach vocational subjects when parents encouraged pursuits of activities associated with vocational concentrations. From there, students began to discover aptitudes for technical areas within specific vocational concentrations. Respondents who discovered strengths and interests in the hands-on aspects of vocational subject matter with their parents were interested in continuing those interests later in life. A technology education student recalled how his grandfather (his parental caretaker) influenced his decision to focus on the specific concentration of technology education by providing access to technology based activities:

> I was always into hands-on activities. Taking stuff apart when I was little.... Sometimes we [grandfather and I] would have contests to see who could put things together the fastest. I realized I was good with that kind of stuff.... When I was deciding on what type of job that I wanted to do, I was considering that.

Implications

In this study, parents or parental caretakers helped develop interests in vocational teaching careers and specific vocational concentrations. Parents accomplished this by serving as role models who enhanced the altruistic desires of respondents, supported respondents' decisions to pursue vocational teaching careers, set high achievement goals that would allow respondents to complete the teacher-preparation process, and introduced the positive aspects of teaching and vocational subject matter at a young age. Additionally, parents involved children in hands-on learning experiences, provided opportunities that nurtured interests in vocational subject matter, and created environments that nurtured the discovery of aptitudes for vocational content.

Although the goal of this study was to determine the influence of parents on their children's decisions to prepare for vocational teaching careers specifically, respondents made numerous references to parents influencing their decisions to become teachers in general. It is important to note that the desire to teach in general and the desire to teach vocational subjects specifically is not mutually exclusive. For some respondents, parents influenced their desires to become teachers before they discovered a specific vocational subject area. For other respondents, parents fostered love for a specific vocational subject prior to influencing their decision to prepare for teaching. In any respect, the choice to prepare for a career in vocational teaching was attributable to the positive experiences and to the overall support and encouragement provided by parents. Much can be learned from the positive career influences of parents in this study. The behaviors displayed by these parents should be mimicked in vocational educational environments frequented by young African American students. For example, those individuals who work closely with African American students in vocational settings should support students' decisions to enroll in vocational courses and should cultivate learning environments that foster student success.

To support the possible career choice of vocational teaching during years when students are making career choices, the parent–child interactions and learning environments fostered by parents should be duplicated specifically by those who closely interact with African American students such as vocational educators, guidance counselors, administrators, and college and school-system recruitment personnel. These individuals should interact with African American students on a personal level while exposing them to learning activities, projects, and co-curricular activities that will help identify interests, abilities, and aptitudes for vocational subject matter. While doing so, vocational educators and personnel should exhibit a pedagogy of care and concern for African American students' personal and educational success.

The high expectations of parents in this study and the response it caused within respondents should motivate guidance counselors and teachers to set high academic standards and target academically successful students for vocational programs. Because children's perceptions of expectations affect their academic achievement (Gill & Reynolds, 1996), parents, vocational educators, and administrators should expect students to perform well in vocational classes.

Based upon respondents' reverence for their parents' community contributions and the altruistic desires they tweaked, it is beneficial to highlight the community development potential of vocational teaching. Vocational student organizations provide specific implications for community outreach and should be used as a tool for attracting African American students to the profession. Additionally, vocational programs at the secondary and post-secondary levels should be promoted by emphasizing participation in co-curricular organization activities.

In summary, all parental influences derived from this study have implications for vocational education. These influences—which include parents serving as role models of altruism, parental support for career goal achievement, high grade expectations, introductions to the positive aspects of

teaching and vocational subject matter, parents involving children in hands-on learning experiences, and the creation
515 of environments that nurture the discovery of vocational content—are all important in creating interest in vocational education and vocational teaching. Each factor serves as a necessary element that creates excitement in vocational subject matter and incites desires to be a part of vocational
520 teaching. It may not be possible to duplicate all of the parental influences presented in this study, but emphasizing and utilizing these influences may provide ways to motivate African Americans to become vocational teachers and may provide answers to alleviating the shortage of African
525 American vocational teachers.

References

American Association of Colleges for Teacher Education. (1994). *Teacher education pipeline III: Schools, colleges, and departments of education enrollments by race, ethnicity, and gender.* (ERIC Document Reproduction Service No. ED 369 780)

Bracey, G. W. (1992). Predicting school success for at-risk children. *Phi Delta Kappan, 74*(2), 104–117.

Dawkins, M. P. (1989). The persistence of plans for professional careers among blacks in early adulthood. *Journal of Negro Education, 58*(2), 220–233.

Denzin, N. K. (1978). *Sociological methods.* New York: McGraw-Hill.

Evans, C. (1976). *Significant other influence and career decisions: Volume I. black and white male urban youth.* Ohio: National Center for Vocational Education Research. (ERIC Document Reproduction Service No. ED 159 332)

Farrell, G. (1998, September). Voc. ed. teacher recruitment at crisis level nationwide. *Education Daily, 31*(182), 1 & 3.

Fields, B. A. (1981). Some influences upon the occupational aspirations of three white-collar ethnic groups. *Adolescence, 16*(63), 663–684.

Gill. S., & Reynolds, A. J. (1996, August). Role of parent expectations in the school success of at-risk children. Paper presented at the biennial meeting of the International Society for the Study of Behavior Development, Quebec, Canada.

Hines, M. S. (1997, March). *Factors influencing persistence among African American upperclassmen in natural science and science related majors.* Paper presented at the Annual Meeting of the American Education Research Association, Chicago, IL.

Irvine, J. J. (1988). An analysis of the problem of the disappearing black educator. *Elementary School Journal, 88*(5), 503–514.

Kimbrough V. D., & Salomone, P. R. (1993). African Americans: Diverse people, diverse career needs. *Journal of Career Development, 19*(4), 265–279.

King, S. H. (1993). The limited presence of African American teachers. *Review of Educational Research, 63*(2), 115–149.

Lee, C. L. (1984). An investigation of the psychosocial variables in the occupational aspirations and expectations of rural black and white adolescents: Implication for vocational education. *Journal of Research and Development in Education, 17*(3), 28–440.

Leong, F. T. L. (1995). *Career development and vocational behavior of racial and ethnic minorities.* New Jersey: Lawrence Erlbaum Associates.

Lincoln, Y. S., & Guba, E. G. (1985). *Naturalistic inquiry.* Newbury Park, CA: Sage Publications.

Miles, M. B., & Huberman, A. M. (1994). *Qualitative data analysis* (2nd ed.). Thousand Oaks, CA: Sage Publications, Inc.

Newby, D., Smith, G., Newby, R., & Miller, D. (1995). The relationship between high school students' perceptions of teaching as a career and selected background characteristics: Implications for attracting students of color to teaching. *The Urban Review, 27*(3), 235–249.

Orfield, G., & Paul, F. G. (1995). *High hope and long odd: A major report on Hoosier teens and the American dream.* Indianapolis, IN: Indiana Youth Institute. (ERIC Document Reproduction Service No. ED 378 463)

Osipow, S. H. (1983). *Theories of career development* (3rd ed.). Englewood Cliffs, NJ: Prentice-Hall.

Otto, L. B. (1989). *How to help your child choose a career.* Florida: State Department of Education. (ERIC Document Reproduction Service No. ED 336 506)

Parham, T. A., & Austin, L. A. (1994). Career development and African Americans: A contextual reappraisal using the nigrescence construct. *Journal of Vocational Behavior, 44*(2), 139–154.

Silverman, D. (1993). *Interpreting qualitative data.* London: Sage Publications.

Simpson, G. (1996). Factors influencing the choice of law as a career by black women. *Journal of Career Development, 22*(3), 197–209.

Exercise for Article 2

Factual Questions

1. Does the researcher regard teaching as a career that is widely available for African Americans today?

2. Are there other current studies that focus on increasing the number of African American vocational teachers?

3. How many African American respondents met the *initial* criteria for being included in the study?

4. According to Patton (1990), qualitative data consists of detailed descriptions of what things?

5. Were respondents assured of confidentiality? If yes, how were they assured?

6. How was triangulation accomplished?

Questions for Discussion

7. In your opinion, are the initial selection criteria described in sufficient detail? Explain. (See lines 159–176.)

8. Respondents validated transcribed interview data by verifying that their thoughts and actions were accurately represented. To what extent does this increase your confidence in the validity of the results reported in this research report?

9. If you had conducted this study, would you have chosen qualitative *or* quantitative methodology? Explain.

10. Do you regard this study as "scientific" even though it does not contain statistical results? Explain.

11. Were any of the results especially surprising to you? Were any specially interesting? Explain.

12. Based on your insights gained from reading this study, what recommendations would you make to someone who might want to conduct future research on this topic?

Quality Ratings

Directions: Indicate your level of agreement with each of the following statements by circling a number from 5 for strongly agree (SA) to 1 for strongly disagree (SD). If you believe an item is not applicable to this research article, leave it blank. Be prepared to explain your ratings.

A. The introduction establishes the importance of the study.

SA   5   4   3   2   1   SD

B. The literature review establishes the context for the study.

SA   5   4   3   2   1   SD

C. The research purpose, question, or hypothesis is clearly stated.

SA   5   4   3   2   1   SD

D. The method of sampling is sound.

SA   5   4   3   2   1   SD

E. Relevant demographics (for example, age, gender, and ethnicity) are described.

SA   5   4   3   2   1   SD

F. Measurement procedures are adequate.

SA   5   4   3   2   1   SD

G. All procedures have been described in sufficient detail to permit a replication of the study.

SA   5   4   3   2   1   SD

H. The participants have been adequately protected from potential harm.

SA   5   4   3   2   1   SD

I. The results are clearly described.

SA   5   4   3   2   1   SD

J. The discussion/conclusion is appropriate.

SA   5   4   3   2   1   SD

K. Despite any flaws, the report is worthy of publication.

SA   5   4   3   2   1   SD

Article 3

The Developmental Progression of Children's Oral Story Inventions

EUGENE GEIST
Ohio University

JERRY ALDRIDGE
University of Alabama, Birmingham

ABSTRACT. This study investigated stories that children created after being told the Grimm version of selected tales. These stories were told as an instruction to the children on story structure and to familiarize children with ideas of plot, character, and conflict in stories. This cross-sectional study considered what differences are evident in the oral fairy tales that children tell at different ages. Stories from children in kindergarten, first grade, second grade, and third grade were collected and analyzed.

For the purpose of this study, the following research questions were asked. These questions guided the research and eventually became the major coding categories.

1) Is there a developmental difference in the type of story (i.e., personal narrative, fantasy, realistic fiction) children tell when they are asked to invent a fairy tale?
2) Are there developmental differences in the content of children's stories among age groups?
3) Are there developmental differences in how children organize the content of their invented fairy tales?

A qualitative research methodology was used for this study. Children's orally invented stories were tape-recorded and transcribed. The data were analyzed using content analysis of the transcripts.

This study indicates that children's orally told invented fairy tales can be used (a) to promote cognitive development, (b) to assess cognitive development, and (c) to identify emotional conflicts that children are experiencing. This study also indicates that second grade is a good time to promote creativity and imaginations as this was the age in which children were most confident in their imaginative abilities.

From *Journal of Instructional Psychology*, 29, 33–39. Copyright © 2002 by *Journal of Instructional Psychology*. Reprinted with permission.

Few studies have been conducted on children's oral story inventions (Aldridge, Eddowes, Ewing, & Kuby, 1994). Studies on children's interest in folk and fairy tales have not touched on children's invented "fairy tales" and how they can reflect developmental issues. There have been many examinations of written retellings of fairy tales (Boydston, 1994; Gambrell, Pfeiffer, & Wilson, 1985; Morrow, 1986). However, few works have examined oral stories invented by children. Invented oral stories can give a valuable insight into a child's cognitive, affective, and creative development (Allan & Bertoia, 1992; Markham, 1983; Sutton-Smith, 1985).

This study investigated stories that children created after being told the Grimm version of selected tales. These stories were told as an instruction to the children on story structure and to familiarize children with ideas of plot, character, and conflict in stories. The Grimm (1993) versions were chosen because the literature suggests that they are the closest to the oral tradition (Zipes, 1988). This cross-sectional study considered what differences are evident in the oral fairy tales that children tell at different ages. Stories from children in kindergarten, first grade, second grade, and third grade were collected and analyzed (Geist & Aldridge, 1999).

For the purpose of this study, the following research questions were asked. These questions guided the research and eventually became the major coding categories.

1) Is there a developmental difference in the type of story (i.e., personal narrative, fantasy, realistic fiction) children tell when they are asked to invent a fairy tale?
2) Are there developmental differences in the content of children's stories among age groups?
3) Are there developmental differences in how children organize the content of their invented fairy tales?

Method

A qualitative research methodology was used for this study. Children's orally invented stories were tape-recorded and transcribed. The data were analyzed using content analysis of the transcripts. According to Carney (1972), "content analysis is any technique for making inferences by objectively and systematically identifying specified characteristics of messages" (p. 25).

A semistructured interview format was used to collect data. The children were asked to make up a fairy tale and tell it to the researcher. The researcher prompted the subject if there was a long pause. The researcher also had the child start over if the child was engaging in a retelling of a story that the researcher recognized. The data were then analyzed using a content analysis.

Participants

Convenience sampling was the method used to select study participants. The classrooms chosen were believed to facilitate the expansion of a developing theory because the sample was homogeneous. All subjects were African American and from low socioeconomic families. The subjects for this study were students in four classrooms at an elementary school in a low socioeconomic area of an urban city in the

55 southeastern United States. The racial makeup of the sample was 100% African American.

Data Collection

Each classroom participated in a 45-minute lesson on fairy tales and story structure each day for 4 days. The les-
60 son consisted of reading and discussing the plots and characters of fairy tales. After the 4 days, the children were asked, individually, to make up a fairy tale and tell it orally. The stories were tape-recorded and transcribed. A content analysis of the transcripts was performed as described by Carney (1992).
65 One kindergarten, one first-grade, one second-grade, and one third-grade classroom, each with approximately 15 students, participated in this study. Each classroom was given an identical session on fairy tales and story structure. This session consisted of reading fairy tales to the students and
70 discussing the aspects of the story. The specific description of the 5 days of storytelling and discussion are found in Geist and Aldridge (1999). These procedures were modified from Allan and Bertoia (1992) by Boydston (1994). Allan and Bertoia developed a procedure to initiate the discussion
75 of fairy tales. This outline was used for seventh graders; however, because this study was interested in students in kindergarten, first, second, and third grades, a procedure modified by Boydston (1994), was used for this study. Boydston's outline was developed for second graders but is
80 appropriate for the ages targeted in this study.

Data Analysis

Analysis of the data was generated from the transcripts of the audiotapes. The research questions served as a guide for conducting the analysis. Each question became a major coding category broken down by age. The results of each
85 age were then compared to each other to build a model of children's invented fairy tales. Bogdan and Biklen (1992) stated that preassigned coding systems are developed when researchers explore particular topics or aspects of the study.

Inter-rater reliability was conducted on this study by hav-
90 ing an educational professional with extensive knowledge of fairy tales and their form, function, and uses independently categorize the data. Another rater was trained in content analysis and was experienced in the content analysis method. This researcher had performed qualitative studies on fairy
95 tales and children's storytelling in the past. The two raters participated in two practice sessions of reading and analyzing children's oral invented stories.

The recordings were transcribed and copied. The independent rater and the researcher received identical copies of
100 the transcripts. Because the three foreshadowed questions that were used as a framework for the categories, the independent rater was given a copy of the foreshadowed questions. Each rater read the transcripts as many times as needed and noted themes related to genre, content, and or-
105 ganization. Each rater then independently compared the common themes from each grade and constructed a model for genre, content, and organization.

Both raters discussed the method for analysis before beginning. When a theme or thread was identified, it was high-
110 lighted by a colored marker that identified it with other items that belonged with that thread. The rater wrote notes in the margin next to this highlighted text. Then all of the text passages with the same color highlight were collected by grade. The rater then reread the passages and came up with a phrase
115 or word that best described the common characteristics of those passages. The descriptive phrases were then compared to the phrases for the other grades to determine if a model could be constructed. Often, there was more than one model that was evident in each of the categories.
120 These themes and models were then compared. The themes and models that were consistent between the two raters were retained and clarified. The themes and models that were not consistent between the two raters were not included. Each story was then categorized independently by
125 each rater into the rough model that had been developed.

Results

Findings from this study suggest a developmental shift in the genre, content, and organization of children's oral invented stories. The genre of the children's stories moved from the fantastical to stories based on personal experiences.
130 Kindergarten children told mostly fantasy stories, first and second graders told mostly realistic fiction, and third graders told mostly personal narratives.

The content of the children's stories showed development in two areas. First, there was development in the basis
135 of their stories. Kindergarten children based their stories on previously heard material, first graders based theirs on familiar surroundings, second graders based their inventions on their imagination, and third graders tended to base their stories on personal experiences.
140 Second, there was development in how parents were depicted in the stories. Kindergartners, first, and second graders depicted parents as heroes and comforters. Third graders depicted parents as authority figures.

The content of the stories of all the grades contained re-
145 flections of the children's fears and concerns from everyday life. Fears about being kidnapped or other stresses, such as performance anxiety and social pressures, were reflected in their stories.

The organization of the stories moved from disjointed
150 sentences to a coherent whole story. States that could be delineated were (a) disjointed, (b) phrase disjointed, (c) short-utilitarian, (d) sidetracked, and (e) coherent whole.

Genre

The development of genre moved from the fantastical notions of kindergartners to the realistic personal narratives
155 of third graders. Kindergartners told fantastical stories of talking umbrellas, flying to Mars, magic, and evil witches that turned children into food. First and second graders told realistic fiction stories about hunters, kings, queens, and an occasional witch; however, almost all of the actions of the
160 characters were in the realm of possibility. Third graders tended to tell personal narratives that related directly to their life experiences; they were simply retelling events that happened to them or to someone they knew.

The study suggests the genre was influenced by three things. First, it was influenced by the classroom context. In the kindergarten classroom, the researcher observed a lot of fantasy literature. Children heard stories daily about talking animals and fantastical actions in the books the teachers read to them. However, as the grades progressed, the researcher observed that the teachers provided more realistic literature and less fantasy. This, in turn, affected the genre of the stories that the children told. Second was the children's developing understanding of the difference between fantasy and reality. As children begin to understand the concept of causality and move into concrete operations, the concept of what is possible and logical versus what is illogical, magical, and impossible becomes more delineated. The second- and third-grade stories reflect this move toward reality based stories. Third was the base material that children chose. As we have already mentioned, children tended to choose more personal material as they got older until at third grade they tell personal, true to life personal narratives. Obviously, this shift is going to affect the genre of the story that they tell. This will be discussed further in the examination of the content of the children's stories.

Content

There were three developmental themes that could be delineated in the content of the children's stories. The first was the basis that the children used to construct their stories. The second was the role of parents in the children's stories. Third, the content of all the grades contained reflections of children's fears and concerns.

Children in kindergarten based their stories on previously heard material. They did not appear confident in their ability to be successful in making up a story on their own, so they used stories that they had heard or read recently to build their story around. First graders were a little more sure of themselves so they did not need specific stories on which to base their inventions. However, they still needed to base the settings and characteristics on things that were familiar to them. This gave them the framework for their stories. By second grade, the children did not need outside structure on which to build their stories. They could rely on their imagination completely as the basis for their stories. In third grade, the surge of imagination noted in second grade appeared to be gone. Either by discouragement or development, children had given up on imagination as the basis of their stories. These children told personal narratives that used personal experiences as the basis for their inventions. These types of stories required little or no imagination.

A second developmental theme evident in the content of the children's orally invented stories was that at around third grade children began to consider peers, rather than parents, as their primary social contacts. This transition was reflected in their stories. In kindergarten and first grade, children were still primarily dependent on their parents for social and emotional interaction. However, around second grade they began to bond with peers, and the peer group became their primary social group with many third graders.

Before third grade, parents in children's stories were heroes and comforters. It was they who rescued the child from the grasp of the monster. A major shift had occurred in the third graders' stories, when parents were depicted as strict authority figures who were present to judge and punish. Third grade children's stories showed a common theme of fear of parental reprisals in this sample.

The stories also show a reflection of children's fears and anxieties. Children are surrounded with stress that is often not released. Stories offer children this release. The stories of all the grades contained personal reflections of fears and stresses. Especially prevalent were fears of kidnap and murder. The children in this particular school had experience with a classmate being kidnapped and murdered, so it is not surprising that this fear appeared in their stories.

Organization

Three developmental aspects of children's organization of invented stories were determined in this study. These included:

1) There was a clear developmental sequence to the way children organized their stories.
2) Egocentrism decreased through interactions in the social environment.
3) The distinction of the difference between fantasy and reality developed with age.

Even after the children were involved in the 4-day workshop on fairy tales, a developmental pattern still emerged. This suggests that there are aspects to children's understanding of story structure that are developmental and cannot be totally directly taught. The workshop focused on the characters, settings, plot, and organization of fairy tales. The children were instructed that fairy tales have a clear beginning, middle, and end; the beginning contains an introduction of the characters, setting, and problems; the middle of the story discusses how the characters go about solving the problems; and the end of the story contains the resolution. Thus, the children were familiar with the parts of the stories, and still a majority of the children were unable to use the information given in the workshops to construct a coherent whole story. This suggests that the progression through stages of organization is developmental and not based on training.

There was a cognitive developmental sequence in the organization of children's oral invented stories. So distinct were the differences, a developmental model can be proposed based on the data. The first stage can be characterized by the children being unable to form a coherent, ordered whole story. They told disjointed stories in which individual thoughts were juxtaposed. This is consistent with the findings of Piaget (1958) that children could not order a story into a coherent whole until about the age of 8.

In the second stage, the children could string a series of thoughts together into coherent phrases; however, the phrases of about two or three sentences were juxtaposed against other phrases to which they had little relationship. In the third stage, children told short, utilitarian stories that just included the basics of a story with no elaboration. The children were attempting to keep their stories ordered and co-

275 herent and, if there was too much information, they got confused.

The fourth stage showed the result of this confusion. Children got sidetracked because they included more elaboration and lost track of the original storyline. Eventually,
280 they got back on track and ended the story on the same theme with which they started. The final stage was characterized by children telling a coherent, elaborate story from beginning to end without getting sidetracked.

Conclusions and Implications

This study showed that literacy is not totally in the do-
285 main of social knowledge. The learning of words, letters, and rules of language must be passed down through the culture; these aspects of literacy cannot be invented by children without help. However, there are aspects of literacy that involve what Piaget deemed logico-mathematical knowledge.
290 This study suggests that story structure is, at least partially, logico-mathematical knowledge. The part–whole relationship (Piaget, 1970) plays a part in the structure of children's stories. The children in this study all received direct instruction on story structure, but still a developmental sequence
295 was evident. Children's understanding of story structure is dependent on more than direct instruction.

Story structure is learned through interaction with text and words rather than through direct instruction. Children will invent story structure by telling and writing stories. The
300 reactions from the audience and from their rereading or listening to other students' stories cause disequilibrium, which according to Piaget (1970), leads to development.

This study indicates that children's orally told invented fairy tales can be used (a) to promote cognitive develop-
305 ment, (b) to assess cognitive development, and (c) to identify emotional conflicts that children are experiencing. This study also indicates that second grade is a good time to promote creativity and imagination, as this was the age in which children were most confident in their imaginative abilities.

310 Orally invented stories can be used to promote cognitive development. Each time children tell a story, they must attempt first to order it mentally. This mental activity promotes the construction of knowledge. A developmental sequence to the organization of orally told stories appears evi-
315 dent from the stories children told in this study. To promote the movement through these developmental stages, children must be provided with the opportunity to tell stories to an audience and receive social interaction. Each time the child tells a story, the reaction from the audience causes disequi-
320 librium. If the audience does not understand the story, the child must examine why the audience did not understand it. This type of construction through social interaction was also described by Kamii (2000) in math development. This works just as well for storytelling. The feedback from peers helps
325 the child to overcome the limitations of egocentrism and egocentric thought.

Orally told invented fairy tales can also be used for assessment of children's cognitive abilities. This can give a teacher an idea of the areas in which a child might need
330 work. This study was consistent with Piaget (1952) with regard to developmental sequences through which children must progress. This sequence can be used to assist in screening students who might need assistance.

These stories can be used to identify emotional differ-
335 ences or possible traumas in children's lives. As this study and others have shown (Allan, 1988; Allan & Bertoia, 1992), children include stressful events and emotional problems they are dealing with in their stories. These orally told stories could help screen for physical and sexual abuse, fears
340 and concerns, and emotional problems.

While this study showed promise for identifying developmental changes in children's oral storytelling inventions from kindergarten through third grade, much more research needs to be done. Researchers should also seek to "identify
345 individual and cultural variations in the discourse and oral inventions of young children" (Geist & Aldridge, 1999, p. 822).

References

Aldridge, J., Eddowes, A., Ewing, J., & Kuby, P. (1994). Analytical psychology, constructivism, and education. *Journal of Instructional Psychology, 21*, 359–367.

Allan, J. (1988). *Inscapes of the child's world.* Dallas, TX: Spring Publications.

Allan, J., & Bertoia, J. (1992). *Written paths to healing.* Dallas, TX: Spring Publications.

Bogdan, R., & Biklen, S. (1992). *Qualitative research for educators* (2nd ed.). Boston: Knopp.

Boydston, R. (1994). *Written retellings of fairy tales.* Unpublished doctoral dissertation, University of Alabama at Birmingham, Birmingham, Alabama.

Carney, T. F. (1972). *Content analysis: A technique for systematic inference from communication.* Winnipeg, Manitoba: University of Manitoba Press.

Gambrell, L. B., Pfeiffer, W. R., & Wilson, R. M. (1985). The effects of telling upon reading comprehension and recall of text information. *Journal of Educational Research, 78*, 216–220.

Geist, E. A., & Aldridge, J. (1999). Genre, content, and organization of kindergarten children's oral story inventions. *Psychological Reports, 85*, 817–822.

Grimm Brothers. (1993). *The complete Brothers Grimm fairy tales.* New York: Pantheon Books.

Kamii, C. (2000). *Young children reinvent arithmetic* (2nd ed.). New York: Teachers College Press.

Markham, R. H. (1983). The fairy tale: An introduction to literature and the creative process. *College English, 45*, 31–45.

Morrow, L. M. (1986). The effect of structural guidance in story retellings of children's dictation of original stories. *Journal of Reading Behavior, 18*, 135–151.

Piaget, J. (1952). *The thought and language of the child.* London: Humanities Press.

Piaget, J. (1958). *The growth of logical thinking from childhood to adolescence.* New York: Basic Books.

Piaget, J. (1970). *Structuralism.* New York: Basic Books.

Sutton-Smith, B. (1985). The development of fictional narrative performances. *Topics in Language Disorders, 7*, 1–10.

Zipes, J. (1988). *The Brothers Grimm.* New York: Routledge.

Address correspondence to: Dr. Eugene Geist, Ohio University, W324 Grover Center, Athens, OH 45701.

Exercise for Article 3

Factual Questions

1. According to Carney (1992), what is "content analysis"?

2. How many first-grade classrooms participated in this study?

3. The themes and models that were included had to be consistent among how many raters?

4. Children at what grade level told mostly fantasy stories?

5. At what grade level(s) did the children's stories reflect children's fears and concerns of everyday life?

6. At what grade level did children begin to consider peers, rather than parents, as their primary social contacts?

Questions for Discussion

7. The researchers state that they used a "convenience sample." What do you think this term means?

8. The researchers state that all four classrooms were given an identical session on fairy tales and story structure. Is it important to know that they were "identical"? Explain.

9. In your opinion, is the description of the lessons adequate? If no, what else would you like to know about them? (See lines 57–80.)

10. The authors discuss "inter-rater reliability." In your opinion, how important is this information for evaluating the reliability of the results of this study? Explain. (See lines 89–125.)

11. Do you agree with the researchers that orally told stories could help screen for physical and sexual abuse, fears and concerns, and emotional problems? (See lines 338–340.)

12. This study is qualitative and does not report any statistical analyses. In your opinion, is the study "scientific"? Explain.

13. If you were conducting a study on the same topic, what changes, if any, would you make in the research methodology? Explain.

Quality Ratings

Directions: Indicate your level of agreement with each of the following statements by circling a number from 5 for strongly agree (SA) to 1 for strongly disagree (SD). If you believe an item is not applicable to this research article, leave it blank. Be prepared to explain your ratings.

A. The introduction establishes the importance of the study.

       SA   5   4   3   2   1   SD

B. The literature review establishes the context for the study.

       SA   5   4   3   2   1   SD

C. The research purpose, question, or hypothesis is clearly stated.

       SA   5   4   3   2   1   SD

D. The method of sampling is sound.

       SA   5   4   3   2   1   SD

E. Relevant demographics (for example, age, gender, and ethnicity) are described.

       SA   5   4   3   2   1   SD

F. Measurement procedures are adequate.

       SA   5   4   3   2   1   SD

G. All procedures have been described in sufficient detail to permit a replication of the study.

       SA   5   4   3   2   1   SD

H. The participants have been adequately protected from potential harm.

       SA   5   4   3   2   1   SD

I. The results are clearly described.

       SA   5   4   3   2   1   SD

J. The discussion/conclusion is appropriate.

       SA   5   4   3   2   1   SD

K. Despite any flaws, the report is worthy of publication.

       SA   5   4   3   2   1   SD

Article 4

Teacher Beliefs About Instructional Choice:
A Phenomenological Study

TERRI FLOWERDAY
University of Nebraska, Lincoln

GREGORY SCHRAW
University of Nebraska, Lincoln

ABSTRACT. We interviewed 36 practicing teachers using phenomenological methods to examine what, when, where, and to whom teachers offer choice. Teachers participated in pilot, interview, and member-check phases. Our final results focused on the following main points: (a) Teachers believe that choice promotes learning and motivation; (b) choice is used in a number of ways; (c) teachers have a variety of reasons for giving choices; and (d) teachers imposed limits on classroom choice based on (e) student age, ability, and prior knowledge and (f) teacher experience, efficacy, and management style.

From *Journal of Educational Psychology*, 92, 634–645. Copyright © 2000 by the American Psychological Association. Reprinted with permission.

(Editor's Note: Due to limitations, there are no line numbers from 995 on.)

This study examines teachers' beliefs about instructional choice in the classroom. We undertook this study because we are frequently asked by preservice teachers to comment on the role of choice in the classroom. Unfortunately, we
5 have had very little to say on this topic because there is virtually no research base on either the effects of choice on learning or on how teachers implement choice in the classroom. Our goal in this study is to describe in teachers' own words what types of choices they offer students, how they
10 decide when and to whom choices should be given, and why they offer these choices.

The present research uses semistructured interviews to examine teachers' beliefs about the use of choice in their classrooms. We draw on phenomenological methodology in
15 which a select group of participants describe a phenomenon in their own words. The purpose of this methodology is to generate rather than test theory. Below, we summarize previous research on choice and highlight some of the limitations of these studies. We then describe our methodology in
20 more detail and summarize our main findings. Theoretical consequences of our findings, as well as their relationship to existing psychological theories, are reserved for the Discussion section of this article.

Empirical Research on Choice and Learning

There is little research on choice. However, there is ex-
25 tensive literature that examines the role controlling environments (e.g., teachers and structured classroom settings) play

in autonomy and learning (Flink, Boggiano, & Barrett, 1990; Grolnick & Ryan, 1987; Miserandino, 1996; Ryan, Connell, & Grolnick, 1992). These studies suggest that controlling
30 environments reduce a sense of personal autonomy and intrinsic motivation and result in decreased learning and poorer attitudes about school (Enzle & Anderson, 1993; Weinert & Helmke, 1995). A number of other studies have examined the role that perceived control (i.e., self-judgments
35 of personal competence or autonomy) plays in intrinsic motivation (Boggiano, Main, & Katz, 1988; Skinner, Wellborn, & Connell, 1990; Williams & Deci, 1996). These studies indicate that greater perceived autonomy results in higher levels of intrinsic motivation and enjoyment, especially
40 when the desire for control is high (Law, Logan, & Baron, 1994).

A small but important set of choice-related studies has appeared in the computerized testing literature. These studies typically compare computer-adapted tests (CAT; i.e.,
45 those in which a computer selects test items for an examinee) with self-adapted tests (SAT; i.e., those in which examinees select test items from one of several preassigned difficulty levels). Rocklin and O'Donnell (1987) and Rocklin, O'Donnell, and Holst (1995) found that college students
50 performed better on a self-adapted test compared with a computer-adapted version. Wise, Plake, Johnson, and Roos (1992) showed that individuals taking the self-adapted version reported significantly lower posttest anxiety. Wise, Roos, Plake, and Nebelsick-Gullet (1994) found that the
55 type of test one completes has no effect on posttest anxiety provided one is allowed to choose the test's format (i.e., CAT vs. SAT). In a follow-up study, Wise, Roos, Leland, Oats, and McCrann (1996) reported that individuals with a high desire for control were significantly more likely to se-
60 lect a self-adapted rather than a computer-adapted test. Thus, the ability to choose how one is tested appears to reduce anxiety, regardless of the type of test one takes, and especially if one has a high desire for control. It can be concluded that choice, under these conditions, leads to a de-
65 crease in negative affect (anxiety) or improved affect.

We also identified four studies that examined the effect of choice on learning outcomes. Zuckerman, Porac, Lathin, Smith, and Deci (1978) asked 80 college students to select puzzles they would like to work on during an experimental
70 session. Forty yoked pairs were created such that each individual in the choice condition selected three of six puzzles to

work on, then indicated how much time he or she would allot to each puzzle. Individuals in the yoked group were assigned the puzzles and the same time allotments selected by individuals in the choice group. Individuals who were allowed to choose reported a greater feeling of control, indicated that they would be more willing to return for another session of puzzle solving, and spent significantly more time solving similar puzzles in a free-choice period at the end of the experiment.

Cordova and Lepper (1996) examined the role of choice when elementary school children used computer-aided learning environments to improve arithmetical and problem-solving skills. Allowing children to make choices positively affected several measures of affective engagement, including perceived competence, a preference for greater task difficulty, overall liking, and a greater willingness to stay after class compared with students in a control group. In contrast, there were few significant effects for choice with respect to cognitive engagement variables. Specifically, choice had no impact on use of hints, use of complex problem-solving operations, or the amount of strategic play, although those students given choice performed significantly better on a follow-up math test. A related study by Parker and Lepper (1992) also failed to report differences in cognitive engagement as a function of choice.

Schraw, Flowerday, and Reisetter (1998) conducted two experiments that examined the effect of choice on reading engagement among adults. Experiment 1 compared three groups: those who chose from among three equivalent texts (i.e., free choice), those who were assigned a text under the assumption that other readers declined to read it (i.e., forced choice), and those who were assigned a text without additional information (i.e., control group). None of the groups differed with respect to multiple choice test performance, essays written about the text, or holistic understanding of the text's meaning. Groups did not differ either with respect to interest and personal reactions but differed on several self-report indices of postexperimental satisfaction. Experiment 2 divided a large group into two subgroups, half receiving the option to choose what to read, the other half being assigned a text. The two groups did not differ on any of the cognitive measures or on affective reactions to the text. The free choice group, however, reported more interest in the text and more satisfaction with their research participation experience.

Research results show that choice has mixed effects on engagement and learning. Most studies report an increase in positive affect when individuals are given choices, even when choice has no simultaneous effect on learning. In contrast, few studies report consistently positive effects of choice on learning. Typically, choice had no effect at all on learning, although it appears, on the basis of research from the computerized adaptive testing literature, that choice may have a positive effect if the test taker has a strong desire for control. The main conclusion to emerge from this research is that choice positively effects affect but has little impact on performance.

The research described above has three general limitations. One is that all of these studies examined the consequences of choices rather than reasons for giving choices in the first place. Second, none of these studies examined the role of teachers in the choice-implementation process. Third, there is no explicit theory of choice stated in any of these studies, either in terms of how to administer choices or what to expect once one does so. Thus, after conducting this review, we still were no closer to answering the basic question posed by so many of our teachers: "Should I give my students choices, and if so, what kind?"

The Present Study

We conducted the present research to understand better the role of teachers in the choice-implementation process. We were interested especially in teachers' beliefs about why they give their students choices, although we also asked teachers to describe the use and consequences of those choices. Our main goal was to codify teachers' beliefs about choice. A secondary goal was to discuss the implications of the present research for an emergent theory of choice.

We focused on three aspects of teacher choice, including what choices teachers offer to their students, when and to whom teachers offer choice, and how teachers perceive the effectiveness of the choices they offer students. We used the qualitative tradition of phenomenology to construct a data-driven account of teachers' beliefs about choice (Creswell, 1998; Moustakas, 1994). The purpose of phenomenological research is to describe a phenomenon using the participants' own words.

The present study included three main stages. Semistructured (i.e., open-ended) interviews were conducted in a pilot study ($N = 8$), and a second interview protocol was developed on the basis of teacher feedback obtained in the pilot study. The revised interview questions were used in Stage 2 of the study, which consisted of preliminary written responses by 36 teachers to seven questions, followed by in-depth, one-on-one interviews of teachers using the same seven questions. These items were designed to address the three main research questions described above. Consistent with phenomenological methods (Creswell, 1998; Moustakas, 1994), we present our findings at three levels of specificity, including descriptive analysis, thematic analysis, and interpretive analysis of underlying models (Wolcott, 1994). The purpose of descriptive analysis is to summarize the range of responses and emergent points of agreement to each of the seven questions in the structured interviews. The purpose of thematic analysis is to interpret emergent themes across the full set of interviews. The purpose of interpretive analysis is to propose a preliminary model of teacher choice. The third stage consisted of member checks in which three teachers reviewed and critiqued our final results.

Method

Methodological Framework

We used the qualitative method of phenomenology in this study because there is no existing theory of choice. Phenomenological design is appropriate when one's goal is to explore a phenomenon about which little has been written.

The researcher collects information from knowledgeable participants who are asked to describe the phenomenon, and the researcher then analyzes themes and interprets the data. The results can be used to build a theory that can later be tested. According to Creswell (1998, p. 15), "qualitative research is multi-method in focus, involving an interpretive, naturalistic approach in which the researcher attempts to make sense of or interpret phenomena in terms of the meanings people bring to them." The data are, by nature, descriptive and composed of words or pictures rather than numbers, as is the case in quantitative research. The researcher's purpose is to describe and interpret the perspective of the participant (Bogdan & Biklen, 1992). Toward this end, the researcher begins to collect in-depth experiential information from a select group of participant informants.

Participants

The purpose of phenomenological research is to explore and describe a phenomenon, such as instructional choice in the classroom, from the perspective of a target group made up of individuals who have insight into the specific phenomenon being examined. A semistructured interview format is utilized. The use of criterion sampling (Creswell, 1998) gives the researcher access to in-depth information on the target topic recorded from the perspective of a specific group of participants. This necessitates the use of informants who have considerable experience with the phenomenon. Participants are selected on the basis of their ability to speak directly to the topic under investigation.

Participants for the pilot study ($N = 8$) and participants for the main study ($N = 36$) were classroom teachers attending summer classes at a large midwestern university. Criteria for participation included enrollment in graduate courses in educational psychology, learning theory, or research methods, in addition to at least 1 year of K–12 classroom teaching experience. All participants had bachelor's degrees, and approximately one-third also held master's degrees. A variety of content areas were represented, including science, math, social studies, special education, elementary education, technology, art, music, and foreign language. Both rural and urban school districts were represented, as were small and large schools. Years of experience in the classroom ranged from 1 year to 29 years. Approximately 60% of the participants were female, and 40% were male. Complete demographic information is provided in the Appendix.

Data Collection

The primary source of data is verbal responses from a series of in-depth interviews with participants. Terri Flowerday entered into dialogue with each informant, gathering information, reviewing the information for clarity and intent, and finally, checking for accuracy of interpretation through participant feedback. In the initial series of interviews, responses were tape-recorded, then transcribed into narrative text, and data were analyzed using phenomenological methods outlined in Moustakas (1994). Responses were coded and themes established, which resulted in an interview protocol consisting of seven questions. Additionally, it was decided that future participants would be given these questions prior to the taped portion of the interview. In this way, the teachers would be able to preview the questions, formulate answers, and write brief responses to serve as cues for the taped portion of the interview.

The second series of interviews consisted of 1-hr interviews with each of the 36 teacher–participants. Each participant was given a three-page handout that included six personal profile items (subjects taught, years teaching experience, grade levels taught, number of students per class, degrees held, size and setting of school), and the following seven interview questions:

1a. What types of instructional choices do you give your students? Examples might include choices of reading materials, topics of study, forms of assessment, etc.

1b. Are these choices unlimited or limited? Please describe.

2. Why do you give students choices? What is your rationale for doing so?

3. Is giving choices a good strategy for accomplishing your goals for student learning? Is it successful? Please explain.

4. How do students respond to being given choices?

5. To whom do you give choices? Are there individual differences that you consider such as (a) developmental level or age of students, (b) ability or achievement level of students, (c) course content, and (d) level of motivation, etc.

6. Do you think more or less choice is being given in classrooms today as opposed to when you were in K–12? Why do you say this?

7. When is choice a good idea? Is choice ever a bad idea? Please explain.

Participants were asked to spend 20 min previewing the questions and completing the demographic information. The researcher encouraged participants to write brief responses for each question to serve as cues. After 20 min, the researcher returned and the interview began. The discussion focused on the seven protocol questions. Participants were instructed to respond as openly and honestly as possible and were encouraged to add any information they believed to be relevant. Interviewing took place in two conference rooms in a building on campus, and each session lasted approximately 1 hr.

After finishing the teacher interviews, the tape recordings were transcribed. The researcher carefully read the transcripts and listened to the tapes, looking for significant statements reflecting participant experiences and beliefs about choice. The statements were coded and categories established. This process of horizontalization of the data culminated in a list of nonrepetitive themes. A structural description of the phenomenon was developed, and Terri Flowerday interpreted the results such that a composite description was arrived at. Gregory Schraw reviewed a random sample of transcripts and listened to the tapes. The researchers met to discuss interpretation and revise categories and themes. The discussion continued until complete agreement was reached.

Triangulation

A number of steps were taken to triangulate the data. First, data from the initial eight teacher interviews were

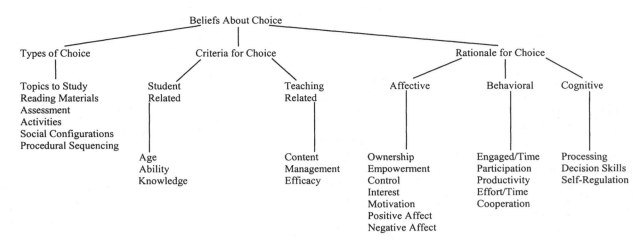

Figure 1. Teacher beliefs about choice.

compared with data obtained from the later 36 interviews. Consistent patterns emerged. Second, both written and verbal responses were obtained from the participants. Verbal responses were later transcribed into written form. The researcher compiled written fieldnotes during and immediately following each interview with regard to contextual observations. There were consistent themes cutting across the verbal and written data. Third, researcher interpretations were checked for accuracy by asking participants to confirm researcher interpretations and to provide clarification when necessary. The fourth step was to have Gregory Schraw review the written responses and fieldnotes, listen to a random sample of taped interviews, and make a separate determination of themes and interpretations (i.e., conduct an audit). The researchers then met to discuss the data, thematic analysis, and interpretive conclusions. Dialogue continued until consensus was reached.

A fifth step was to conduct individual member checks with three additional classroom teachers. Participants were recruited from a different section of the same class taught during the spring semester. Criteria for participation were the same as for the main study. The purpose of the member check was to verify that our final results were consistent with teachers' beliefs and classroom experiences. Teachers were debriefed about the purpose of the member check process and about our final results. Debriefing focused on five aspects of our results: (a) teachers believe that choice promotes learning and motivation; (b) choice was used in a number of ways; (c) teachers had a variety of reasons for giving choices and implemented choice on the basis of this rationale; (d) student age, ability, and prior knowledge were factors to be considered; and (e) teacher experience, efficacy, and management style influenced beliefs about choice.

Teachers participating in the member-check phase of the study represented elementary, middle level, and senior high schools. Both female and male teachers were interviewed. The member-check phase consisted of individual 1-hr interviews that were tape-recorded and transcribed. Teachers were informed about the purpose and procedures of the two initial interview phases, and teacher responses were de-

scribed. Participants were shown a thematic representation of teacher responses (see Figure 1), and the researcher explained the key points and rationale for the model. Participants were encouraged to ask questions and provide feedback. Next, teachers were given approximately 15 min to reflect on the model and write comments. The final 30 min were devoted to participant–researcher dialogue during which teacher input was solicited and clarification provided. Determining the degree to which participants endorsed or wanted revisions in the model was our goal. Participant notes and verbal responses were analyzed using qualitative methods consistent with phenomenological design. We met to discuss the results and concluded that participants in the member check overwhelmingly endorsed the themes represented in Figure 1 and the interpretations we made.

Results

Thematic Analysis

Thirty-six teachers responded individually to each of the seven questions described above. Responses were categorized around three broad thematic topics, shown in Figure 1. The *types-of-choice* category refers to six areas of choice that teachers commonly offer to students. The *criteria-for-choice* category refers to characteristics of students and teachers that affect choice. The *rationale-for-choice* category refers to affective, behavioral, and cognitive reasons for giving choices to students.

Types of Choices

All participants were asked to describe the types of instructional choices they gave to their students. Choices varied as a function of content areas (e.g., science, literature, elementary education, music, social studies) and educational levels (e.g., kindergarten, fourth grade, middle school, senior high school), although all teachers agreed on six main types of choice, including: (a) topics of study; (b) reading materials; (c) methods of assessment; (d) activities; (e) social arrangements; and (f) procedural choices. These themes are consistent with the recommendations for student choice made by educational researchers. For example, Shevin and Klein (1984) suggested giving choice among various objects

370 and activities, choice of whether or not to engage in an activity, choice of when to terminate an activity, choice of partners for activities, and choice of sequence of activities as appropriate for novice decision makers in educational settings.

375 Choices of topics for study and of reading materials were mentioned most frequently. Topics were chosen for research papers, in-class projects, and presentations. Choice of reading materials included type of genre (e.g., fiction or biography) and choice of authors. For example, one teacher stated,

380 "I generally lay out an overall plan of topics and let students make decisions about material within the topics." Assessment choices included the type and frequency of assessments and criteria for evaluation, such as rubric development. A typical teacher response was to let students select

385 "from among different forms of assessment such as essay test questions, exams, or book reports versus final projects." Choice of activities varied substantially depending on the age of students. Younger students were given choices about what to do, whereas older students were given more choices

390 about how to do it. These choices centered around how to allocate one's learning time in the classroom. One physical education teacher indicated how she allowed students to "choose what type of equipment they want to use, like basketball or yellow ball or activities such as dribbling or shoot-

395 ing." Choice of social arrangement was important to students and included decisions about working in pairs or small groups, seating arrangements, and choosing group members when collaborative projects were assigned. Students were allowed to make a number of procedural choices as well,

400 including when to take tests, what order to study prescribed topics, and when assignments were due.

Criteria for Choices

Teachers described a number of factors that affected the use of choice in the classroom. Student-related themes focused on characteristics of students, such as age, ability

405 level, and amount of prior knowledge, that influence teacher decisions about the use of choice. Teaching-related themes focused on characteristics of the teaching environment, such as course content, teacher management style, and teaching efficacy, that affect the use of choice.

410 *Student-related themes.* Most teachers stated that older students need more choices than younger students. Seventy-six percent of the teachers who discussed student age as a determining factor in their use of choice said that older students were better candidates for instructional choice due to

415 maturity and better decision-making skills. Older students also have well-established interests and should be allowed to pursue those interests. Teachers were concerned that younger students could be overwhelmed by too many choices. Typical responses included the following:

420 "I give more choices to older students; younger children need more structure and can't deal as well with decisions."

"I give [fewer] choices to younger students since their responses tend to be predictable and less mature."

"Choice is a bad idea when students are developmentally not
425 ready to decide what to learn."

"Choice is negative when maturity of students is too low."

In contrast to the majority position, some teachers argued that choice should be increased in elementary classrooms. Four of the 36 teachers stated that choice is more important
430 for younger children than for older children. These teachers suggested that it is never too early to start teaching decision-making and self-regulation skills that spontaneously emerge from choice making, and that even 5 year olds benefit from frequent presentation of choice. They argued that younger
435 students need choice at least as much, if not more, than older students because they have little experience with decision making. One teacher claimed that "students need to be able to think for themselves, so we need to start providing choices when they are younger." Another stated succinctly
440 that "little kids need to explore; they are interested in everything; they need choices."

Student ability was an important variable as well. The majority of teachers (11 of 13) who discussed ability level indicated that higher achieving or higher ability students
445 benefit more from choice than do their lower ability peers because they are better able to utilize the choices they are given. A high school math and computer teacher offered a common response when he stated,

My more capable students will take that choice and use it crea-
450 tively. I think with my less capable students, especially in math, there are so many fundamentals you have to cover. You know choice is going to make them more interested but they have to have a minimal level of information first.

Additional comments included the following statements:

455 "More and different types of choices can be given to high achievers."

"More capable students get more choices."

"The higher the achiever, the more choice. Low achievers need more structure."

460 "High ability means more choice in my class."

"I think the gifted kids need to be challenged; they need lots of options."

Teachers suggested prior knowledge has a significant impact on the degree to which students benefit from choice.
465 Most teachers indicated that students use choice most effectively when they possess a certain degree of background knowledge in a subject area or have attained a basic level of procedural skill. A variety of teacher comments indicated that choices have less utility when students are relative nov-
470 ices:

"Giving choices depends on the student's level of learning, the material, and on how far into the course the student has gone."

"I give them choices once I feel they have a good grasp of the foundations."

475 "Choice is a good idea when students have a good foundation of principles and they need to learn to apply them."

"Students benefit from choice when they have familiarity with content, with me and my expectations, and have a certain amount of background information."

480 "Choice is a good idea when they (the students) have some background knowledge to go off of and not a good idea when they have no knowledge to make a good choice with."

Teaching-related themes. Course content affects the use of choice in the classroom. Topics that require sequencing, 485 such as mathematics, were deemed less amenable to choice. One high school math teacher said, "Certain material needs to be covered and in a systematic, orderly way," adding, "There is little room for choice." Another teacher agreed: "In my math classes, I give choices of which problems to 490 work but that's about all."

Other subject areas, such as history and literature, were believed to be better suited to instructional choice. Choices were given on what topic to study, such as the Civil Rights Movement or the Cold War, and how to assess learning us-495 ing a variety of measures, such as written tests, class presentations, and projects. One high school psychology teacher told us, "Because everything is interesting in psychology, students need to choose what to research" and, because it is an elective course, "Students are more invested and need 500 more choices." A high school creative writing teacher said, "Students need to choose topics they are interested in so they will be motivated to write about them." Business teachers also discussed the importance of instructional choice as a way of making projects relevant. "Students need to select 505 companies or products to study that are meaningful to them." They can "choose the newspaper articles they want to bring in for discussion," and "they choose the software they want to use." Art, music, and drama teachers indicated that choice is essential for the development of creativity:

510 "Choices are given in music selection, in what uniforms to wear, and in what types of groups we will form."

"Students have choices of which play to do, and what parts to try out for."

"My art students are given choices of subject matter and im-515 agery; choice benefits those who have skill and creativity in the visual arts."

The physical education teachers who were interviewed offered choices of "activities to focus on," "equipment to use," and "partners or groups to practice drills with." 520 Teachers' classroom management styles affected the use of choice. Teachers who valued student autonomy were most likely to support the use of choice. Nevertheless, all teachers believed that choice could be used effectively even in tightly controlled classrooms. Most teachers also believed it was 525 important to yield some control of the classroom to students and that choice was an important way to do so. For example, one teacher stated that "choice allows students to be accountable for their actions; they made the choice so they follow through." Making choices also helps students learn 530 about consequences. As one teacher said, "Basically, students always have a choice of doing or not doing, of studying or not studying, but they also have to face the consequences." Teachers also reported using choice to reinforce positive behavior, as the following quotes indicate:

535 "I give my kids choices after they have done a good job on an assignment."

"I let my students choose as a positive consequence based on earlier behavior."

"Giving my students choice helps build rapport between them 540 and me; they show more respect."

Students who are allowed to make choices "invest more energy in learning" and "feel a certain responsibility to participate." Students respond to choice by "becoming very trustworthy," by "making good decisions," and by "working 545 cooperatively together."

The use of choice was linked to teachers' efficacy. Most teachers reported using more choice as they became more experienced over the years and as they became more comfortable throughout the course of each academic year. Sev-550 eral teachers mentioned that choice giving in their classrooms had not truly been incorporated until after they had multiple years of teaching experience. As the following comments indicate, more choices were offered to students as teachers became more efficacious:

555 "At first, I didn't give many choices but gradually I started adding options and alternatives."

"I think it's more work to give choices and new teachers have enough to deal with already."

"I give more choices than I used to because I've learned how to 560 handle their reactions."

"I am more comfortable giving choices now and have more of them built into my lessons."

Rationale for Choice

Teachers' responses fell into one of three subcategories that reflected affective, behavioral, and cognitive rationales 565 for choice. "Affective" rationales focused on changing attitudes and increasing affective engagement. "Behavioral" rationales emphasized the role of choice in increasing student effort and participation. "Cognitive" rationales highlighted the effect of choice on levels of processing and cog-570 nitive engagement. Additionally, teachers cited increased self-regulation and improved decision-making skills.

Affective rationales for choice. Teachers give students choices because choices have a positive effect on attitude and affective engagement. Words and phrases that were used 575 to describe student response to choice included *empowered, sense of control, responsibility, ownership, motivated, enthusiastic, satisfaction, excited, appreciative,* and *sense of purpose.* The majority of teachers said that choice produces positive effects on students most of the time. However, 580 teachers also conceded that some students react negatively to choice, preferring to be "just told what to do." Terms such as *overwhelmed, confused,* and *nervous* were used to describe negative affective response.

Roughly 70% of teachers mentioned student *ownership* 585 as the most important affective consequence of choice. One teacher said of her students, "It gives them more ownership of learning, promotes collaboration (sometimes) and more buy in." Another teacher said the reason for giving students choice was that they developed "ownership, (became) more 590 motivated and committed to learning. Ownership is a factor; children are more likely to follow through on a choice they feel they made." The belief that ownership is positive and leads to an increase in learning provides the basis for their rationale of choice giving. One teacher said,

595　I believe that students feel a sense of ownership to a project if they have chosen it. In turn, I believe, the ownership factor leads to more enthusiasm, better quality work, and the student will be more likely to remember something they value.

Another teacher reported "On projects where they (the
600　students) had a choice, they had more ownership in them and put forth more effort."

Empowerment was a second term used frequently to explain why choice is important for students. Various teachers reported, "Because students feel empowered, they respond in
605　a responsible way"; "Students who are given choices feel empowered and when they feel empowered, they are more apt to take control of or responsibility for their own learning"; and "I think young children might have a more difficult time (making choices); however, this might still make
610　them feel empowered."

Many participants also used choice to give students control of the learning process. One teacher said choice is important because "most times, it promotes success; control of learning," and another teacher simply stated, "It gives the
615　students more control of their learning. I like them to feel they have an element of control in what they're doing; they'll do a better job." One high school teacher commented, "I give choices because it works. Especially in high school, students need to take some control of their learning [and] the
620　environment. Students need to have some control; a sense of their own directedness."

Teachers claimed that choice enhances motivation by increasing interest and that this can occur in two ways. First, choice increases interest by providing the opportunity for
625　students to select what they are already interested in. Second, choice may generate interest where previously it did not exist. A large number of teachers discussed the motivational properties of choice and the potential for interest generation. These teachers believe that choice has a positive motiva-
630　tional effect on students because it increases interest and engagement. One high school teacher stated that choice "promotes involvement, matches student interests; there is less groaning." Choice also "taps creativity, interest, and adds variety." Choice gives students the "satisfaction of
635　solving a problem that they are interested in." Teachers also reported that "choice is a good idea when a student is able to tailor assignments to their own interests" and "students are given choices so they will be interested in the subject, motivated." A computer teacher said, "If they (students) are al-
640　lowed to pick a topic, they have more interest in what they're doing; they're not going to choose a topic they aren't interested in." She added, "Any time a student is interested in what they're learning, they seem to be more motivated."

One participant stated that "choice is good for motiva-
645　tion. A nonmotivated student will get choices in hopes of motivating him." Another teacher reported, "Student self-efficacy and motivation are positively affected by giving students a feeling they are invested in the course." Yet another teacher indicated that he gives his students choice be-
650　cause of "the motivation factor," which "causes students to stick with it and they seem to learn more." A secondary school teacher, when asked why she gives students choices, responded "motivation; taking time to choose helps them focus, it seems to give them a feeling of responsibility, a
655　vested interest; it's *my* topic. It motivates them to get started and I can usually see a sense of pride as they work."

Many teachers also linked the opportunity for choice to positive affect or the alleviation of negative affect. One participant stated that students are "usually more excited and
660　willing to start their research when they have chosen their own topic." In computer class, "they are thrilled when they get to choose their activity." Additionally, "many seem relieved; it eases pressure." One teacher reported, "Most students say that learning is more fun, meaningful, and they
665　feel proud of their work." Another participant stated that it "gives students more confidence if they get to make the choices instead of always being told what to do." An industrial technology instructor mentioned that "students don't feel threatened when you give them choices; it works really
670　well that way."

Although teachers agreed that giving students choice is usually a good strategy for improving attitude and learning, several also pointed out that occasionally there is a student who reacts negatively to choice. When asked how students
675　react to choice, one middle school teacher responded, "Some of them, when you say you're giving them a choice, say, 'We'd rather just be given a normal assignment.' They really don't know what they're going to do." She continued, "I don't let them off the hook right away but I try to give them
680　suggestions and if I know the student, I know what they might be interested in." Another participant reported, "Sometimes, they (students) respond with skepticism, like 'what's the catch?'" One teacher explained, "Some of my students don't like having to make a choice; they feel that I
685　should facilitate entirely."

Behavioral rationales for choice. Most teachers claimed that choice is related positively to student behaviors such as time on task, participation in classroom activities, demonstration of effort, cooperation, and respect. "The class comes
690　together tremendously; when students choose, they generally participate more fully," said one teacher. Choice "helps them to be more actively engaged," and students "usually work harder, give better effort" when they have chosen the activity. Other teachers said, "Choice makes students responsible
695　for their behavior" and "in math, some students can meet more objectives if they don't have to repeat learned activities but can work at their own pace." One middle school teacher explained that as a result of choice, "reports and presentations are always extremely well done but sometimes impor-
700　tant topics aren't chosen." A high school teacher said, "We know from business research that if you give everyone the opportunity to make decisions, their productivity will increase; that's what I see."

In most but not all cases, the behavioral responses to
705　choice were perceived positively. Some teachers, however, pointed out that there can also be behavioral pitfalls associated with choice. For example, when given choices, "Some

students fall back on easy, comfortable topics and don't push themselves; they get lazy." Choice can "allow the student to stagnate on a favorite topic or activity; not explore new territory." Giving students a choice of topics for a research paper can provide an opportunity "to avoid the assignment" by turning in a previously written piece of work.

Cognitive rationales for choice. When teachers were asked specifically about the effects of choice on student learning, nearly everyone indicated they believed their students learn more when choices are offered, even though this conclusion is not supported by empirical findings (Schraw et al., 1998). Teachers emphasized two cognitive subthemes: (1) greater level of cognitive engagement with deeper processing, and (2) greater self-regulation and the development of decision-making skills. First, choice is believed to be responsible for increasing student engagement with learning materials and classroom activities. Choice is believed to be beneficial because it provides students with the opportunity to explore topics for which they have intrinsic interest, leads to greater engagement, deeper processing, and better recall. A special education teacher whose students she described as "at-risk teens" said that giving students appropriate choices encouraged them to interact with the material. She indicated that they spend more time studying "if they are interested, if they want to know more about the issue." A middle school science teacher said he believes that when students are given choices "they definitely make the commitment to learning, use higher level thinking." He went on to say, "They (the students) think more about the way the whole thing fits together, especially when you give choices for assessment." Another teacher said of the relationship between choice and learning, "Choice makes education more meaningful. There is more permanence, more learning."

Teachers also suggested that choice encourages self-regulation and is necessary for the development of decision-making skills. The perception of learning as self-determined causes the student to invest more time, energy, and effort in the process because it is "uncool to fail at something you have chosen." This feeling of responsibility for producing a desirable outcome may be the mechanism by which engagement, strategy use, and learning are increased. One teacher reported, "I believe choice leads to self-regulation of learning." A foreign language teacher commented, "I think it is more likely to lead to the use of metacognitive skills as students make decisions about the direction of their learning." Participants said that choice is associated with "increased self-monitoring" and "thinking and decision-making skills." Choice, participants said, allows students to learn to "evaluate options and develop decision-making skills." Students "learn from their choices; even if they make a bad choice, they can learn from it." Simply put, "Choice builds learning skills."

Summary

The themes summarized above make it clear that teachers possess a variety of beliefs about use of choice in the classroom. Most teachers have spent a great deal of time thinking about the implementation and consequences of

choice. Typically, several student-related factors are considered. These factors or themes shown in Figure 1 are consistent with educational research as well. For example, Shevin and Klein (1984) concluded that students' ages and ability levels affect the use of choice in the classroom. Shapiro and Cole (1994, p. 136) reported that "not all choices are appropriate for all students." Shapiro and Cole (1994, p. 137) went on to say, "As students increase in age and ability level, they may benefit from expanded choice." Zimmerman and Martinez-Pons (1990) concluded that high-ability students were better able to use self-regulation strategies when allowed to do so. Sweet, Guthrie, and Ng (1998) concluded that low-achieving students benefit less from choice than their high-achieving counterparts. Aguilar and Petrakis (1989) found that prior experience and skill level were influential factors in students' choice of sports and in their level of participation in sports-related activities.

Support for teacher-related variables (e.g., course content, management style, experience, and efficacy) can be found in the research literature as well. Choice has been used successfully in many content areas, including art (Amabile & Gitomer, 1984), reading (Guthrie & McCann, 1997; Pressley, Yokoi, Rankin, Wharton-McDonald, & Mistretta-Hampston, 1997; Turner, 1995), and foreign language (Bruning, Flowerday, & Trayer, 1999). Teachers' management styles, experiences, and efficacies play a role in implementation of choice. Woolfolk and Hoy (1990) reported that teachers' beliefs about their personal teaching efficacies (their personal abilities to influence student learning outcomes) affects their philosophies of classroom management and instructional style. Teachers with greater personal efficacy tend to operate from a humanistic orientation in which "self-discipline is substituted for strict control" (Woolfolk & Hoy, 1990, p. 84). Bandura (1993) concurred that "teachers' beliefs in their personal efficacy to motivate and promote learning affect the types of learning environments they create and the level of progress their students achieve" (p. 117). Bandura (1997) and Lent, Brown, and Hackett (1994) also suggested that self-efficacy is instrumental in the appraisal and implementation of occupational and academic choices.

Final Results

The thematic results reported above provide a descriptive account of teachers' beliefs in their own words. This section organizes those themes into an integrated structural description of teacher beliefs about choice (Moustakas, 1994). The purpose of the structural description is to provide an analysis of themes reported by teachers.

Teachers discussed at length their beliefs about choice, distinguishing between positive and negative effects of choice on affective (e.g., engagement and motivation) and cognitive (e.g., learning) engagement. Teachers strongly agreed that choice improves affective response by increasing students' ownership, interest, creativity, and personal autonomy. This claim has been made by a number of choice proponents (Deci, 1992; Kamii, 1991; Kohn, 1993). Many teachers stated that choice increases student creativity and flow as well, a claim consistent with recent qualitative

820 analyses of the creative process (Amabile, 1996; Csikszent-mihalyi, 1996). There also was a consensus among teachers that judicious use of choice in the classroom improves student–teacher relationships by demonstrating that teachers have confidence in students' ability to self-regulate their
825 learning. Teachers agreed that choice improves cognitive processes such as student engagement, strategy use, and decision making because students are more motivated to perform well when they set their own goals and decide how to reach them. These claims have not been supported with any
830 degree of consistency, although there have been a few empirical studies that specifically address these issues (Hannifin & Sullivan, 1996; Schraw et al., 1998).

All of the teachers we interviewed held positive beliefs about the use of choice in the classroom. However, most of
835 the same teachers expressed some concerns about the overuse of choice. One concern was that too much choice becomes counterproductive. Teachers believed that too many choices can overwhelm students, especially younger students who are less skilled at making their own educational deci-
840 sions. There was consensus as well that choice may allow unmotivated students to take the path of least resistance. These claims are consistent with findings in business (Williams, 1998) and psychology (Tafarodi, Milne, & Smith, 1999) that indicate that choice is most effective when it in-
845 cludes two equally valued alternatives. Choices between two unequal alternatives or alternatives that are not valued may result in negative outcomes because of what Kohn (1993) refers to as "pseudo-choice."

Teachers offered students choices in six areas. Choices
850 were offered most frequently with respect to topics for term papers and research projects and what to read during recreational reading periods throughout the day. Teachers consistently reported that choice promotes engagement and learning because students select topics they are knowledgeable
855 about and are interested in. Classroom assessment was another area where teachers offered a variety of choices. Most choices concerned the type, frequency, and criteria for assessment. Teachers felt it was motivating for students to help select the criteria used to evaluate their work even though
860 teachers did not do so frequently. Teachers also offered a variety of choices regarding classroom social arrangements. These choices typically concerned seating arrangements, choosing group members, and whether students would work alone or in pairs. Although teachers felt that choice in social
865 arrangements was important, choice was limited to ensure that students had a variety of social experiences and interacted in an academic work setting with other students they would not interact with if they were not required to do so. Previous research has suggested that a variety of social ex-
870 periences are advantageous for students compared with a more limited array of experiences that would result if students consistently selected in-class partners (Cooper, 1999; Zimmerman, 2000). Teachers offered students a variety of choices regarding classroom procedures such as when to
875 complete assignments, what order the class would cover main topics, and when to be tested. Procedural choice facilitated learning because it gave students an opportunity to

better accommodate individual academic interests and extra-curricular activities such as athletics, music, and performing
880 arts.

Teachers gave students choices for two main reasons, one of which they discussed at length (i.e., enhancement of classroom experience), and one of which they rarely discussed explicitly (i.e., reward of effort and good behavior).
885 Teachers indicated that choice resulted in increased student engagement, sense of control, and motivation. This claim is supported by a number of empirical studies based on self-determination theory (Deci, Vallerand, Pelletier, & Ryan, 1991; Ryan & Deci, 2000). Choice is used as well to pro-
890 mote deeper cognitive processing and creativity (Kamii, 1991; Kohn, 1993). Teachers also use choice to improve students' decision-making skills. Teachers frequently commented that many of their students were rather unskilled in this regard, presumably because they are rarely given mean-
895 ingful choices in academic settings. There are no empirical studies that have examined this relationship.

Teachers also used choice as a reward for effort or good behavior. Few of the teachers we interviewed discussed this aspect of choice explicitly, although it became apparent,
900 based on their comments about when and where they used choice, that it was used frequently as a reward. Teachers were most likely to give choices to older, competent, self-regulated students who had previously demonstrated the ability to use choice wisely. In addition, some teachers gave
905 students choices as a reward for extra effort, improved achievement, or attempts to comply with rules or circumstances they did not enjoy.

Although teachers said they offered choices to every student, and did so regularly, they also stated that options
910 should be limited to increase chances of a positive outcome. Most teachers provided a limited-choice menu to students in which they were required to choose from an array of teacher-selected options.

Teachers repeatedly indicated that several student-related
915 and teacher-related variables affect the use of choice. Age, prior knowledge, and student achievement were mentioned by participants as factors to be considered when making decisions about choice. Older students are given more choices than are younger students because they possess more
920 knowledge and decision-making skills. Teachers also suggested that older students have a stronger need for autonomy and control of their academic progress. This claim is supported by a variety of studies indicating that older students respond more favorably in less controlling environments
925 compared with younger students (Flink et al., 1990; Grolnick & Ryan, 1987). Level of prior knowledge should be considered. High-knowledge students are entrusted with more important choices such as selecting a topic for a major research or creative project than are low-knowledge stu-
930 dents. Achievement level affects the number and scope of classroom choice. Self-regulated students are given more choices than are less-regulated students. Choices did not appear to differ as a function of gender or social competence.

935 　　The amount of choice given to students is influenced by a number of teacher-related variables. Perhaps the most important of these is teacher self-efficacy. Many teachers indicated that they increased the use of choice throughout their careers, in part due to the extra time and effort needed to
940 administer choices and in part because they felt a greater need for control in their early years. Teachers continue to give more choices to their students in academic settings where they themselves feel intellectually and psychologically autonomous. A second closely related factor is experi-
945 ence. The more experience a teacher has in a particular topic area, the more likely she or he is to offer choice. Course content is another important variable. Teachers in the physical or biological sciences and in mathematics offered fewer choices overall than teachers in the arts and social sciences.
950 This phenomenon was due to two factors: the crucial role of foundational knowledge in the sciences and the naturally occurring instructional sequence implicit in math and science courses. Last, teachers' management styles affected the use of choice. Some teachers believed that classrooms were
955 more efficient when teachers assumed control for student learning. These teachers offered less choice, although even the most teacher-centered individuals believed that regular choices were of benefit to motivation and learning. In contrast, some teachers believed in student-centered classrooms
960 that offered more choices. Although teachers differed in their management styles and usage of choice, there did not appear to be noticeable differences in their attitudes about the effectiveness of choice. Thus, whether teachers use choice a little or a lot, when they do use it, most feel that it
965 promotes motivation and learning.

Feedback from Final Member Checks

　　Teachers interviewed in the final member-check phase of the study enthusiastically supported the thematic representation of teacher practices and beliefs as presented in Figure 1. All three participants indicated that results were consistent
970 with their understanding and perceptions of instructional choice in the classroom. A fifth-grade teacher stated, "I think it is very thorough; I think it covers everything in depth." He indicated that he uses many of the choices represented with his own students. The rationale-for-choice section was par-
975 ticularly well received. Participants commented that the categories were useful for thinking about rationale and that they had used similar reasoning when deciding about choices for their students. One middle school language arts teacher was especially interested in the types of choices be-
980 ing offered and indicated agreement with all the categories and themes. A high school social studies and Spanish teacher was interested in the teaching-related themes, suggesting that management style and teacher efficacy were very important determinants of decision making about provi-
985 sion of choice. She stated, "Some teachers are very teacher-centered, controlling, and don't provide these opportunities; it might overwhelm some." Also, the secondary teacher reinforced the belief that there was potential for choice to backfire, leading to negative affective, behavioral, and cognitive
990 effects. Member-check participants overwhelmingly en-dorsed the teacher-belief themes and made no recommendations for substantial additions or deletions from the model.

Discussion

　　We focus on three main points in this discussion: (1) summarization of our initial research questions, (2) a sum-
995 marization of guidelines for the use of choice in the classroom on the basis of our findings, and (3) implications for future research.

Summary of Findings

　　This study examined three questions related to teachers' beliefs about instructional choice. These questions focused on what kind of choices teachers give to students, when and to whom they give them, and why they give them. We explored these questions for two reasons. The first reason is that we are frequently asked questions by preservice and practicing teachers about how to use choice in the classroom. Thus far, we have relied solely on our own personal experiences to answer these questions because there are no systematic research findings to draw from. We believe the present findings, based on the classroom practices of 36 teachers, offer a number of explicit guidelines. A second reason is that there is no existing theory of teacher choice. We undertook the present study in part to begin to generate a preliminary model of teacher choice that can be refined and tested by subsequent research.

　　Our first question focused on what kinds of choices teachers offer their students. Most choices fall into one of six categories, including topic of study, reading materials, methods of assessment, order of activities, social arrangements, and procedural choices. Most choices center on topic of study or reading materials. Fewer choices were given with regard to classroom assessment, in part because teachers were required to conduct certain kinds of assessment and in part because students often lacked a clear idea of what needed to be assessed or how to do so. Nevertheless, teachers felt that some choice of assessment greatly enhanced a students' sense of autonomy and personal control. Choice of learning activities was also common. Teachers offered students a variety of choices with respect to homework, in-class free time, as well as alternative ways to demonstrate their knowledge. A number of social relationship choices were given, although these choices were given cautiously. In general, teachers did not give students social options until a certain degree of competence had been demonstrated. We discuss this phenomenon in more detail below.

　　Three factors emerged as important constraints on who is given choice: age, ability, and prior knowledge. This pattern closely matched previous research (Shapiro & Cole, 1994). Teachers give older students more choices even though many teachers emphasized the need for authentic choices for younger students. Students of higher ability or those who demonstrate higher performance are given more choices as well. The rationale is that self-regulated students can be trusted to make wise choices and use the opportunities provided by choice more efficiently. This assumption is supported by recent empirical findings (Zimmerman, 2000).

Prior knowledge was also considered in making decisions about who is given choice. Teachers had strong beliefs that knowledgeable students are best able to make wise choices and work autonomously once given a choice. Teachers were aware of the potential interactions among age, ability, and prior knowledge. A number of participants indicated that knowledge compensates in part for age and ability; thus, it was possible to give high-knowledge younger students more choices than low-knowledge older students. Nevertheless, teachers also emphasized the role of "choice equity" in the classroom, indicating choice can be appropriately structured in such a way as to benefit all students regardless of age, ability, or level of prior knowledge.

Teachers' comments about when they give choices were especially interesting. Participants agreed that all students should be given choices on a regular basis even when they are young. However, a closer analysis of teachers' comments indicated they made an implicit distinction between generative and maintenance functions of choice, often opting for the latter. By generative function, we mean the assumption that choice causes (i.e., generates) self-determination because it gives students a greater sense of control, interest, and better decision-making skills. Agreeing with this assumption suggests that teachers should use choice in a proactive manner to motivate their students. In contrast, many teachers used choice as a reward to "maintain" existing behaviors; that is, choice was used in the classroom as a consequence rather than as a causal antecedent of self-determined behaviors. For example, students who were performing well could choose their partner for an upcoming class project, or students who performed well on one assignment were given more choices on the next assignment. This pattern seemed somewhat contradictory to us given the explicit theoretical emphasis on the generative function of choice in research literature. From our perspective, it appears that teachers implicitly believe that choice causes self-determination but paradoxically act as if self-determination should be rewarded by choice. Future research will look more closely at this inconsistency between theory and practice. It may be that choice serves as a cognitive–behavioral reinforcer as well as a source of intrinsic motivation.

Teachers gave students choices for three main reasons. The first was to increase student self-determination. All teachers felt the self-determined students were more motivated and more likely to be deeply engaged in classroom learning. This assumption is closely aligned with the main assumptions of self-determination theory (Deci & Ryan, 1987; Deci et al., 1991). The second reason for giving choice was to increase personal interest, which was seen as a major catalyst for improving learning. Teachers felt that interest was necessary for total engagement (Deci, 1992). A third reason was to provide an opportunity for students to practice their decision-making skills. Teachers stressed that students would not become facile at making wise choices unless they were given the opportunity to do so and gained feedback about their progress (Reeve, Bolt, & Cai, 1999).

Guidelines for Classroom Practice

The present findings have a number of implications for teaching. The most obvious of these is that teachers believe that choice matters to students. All teachers in the study offer their students choices, and most do so regularly. On a day-to-day basis, teachers offer more choices to older, higher ability, and more knowledgeable students than others, although all teachers felt it is important to maintain some degree of choice equity. A second implication concerns what kinds of choices to give students. All of the teachers we interviewed gave students choices about what to study, especially in their free time or when they were working in small groups. The rationale is that students will select tasks and materials that are of interest to them and therefore experience greater motivation to learn. None of the teachers expressed any misgivings about this strategy. A third implication concerns how to sequence choices. Participants agreed that simple choices were most appropriate for younger or less capable students and that all students should be eased into the year with simple choices.

Our interviews yielded a considerable amount of data in which a wide variety of suggestions were made for using choice in the classroom. We offer a number of general conclusions that most or all teachers agreed with.

When to use choice: (a) in all grades, but older students need more choices as student competence and self-regulation increase; and (b) when students know a lot about the task or topic.

Where to use choice: (a) in a variety of settings (e.g., math, history); (b) on different tasks (e.g., homework, assessment); and (c) for academic and social activities.

How to use choice: (a) offer simple choices at first; (b) help students practice making good choices; (c) provide feedback about the choice; (d) use team choices for younger students; (e) provide information that clarifies the choice; and (f) offer choices within a task (e.g., ordering, sequence, topic).

Implications for Future Research

The present findings raise several broad issues for future research. One concerns the extent to which teachers' beliefs about choice can be validated empirically. Current research supports many of the claims that teachers make regarding positive affective engagement, satisfaction, and empowerment. However, there is less support for the claim that choice significantly improves deeper learning. A second issue is whether the use of choice in a generative or maintenance manner affects intrinsic motivation, engagement, or learning. One possibility is that choice used as a reward could undermine intrinsic motivation (Kohn, 1993). Studies are needed to determine whether performance contingencies attached to choice undermine its potentially positive effects. A third issue pertains to how teachers' usage of choice is related to their own teaching self-efficacies. None of the teachers in this study explicitly addressed this issue, although many mentioned that they offered more choices as their careers advanced and students became more self-regulated. We suspect that high-efficacy teachers offer more choices to their students than do low-efficacy teachers (Calderhead, 1996; Pajares, 1992). Fourth, a much better understanding is needed of the relationship between choice and interest. All of the teachers we interviewed stated that choice increased interest because it allowed students to select what they liked and already knew about. However, it is unclear presently whether choice exerts a causal influence on interest, or if interest contributes to learning separate from choice.

Appendix

Demographic Information from Current Study (N = 36)

Item	Total
Male	14 (39%)
Female	22 (61%)
Grade levels taught	
Elementary (K–5)	8 (22%)
Secondary (6–12)	28 (78%)
Degrees held	
Bachelors only	24 (67%)
Bachelors and masters	12 (33%)
Description of schools	
Small	15 (41%)
Medium–large	21 (59%)
Rural	18 (50%)
Urban	18 (50%)
Subjects represented	
Elementary curriculum	7
Business	5
Computer technology	10
Language arts–English	12
Math	6
Music–art	2
Physical education	6
Science	11
Social sciences	8
Special education	4
Industrial technology	1
World languages	5

Item	N	Minimum	Maximum	M	SD
Number of students per class	36	1.00	35.00	20.77	7.54
Years of teaching experience	36	1.00	29.00	8.06	7.58

References

Aguilar, T. E., & Petrakis, E. (1989). Development and initial validation of perceived competence and satisfaction measures for racquet sports. *Journal of Leisure Research, 21,* 133–149.

Amabile, T. M. (1996). *Creativity in context.* Boulder, CO: Westview.

Amabile, T. M., & Gitomer, J. (1984). Children's artistic creativity: Effects of choice in task materials. *Personality and Social Psychology Bulletin, 10,* 209–215.

Bandura, A. (1993). Perceived self-efficacy in cognitive development and functioning. *Educational Psychologist, 28,* 117–148.

Bandura, A. (1997). *Self-efficacy: The exercise of control.* New York: Freeman.

Bogdan, R. C., & Biklen, S. K. (1992). *Qualitative research for education: An introduction to theory and methods.* Boston: Allyn & Bacon.

Boggiano, A. K., Main, D. S., & Katz, P. A. (1988). Children's preference for challenge: The role of perceived competence and control. *Journal of Personality and Social Psychology, 54,* 134–141.

Bruning, R., Flowerday, T., & Trayer, M. (1999). Developing foreign language frameworks: An evaluation study. *Foreign Language Annals, 32,* 159–176.

Calderhead, J. (1996). Teachers: Beliefs and knowledge. (In D. C. Berliner & R. C. Calfee (Eds.), *Handbook of educational psychology* (pp. 709–725). New York: Simon & Schuster Macmillan.

Cooper, M. A. (1999). Classroom choices from a cognitive perspective on peer learning. (In A. M. O'Donnell & A. King (Eds.), *Cognitive perspectives on peer learning* (pp. 215–234). Mahwah, NJ: Erlbaum.

Cordova, D. I., & Lepper, M. R. (1996). Intrinsic motivation and the process of learning: Beneficial effects of contextualization, personalization, and choice. *Journal of*

Educational Psychology, 88, 715–730.

Creswell, J. W. (1998). *Qualitative inquiry and research design: Choosing among five traditions.* Thousand Oaks, CA: Sage.

Csikszentmihalyi, M. (1996). *Creativity: Flow and the psychology of discovery and invention.* New York: Harper-Collins.

Deci, E. L. (1992). The relation of interest to the motivation of behavior: A self-determination theory perspective. (In A. Renninger, S. Hidi, & A. Krapp (Eds.), *The role of interest in learning and development* (pp. 43–70). Hillsdale, NJ: Erlbaum.

Deci, E. L., & Ryan, R. M. (1987). The support of autonomy and control of behavior. *Journal of Personality and Social Psychology, 53,* 1024–1037.

Deci, E. L., Vallerand, R. J., Pelletier, L. G., & Ryan, R. M. (1991). Motivation and education: The self-determination perspective. *Educational Psychologist, 26,* 325–346.

Enzle, M. E., & Anderson, S. C. (1993). Surveillant intentions and intrinsic motivation. *Journal of Personality and Social Psychology, 64,* 257–266.

Flink, C., Boggiano, A. K., & Barrett, M. (1990). Controlling teaching strategies: Undermining children's self-determination and performance. *Journal of Personality and Social Psychology, 59,* 916–924.

Grolnick, W. S., & Ryan, R. M. (1987). Autonomy in children's learning: An experimental and individual difference investigation. *Journal of Personality and Social Psychology, 52,* 890–898.

Guthrie, J. T., & McCann, A. D. (1997). Characteristics of classrooms that promote motivations and strategies for learning. (In J. T. Guthrie & A. Wigfield (Eds.), *Reading engagement: Motivating readers through integrated instruction* (pp. 128–148). Newark, DE: International Reading Association.

Hannafin, R. D., & Sullivan, H. J. (1996). Preferences and learner control over amount of instruction. *Journal of Educational Psychology, 88,* 162–173.

Kamii, C. (1991). Toward autonomy: The importance of critical thinking and choice making. *School Psychology Review, 20,* 382–388.

Kohn, A. (1993, September). Choices for children: Why and how to let students decide. *Phi Delta Kappan,* 8–20.

Law, A., Logan, H., & Baron, R. S. (1994). Desire for control, felt control, and stress inoculation training during dental treatment. *Journal of Personality and Social Psychology, 67,* 926–936.

Lent, R. W., Brown, S. D., & Hackett, G. (1994). Toward a unifying social cognitive theory of career and academic interest, choice, and performance. *Journal of Vocational Behavior, 45,* 79–122.

Miserandino, M. (1996). Children who do well in school: Individual differences in perceived competence and autonomy in above-average children. *Journal of Educational Psychology, 88,* 203–214.

Moustakas, C. (1994). *Phenomenological research methods.* Thousand Oaks, CA: Sage.

Pajares, M. F. (1992). Teachers' beliefs and educational research: Cleaning up a messy construct. *Review of Educational Research, 62,* 307–322.

Parker, L. E., & Lepper, M. R. (1992). The effects of fantasy contexts on children's learning and motivation: Making learning more fun. *Journal of Personality and Social Psychology, 62,* 625–633.

Pressley, M., Yokoi, L., Rankin, J., Wharton-McDonald, R., & Mistretta-Hampston, J. (1997). *A survey of the instructional practices of Grade-5 teachers nominated as effective in promoting literacy* (Reading Research Report No. 85). Athens, GA: University of Georgia and University Maryland, with the National Reading Research Center.

Reeve, J., Bolt, E., & Cai, Y. (1999). Autonomy-supportive teachers: How they teach and motivate students. *Journal of Educational Psychology, 91,* 537–548.

Rocklin, T., & O'Donnell, A. M. (1987). Self-adapted testing: A performance-improving variant of computerized adaptive testing. *Journal of Educational Psychology, 79,* 315–319.

Rocklin, T. R., O'Donnell, A. M., & Holst, P. M. (1995). Effects and underlying mechanisms of self-adapted testing. *Journal of Educational Psychology, 87,* 103–116.

Ryan, R., Connell, J., & Grolnick, W. (1992). When achievement is not intrinsically motivated: A theory of internalization and self-regulation in school. In K. Boggiano & T. Pittman (Eds.), *Achievement and motivation: A social developmental perspective* (pp. 167–188). Cambridge, UK: Cambridge University Press.

Ryan, R. M., & Deci, E. L. (2000). Self-determination theory and the facilitation of intrinsic motivation, social development, and well-being. *American Psychologist, 55,* 68–78.

Schraw, G., Flowerday, T., & Reisetter, M. (1998). The role of choice in reader engagement. *Journal of Educational Psychology, 90,* 705–714.

Shapiro, E. S., & Cole, C. L. (1994). *Behavior change in the classroom: Self-management intervention.* New York: Guilford Press.

Shevin, M., & Klein, N. K. (1984). The importance of choice-making skills for students with severe disabilities. *Journal of the Association for Persons with Severe Handicaps, 9,* 159–166.

Skinner, E. A., Wellborn, J. G., & Connell, J. P. (1990). What it takes to do well in school and whether I've got it: A process model of perceived control and children's engagement and achievement in school. *Journal of Educational Psychology, 82,* 22–32.

Sweet, A. P., Guthrie, J. T., & Ng, M. M. (1997). Teacher perceptions and student reading motivation. *Journal of Educational Psychology, 90,* 210–223.

Tafarodi, R. W., Milne, A. B., & Smith, A. J. (1999). The confidence of choice: Evidence for an augmentation effect on self-perceived performance. *Personality and Social Psychology Bulletin, 25, 11,* 1405.

Turner, J. C. (1995). The influence of classroom contexts on young children's motivation for literacy. *Reading Research Quarterly, 30*, 410–441.

Weinert, F. E., & Helmke, A. (1995). Learning from wise mother nature or big brother instructor: The wrong choice as seen from an educational perspective. *Educational Psychologist, 30*, 135–142.

Williams, G. C., & Deci, E. L. (1996). Internalization of biopsychosocial values by medical students: A test of self-determination theory. *Journal of Personality and Social Psychology, 70*, 767–779.

Williams, S. (1998). An organizational model of choice: A theoretical analysis differentiating choice, personal control, and self-determination. *Genetic, Social, and General Psychology Monographs, 124*, 465–491.

Wise, S. L., Plake, B. S., Johnson, P. L., & Roos, L. L. (1992). A comparison of self-adapted and computerized adaptive tests. *Journal of Educational Measurement, 29*, 329–339.

Wise, S. L., Roos, L. L., Leland, V. L., Oats, R. G., & McCrann, T. O. (1996). The development and validation of a scale measuring desire for control on examinations. *Educational and Psychological Measurement, 56*, 710–718.

Wise, S. L., Roos, L. L., Plake, B. S., & Nebelsick-Gullet, L. J. (1994). The relationship between examinee anxiety and preference for self-adapted testing. *Applied Measurement in Education, 7*, 81–91.

Wolcott, H. F. (1994). *Transforming qualitative data: Description, analysis, and interpretation.* Thousand Oaks, CA: Sage.

Woolfolk, A. E., & Hoy, W. K. (1990). Prospective teachers' sense of efficacy and beliefs about control. *Journal of Educational Psychology, 82*, 81–91.

Zimmerman, B. J. (2000). Attaining self-regulation: A social–cognitive perspective. In M. Boekarts, P. Pintrich, & M. Zeidner (Eds.), *Handbook of self-regulation* (pp. 13–39). San Diego: Academic Press.

Zimmerman, B. J., & Martinez-Pons, M. (1990). Student differences in self-regulated learning: Relating grade, sex, and giftedness to self-efficacy and strategy use. *Journal of Educational Psychology, 82*, 51–59.

Zuckerman, M., Porac, J., Lathin, D., Smith, R., & Deci, E. L. (1978). On the importance of self-determination for intrinsically-motivated behavior. *Personality and Social Psychology Bulletin, 4*, 443–446.

Acknowledgments: Special thanks go to Douglas Kauffman for his helpful assistance on an earlier version of this article.

Address correspondence to: Terri Flowerday, University of Nebraska—Lincoln, 309 Bancroft Hall, Lincoln, NE 68588-0384. E-mail may be sent to Gregory Schraw at gschraw@unl.edu

Exercise for Article 4

Factual Questions

1. According to the researchers, the purpose of phenomenological methodology is to
   A. test theory.   B. generate theory.

2. In their review of empirical research on choice and learning, the researchers state that the research they describe has three general limitations. What is the first one they mention?

3. According to the researchers, the purpose of phenomenological research is to describe a phenomenon using what?
   A. The researchers' own words.
   B. The participants' own words.
   C. The words of previous researchers.

4. What were the participants for the pilot study and the main study attending?

5. What did the participants do immediately before being interviewed?

6. "Triangulation of data" refers to collecting and/or interpreting data using more than one method. What was the third method used to triangulate the data in this study?

7. Most teachers (i.e., participants) stated that which group of students were given more choices?
   A. Younger students.   B. Older students.

8. What was the mean (*M*) number of years of teaching experience?

Questions for Discussion

9. In the first stage of their research, the researchers conducted a pilot study using eight participants. In your opinion, how important is this aspect of the research? Does it give you more confidence in the results of the study? Explain.

10. Have the researchers described their "methodological framework" in lines 179–197 adequately? Have they adequately justified the use of qualitative methodology instead of quantitative methodology? Explain.

11. To what extent does the use of "member checks" by the researchers increase your confidence in the validity of the results of this study? (See lines 311–348.)

12. What aspects of the results, if any, surprised you? Were any of the results especially interesting to you? Explain.

13. According to the Appendix just above the references for this article, 78% of the participants were secondary school teachers. Does this fact influence your interpretation of the results? Explain.

14. If you were to conduct a follow-up study on the same topic, would you build on this study by conducting an additional qualitative study *or* would you conduct a quantitative study? Explain.

Quality Ratings

Directions: Indicate your level of agreement with each of the following statements by circling a number from 5 for strongly agree (SA) to 1 for strongly disagree (SD). If you believe an item is not applicable to this research article, leave it blank. Be prepared to explain your ratings.

A. The introduction establishes the importance of the study.

SA   5   4   3   2   1   SD

B. The literature review establishes the context for the study.

        SA   5   4   3   2   1   SD

C. The research purpose, question, or hypothesis is clearly stated.

        SA   5   4   3   2   1   SD

D. The method of sampling is sound.

        SA   5   4   3   2   1   SD

E. Relevant demographics (for example, age, gender, and ethnicity) are described.

        SA   5   4   3   2   1   SD

F. Measurement procedures are adequate.

        SA   5   4   3   2   1   SD

G. All procedures have been described in sufficient detail to permit a replication of the study.

        SA   5   4   3   2   1   SD

H. The participants have been adequately protected from potential harm.

        SA   5   4   3   2   1   SD

I. The results are clearly described.

        SA   5   4   3   2   1   SD

J. The discussion/conclusion is appropriate.

        SA   5   4   3   2   1   SD

K. Despite any flaws, the report is worthy of publication.

        SA   5   4   3   2   1   SD

Article 5

Student Perceptions of the Transition from Elementary to Middle School

PATRICK AKOS
University of North Carolina

From *Professional School Counseling*, 5, 339–345. Copyright © 2002 by American School Counselor Association. Reprinted with permission.

Transitions are often a difficult time of life. The stress and challenge inherent in adjustment can create developmental crises for even the heartiest individuals. Helping students in transition is similarly challenging. To facilitate successful transitions, helping professionals such as school counselors should consider the developmental tasks of various stages, the coping abilities and flexibility of individuals, and the potent systemic and contextual factors of influence.

School personnel recognize the difficult transition students undertake when moving from one level of schooling to another. The transition from elementary to middle school may be especially challenging because it often involves significant school and personal change. One consideration is that most middle school environments differ significantly from the elementary environment (Perkins & Gelfer, 1995). Contextual transitions commonly include additional and unfamiliar students and school staff, and multiple sets of behavioral and classroom rules and expectations.

This contextual change during the transition to middle school is heightened by personal change. Physical, emotional, and social changes that occur in puberty have been associated with heightened emotionality, conflict, and defiance of adults (Berk, 1993). Although pubertal changes have been viewed more as an opportunity than a crisis (Papalia, Olds, & Feldman, 2001), the varied timing of preadolescent development is difficult for students (Berk, 1993). Pubertal changes occur at different times and at different rates for students in the same grade. Therefore, as students transition to middle school, they confront both external contextual changes and internal pubertal changes.

Research has highlighted the developmental and academic difficulties often associated with the transition from elementary to middle school. Both boys and girls show a significant increase in psychological distress across the transition to middle school (Chung, Elias, & Schneider, 1998; Crockett et al., 1989). Even though declines in achievement and increased distress are not gender exclusive, boys tend to show a significant drop in academic achievement, while girls seem to experience a greater level of psychological distress after the transition (Chung et al., 1998). Also during the transition, girls find peer relationships most stressful, whereas boys find peer relationships, conflict with authority, and academic pressures as equal stressors (Elias, Ubriaco, Reese, Gara, Rothbaum, & Haviland, 1992).

Along with psychological and academic outcomes, studies have shown that student motivation and attitudes toward school tend to decline during the transition to middle school (Anderman, 1996; Harter, 1981; Simmons & Blyth, 1987). Eccles et al. (1993) used "stage-environment fit" to describe the poor fit between the developmental needs of preadolescents and the environment of middle school or junior high school (e.g., academic tracking, increasing competition, and awareness of personal peer group status). Declining student motivation and attitude were highlighted by Simmons and Blyth, who found more negative consequences for students in the transition from elementary to middle school as compared to students making the same grade transition in K–8 schools.

While most of the research describes the negative outcomes associated with the transition to middle school, several authors also suggested interventions to reduce negative outcomes. Schumacher (1998) identified social, organizational, and motivational factors as important aspects of successful interventions. Eccles et al. (1993) suggested strategies designed to create a school context appropriate to developmental levels of preadolescents. These included building smaller communities within the school, using teaming and cooperative learning, eliminating tracking, empowering teachers, and improving student/teacher relationships. Similarly, Felner et al. (1993) found teaching teams and advisory programs as important preventative interventions for students in transition.

Although much of the research has either noted the detrimental effects of the school transition or suggested interventions, few investigations have sought student perceptions during the transition to middle school. Arowosafe and Irvin (1992) interviewed students about the transition at the end of the sixth-grade year. They asked students about stressors, school safety, perceptions of school, and what people told them about middle school. Students reported heightened levels of stress related to safety concerns in the school. They also noted that students report friends and the information they received from others as critical factors that affect the transition experience.

85   The purpose of the current investigation was to learn more about student perceptions during the transition from elementary to middle school. The research questions were:

- What questions do students have about middle school?
90   - What specific concerns do students have about middle school?
- What aspects of middle school do students see as positive?
- What do students think middle school will be like?
95   - Whom do students turn to for help during the transition into middle school?
- What is important for students to know about coming to middle school?

Method

Participants

The research was conducted in four phases. For phases I and II, participants included all 331 fifth-grade students in a
100   large, rural, southeastern public school district. Participants included students from three different elementary schools that were scheduled to enter one large middle school (sixth to eighth grade). The mean age was 11.8 years, with a range of 10 to 13 years old. Racial composition of the participants
105   included 59% White students ($n = 195$), 37% Black students ($n = 122$), and 4% Other ($n = 14$). There were 175 females (53%) and 156 males (47%). Approximately 45% ($n = 149$) were on free or reduced lunch during the fifth-grade year.

At the start of the sixth-grade year (phase III), 103 stu-
110   dents (four home-base classrooms) were randomly selected from the 331 fifth-grade students. Demographic information mirrored that of the first sample. Phase IV included a purposeful sample of participants ($n = 97$), again from the 331 fifth-grade students, who experienced success at the middle
115   school. The sample was selected in December of the sixth-grade year. Success was defined by average or better grades (no grade lower than a C), appropriate behavior (no more than one behavior referral), and regular attendance (no more than two unexcused absences) during the first academic
120   marking period (9 weeks) of sixth grade. The researcher felt that perceptions and insight from students with generally positive records, rather than a random or complete sample, would be valuable for understanding student perceptions of the transition. The phase IV sample included students with
125   similar demographics as compared to the participants for the earlier phases.

Setting

Due to the contextual influence on this research (i.e., the significance of elementary school and middle school context), it is important to provide data about the setting. In the
130   participating elementary schools, students attend neighborhood schools that use self-contained classrooms. This middle school is centrally located in the large rural county. The middle school uses teaching teams, four teachers per team that cover primary subjects, and each student has one of
135   those teachers for a home base. As with most middle schools, students move between four to six teachers and are introduced to lockers, showering in gym class, and more

responsibility than in elementary school. Students from this district can also travel for up to one and one-half hours each
140   way on a bus to and from their middle school. Although middle school students commute to school on a bus with students from similar geographic areas, students also ride with all students in grades 6 to 12 in the school district.

Procedure

A longitudinal analysis of student perceptions occurred
145   in four phases, starting in January of fifth grade and concluded in December of sixth grade. In phase I (January of the fifth-grade year), the participants submitted questions about middle school. In phase II (May of the fifth-grade year), the participants completed a questionnaire designed to
150   discover more information about student perspectives. In phase III (in August—the start of the sixth-grade year in middle school), students completed a questionnaire similar to the one used in phase II. The phase III questionnaire was administered in home base at the conclusion of the first two
155   weeks of school. In the last phase, phase IV (December of the sixth-grade year), a purposeful sample of selected successful students completed a questionnaire that repeated questions from phases II and III. The phase IV questionnaire was administered at a meeting of selected students led by the
160   school counselor to assist in planning for the upcoming year.

Data Collection

One writing assignment and three questionnaires were used to elicit student perspectives during the transition. In phase I, participants were asked to write any questions they had about middle school. In phase II, the participants com-
165   pleted a five-item questionnaire. One item of the questionnaire asked students to select concerns from a list of 13 themes. A second item, consisting of the same 13 themes, asked students to select positive aspects. The checklist items were generated from themes written by students in phase I,
170   and each checklist included an open-ended response. The checklists were identical and included items such as changing classes, using your locker, getting good grades, older students, and making friends. The questionnaire also assessed general feelings about coming to middle school. One
175   question asked students to indicate how they feel about coming to middle school (worried, a little worried, a little excited, or excited). Additionally, an open-ended question was included to assess perceptions of what middle school would be like. Finally, one question asked students to select the
180   person or persons they felt were most helpful to them during the transition to middle school (teachers, counselors, parents, friends, or someone else).

During phase III, students completed a second questionnaire in home base. This seven-item questionnaire inquired
185   about academic strategies and goals for sixth grade. Included in the questionnaire were items replicated from previous phases. Students were asked what, if any, questions they had about middle school and what concerns they had about middle school.

190   The third questionnaire again replicated previous questions. This six-item questionnaire included open-ended questions about concerns and best aspects of middle school. The

questionnaire also replicated the question about the person or persons who helped students during the transition to middle school. These questions were worded as reflections over the past transition year (e.g., "What were the best aspects about coming to middle school?"). The questionnaire also included an open-ended question to seek students' recommendations for helping fifth-grade students in the transition to middle school for the next academic year. Finally, the questionnaire concluded with one question about class schedule and one about team membership.

Data Analysis

The open-ended writing assignment and series of questionnaire responses were analyzed for content and qualitative themes concerning the transition. Data were subjected to content analysis to identify emergent themes in the responses. Because categories in a content analysis should be completely exhaustive and mutually exclusive, a step classification system (Holsti, 1969) was used. First, each participant's response was categorized into a meaning unit. Meaning units are described as perceived shifts in attitude or a shift in the emotional quality of a response (Giorgo, 1985). These units are not meant to be independent, but rather expressions of aspects of the whole response. For the writing assignment, each question listed by students was coded as a meaning unit. In questionnaires, individual question responses were also coded as meaning units. Open-ended questions on the questionnaires were analyzed for meaning shifts and coded accordingly. For example, a response such as "both scary and fun" would be coded as two separate meaning units. The data, divided into meaning units, describe meaningful aspects of the response, with minimal inferences from the researcher (Seidman, 1991).

After meaning units were coded and tabulated for all data, the researcher examined the coding for their thematic meaning and collapsed coded content into larger themes. Larger themes were identified from the most frequent responses emerging from the initial coding. For example, one student wrote eight separate questions. Although all eight questions were distinct meaning units, the first five focused on rules and procedures, while the last three listed concerns about bullies and older students. Additionally, several responses did not collapse into larger categories and were judged atypical. These responses represented less than 3% of the total responses.

Researcher and Researcher Bias

The researcher is a White male who at the time of the study was a practicing school counselor at the middle school. Although student perceptions formed the base of all conclusions, the researcher also had assumptions that may have influenced the results. As a school counselor, research bias included an increased focus on personal/social adjustment during the transition. The researcher also assumed a level of anxiety concerning the transition to middle school.

Results

Phase I—January of Fifth-Grade Year

What questions do students have about going to middle school? Three hundred thirty-one participants submitted a total of 555 questions. Most students submitted 3 to 5 questions, with a range from 1 to 15. Twenty-eight percent ($n = 156$) of the questions focused on rules and procedures (e.g., "What's the consequence for being late?"), 16% ($n = 90$) on class schedules in sixth grade (e.g., "Do sixth graders get to do chorus?"), 11% ($n = 60$) on PE or gym class (e.g., "Do you get to play basketball in gym class?"), 9% ($n = 52$) on expectations for sixth graders (e.g., "Do you have a lot of work to do?"), and 9% ($n = 52$) on lunch (e.g., "If you have last lunch, do you always have pizza?"). The remaining questions (27%) addressed topics (each one comprised less than 5% of the total) that included lockers, extracurricular programs, recess, teachers, and sports. Of particular note and consistent with current events in schools today, a few of the questions concerned school violence or safety. For example, two questions included "What happens if you threaten to hurt a teacher?" and "Do people kill people in middle school?"

Phase II—May of Fifth-Grade Year

What specific concerns do students have about coming to middle school? A total of 735 concerns were selected by the 331 participants. The frequency of selected concerns was spread somewhat evenly over the 13 choices provided in the questionnaire. In fact, no one response comprised more than 15% of the total selections. The most frequent responses included older students, 14% ($n = 102$); homework, 13% ($n = 98$); using one's locker, 12% ($n = 88$); and getting good grades, 12% ($n = 85$). Only lunchroom, bathrooms, and the open-ended choice received little attention (comprised less than 1%).

Which aspects of middle school do students see as positive? A total of 808 items were selected by the 331 participants. Parallel to the worries of fifth-grade students, students selected a variety of potential positive aspects of middle school. The most mentioned aspects included making friends, 16% ($n = 130$); gym/PE class, 15% ($n = 124$); using your locker, 11% ($n = 90$); and both changing classes and getting good grades, 10% ($n = 82$ for each). Only the open choice received less than 1% ($n = 10$).

What do students think middle school will be like? A total of 329 meaning units were coded from the responses by the 331 participants. Forty-five percent of the responses listed that middle school will be "fun" ($n = 148$), 14% of the responses mentioned that middle school will be "exciting" ($n = 46$), 11% of responses suggested it will be "cool" ($n = 36$), while 9% of the responses listed "hard" or "scary" ($n = 31$). A variety of other responses (each category represented less than 5% of the total) included "weird," "tight," "good," "awesome," and "like a maze."

Whom do students turn to for help during the transition to middle school? A total of 480 choices were selected by the 331 participants. Thirty-five percent of the responses specified friends ($n = 166$), 22% parents ($n = 105$), 21% teachers ($n = 103$), 14% school counselor ($n = 68$), while 8% mentioned other sources including "cousins," "siblings," and "other family" ($n = 38$).

Phase III—August of the Sixth-Grade Year

What questions do students have about middle school? A total of 91 responses were reported by 103 randomly selected participants from phases I and II. Thirty-four percent of the responses indicated no questions about middle school (*n* = 31), 16% of responses centered on rules and procedures (*n* = 15; e.g., "Can I have one more minute extra to change classes?"), 15% of the responses focused on homework (*n* = 14; e.g., "How much homework do we get?"), and 7% of the responses focused on classes (*n* = 6; e.g., "Do I have to take an elective?"). The remaining responses (*n* = 31) were varied, and each category accounted for less than 5% of the total.

What specific concerns do students have about middle school? A total of 115 responses were tabulated from the 103 randomly selected participants from phases I and II. Twenty-four percent of the responses focused on bullies or older students (*n* = 28; e.g., "Being picked on on the bus with the older kids"), 19% about getting lost in the building (*n* = 22; e.g., "Getting lost"), and 19% about doing well in classes (*n* = 22; e.g., "I am worried that I might not do as well as I have in the past years"). Fourteen percent of the responses suggested there were no concerns (*n* = 16) and 7% of the responses centered on being tardy to class (*n* = 8; e.g., "What happens if I am a minute late to class?"). The remaining responses (*n* = 27) were varied, and each category accounted for less than 5% of the total responses.

Phase IV—December of Sixth-Grade Year

What were the most difficult aspects of middle school? A total of 152 responses were listed by the 97 participants from a purposeful sample of successful students in phases I and II. Twenty-six percent of the responses focused on getting lost (*n* = 40; e.g., "Fear of getting lost"), 13% on making friends (*n* = 19; e.g., "Getting to know people"), 11% on learning the class schedule (*n* = 17; e.g., "Knowing how to change classes"), 10% on lockers (*n* = 16; e.g., "Opening your locker"), 8% on getting to class on time (*n* = 12; e.g., "Tardies, all of them you can get"), and 5% of responses indicated there were no difficulties. The remaining responses (*n* = 50) were varied, and no category accounted for more than 5% of the total.

What were the best aspects of being in middle school? A total of 118 responses were reported from 97 participants of a purposeful sample of successful students from phases I and II. Forty-three percent centered on freedom/choices (*n* = 51; e.g., "You get more freedom, like not having to walk in lines"), 18% focused on friends (*n* = 21; e.g., "Get more time to talk to friends"), 16% on classes (*n* =19; e.g., "Different and better classes"), and 13% on lockers (*n* = 15, e.g., "You get your own space and can put stuff in your locker"). The remaining responses (*n* = 12) were varied, and each category accounted for less than 5% of the total.

Who helped students the most with the transition to middle school? A total of 131 choices represented the people most helpful to the 97 participants. Forty percent of the responses selected friends (*n* = 52), 23% chose teachers (*n* = 30), 19% selected parents (*n* = 25), 11% selected other family (*n* = 14; e.g., "brothers," "cousins"), while 8% selected the school counselor (*n* = 10).

What is important to tell fifth-grade students about coming to middle school? Of the 158 responses from the 97 participants, 23% felt it was most important to tell fifth-grade students about rules (*n* = 36; e.g., "You can't chew gum"), 18% reported expectations/responsibilities (*n* = 29; e.g., "You have to do your homework to go to incentive day"), 10% where classes and other items are located (*n* = 16; e.g., "Art is on the eighth-grade hall"), 9% that it is fun (*n* = 14; e.g., "It is more fun than elementary school"), 8% there are nice teachers (*n* =12; e.g., "Teachers are pretty nice"), and 6% that it is not hard (*n* = 9; e.g., "Most of the classes are easy, except social studies"). The remaining responses (*n* = 69) accounted for categories represented by less than 5% of the total.

Discussion

Students' questions about middle school were dominated by rules and procedures throughout the transition from fifth to sixth grade. Although school rules may be a typical part of orientation programs, being explicit and thorough about rules and procedures seems crucial. The data suggest that students are keenly aware of the contextual change in the transition. Although sixth-grade students at times may exhibit adolescent characteristics, it seems important to remember that these students need an "elementary" orientation concerning rules and procedures. Rules such as walking in the halls or keeping one's hands to oneself, or procedures such as reporting to class before the tardy bell seem simplistic, but these rules and procedures are what students asked about the most. In fact, students 9 weeks into the sixth grade still reflected that expectations and responsibilities were most important to tell fifth-grade students. Although class scheduling is often the start and focus of the orientation process for students in fifth grade, these data suggest that rules/procedures and expectations are most important to students.

Student worries about middle school include a wide variety of topics. Although orientation programming attempts to minimize these concerns, these data indicate that it is important to address a variety of worries involved in the transition. In fact, the spread and frequency of reported worries suggest that there is a generalized or overall persistent level of worry for most students in transition. This conclusion is similar to research suggesting the difficulty of school transitions (Chung et al., 1998; Crockett et al., 1989).

It is also noteworthy both in the fifth grade and at the start of the sixth-grade year that older students or bullies were a particular concern. This echoes findings from Arowosafe and Irvin's (1992) study in which students reported safety as a concern because of rumors about older students. Orientation programming could address this persistent concern by including older students as tour guides or peer mentors in the school to ease the transition. Alternatively, schoolwide bullying programs may help alleviate student concerns about school safety. It is also important to note that homework and doing well in classes seem to be of particular concern to students in both fifth grade and the start of sixth grade. Students' academic concerns may suggest that it is important to build students' confidence in the classroom by teaching homework and study skills. In light of research (Anderman, 1996; Harter, 1981; Simmons & Blyth, 1987) that suggests academic and motivational declines in the transition, addressing these concerns seems especially important. Additionally, getting lost in middle school is a main concern of students upon reflection in December of the sixth-grade year. This fear could be addressed by providing school tours or comprehensive class schedule-based orientations.

Although intervention or orientation programming can be useful to address questions and worries, designing orientation programs that facilitate and build upon student enthusiasm and confidence might provide encouragement to overcome worries and build motivation during the transition. Students recorded more entries for positive aspects than concerns and indicated excitement about a variety of aspects of middle school. In fact, 70% of the student responses were positive to the open-ended question, "What will middle school be like?" During the transition, orientation leaders should highlight aspects of middle school that students seem to enjoy, including increased freedom and choices, the opportunity to change classes, and having their own lockers. Also, it is important to note that students mentioned friends as the top source of help during the transition. This finding supports the need to include peers in transition interventions and orientation programming. Upon reflecting about the transition, sixth-grade students suggest it is important to tell fifth graders that middle school is fun and there are nice teachers.

Although a few studies have found students that thrive in the transition (Crockett et al., 1989; Hirsch & Rapkin, 1987), these data contradict most of the previous research reporting the transition as a rather negative event for students (Anderman, 1996; Chung et al., 1998; Crockett et al., 1989; Elias, Gara, & Ubriaco, 1985; Harter, 1981; Simmons & Blyth, 1987). This study suggests that there are equal, if not more positive, aspects related to the transition to middle school from the student perspective.

This study revealed the importance of including a variety of people in the transition or orientation program. Although school counselors are often responsible for transition planning, students reported that friends, parents, and teachers are all sources of help in the transition. Again, friends and peers are reported as the most frequent resource for students in transition. However, some peers may not provide accurate or helpful information. In this way, it may be useful to identify role-model students who exhibit a desire and skill set that would make them good candidates to help students in transition. An ambassador or peer-helping program may be extremely helpful in the transition (Arowosafe & Irvin, 1992). In fact, Mittman and Packer (1982) found that students attribute a good start frequently to the presence of old friends and the making of new friends. This type of peer support has a strong relationship with adolescent mental health (Hirsch & DeBois, 1992).

Similarly, including teachers and parents in programming is important. Although teachers often provide an orientation to their individual classrooms, integrating teachers in a systemic way may be useful. For example, teachers may have unique classroom rules or procedures, but perhaps a combined orientation can be presented by teachers about general topics such as hall passes or discipline referrals. Arowosafe and Irvin (1992) suggested that teachers can be integrated in advisor/advisee activities. Similarly, although parents are included in open house and class scheduling in most cases, it seems important that parents are informed about rules/procedures and expectations in the middle school.

Arowosafe and Irvin (1992) also suggested it is important to provide parent consultation on the transition to middle school, as they found most parents tended to provide warnings rather than positive information about middle school. In this way, parent orientation can strengthen and support student orientation to the middle school. Students look for help from parents during the fifth-grade year, while teachers replace parents to become more important during the sixth-grade year. This shift in adult influence fits developmentally as preadolescents struggle to form an identity independent of family. Interestingly, students still continue to desire adult assistance throughout the transition.

Limitations

With only one primary researcher, qualitative data coding is limited. No researcher can enter into a study without bias (Rowan, 1981). With only one researcher involved with data analysis and only one school district, this study requires replication. Interviews, rather than questionnaires, with students may also elicit richer information about difficulties and positive aspects of the transition. All of the data are self-report, which has inherent limitations.

Implications for School Counselors

Data from this research and the research to date (e.g., Arowosafe & Irvin, 1992; Crockett et al., 1989; Eccles & Midgley, 1989) on school transition suggest that preventive or proactive programming is needed to assist students with the elementary to middle school transition. The transition provides both a challenge and opportunity for school counselors. This research suggests the following guidelines for school counselors coordinating transition programs: (a) rules, expectations, and responsibilities are the primary concern of students and should be presented early in fifth grade and infused throughout the transition year (this is also an excellent opportunity to include administrators and teachers in transition programming), (b) school counselors have an opportunity both to address concerns and stressors and to promote positive aspects of the transition to middle school, (c) transition programs should include peers, family, and teachers as students look to significant others for help, and (d) transition programs should evolve throughout the transition year as student perceptions and needs change.

References

Anderman, E. (1996). The middle school experience: Effects on the math and science achievement of adolescents with LD. *Journal of Learning Disabilities, 31*, 128–138.

Arowosafe, D., & Irvin, J. (1992). Transition to a middle level school: What kids say. *Middle School Journal, 24*(2), 15–19.

Berk, L. (1993). *Infants, children, and adolescents.* Needham Heights, MA: Allyn & Bacon.

Chung, H., Elias, M., & Schneider, K. (1998). Patterns of individual adjustment changes during the middle school transition. *Journal of School Psychology, 36,* 83–101.

Crockett, L., Peterson, A., Graber, J., Schulenburg, J., & Ebata, A. (1989). School transitions and adjustment during early adolescence. *Journal of Early Adolescence, 9,* 181–210.

Eccles, J., & Midgley, C. (1989). Stage/environment fit: Developmentally appropriate classrooms for early adolescents. In R. Ames & C. Ames (Eds.), *Research on motivation in education* (Vol. 3, pp. 139–186). New York: Academic.

Eccles, J., Wigfield, A., Midgley, C., Reuman, D., Mac Iver, D., & Feldlaufer, H. (1993). Negative effects of traditional middle schools on students' motivation. *The Elementary School Journal, 93,* 553–574.

Elias, M., Gara, M., & Ubriaco, M. (1985). Sources of stress and support in children's transition to middle school: An empirical analysis. *Journal of Clinical Child Psychology, 14,* 112–118.

Elias, M., Ubriaco, M., Reese, A., Gara, M., Rothbaum, P., & Haviland, M. (1992). A measure of adaptation to problematic academic and interpersonal tasks of middle school. *Journal of School Psychology, 30,* 41–57.

Felner, R., Brand, S., Adan, A., Mulhall, P., Flowers, N., Sartain, B., & DuBois, D. (1993). Restructuring the ecology of the school as an approach to prevention during school transitions: Longitudinal follow-ups and extensions of the School Transition Environment Project (STEP). *Prevention in Human Services, 10*(2), 103–136.

Giorgo, A. (1985). *Phenomenology and psychological research.* Pittsburgh, PA: Duquesne University.

Harter, S. (1981). A new self-report scale of intrinsic versus extrinsic orientation in the classroom: Motivational and informational components. *Developmental Psychology, 17,* 300–312.

Hirsch, B., & DeBois, D. (1992). The relation of peer support and psychological symptomatology during the transition to junior high school: A two-year longitudinal analysis. *American Journal of Community Psychology, 20,* 333–347.

Hirsch, B., & Rapkin, B. (1987). The transition to junior high school: A longitudinal study of self-esteem, psychological symptomatology, school life, and social support. *Child Development, 58,* 1235–1243.

Holsti, O. (1969). *Content analysis for the social sciences and humanities.* Reading, MA: Addison-Wesley.

Mittman, A., & Packer, M. (1982). Concerns of seventh graders about their transition to junior high school. *Journal of Early Adolescence, 2,* 319–338.

Papalia, D., Olds, S., & Feldman, R. (2001). *Human development* (8th ed.). New York: McGraw-Hill.

Perkins, P., & Gelfer, J. (1995). Elementary to middle school: Planning for transition. *The Clearing House, 68,* 171–173.

Rowan, J. (1981). A dialectical paradigm for research. In P. Reason & J. Rowan (Eds.), *Human inquiry* (pp. 93–112). New York: John Wiley.

Schumacher, D. (1998). *The transition to middle school* (Report No. EDO-PS-98-6). Washington, DC: Clearinghouse on Elementary and Early Childhood Education. (ERIC Document Reproduction Service No. ED 422 119)

Seidman, I. (1991). *Interviewing as qualitative research: A guide for researchers in education and the social sciences.* New York: Columbia Teachers Press.

Simmons, R., & Blyth, D. (1987). *Moving into adolescence: The impact of pubertal change and school context.* Hawthorne, NY: Aldine de Gruyter.

Acknowledgment: This research was sponsored by the American School Counselor Association Practitioner Grant.

Exercise for Article 5

Factual Questions

1. According to the literature review, after the transition, girls seem to experience a greater level of what (in comparison with boys)?

2. The students were in which grade when phase I of the study was conducted?

3. How were the 103 students for phase III selected from the 331 fifth-grade students?

4. "Meaning units" are described as perceived shifts in what?

5. For Phase I, what is the total number of questions submitted by participants?

6. In Phase III, what percentage of the respondents indicated no questions about middle school?

7. In his discussion of the results, the researcher indicates that the participants' questions about middle school were dominated by what?

Questions for Discussion

8. Phase IV of the study was limited to students who had experienced success at the middle school. What is your opinion on the researcher's decision to limit this phase to just those who were successful? (See lines 109–126.)

9. What is your opinion on the researcher's definition of "success," which is stated in lines 116–120?

10. Some of the data collection was open-ended (e.g., asking students to write their questions about middle school). In addition, there were closed-ended questions in which students selected from choices. What is your opinion on these two approaches to data collection? Are they both needed in a study of this type? Explain.

11. The researcher describes the qualitative data analysis in lines 203–235. In your opinion, is it described in adequate detail? Explain.

12. In your opinion, how important is the material on "Researcher and Researcher Bias"? (See lines 236–243.)

13. The researcher describes the limitations of the research in lines 495–502. Do you think that the results of this research are valuable despite the limitations? Explain.

14. If you were to conduct research on the same topic, what changes in the research methodology, if any, would you make?

Quality Ratings

Directions: Indicate your level of agreement with each of the following statements by circling a number from 5 for strongly agree (SA) to 1 for strongly disagree (SD). If you believe an item is not applicable to this research article, leave it blank. Be prepared to explain your ratings.

A. The introduction establishes the importance of the study.

      SA   5   4   3   2   1   SD

B. The literature review establishes the context for the study.

      SA   5   4   3   2   1   SD

C. The research purpose, question, or hypothesis is clearly stated.

      SA   5   4   3   2   1   SD

D. The method of sampling is sound.

      SA   5   4   3   2   1   SD

E. Relevant demographics (for example, age, gender, and ethnicity) are described.

      SA   5   4   3   2   1   SD

F. Measurement procedures are adequate.

      SA   5   4   3   2   1   SD

G. All procedures have been described in sufficient detail to permit a replication of the study.

      SA   5   4   3   2   1   SD

H. The participants have been adequately protected from potential harm.

      SA   5   4   3   2   1   SD

I. The results are clearly described.

      SA   5   4   3   2   1   SD

J. The discussion/conclusion is appropriate.

      SA   5   4   3   2   1   SD

K. Despite any flaws, the report is worthy of publication.

      SA   5   4   3   2   1   SD

Article 6

A Comparison of Alternatively and Traditionally Prepared Teachers

JOHN W. MILLER
Florida State University

MICHAEL C. MCKENNA
Georgia Southern University

BEVERLY A. MCKENNA
Georgia Southern University

From *Journal of Teacher Education, 49,* 165–176. Copyright © 1998 by the American Association of Colleges of Teacher Education and Corwin Press, Inc., a Sage Publications Company. Reprinted with permission of Corwin Press, Inc.

By 1993, 40 states had instituted alternative certification (AC) programs for degree holders wishing to teach (Sindelar & Marks, 1993). Although these alternative certification programs have occasioned controversy over their value, researchers have conducted very few substantive investigations on their effectiveness. The few extant studies have somewhat contradictory results.

One problem with investigations and even discussion of AC and traditional certification (TC) is the variety of the former. Cornett (1990) provides useful descriptions of the broadly differing ends of the spectrum of AC programs: [Some AC programs] *simply give teachers without the proper credentials (requirements such as education hours completed) an interim status and allow them to be employed while they work to earn the college credits that are equivalent to standard requirements for teacher education programs. On the other hand, several states have developed* **alternative certification programs**—*ones that permit Arts and Sciences graduates to go through intensified but shorter programs (not requiring the typical accumulation of education hours), or meet requirements by demonstrating competencies, or by gaining the necessary expertise through field-based experiences while holding a teaching position* (p. 57, emphasis in original).

In this article, we compare TC program graduates with individuals completing a carefully constructed AC program. The AC program required condensed coursework to meet provisional certification standards, an induction mentoring program, and ongoing casework to meet minimal state certification guidelines. It did not meet the full requirements for a degree program in middle-level education.

Darling-Hammond (1992), reviewing the literature on alternative teacher certification programs, reports: *Studies of teachers admitted through quick-entry alternate routes frequently note that the candidates have difficulty with curriculum development, pedagogical content knowledge, attending to students' differing learning styles and levels, classroom management and student motivation (Feiman-Nemser & Parker, 1990; Grossman, 1989; Lenk, 1989; Mitchell,* *1987). Novice teachers without full training show more ignorance about student needs and differences and about teaching basics than trained beginners (Rottenberg & Berliner, 1990)* (Darling-Hammond, 1992, p. 131).

Some researchers question the content preparation of AC teachers, a supposed strength of AC programs. McDiarmid and Wilson (1991) compared the mathematical knowledge of teachers from two different AC programs with that of TC teachers and noted that teachers with AC preparation lacked depth of content knowledge.

They did not improve appreciably through teaching the content: *Our analyses should raise questions about assumptions that underlie policy initiatives such as alternate routes: Specifically, should a major in mathematics—or in any discipline—be accepted as a proxy for the kinds of understandings of the subject essential to helping diverse learners understand critical ideas and concepts* (McDiarmid & Wilson, 1991, p. 102)?

Several studies support the equivalence and occasional advantages of AC programs when compared with TC programs. Adelman (1986) found that AC programs attract individuals with greater classroom effectiveness than that possessed by TC teachers. In an evaluation of Texas programs, Wale and Irons (1990) found that administrators held favorable opinions of AC teachers. Hawk and Schmidt (1989) found no difference between AC and TC teachers, either in observed classroom performance or National Teacher Examination scores. Other researchers (Barnes, Salmon, & Wale, 1989; Dewalt & Ball, 1987; Etheridge, Butler, Etheridge, & James, 1988; Guyton, Fox, & Sisk, 1991; Hutton, 1987; Mishima, 1987; Soares, 1989, 1990) report similar findings. Comparisons based on achievement test performance suggest that AC programs do not necessarily lead to lower student outcomes (Barnes, et al., 1989; Denton & Peters, 1988; Gomez & Grobe, 1990; Stafford & Barrow, 1994).

Yet, legitimate reasons exist to continue examining the value of alternative programs, especially those employing innovative methodologies. First, a substantial database suggests that AC teachers are not inherently inferior to their TC colleagues. Second, alternative certification programs have been in place as long as there have been certification programs of any kind. All states award probationary certificates in areas of shortage of people from TC programs. Third, widespread desire exists to create diversity in the teaching

85 force by recruiting people with a variety of life experiences. AC populations are demonstrably more diverse than TC populations (McKibbin & Ray, 1994; Sindelar & Marks, 1993). Fourth, the periodic need to meet specific teacher shortages is likely to continue. Fifth, conflicting results of 90 comparative studies suggest that AC programs cannot be easily lumped together for generalization. McKibbin (1995), for example, has listed nine different alternative routes to teaching in California. Alternative certification is here to stay; researchers should investigate not whether such pro-95 grams work, but which ones work best.

The present research evidence comparing AC with TC teachers is inconclusive and somewhat contradictory. Numerous reasons for such inconsistent results exist: methodological differences across studies, lack of accepted 100 dependent variables, problems with operationally defining the term *alternative certification,* and other measurement problems. Hawley (1990) cites key problems with such studies:

- *Alternative certification teachers from a given district are*
105 *not compared with TC teachers from that district, but with teachers statewide or nationally or some other jurisdiction that is very different from the district being studied.*

- *Demonstrating that, on average, AC teachers have higher test scores, or grade point averages, or knowledge of sub-*
110 *ject matter when such criteria are used to screen out AC applicants, attests not to the superiority of AC programs in attracting candidates, but to the simple fact that different requirements for entry result in different entrants.*

- *Measures of teaching performance are often administered*
115 *by principals. Principals usually must commit to support of the AC program before AC teachers are assigned to their schools. And they must devote resources to mentoring and other support.*

- *Most studies of AC do not try to systematically assess*
120 *teacher performance. When such assessments do take place, they typically rely on measures that are required by the district or the state.*

- *Some of the more interesting studies comparing TC teachers with those who enter teaching through alternate routes*
125 *involve very small numbers of teachers and the reader has no way of knowing whether the teachers studied are representative.*

- *Some studies fail to distinguish between types of (AC) programs when the data are analyzed* (pp. 7–8).

130 In the remainder of this article, we report our studies investigating the efficacy of an AC program for middle-grade teachers designed by faculty at a southeastern university and funded by the BellSouth Foundation. We designed these studies to overcome the methodological limitations Hawley 135 (1990) cited to answer questions about programmatic strengths on which to capitalize and weaknesses to reduce or eliminate in AC programs.

The Alternative Program

In May 1989, the university initiated an AC training model for 70 middle-grade teachers. The program included 140 individualized and intensive programs of study that comply

with Georgia Certification Standards (provisional). Coursework was undertaken in the 1989 summer quarter to qualify the 70 participants for provisional certification and fall 1989 employment in Georgia public schools. Sixty-seven partici-145 pants successfully completed the coursework and were in classrooms in Fall 1989. Depending on initial assessments, students took between 15 and 25 quarter hours (the equivalent of 9–15 semester hours) prior to the beginning of their teaching assignments in the fall.

150 During their initial year as teachers, participants were heavily involved with additional coursework and mentoring from university and public school faculty to support their initial instruction. The experiences were designed recognizing that placing teachers in classrooms without university 155 supervision or carefully controlled mentor interaction can lead to ineffective practices (Grossman, 1989; Hawley & Rosenholtz, 1984; McKibbin & Ray, 1994) and in the belief that on-the-job feedback from supervisors and mentors is a distinguishing feature of effective AC programs.

160 Interns had their own classrooms; they received a substantial amount of supervision. A university supervisor observed each teacher eight times during the year and held post-observation conferences. The supervisor met with mentors individually to monitor the success of the teacher–165 mentor relationship. During their first year, teachers took a biweekly class taught by the university supervisor that focused on examining common problems, exploring solutions collaboratively, and providing support. Teachers took regular course offerings depending on their assessed needs for 170 certification.

In subsequent years, university support ceased except for additional coursework required of some participants to earn regular certification. Mentor relationships continued on an informal basis.

Study 1

175 We conducted the initial study to examine differences in teaching practices between those educated in TC and AC programs. We examined behavioral differences of teachers in relationship to training differences.

Subjects

Sixty-seven of the 70 summer participants were placed in 180 classrooms in Fall 1989. Three years later, we traced 41 of the 67 AC students to teaching positions accessible to the campus. They became the AC sample. We matched them with TC counterparts, teachers who began in the same year and thus had 3 years of teaching experience. They taught the 185 same subjects, at the same grade level, at the same school; all had graduated from varying TC programs from instate and out-of-state public and private institutions.

Instrument and Data Collection

We used a 15-item, 4-node rating scale to evaluate observed lessons for specific dimensions of instruction known 190 to be causally related to learning (e.g., Hunter & Russell, 1977; Rosenshine, 1986). The instrument has two subscales, Effective Lesson Components (9 items) and Effective Pupil-Teacher Interaction Components (6 items). The Effective

Lesson Components include Focus, Objective and Purpose, Goal Direction, Exposition, Modeling, Practice, Monitoring, Feedback and Adjustment, and Closure. The Effective Pupil-Teacher Interaction Components include Questioning Strategies, High Pupil Participation, Creative and Enthusiastic Presentation, Appropriate Reinforcement, Appropriate Constructive Criticism, and Appropriate Negative Consequences.

We labeled rating-scale nodes as follows:
1 = *No attempt to exhibit the behavior*
2 = *Limited effectiveness in exhibiting the behavior*
3 = *Moderate effectiveness in exhibiting the behavior*
4 = *High effectiveness in exhibiting the behavior*
We allowed an NA rating (no appropriate opportunity to exhibit the behavior) for some categories (e.g., Focus, Practice) because circumstances might have prevented the teacher from applying the categories during a given observation. For other categories (e.g., Monitoring, High Pupil Participation), we assumed that evaluation was possible during any observation, and we did not permit the NA.

Prior to the study, we precisely defined each category of teacher behavior and developed instructional materials (including printed manuals and videotaped lessons) to train observers in script taping and converting completed script tapes into viable ratings. The instrument and the training program had been carefully and systematically validated prior to the present study (Miller & McKenna, 1988; Miller, McKenna, & Davison, 1990; Miller, McKenna, & Harris, 1989). We trained two certified teachers as observers because of their extensive classroom experience and because the instrument had been validated on the basis of practitioner observers. Each observer observed and evaluated all 82 of the subjects. The observations were blind; observers did not know that 41 subjects were alternatively certified and 41 were traditionally certified. They were informed that they would be observing teachers to establish an evaluation data base for the instrument. The observations were unscheduled; if an intact lesson was not being taught, the observer would stay until an intact lesson was begun or return on another occasion. They then arranged observations of each pair of teachers. Two observers were present for all lessons observed so that ratings for each category could be juried in case of disagreement after the completion of their script tapes. In nearly all cases, jurying was unnecessary because the two ratings coincided. Observers visited both teachers in each pair on the same day. They observed at a time the teachers had suggested; teachers were encouraged to select a time when they were introducing new material. Both observers had their observational skills validated prior to any data collection.

Results

We conducted preliminary analysis steps to identify outliers and assess assumptions for the multivariate analysis of variance (MANOVA) procedure. First, inspection of histograms of each dependent variable for each group did not suggest the presence of outlier observations. Second, we assessed the assumption of multivariate normality by examining the histograms mentioned above. Inspection of the plots suggested the assumption of multivariate normality was tenable. Finally, we considered the scores of each teacher to be independent. Thus, we identified no unusual data values, and MANOVA assumptions appeared to be met.

We computed means and standard deviations for all 15 categories of teacher behavior for both groups. Occasional ratings of NA caused the number of subjects to vary for some categories. We also computed means and standard deviations for the two subscales. We eliminated teachers from the computation of the mean for that subscale who received a rating of NA for any item in one of the two subscales. Descriptive statistics for all categories and for the two subscales appear in Table 1. The difference in sample means between the two groups appears small for all the individual categories, with the largest difference being approximately 0.2.

We used three separate MANOVAs to determine if the small sample differences between groups obtained in the study reflect real differences in the populations or are due to sampling variability. In the first MANOVA, we used the two subscales as the dependent variables. A nonsignificant Wilks's lambda resulted, Wilks's lambda = .98, $F(2,31) = 0.4$, $p = .69$. No group differences on the two subscales were present. In the second MANOVA, the nine Effective Lesson Component categories were used as the dependent variables. Again, we detected no significant differences, Wilks's lambda = .76, $F(9,24) = 0.8$, $p = .59$. Finally, we used the six Effective Pupil-Teacher Interaction measures as dependent variables. Once again, we observed no significant differences, Wilks's lambda = .93, $F(6, 66) = 0.9$, $p = .53$. The analyses suggest that the differences obtained in the study between traditional and alternative groups were due to sampling variability and do not reflect true differences in the populations.

We performed follow-up analyses to identify whether the study had adequate precision to support a finding of no practical importance in the population. To identify whether the study had adequate precision, we computed 99% confidence intervals for each of the contrasts. We selected the more stringent 99% confidence level to protect against the inflation of family-wise error rate. We then compared intervals against a threshold value of 1 for the individual categories and values of 9 and 6 for the two subscales, respectively, with the belief that a 1-unit change on the 4-node rating scale reflects an important difference. Confidence intervals that lie completely below the value of practical importance allow us to conclude that we have high confidence that the true population difference is of no practical importance. The results, shown in Table 1, suggest that this study had sufficient precision of estimation, as the range of each of the confidence intervals lies entirely below the threshold values of importance. There appear to be no reliably important differences between the alternative and traditional teaching groups for the behavior examined in this study. We accept the null hypothesis that groups do not differ on these sets of teaching behaviors.

Table 1
Contrasts Between the Traditional and Alternative Groups

| | Group | | | | | | Point estimate of contrast | SE | 99% confidence interval |
| | TC | | | AC | | | | | |
Variable	N	M	SD	N	M	SD			
Focus	32	2.9	1.0	41	2.8	0.9	0.15	0.27	(−0.57, 0.87)
Objective and purpose	16	2.6	1.0	18	2.7	0.9	−0.14	0.26	(−0.81, 0.54)
Goal direction	41	3.4	0.6	41	3.3	0.6	0.12	0.14	(−0.25, 0.49)
Exposition	41	3.1	0.4	41	3.1	0.6	0.03	0.12	(−0.29, 0.35)
Modeling	41	3.1	0.6	41	3.0	0.7	0.09	0.16	(−0.34, 0.52)
Practice	34	3.2	0.5	41	3.3	0.5	−0.10	0.13	(−0.45, 0.25)
Monitoring	41	3.2	0.7	41	3.2	0.7	0.01	0.15	(−0.37, 0.39)
Feedback and adjustment	41	3.3	0.6	41	3.1	0.7	0.19	0.15	(−0.20, 0.58)
Closure	34	2.1	1.0	40	2.2	0.9	−0.01	0.25	(−0.66, 0.64)
Effective lessons subscale		27.9	4.4	N/A	26.8	4.2	1.16	1.47	(−2.87, 5.19)
Questioning strategies	27	3.2	0.5	38	3.1	0.6	0.06	0.13	(−0.28, 0.40)
High pupil participation	41	3.4	0.7	41	3.5	0.6	−0.05	0.15	(−0.45, 0.35)
Creative and enthusiastic presentation	41	3.1	0.7	41	3.0	0.7	0.12	0.16	(−0.31, 0.55)
Appropriate reinforcement	40	3.1	0.5	35	2.9	0.5	0.16	0.12	(−0.16, 0.48)
Appropriate constructive criticism	41	3.1	0.5	36	2.9	0.6	0.22	0.14	(−0.15, 0.58)
Appropriate negative consequences	33	2.8	0.6	41	2.8	0.6	0.09	0.14	(−0.28, 0.46)
Effective pupil-teacher interaction subscale		18.7	2.6	N/A	18.2	2.6	0.49	0.60	(−1.10, 2.08)

Discussion

That the two groups did not significantly differ on any of the dimensions surveyed suggests alternative explanations. The most apparent is that certification programs did not dif-
310 ferentially affect teachers' performance. Two conditions affected this result: Data were gathered 3 years after preservice preparation for TC teachers had ended, and intervening professional experiences may have had an equalizing effect. Ongoing mentorship was designed to accomplish this result.
315 A second factor is that the AC teachers, like their traditional colleagues, faced annual evaluations based on a rating scale that, while different from the instrument used in the study, drew on the same effectiveness literature.

An unlikely alternative explanation is that the two ob-
320 servers exhibited a response set in which ratings clustered around the moderate node (rating = 3) even when observed evidence suggested otherwise. Examination of Table 1 reveals sizeable standard deviations (for a scale spanning only three units), indicating considerable variance in the ratings.
325 In Closure, the mean for both groups differed markedly from the means for most other categories. Finally, the training program to prepare the observers had been validated through studies establishing its effectiveness in developing the ability to produce ratings consistent with observed evidence (Miller
330 & McKenna, 1988).

The most reasonable conclusion is the most obvious: Alternative certification did not lead to inferior practice among teachers evaluated 3 years into their careers. The program through which these teachers passed did not end with
335 graduation but included a two-part mentoring component supporting them through their initial year. Preparatory coursework followed by supervised application of what is learned exemplifies the direct instruction model on the basis of which these teachers were evaluated.

Study 2

340 We conducted a second study to examine the effects of AC versus TC teachers on the achievement outputs of their students. The treatments previously discussed in relation to Study 1 remain the same in Study 2. The sample, instrument, data collecting, and statistical analysis all differ.

Sample

345 From the 41 AC teachers and 41 TC teachers from the observational analysis, we selected only those in self-contained fifth- and sixth-grade classrooms. We did so to have students taught all of their basic subject matter competencies in a given year by a single teacher. Teachers in subject-
350 matter-defined middle-grade classrooms, such as middle-grade science, could not be fairly evaluated because of the indirect alignment between their teaching, the teaching of others, and the focus of the achievement test score. In the self-contained classrooms, where both pre- and post-
355 achievement test scores were available, we could determine entry level differences to control for prior differences of achievement based on interaction with other teachers or any other related factors. We could attribute posttest gains to the instruction of a single teacher rather than that of several
360 teachers for each individual student.

Eighteen classrooms of students participated in the achievement test score analysis done in Study 2. For each of these 18 classrooms, we utilized all students present for the entire year and having pretest and posttest scores. This re-
365 sulted in a sample of 188 students taught by AC teachers and 157 students taught by TC teachers.

There were no apparent systematic biases in the way students were placed into these classrooms. They were not ability grouped; therefore, there was no systematic reason to
370 suspect that there would be pretest differences. Nevertheless, we collected pretest scores for all subjects and analyzed differences between the AC and the TC distributions of students' scores. There were no entry level differences approaching significance on either the total reading or total
375 math variables, or on any of the other subtest scores.

Instrument and Data Collection

Students took the Iowa Test of Basic Skills (ITBS) as a posttest at the conclusion of the academic year. The total reading and total math subtest normal curve equivalent scores (NCEs) were the primary bases of analysis. To provide general indicators of some different types of thinking skills, we analyzed three other math subtests: concepts, problem solving, and computation NCE scores.

The achievement tests were administered under normal standardized procedures by the classroom teachers and were retrieved from the district's database. Students with posttest scores in AC and TC teachers' classrooms were then traced backwards to pretest scores.

Results

NCE means and standard deviations for total math and total reading subtests, and the three additional math subtests are in Table 2. After determining that there were no preexisting differences based on pretest measures, we concluded no covariate was necessary. The data met the same major assumptions for MANOVA as the data analyzed for Study 1. We used the posttest MANOVA procedure to control for family-wise error rate and test the hypothesis that group population means did not differ for any of the dependent measures and combinations. A conceptual relationship existed between the nature of the dependent variables; a statistical test of the quality of variance assumption was conducted and met. The normality of the distributions was examined with histograms and appeared to be met. Comparison between the AC and TC students' test score means were then conducted by a multivariate analysis of variance (MANOVA). A nonsignificant Wilks's lambda resulted, $F(1,158) = .99$, $p = .83$. No significant difference was observed in the effect of the independent variable (method of training) on the collective dependent measures. Further examination of the five posttest means indicated that there were virtually no differences on any of the dependent measures.

Table 2
Means and Standard Deviations of NCEs for Total Math, Total Reading, and Math Subtests

Test	Group			
	TC		AC	
	M	SD	M	SD
Total math	47.6	18.4	46.9	19.1
Total reading	44.5	16.2	45.9	16.1
Math concepts	46.1	17.2	46.0	16.9
Math problem solving	44.5	15.8	46.3	17.6
Math computation	41.3	15.1	45.2	15.2

N: TC = 157, AC = 188

Follow-up analyses indicated that Study 2 had adequate precision to support a finding of no practical importance in the population.

Discussion

The results of the student output measures closely parallel those of the observational study. There was no difference in average student achievement test score levels, based upon whether students had been taught by AC or TC teachers.

Although this was not an experiment in that there was no random assignment of classrooms, little indication exists that any entry-level biases would have affected these test scores. The school district did not use any grouping or clustering assignment processes that would create differences and used a random procedure within grade levels and within buildings to assign students to classrooms. Insofar as the ITBS reflects student learning in reading and mathematics, there were no relative advantages or disadvantages in terms of student mean output whether AC or TC teachers taught them.

Although the value of these achievement test scores may be questioned, no indications existed of trends of differences in student output based on these measures used in a district-wide procedure. There appeared to be no effect of type of teacher training on student achievement.

Study 3

The third study was qualitative. We conducted it to gain insight into AC and TC teachers' perceptions of their teaching abilities.

Subjects

The 82 teachers in the 41 pairs of matched subjects in Study 1 were the total sample for Study 3. The same selection and matching procedures in Study 1 apply in Study 3.

Instrument and Data Collection

We developed a direct interview protocol to collect qualitative data. The protocol contained three major areas of questions and some recommended supportive probes in each of these three areas.

The interviews were face-to-face meetings between trained interviewers and all subjects in their classrooms. To avoid formalization of response and to create a more discussion-oriented atmosphere, interviewers did not tape-record the interviews. They conducted the interviews as informal discussions between teachers concerning perceptions of their experiences. We used practicing teachers to gather data because of their classroom experience and because interviewees might be forthcoming reflecting with a peer. The three major areas discussed included teachers' perceptions of their preparation level when they began teaching 3 years previously, their perception of their current level of competency, and their perception of problems encountered across their 3-year careers. Interviewers kept complete notes; these notes were later transcribed. Interviewers did not know that some subjects were AC teachers and some were TC. Questions in the interview protocol were composed to not reveal to the interviewer the type of preparation the interviewee had undergone.

Results and Discussion

All 82 subjects responded to discussion probes in each of the three areas. Content analysis of the resulting commentary reveals interesting trends. Although there were differences in the qualitative aspects of the AC and TC teachers' responses, differences within those categories were greater than differences across the categories. The following are generalizations about teachers' feelings of adequacy of preparation at the beginning of their teaching experience.

470 Neither AC nor TC teachers felt particularly well prepared. TC teachers sometimes tried to explain this more as
the natural tendency to feel inadequate at the beginning of a
career, whereas AC teachers felt that something was missing. Typical comments from TC teachers, when asked, *How*
475 *prepared did you feel as a teacher when you started your*
job? included

- *I did not feel very prepared. Of course, no one ever*
  feels truly prepared.
- *Not too prepared, but not because of the program I*
480 *was in—it's just the nature of teaching.*
- *I'm sure that like all first-year teachers I had some*
  problems and felt uneasy.
- *Like anyone, there was the uncertainty of a new job.*
- *I had all the theories for teaching, but lacked any*
485 *real classroom experience in my undergraduate*
  program.

Some AC teachers also felt inadequate. They believed
they had gaps that could be traced to their preparation.

- *I did not know how to control behavior.*
490 - *I did not know how to write a lesson plan.*
- *Very unprepared. I'm not sure whether student*
  teaching would have helped, but I think so.
- *Very shaky. I don't think I would have made it with-*
  out my mentor.
495 - *Some hands-on experience would have been helpful.*
  I had no earthly idea of how to do a lesson.

More TC teachers felt adequately prepared than not. The
percentage expressing confidence was higher for TC than
AC teachers. They made comments like

500 - *I was very confident. I felt pleased with how my un-*
  dergraduate program prepared me.
- *Fairly prepared. I had been involved some with the*
  schools beforehand.
- *Pretty prepared, but then I guess no one goes in*
505 *completely prepared.*

Responses to the first question indicated that both groups
were somewhat unsure of themselves. Some TC teachers had
a higher confidence level, whereas others felt similarly to
AC teachers. TC teachers explained some of their inadequa-
510 cies as the natural by-product of beginning a new job.

Question 2 concerning the current feeling of competence
to practice elicited little or no differences between the
groups. The TC teachers said things like

- *I feel very prepared. On-the-job experience does*
515 *wonders.*
- *I owe a great deal to my mentor. I feel very confi-*
  dent now.
- *Experience is the best teacher. There is no substitute*
  for actual classroom experience.
520 - *Now I am very prepared. I feel the comfort that*
  comes from experience.

AC teachers, who might have been expected to place
even more value in the more practical experience, did not
differ from their TC counterparts who also placed a great
525 deal of faith in on-the-job practice. AC teachers made comments like

- *I am very prepared now. I have learned how to have*
  good rapport with my students.
- *Now I feel I am on equal footing with the teachers*
530 *who went through the traditional route.*
- *I have taught several years at the same school, so*
  now I feel confident.
- *I am very grateful for the opportunity that this pro-*
  gram created for me and for all the help that was
535 *provided in the induction program.*
- *I enjoy teaching more now, I am more relaxed and*
  prepared. The veteran mentor really helped.

Both TC and AC teachers, after having had experience,
felt competent. At the end of the 3-year experimental period,
540 TC and AC teachers were not distinguishable based upon
their comments concerning their competence.

The types of problems TC and AC teachers encountered
seem not to differ. Discipline and classroom management
were by far the most common problems both cited. Both
545 groups cited the ability to deal with special need students, to
work with emerging technologies, and to deal with parents
less often, but equally frequently. A number of the AC
teachers commented favorably on the induction program and
the help of their mentors in overcoming some of their initial
550 difficulties.

Summary and Implications

We conducted three studies to address basic issues of research design Hawley (1990) identified as characteristic of
comparative investigations of AC and TC teachers. We addressed his observation that AC teachers are too often com-
555 pared with TC teachers from other districts by using
same-school pairs of TC and AC teachers. We further
matched each pair by subject matter taught and years of experience. Hawley's observation that different screening criteria for AC and TC trainees may skew samples even before
560 training begins was not a problem in these studies because
the AC cohort was not subject to special admission requirements, such as higher test performance. We met his concern
that classroom observation data often come from principals
through using trained observers who were outsiders to the
565 school and who visited classrooms without knowledge of the
certification history of those observed. We used a well-vali-
dated instrument with which none of the teachers was familiar.

Hawley also noted that the small sample sizes in some
570 studies raise questions about the representativeness of the
teachers included as subjects. We consistently used a relatively large cohort of AC teachers. Finally, Hawley noted
some studies fail to distinguish types of AC programs in data
analysis, a difficulty occurring when results of several inves-
575 tigations are aggregated. Our results are limited to a single
AC program with well-defined characteristics. This clarity
of identity gives the results their strength.

The preceding does not mean no design limitations were
present. Examining the trainees of a single program and after
580 an interval of only 3 years constrains the generalizability of
finding and leaves unaddressed such matters as first-year
efficacy. Nevertheless, two circumstances make it possible

to arrive at important conclusions about alternative certification on the basis of these results. The first is that we systematically accounted for notable past difficulties with research. The second is the logical progression in planning the second and third studies to extend and clarify the results.

The combined results of Study 1, dealing with observable differences in classroom teaching behaviors; Study 2, dealing with achievement test score performance of students; and Study 3, dealing with qualitative differences in the perceptions of teachers, support the conclusion that, after 3 years of experience and mentoring, no major differences exist between AC and TC teachers. Yet, these studies provide no solace for those who believe that anyone with a bachelor's degree can be placed in a classroom and expect to be equally as successful as those having completed traditional education programs.

We can clearly say that after 3 years, there appear to be no observable teaching behavior differences, student output differences, or attitudinal differences concerning perceptions of competence of people prepared under the two conditions. Other indicators might have revealed differences between the two groups of teachers compared in these studies. Student behaviors, for example, might have been examined with respect to library use, cooperative group work, engaged time, and many other potential impact measures. Teacher behaviors might have been more broadly indexed to include professional memberships, integration into the school culture, emergent philosophical orientations, and any number of other conceivable outcomes. Although interesting, such possibilities seem less central to the principal issues involving issues addressed by the outcomes examined in the present systematic series of investigations. Carefully constructed induction programs may be a good means of including a broader, more diverse teaching population than limiting all avenues of entrance to the profession through TC preparation. The three studies reported here support carefully constructed AC programs with extensive mentoring components, post-graduation training, regular inservice classes, and ongoing university supervision.

A most constructive result of data interpretation would be to examine the relevance of the induction program presented to AC teachers as a model for all beginning professionals. Extensive mentoring with peer professionals, continued university support, and specifically constructed inservice classes during the first 3 years of preparation may be a model that would enhance the teaching abilities of all. Rather than construing these results as supporting a means of diminishing potential differences, it may be more appropriate to envision a comprehensive induction model that provides a baseline of support for those entering service through AC routes and enrichment or even remediation for those entering via TC programs.

References

Adelman, N. E. (1986). *An exploratory study of teacher alternative certification and retraining programs* (U.S. Department of Education, Data Analysis Support Center, Contract No. 300-85-0103). Washington, DC: Policy Studies Associates.

Barnes, S., Salmon, J., & Wale, W. (1989, March). *Alternative teacher certification in Texas.* Paper presented at the meeting of the American Educational Research Association, San Francisco. (ERIC Document Reproduction Service No. 307 316)

Cornett, L. M. (1990). Alternative certification: State policies in the SREB states. *Peabody Journal of Education, 67*(3), 55-83.

Darling-Hammond, L. (1992). Teaching and knowledge: Policy issues posed by alternate certification for teachers. In W. D. Hawley (Ed.), *The alternative certification of teachers* (Teacher Education Monograph No. 14, pp. 123-154). Washington, DC: ERIC Clearinghouse on Teacher Education.

Denton, J. J., & Peters, W. H. (1988, September). *Program assessment report: Curriculum evaluation of a non-traditional program for certifying teachers.* College Station: Texas A & M University. (ERIC Document Reproduction Service No. 300 361)

Dewalt, M., & Ball, D. W. (1987). Some effects of training on the competence of beginning teachers. *Journal of Educational Research, 80,* 343-347.

Etheridge, C. P., Butler, E. D., Etheridge, G. W., & James, T. (1988, February). *The effects of type of teacher preparation program on internships in secondary schools.* Paper presented at the meeting of the American Association of Colleges for Teacher Education, New Orleans. (ERIC Document Reproduction Service No. 293 807)

Feiman-Nemser, S., & Parker, M. B. (1990). *Making subject matter part of the conversation or helping beginning teachers learn to teach.* East Lansing, MI: National Center for Research on Teacher Education.

Gomez, D. L., & Grobe, R. P. (1990, April). *Three years of alternative certification in Dallas: Where are we?* Paper presented at the meeting of the American Educational Research Association, Boston.

Grossman, P. L. (1989). A study in contrast: Sources of pedagogical content knowledge for secondary English teachers. *Journal of Teacher Education, 40*(5), 24-31.

Guyton, E., Fox, M. C., & Sisk, K. A. (1991). Comparison of teaching attitudes, teacher efficacy, and teacher performance of first year teachers prepared by alternative and traditional teacher education programs. *Action in Teacher Education, 13(2),* 1-9.

Hawk, P. P., & Schmidt, M. W. (1989). Teacher preparation: A comparison of traditional and alternative programs. *Journal of Teacher Education, 40*(5), 53-58.

Hawley, W. D. (1990). The theory and practice of alternative certification: Implications for the improvement of teaching. *Peabody Journal of Education, 67*(3), 3-34.

Hawley, W. D., & Rosenholtz, S. (1984). Good schools: What research says about improving student achievement. *Peabody Journal of Education, 61*(4), 1-178.

Hunter, M., & Russell, D. (1977). How can I plan more effective lessons? *Instructor, 87*(2), 74-75, 88.

Hutton, J. B. (1987). *Alternative teacher certification: Its policy implications for classroom and personnel practice.* Austin: University of Texas. (ERIC Document Reproduction Service No. 286 264)

Lenk, H. A. (1989). *A case study: The induction of two alternate route social studies teachers.* Unpublished doctoral dissertation, Teachers College, Columbia University.

McDiarmid, G. W., & Wilson, S. M. (1991). An exploration of the subject matter knowledge of alternate route teachers: Can we assume they know their subject? *Journal of Teacher Education, 42*(2), 93-103.

McKibbin, M. D. (1995, April). *A longitudinal study of the effectiveness of district intern alternative certification programs in California.* Paper presented at the meeting of the American Educational Research Association, San Francisco.

McKibbin, M., & Ray, L. (1994). A guide for alternative certification program improvement. *The Educational Forum, 58,* 201-208.

Miller, J. W., & McKenna, M. C. (1988, April). *Effects of a training program on the ability to observe and analyze instruction.* Paper presented at the meeting of the American Educational Research Association, New Orleans.

Miller, J. W., McKenna, M. C., & Davison, R. G. (1990, April). *The relationship of observational notes to the quality of post-observation teacher conferences.* Paper presented at the meeting of the American Educational Research Association, Boston.

Miller, J. W., McKenna, M. C., & Harris, B. (1989, March). *The utility of differing scripting strategies in evaluating teaching performance.* Paper presented at the meeting of the American Educational Research Association, San Francisco.

Mishima, P. (1987). *The California teacher trainee program: A review.* Sacramento, CA: California State Office of the Legislative Analyst. (ERIC Document Reproduction Service No. 293 801)

Mitchell, N. (1987). *Interim evaluation report of the alternative certification program* (REAB7027-2). Dallas, TX: DISD Department of Planning, Evaluation, and Testing.

Rosenshine, B. V. (1986). Synthesis of research on explicit teaching. *Educational Leadership, 43*(7), 60-69.

Rottenberg, C. J., & Berliner, D. C. (1990, April). *Expert and novice teachers' conceptions of common classroom activities.* Paper presented at the meeting of the American Educational Research Association, Boston.

Sindelar, P. T., & Marks, L. J. (1993). Alternative route training: Implications for elementary education and special education. *Teacher Education and Special Education, 16,* 146-154.

Soares, L. M. (1989, February). *Correlates of self-attribution and competency of liberal arts graduates in teacher training programs.* Paper presented at the annual meeting of the Eastern Educational Research Association, Savannah, GA. (ERIC Document Reproduction Service No. 304 408)

Soares, L. M. (1990, April). *Comparisons of student teachers and alternative route candidates.* Paper presented at the meeting of the American Educational Research Association, Boston.

Stafford, D., & Barrow, G. (1994). Houston's alternative certification program. *The Educational Forum, 58,* 193-200.

Wale, W. M., & Irons, E. J. (1990, April). *An evaluative study of Texas alternative certification programs.* Paper presented at the meeting of the American Educational Research Association, Boston.

About the authors: John W. Miller is dean of the College of Education at Florida State University, Tallahassee. His specializations include administration of teacher education programs. Michael C. McKenna is professor at Georgia Southern University, Statesboro. His specializations include teacher education and literacy education. Beverly A. McKenna is instructor at Georgia Southern University, Statesboro. Her specializations include internships in elementary and middle-level education.

Exercise for Article 6

Factual Questions

1. Why do the authors say that "AC programs cannot be easily lumped together for generalization"?

2. According to Hawley (1990), which is cited in the literature review, what are the problems with some of the "more interesting studies" that compare TC teachers with AC teachers?

3. How many of the 70 summer AC participants were used in Study 1?

4. What do the researchers mean when they say that the observations in Study 2 were "blind"?

5. In the results for Study 2, the researchers state that they "accept the null hypothesis." What does this null hypothesis say?

6. Assuming that there is one teacher per classroom, how many teachers were involved in Study 2?

7. In Study 2, what was the "independent variable"?

8. Why did the researchers decide *not* to tape-record the interviews in Study 3?

9. How many of the teachers responded to the discussion probes in Study 3?

Questions for Discussion

10. The researchers use more direct quotations in the introduction to their article than the researchers who wrote other articles in this book. In general, do you think it is a good idea to use direct quotations or to paraphrase as the other researchers did? Explain.

11. This study is based on teachers who began teaching in 1989. Yet, it was not published until 1998. Does this time lag pose any potential problems? Explain.

12. The alternative program is described in lines 138–174. In your opinion, is it described in sufficient detail? If not, what additional types of information might have been included?

13. The AC and the TC teachers were matched on a number of characteristics. (See lines 182–187.) Is this important to know? Are there any other characteristics on which they might be matched? Explain.

14. In Study 2, there were 18 classrooms. However, the researchers do not state how many were taught by AC teachers and how many were taught by TC teachers. Would you be interested in having this information? Explain.

15. The Iowa Test of Basic Skills, which is a major, nationally normed test, was used in Study 2. Do you think that the researchers should have provided more information about this test than they did? (See lines 376–387.)

16. In Study 3, the interviewers did not know that some subjects were AC teachers and some were TC. If you had conducted this study, would you have given this information to the interviewers? Explain.

17. This article does not provide data on possible differences between the two groups of teachers during their first two years of teaching. Do you think that it would be wise to collect such data in future studies? Explain.

18. Studies 1 and 2 are quantitative, while Study 3 is qualitative. In your opinion, do the two types of studies contribute equally to furthering knowledge of this topic? Are both important or should one type be dropped from this report? Explain.

19. To what population(s), if any, would you be willing to generalize the results of this study? Explain.

Quality Ratings

Directions: Indicate your level of agreement with each of the following statements by circling a number from 5 for strongly agree (SA) to 1 for strongly disagree (SD). If you believe an item is not applicable to this research article, leave it blank. Be prepared to explain your ratings.

A. The introduction establishes the importance of the study.

    SA   5   4   3   2   1   SD

B. The literature review establishes the context for the study.

    SA   5   4   3   2   1   SD

C. The research purpose, question, or hypothesis is clearly stated.

    SA   5   4   3   2   1   SD

D. The method of sampling is sound.

    SA   5   4   3   2   1   SD

E. Relevant demographics (for example, age, gender, and ethnicity) are described.

    SA   5   4   3   2   1   SD

F. Measurement procedures are adequate.

    SA   5   4   3   2   1   SD

G. All procedures have been described in sufficient detail to permit a replication of the study.

    SA   5   4   3   2   1   SD

H. The participants have been adequately protected from potential harm.

    SA   5   4   3   2   1   SD

I. The results are clearly described.

    SA   5   4   3   2   1   SD

J. The discussion/conclusion is appropriate.

    SA   5   4   3   2   1   SD

K. Despite any flaws, the report is worthy of publication.

    SA   5   4   3   2   1   SD

Article 7

The Portrayal of Older People in
Award-Winning Literature for Children

MARY DELLMANN-JENKINS
Kent State University

LISA YANG
Kent State University

ABSTRACT. This study extended previous research on picture books receiving the prestigious Caldecott Medal by examining illustrations for the portrayal of older adult characters. Comparison of the 1972–1983 and 1984–1995 groups of Caldecott winners revealed significant changes in the depiction of older people in the more recent group of award books. Recent books portray them in a more positive manner. In addition, only two significant gender differences in a field of 36 possibilities were found over the entire 23-year period of Caldecott award-winners. Implications are drawn regarding the important role picture books play in the construction of young readers' positive attitudes toward old age and older people.

From *Journal of Research in Childhood Education, 12*, 96–100. Copyright © 1997 by the Association for Childhood Education International. Reprinted with permission.

"All wrinkled and short," "chew funny," "don't go out much," and "have heart attacks and die." These are typical responses of preschool-age children when asked to describe how older people look and act (Jantz, Seefeldt, Galper, & Serock, 1976). Similarly, attributes like "being helpful," "does things well," "thinks carefully," and "knows a lot" are often bypassed by 3- and 4-year-olds when asked to describe the abilities of older adults (Rich, Myrick, & Campbell, 1984). Many of these ideas and images are based on the media experiences young children encounter. Picture books, in particular, are important sources of learning during early childhood, with their storylines and illustrations conveying powerful messages to young readers about the attributes of older people.

Examining the depiction of older adult characters in picture books that have received the prestigious Caldecott Medal was the goal of this study. These award-winning books are very popular and are frequently chosen as teaching materials by early childhood educators, parents of young children, and child care providers (Lacy, 1986). Research is needed on how older people are portrayed in the illustrations of Caldecott Medal books, however. A review of the literature revealed only studies that examined age depiction in the storylines of popular, but non-award-winning books (Ansello, 1977, 1978; Blue, 1978; Janelli, 1988). Although studies have been conducted with samples of Caldecott award-winners, researchers have examined the illustrations of these picture books only in terms of gender-based issues, such as sex-role stereotypes and the frequency of male and female characters in central roles (Collins, Ingoldsby, & Dellmann, 1984; Dellmann-Jenkins, Florjancic, & Swadener, 1993; Weitzman, Eiffer, Hokada, & Ross, 1972; Williams, Vernon, Williams, & Malecha, 1987).

Both the portrayal of gender equality and the accurate depiction of age-related characteristics are of utmost importance to socialization in early childhood. Awareness of both gender and age differences develops very early in life; by age 4 children are ascribing meanings to these differences (Kaplan, 1992; Papalia & Olds, 1993). In addition, the formation of age-related biases and negative attitudes toward old age and old people are also forming at this young age. Children as young as 3 report being both "afraid and disgusted by ideas of growing old" as well as reporting an array of negative stereotypes about the attributes of older people (Rich et al., 1984).

Because research had not determined the types of messages about older people conveyed in the award-winning Caldecott books, the goal of this study was to examine the portrayal of older adult characters in these picture books. This research involved a content analysis of the illustrations of older adult characters in Caldecott Medal and Honor Book (runners-up) winners for over two decades—from 1972 to 1995.

Methods

Sample

A total of 95 picture books received the Caldecott Medal or Honor Book (runner-up) designation from 1972 through 1995. The illustrations of each of these books were content-analyzed for the presence of older people in main or secondary character roles. The results of this analysis were unexpected and revealed that only 12% (11 out of the 95) of the award-winners depicted older adult characters at all. Of these, 3 were Caldecott winners and 8 were Honor Books. In each of these picture books, however, the older adult characters were depicted in central roles. (Figure 1 lists the 11 books that were examined in this study.)

Analysis Procedures

The illustrations of the older adult characters in these 11 books were then content-analyzed based on 36 features. The first 24 features were adapted from the semantic differential section of the Children's Attitudes Toward the Elderly (CATE) scale developed by Jantz et al. (1976). The CATE is often used when assessing young children's per-

ceptions of the attributes and abilities of older people (Dellmann-Jenkins, Lambert, Fruit, & Dinero, 1986; Rich et al., 1984). Features 25 through 36 were identified after performing a pilot analysis of the older adult characters in 4
75 picture books randomly selected from the 1972–1995 sample of Caldecott award-winners.

1995
Honor Book – *John Henry,* ill. by Julius Lester & Jerry Pinkney, written by Brad Kessler (Dial Books for Young Readers).
1994
Caldecott Winner – *Grandfather's Journey,* Allen Say (Houghton Mifflin).
Honor Book – *Peppe, the Lamplighter,* ill. by Ted Lewis, written by Elise Bartone (Lothrop Publishing).
1990
Honor Book – *The Talking Eggs,* ill. by Jerry Pinkney, written by Robert D. San Souci (Dial Books for Young Readers).
1989
Caldecott Winner – *Song and Dance Man,* ill. by Stephen Gammell, written by Karen Ackerman (Alfred A. Knopf).
1986
Honor Book – *The Relatives Came,* ill. by Stephen Gammell, written by Cynthia Rylant (Bradbury Press).
1984
Honor Book – *Little Red Riding Hood,* ill. by Trina Schart Hyman, written by Jacob Grimm (Holiday House).
1982
Honor Book – *A Chair for My Mother,* Vera B. Williams (Greenwillow Books).
1981
Honor Book – *The Grey Lady and the Strawberry Snatcher,* Molly Bang (Four Winds Press).
1977
Honor Book – *Fish for Supper,* M. B. Goffstein (The Dial Press).
1972
Caldecott Winner – *One Fine Day,* Nonny Hogrogian (The Macmillan Company/Collier-Macmillan Ltd., London).

Figure 1. *The 1972–1995 Caldecott Winners and Honor Books Depicting Older Adult Characters.*

The reliability of these measuring criteria was tested by having two child/family studies instructors independently analyze and code the illustrations of 5 of the 11 award-
80 winners that depicted older adults in central or secondary roles. Comparison of their content-analysis of the randomly selected picture books with that of the present researchers revealed interrater reliabilities ranging from 91% to 97%.

When content-analyzing the portrayal of older adults in
85 the 23-year sample of Caldecott Medal and Honor Book winners, it was hypothesized that:

1. A larger number of older adult characters would be

positively depicted in award-winning books from 1984 to 1995 than those books that received awards
90 from 1972 through 1983.
2. In the total sample, a larger number of older male characters would be positively portrayed in the award-winning books than older female characters.

The second hypothesis was based on Janelli's (1988)
95 storyline analysis of popular, but non-award-winning, picture books. Overall, she found that older male characters were more frequently portrayed as active and engaged in respected roles than were older female characters.

A series of Tests of Independent Proportions were per-
100 formed to test Hypothesis 1. Then Z scores were computed to determine whether significant differences existed in the portrayal of older adult characters between the two periods of award-winning children's literature, 1972–1983 and 1984–1995. Z scores were also computed to test Hypothesis
105 2 and to determine whether significant gender differences existed in the depiction of older adult characters in Caldecott and Honor Book winners over the 23-year period.

Results
Time Period Differences in the Depiction of Older People

The results of the Tests of Independent Proportions of the 1972–1983 and 1984–1995 sample groups of Caldecott
110 winners revealed greater positive portrayal of older people in the more recent group of award books. As shown in Table 1, the 1984–1995 group had significantly more older adult characters depicted as "right" ($Z = 4.23$), "wonderful" ($Z = 2.81$), "good" ($Z = 2.11$), and "caring" ($Z = 2.53$) than
115 did the 1972–1983 group. Approaching significance ($p < .10$), the 1984–1995 group of award-winners also had more older adult characters depicted as "happy" ($Z = 1.67$) and "not lonely" ($Z = 1.39$) than did the 1972–1983 group.

Throughout the 23-year period, older adult characters
120 from the Caldecott winners were seldom (less than 25%) or never portrayed as sick, dirty, poor, unfriendly, wrong, terrible, ugly, bad, harmful, passive, irritable, lazy, cold-hearted, ignorant, or boring (see Table 1).

Gender Differences in the Depiction of Older People

The results of the Tests of Independent Proportions of
125 the portrayal of older male as compared to older female characters in the total 1972–1995 sample of award-winning picture books revealed two significant differences (see Table 1). Men were more frequently depicted as "active" than women ($Z = 2.04$), while women were portrayed more often
130 than men as being "frightened" ($Z = 2.03$). Although these findings are not positive, they are consistent with prior studies documenting the negative portrayal of females in storylines in Caldecott Medal winners through the mid-1980s (Collins et al. 1984; Weitzman et al. 1972; Williams
135 et al. 1987).

However, there were only these two significant gender differences in a field of 36 possibilities over the entire 23-year period of Caldecott award-winners. The descriptive data shows that throughout the 1972–1995 period of Calde-
140 cott winners, older men and older women were seldom (less

Table 1

Results of the Test of Independent Proportions on Portrayal of Older People in Award-winning Children's Books from 1972–1995

Characteristic of older people	1972–1983 (N = 8) f (p)	1984–1995 (N = 13) f (p)	Z	1972–1995 Women = 11 f (p)	1972–1995 Men = 11 f (p)	Z
Healthy	8(1.000)	6(.60)	2.041	7(.70)	7(.875)	.888
Sick	0(.000)	2(.20)	1.351	2(.20)	0(.000)	1.351
Clean	8(1.000)	8(.80)	1.351	8(.80)	8(1.000)	1.351
Dirty	0(.000)	1(.10)	.917	1(.10)	0(.000)	.917
Rich	0(.000)	0(.00)	–	0(.00)	0(.000)	–
Poor	0(.000)	0(.00)	–	0(.00)	0(.000)	–
Friendly	6(.750)	9(.90)	.847	7(.70)	8(1.000)	1.695
Unfriendly	1(.125)	0(.00)	1.147	1(.10)	0(.000)	.917
Right	0(.000)	10(1.00)	4.237 ***	5(.50)	5(.625)	.530
Wrong	0(.000)	0(.00)	–	0(.00)	0(.000)	–
Wonderful	2(.250)	9(.90)	2.814 ***	6(.60)	5(.625)	.108
Terrible	0(.000)	0(.00)	–	0(.00)	0(.000)	–
Pretty	1(.125)	0(.00)	1.147	1(.10)	0(.000)	.917
Ugly	1(.125)	0(.00)	1.147	1(.10)	0(.000)	.917
Happy	6(.750)	10(1.00)	1.678 *	9(.90)	7(.875)	.169
Sad	2(.250)	0(.00)	1.678	2(.20)	0(.000)	1.351
Good	5(.625)	10(1.00)	2.119 **	8(.80)	7(.875)	.424
Bad	0(.000)	0(.00)	–	0(.00)	0(.000)	–
Helpful	4(.500)	6(.60)	.424	6(.60)	4(.500)	.424
Harmful	1(.125)	0(.00)	1.147	1(.10)	0(.000)	.917
Active	6(.750)	8(.80)	.254	6(.60)	8(1.000)	2.041 **
Passive	0(.000)	1(.10)	.917	1(.10)	0(.000)	.917
Patient	4(.500)	4(.40)	.424	4(.40)	4(.500)	.424
Irritable	1(.125)	0(.00)	1.147	1(.10)	0(.000)	.917
Diligent	4(.500)	3(.30)	.866	4(.40)	3(.375)	.108
Lazy	0(.000)	0(.00)	–	0(.00)	0(.000)	–
Caring	4(.500)	10(1.00)	2.538 **	8(.80)	6(.750)	.254
Cold-hearted	1(.125)	0(.00)	1.147	1(.10)	0(.000)	.971
Knowledgeable	0(.000)	2(.20)	1.351	1(.10)	1(.125)	.169
Ignorant	0(.000)	0(.00)	–	0(.00)	0(.000)	–
Interesting	3(.375)	2(.20)	.822	3(.30)	2(.250)	.235
Boring	0(.000)	0(.00)	–	0(.00)	0(.000)	–
Brave	1(.125)	0(.00)	1.147	1(.10)	0(.000)	.971
Frightened	2(.250)	2(.20)	.254	4(.40)	0(.000)	2.030 *
Not lonely	5(.625)	9(.90)	1.396 *	7(.70)	7(.875)	.888
Lonely	2(.250)	1(.10)	.847	3(.30)	0(.000)	1.695

*p < .10. ** p < .05. *** p < .01.

than 25%) or never depicted as sick, dirty, poor, unfriendly, wrong, terrible, ugly, sad, bad, harmful, passive, irritable, lazy, cold-hearted, ignorant, or boring (see Table 1).

Discussion and Conclusions

These findings are an indication that illustrators of more recent award-winning picture books are more sensitive to showing their young readers an array of positive and respected attributes that older people possess. In addition, the illustrators of the award-winning picture books were sensitive to portraying the majority (70% or more) of both older women and men throughout the 23-year period as healthy, clean, friendly, happy, good, caring, and not lonely. These results are especially encouraging since previous research on non-award-winning but popular picture books indicates that older adult characters (of both sexes) are frequently portrayed in storylines as physically unattractive, with few positive attributes, and in passive and unrespected roles (Ansello, 1978; Blue, 1978; Janelli, 1988).

Overall, the results of this study suggest that those individuals responsible for selecting Caldecott and Honor Book winners are sensitive to the powerful impact picture books can have on young children. The finding that older adults are being depicted more positively in more recent books is an encouraging trend, while results indicating only two differences in the way male and female older characters are

165 portrayed reveals a positive lessening of adherence to gender role stereotypes.

The results of these statistical comparisons are valuable information for parents, educators, and caregivers who want to provide young children with literature that conveys posi-
170 tive messages about older people. However, the finding of even two differences (males are more active than females and females are more frightened than males) in male/female character portrayal indicates that gender role depictions are not yet comparable.

175 Furthermore, the fact that older adults were portrayed in character roles in only 12% of the sample of Caldecott Medal and Honor Book winners over the 23 years of publication was both unexpected and noteworthy. Early childhood is a critical period in gender role acquisition and it is
180 widely accepted that books contribute significantly to this area of development. At a time when the older adult segment of our population is increasing rapidly, more attention to the presentation of older people in varied and positive roles by authors and illustrators would help children accept
185 the aging of many people in their lives, as well as their own aging process. Many of today's young children have six or seven living grandparents. Unbiased and authentic storylines and illustrations in picture books about older people and old age are well-timed in the construction of young
190 readers' positive, yet realistic, views about their elders and their own aging process.

While this research examined the illustrations in Caldecott and Honor award-winning children's picture books, these books are only a small segment of those in press.
195 Children are exposed to a much wider selection of literature. Thus, there is a need for further research that addresses how older people are characterized in storylines and illustrations in non-award-winning books as well as other award-winning children's literature. In an aging society, the
200 negative (and inaccurate) aging themes of the past (the wicked old witch, the doddering old man) should not continue to shape the attitudes of children toward their elders and toward the process of growing older.

References

Ansello, E.F. (1977). Age and ageism in children's first literature. *Educational Gerontology: An International Quarterly, 2,* 255–274.

Ansello, E. F. (1978). Ageism—The subtle stereotype. *Childhood Education, 54,* 118–122.

Blue, G. F. (1978). The aging as portrayed in realistic fiction for children 1945–1975. *The Gerontologist, 18*(2), 187–192.

Collins, L., Ingoldsby, B., & Dellmann, M. (1984). Sex-role stereotyping in children's literature: A change from the past. *Childhood Education, 60,* 278–285.

Dellmann-Jenkins, M., Florjancic, L., & Swadener, E. B. (1993). Sex roles and cultural diversity in recent award-winning picture books for young children. *Journal of Research in Childhood Education, 7*(2), 74–82.

Dellmann-Jenkins, M., Lambert, D., Fruit, D., & Dinero, T. (1986). Old and young together: Effect of an education program on preschoolers' attitudes toward old people. *Childhood Education, 62,* 206–212.

Janelli, L. M. (1988). Depictions of grandparents in children's literature. *Educational Gerontology, 14,* 193–202.

Jantz, R. K., Seefeldt, C., Galper, A., & Serock, K. (1976). *Children's attitudes toward the elderly: Final report.* College Park, MD: University of Maryland.

Kaplan, P. (1992). *A child's odyssey* (2nd ed.). Chapter 11. New York: West.

Lacy, L. E. (1986). *Art and design in children's picture books.* American Library Association.

Papalia, D. E., & Olds, S. (1993). *A child's world* (6th ed.). Chapter 9. New York: McGraw Hill.

Rich, P. E., Myrick, R. D., & Campbell, C. (1984). Changing children's perceptions of the elderly. *Educational Gerontology, 9,* 483–491.

Weitzman, L., Eiffer, D., Hokada, E., & Ross, C. (1972). Sex-role socialization in picture books for preschool children. *American Journal of Sociology, 77,* 1125–1150.

Williams, J., Vernon, J., Williams, M., & Malecha, K. (1987). Sex-role socialization in children's books: An update. *Social Science Quarterly, 68,* 148–156.

Exercise for Article 7

Factual Questions

1. How many of the 95 books depicted older adults?

2. How many of the books were used to determine interrater reliability?

3. What was the basis for the second hypothesis?

4. How many of the older characters were depicted as healthy in the 1972–1983 sample of books? How many were depicted as healthy in the 1984–1995 sample?

5. Was the difference for being "wonderful" between the 1972–1983 and the 1984–1995 samples statistically significant? If yes, at what probability level?

6. Was there a statistically significant difference between women and men for "Caring"? If yes, at what probability level?

7. According to the researchers, are the results of this study consistent with those of earlier studies on non-award-winning picture books? Explain.

8. The researchers characterize which result as "unexpected and noteworthy"?

Questions for Discussion

9. Were you surprised that older adults were depicted in only 11 of the 95 picture books?

10. When researchers have hypotheses, they usually state them before describing their methods. The researchers who prepared this article did not follow this pattern. Is this important? Why? Why not?

11. Is the interrater reliability adequate? Explain.

12. Is the list of characteristics in Table 1 sufficiently comprehensive? Are there any others you would add to the list in future research? Explain.

13. There was a statistically significant difference on the variable called "Active," with 6 of the female and 8 of the male characters identified as being active. In your

opinion, is the size of the difference large enough to be of practical importance? Explain.

14. The researchers determined significance using probabilities of $p < .10$, $p < .05$, and $p < .01$. If you have studied significance testing, are all three of these levels commonly used in research? (Note that in line 115 the researchers use the term "approaching significance.")

15. This article is an example of a method of research called "content analysis," that is, research in which the contents of written documents are analyzed. In your opinion, is this method of research as interesting and important as other methods that analyze the behavior of individuals and groups of individuals? Explain.

16. If you had helped plan this research, what changes in the research methodology, if any, would you have recommended?

Quality Ratings

Directions: Indicate your level of agreement with each of the following statements by circling a number from 5 for strongly agree (SA) to 1 for strongly disagree (SD). If you believe an item is not applicable to this research article, leave it blank. Be prepared to explain your ratings.

A. The introduction establishes the importance of the study.

SA   5   4   3   2   1   SD

B. The literature review establishes the context for the study.

SA   5   4   3   2   1   SD

C. The research purpose, question, or hypothesis is clearly stated.

SA   5   4   3   2   1   SD

D. The method of sampling is sound.

SA   5   4   3   2   1   SD

E. Relevant demographics (for example, age, gender, and ethnicity) are described.

SA   5   4   3   2   1   SD

F. Measurement procedures are adequate.

SA   5   4   3   2   1   SD

G. All procedures have been described in sufficient detail to permit a replication of the study.

SA   5   4   3   2   1   SD

H. The participants have been adequately protected from potential harm.

SA   5   4   3   2   1   SD

I. The results are clearly described.

SA   5   4   3   2   1   SD

J. The discussion/conclusion is appropriate.

SA   5   4   3   2   1   SD

K. Despite any flaws, the report is worthy of publication.

SA   5   4   3   2   1   SD

Article 8

A Comparison of How Textbooks Teach Mathematical Problem Solving in Japan and the United States

RICHARD E. MAYER
University of California, Santa Barbara

VALERIE SIMS
University of California, Santa Barbara

HIDETSUGU TAJIKA
Aichi University of Education, Japan

ABSTRACT. This brief report compared the lesson on addition and subtraction of signed whole numbers in three seventh-grade Japanese mathematics textbooks with the corresponding lesson in four U.S. mathematics textbooks. The results indicated that Japanese books contained many more worked-out examples and relevant illustrations than did the U.S. books, whereas the U.S. books contained roughly as many exercises and many more irrelevant illustrations than did the Japanese books. The Japanese books devoted 81% of their space to explaining the solution procedure for worked-out examples compared to 36% in U.S. books; in contrast, the U.S. books devoted more space to unsolved exercises (45%) and interest-grabbing illustrations that are irrelevant to the lesson (19%) than did the Japanese books (19% and 0%, respectively). Finally, one of the U.S. books and all three Japanese books used meaningful instructional methods emphasizing (a) multiple representations of how to solve worked-out examples using words, symbols, and pictures and (b) inductive organization of material beginning with familiar situations and ending with formal statements of the solution rule. The results are consistent with classroom observations showing that Japanese mathematics instruction tends to emphasize the process of problem solving more effectively than does U.S. mathematics instruction (Stevenson & Stigler, 1992).

From *American Educational Research Journal, 32,* 443-460. Copyright © 1995 by the American Educational Research Association. Reprinted with permission.

National and international assessments of mathematics achievement have consistently revealed that students in the United States perform more poorly than their cohorts in other industrialized nations, particularly students from Asian nations such as Japan (Robitaille & Garden, 1989; Stevenson, Lee, Chen, Stigler, Hsu, & Kitamura, 1990; Stevenson & Stigler, 1992; Stigler, Lee, & Stevenson, 1990). The relatively poor performance of U.S. students occurs not only on tests of basic computational skills but also on tests of mathematical problem solving.

Converging evidence suggests that an explanation for cross-national differences can be found in the *exposure hypothesis:* cross-national differences in mathematics achievement are related to differences in the quantity and quality of mathematics instruction (Mayer, Tajika, & Stanley, 1991; McKnight et al., 1987; Stevenson & Stigler, 1992). Stevenson, Stigler, Lee, Kitamura, Kimura, and Kato (1986) point out that Japanese students spend approximately twice as many hours per week on mathematics as U.S. students spend. Perhaps even more important, Stevenson and Stigler (1992) provide evidence that Japanese schools tend to emphasize the process of problem solving whereas U.S. schools tend to emphasize the mastery of facts and procedures for computing the correct answer. For example, compared to U.S. elementary school mathematics teachers, Japanese teachers provide more verbal explanations, engage students in more reflective discussion, are more likely to use concrete manipulatives to represent abstract concepts, are more likely to include a real-world problem in a lesson, present more coherent lessons, ask questions that require longer answers, provide more critical feedback, and focus on fewer problems in more depth (Stevenson & Stigler, 1992).

The present study compared how mathematical problem solving is taught in mathematics textbooks used in Japan and in the United States. In particular, we examined the hypothesis that a typical Japanese textbook is more oriented toward teaching conceptual understanding and problem-solving skills whereas typical U.S. textbooks are more oriented toward teaching isolated facts and rote computation. This study extends earlier research comparing how mathematical problem solving is taught in Japanese and U.S. classrooms (Stevenson & Stigler, 1992) and contributes to an emerging research base on cross-national comparisons of textbooks (Chambliss & Calfee, 1989; Okamoto, 1989; Stevenson & Bartsch, 1991).

Cross-national comparisons of mathematics textbooks are important in light of evidence that U.S. textbooks constitute a sort of de facto national curriculum. For example, Armbruster and Ostertag (1993, p. 69) assert that "the powerful role of textbooks in the American curriculum is by now well established." Garner (1992, p. 53) notes that "textbooks serve as critical vehicles for knowledge acquisition in school" and can "replace teacher talk as the primary source of information." Glynn, Andre, and Britton (1986, p. 245) propose that across many disciplines students experience "a heavy reliance on textual materials for a great deal of their knowledge." It follows that examining the content and teaching methods used in American and Japanese mathematics textbooks provides a partial account of how mathematics is taught in the two nations.

Method

Materials

The data source consisted of lessons on addition and subtraction of signed whole numbers taken from three Japanese textbooks (Fukumori et al., 1992, pp. 19–25; Kodaira, 1992, pp. 27–32; Fujita & Maehara, 1992, pp. 17–25) and four U.S. textbooks (Bolster, Crown, Hamada et al., 1988, pp. 354–359; Fennell, Reys, Reys, & Webb, 1988, pp. 428–431; Rucker, Dilley, Lowry, & Ockenga, 1988, pp. 332–335; Willoughby, Bereiter, Hilton, & Rubinstein, 1991, pp. 260–265) commonly used to teach seventh-grade mathematics. The number of pages for the lesson in the Japanese books ranged from 7 to 9 based on an average page size of 5.5 x 7.5 inches, and from 4 to 6 in the U.S. books based on a page size averaging 7 x 9.5 inches. The Japanese books were approved by the Japanese Ministry of Education and were highly similar to one another because they conformed to detailed governmental specifications; the U.S. books were from publishers' series that were approved for adoption by the California State Department of Education. The books were selected as typical based on consultations with teachers and school administrators in Japan and the United States. The lesson in all books described how to add and subtract positive and negative whole numbers, such as $3 + 8 =$ _, $-3 + 8 =$ _, $3 + -8 =$ _, $-3 + -8 =$ _, $3 - 8 =$ _, $-3 - 8 =$ _, $3 - -8 =$ _, and $-3 - -8 =$ _. In each of the Japanese books, the material was contained in the lesson entitled, "Addition and Subtraction," taken from the chapter entitled, "Positive and Negative Numbers" (Fujita & Maehara, 1992; Fukumori et al., 1992; Kodaira, 1992). In the U.S. books, the material was contained in lessons entitled, "Adding and Subtracting Signed Numbers" (Willoughby, Bereiter, Hilton, & Rubinstein, 1991); "Adding Integers" and "Subtracting Integers" (Fennell, Reys, Reys, & Webb, 1988; Rucker, Dilley, Lowry, & Ockenga, 1988); or "Adding Integers: Same Sign," "Adding Integers: Different Signs," and "Subtracting Integers" (Bolster, Crown, Hamada, et al., 1988). We also included the exercises involving addition and subtraction of signed integers in the end-of-the-chapter test. We did not include sections on addition and subtraction of signed fractions, signed decimals, or three or more signed numbers, because this material was not covered in all books. In short, the data source consisted of seven lessons on addition and subtraction of signed integers, ranging from 4 to 9 pages in length.

Procedure

To conduct a quantitative analysis of the instructional methods used for teaching students how to solve signed arithmetic problems, two independent raters broke each lesson into four parts—exercises, irrelevant illustrations, relevant illustrations, and explanation—and resolved conflicts by consensus. First, the raters circled the exercise portions of each lesson using a colored marker. We defined an exercise as a symbol-based problem involving addition or subtraction of two signed integers for which no answer or explanation was provided, such as $-8 + 3 =$ _. In the Japanese books, the exercises were labeled as "Problem" or "Exercise"; con-tained the instructions, "Calculate the following"; and were numbered consecutively. In the U.S. books, the exercises were presented under labels such as "Exercise" or "Practice"; contained instructions such as, "Give each sum," "Give each difference," "Add," or "Subtract"; and were numbered consecutively. The raters counted the number of exercise problems involving addition or subtraction of two signed numbers in each lesson, including exercise problems given at the end of the chapter. We did not include exercises involving fractions, decimals, or more than two numbers. There were no unresolved disagreements between the raters.

Second, the raters circled the irrelevant illustrations in each lesson using a colored marker and circled the relevant illustrations using a different colored marker. We defined an illustration as any line drawing, chart, picture, or photograph. Furthermore, we defined a relevant illustration as any line drawing or chart that represented the steps in the solution of a signed arithmetic problem and an irrelevant illustration as a picture or photograph that did not correspond to the steps in the solution of a signed arithmetic problem. To ensure consistency, the raters maintained a list of illustrations that were classified as relevant and a list of illustrations that were classified as irrelevant. Relevant illustrations included line drawings showing changes in the water level of a water storage tank, changes in position on a number line, or changes in mixtures of negative and positive ions in a beaker; irrelevant illustrations included a picture of a tape measure, a drawing of a ski village, a drawing of a mad scientist, a drawing of a submarine, a mural from an ancient Egyptian pyramid, a photo of a woman swinging a golf club, and a photo of hockey players skating on ice. A series of line drawings about the same problem presented together on a page was counted as one illustration. The raters counted the number of relevant and irrelevant illustrations in each lesson. There were no unresolved disagreements.

Third, the remaining portions of the lesson constituted the explanation and were circled with a colored marker designating explanation. Each rater counted the number of worked-out examples in the explanation portion of the lesson. A worked-out example was defined as a signed arithmetic problem in which the answer and verbal description of how it was generated were given. In most cases, the worked-out examples were presented under the heading, "Example." Each rater also counted the number of words in the explanation section of the lesson; words in headings and in relevant illustrations were included. A word was defined as any letter or letter group found in a dictionary. We did not include mathematical symbols such as numerals, $+$, $-$, or $=$. There were no unresolved disagreements between the raters.

One of the raters used a ruler to measure the space (in square inches) occupied by exercises, irrelevant illustrations, relevant illustrations, and explanation for each lesson. In measuring the areas, margin space was not included. Given the objective nature of these measurements, a second rater was not needed.

In sum, the quantitative data for each lesson included the number of exercises, the number of irrelevant illustrations, the number of relevant illustrations, the number of worked-out examples, the number of words, the area occupied by exercises, the area occupied by irrelevant illustrations, the area occupied by relevant illustrations, and the area occupied by explanation.

Results and Discussion

The instructional lesson is much longer in Japan than in the U.S., but the exercise set is about the same length in both nations. Research on instructional methods has emphasized the role of meaningful explanation rather than unguided hands-on symbol manipulating activities in promoting problem-solving competence (Mayer, 1987). The instructional part of the lesson—that is, the part of the lesson that did not contain to-be-solved exercises—was more than four times longer in the Japanese books than in the U.S. books: The mean number of words in the U.S. books was 208 compared to 925 in the Japanese books. However, the exercise part of the lesson, which emphasizes unguided symbol manipulation, was about the same in the two nations: The Japanese books contained an average of 63 exercises on addition and subtraction of signed numbers, whereas the U.S. books averaged 51 exercises. In both nations, additional worksheets and workbooks are available to supplement the textbook exercises. Overall, these data show a difference in the relative emphasis of Japanese and U.S. books: There were 14.7 words of instruction per exercise in the Japanese books compared to an average of 3.9 words of instruction per exercise in the U.S. books.

Worked-out examples and concrete analogies are more common in Japan than in the U.S. Research on multiple representations, case-based reasoning, and analogical reasoning has demonstrated the important role of worked-out examples and concrete analogies in helping students to improve their problem-solving skills (Mayer, 1987). Worked-out examples serve to model appropriate problem-solving processes, and concrete analogies provide a means for connecting procedures to familiar experience. On average, worked-out examples were three times more common in the Japanese textbooks than in the U.S. textbooks: U.S. books averaged approximately 4 worked-out examples compared to 15 in the Japanese lessons.

The Japanese books employed the same concrete analogy throughout the lesson on addition and subtraction of signed numbers. For example, one book presented a tank for storing water in which a rise in the water level is expressed by a positive number and a fall in the water level is expressed by a negative number. According to this analogy, addition of signed numbers occurs when the water level is changed twice—for example, a first change in the water level plus a second change in the water level produces a total change in the water level; subtraction of signed numbers occurs when one knows the total change and the second change but wants to find the first change. The analogy was represented in multiframe illustrations 9 times, indicating changes that corresponded to arithmetic operations. Another book used the analogy of walking east or west along a path, which was portrayed as arrows along a number line. The book contained 7 multiframe illustrations showing the process of tak-

ing two trips along the number line. For example, the problem (+8) + (−3) = ___ was represented as two parts of a trip: an arrow from 0 to 8 (labeled as +8) and an arrow from 8 to 5 (labeled as −3). Below this figure, the solution was represented as an arrow from 0 to 5 (labeled as +8 − 3). A third book represented addition and subtraction of signed numbers as movement along a number line, including 6 sets of illustrations of number lines.

In contrast, the U.S. books used concrete analogies such as changes in temperature on a thermometer, keeping score in golf or hockey, matter and antimatter annihilation, and beakers containing positive and negative ions. However, in three out of four cases, the analogy used to represent addition was different from the analogy used to represent subtraction, and none of the analogies was represented in a multiframe illustration depicting changes that correspond to addition or subtraction. In the U.S. books, analogies used to describe addition of signed numbers were insufficient to describe subtraction of signed numbers. For example, in the matter/antimatter analogy, combining 5 bricks and 2 antibricks yielded 3 bricks (analogous to 5 + −2 = 3). However, this analogy breaks down for situations in which a negative number is subtracted from another number (such as 5 − −2 = 7), so the textbook used a different analogy, temperatures on a thermometer, to represent subtraction of signed numbers.

Relevant illustrations were more common in Japanese books than in U.S. books, but irrelevant illustrations were more common in U.S. books than in Japanese books. Research on illustrations reveals that some kinds of illustrations have more instructional value than others (Levin & Mayer, 1993; Mayer, 1993). Illustrations that simply decorate the page are instructionally irrelevant, whereas illustrations that explain the process of signed arithmetic are instructionally relevant. Other than the first page of the chapter, the Japanese books contained more relevant and fewer irrelevant illustrations than U.S. books: The Japanese books contained an average of 0 irrelevant and 11 relevant illustrations compared to an average of 2 irrelevant and 4 relevant illustrations in the U.S. books. The irrelevant illustrations in U.S. textbooks may be intended to make the material more interesting, but recent research on seductive details reveals that the addition of highly interesting and vivid material to a text often diminishes students' recall of the important information (Garner, Brown, Sanders, & Menke, 1992; Wade, 1992).

In summary, the foregoing analyses indicate that the Japanese books contain far more worked-out examples and relevant illustrations than the U.S. books, whereas U.S. books contain roughly as many exercises and more irrelevant illustrations than Japanese books. Another way to examine these kinds of differences is to compare the allocation of page space in Japanese and U.S. lessons, which is done in the next section.

Japanese books excel in devoting page space to explanation of problem-solving procedures, whereas U.S. books excel in devoting page space to unsolved exercises and interest-grabbing illustrations. The allocation of space in Japanese and U.S. textbooks represents the values of the cultures that produced them. An emphasis on understanding the process of problem solving is reflected in the use of worked-out examples, which model the problem-solving process in words, symbols, and illustrations. Research on the teaching of problem-solving processes indicates that successful programs rely on the use of cognitive modeling techniques—such as detailed descriptions of worked-out examples (Mayer, 1992). On average, 81% of the page space in Japanese books was devoted to explanation of problem-solving procedures (63% emphasizing worked-out examples and 18% for corresponding illustrations) compared to 36% in U.S. books (25% emphasizing worked-out examples and 11% for corresponding illustrations).

In contrast, an emphasis on the product of problem solving is reflected in the presentation of lists of to-be-solved exercise problems. On average, 45% of the page space in U.S. books was devoted to presenting lists of exercise problems compared to 19% in Japanese books. Perhaps to compensate for what might be considered the boring task of having to solve exercise problems without guidance, authors of U.S. books added interest-grabbing illustrations that were irrelevant to the problem-solving procedures. On average, U.S. books devoted 19% of their space to irrelevant illustrations compared to 0% in Japanese books. Figure 1 summarizes these differences in the use of space in Japanese and U.S. textbooks.

Meaningful instructional methods emphasizing the coordination of multiple representations were more common in Japanese books than in U.S. books. Research in mathematics education emphasizes the importance of helping students build connections among multiple representations of a problem and of helping students induce solution rules based on experience with familiar examples (Grouws, 1992; Hiebert, 1986). To analyze these aspects of meaningful instruction and to supplement the foregoing quantitative analyses, we analyzed the ways that the textbooks explained one type of signed arithmetic—namely, adding two numbers with different signs, such as $(+ 3) + (–8) = –5$ or $(–4) + (+3) = –1$. To assess the use of multiple representations in each lesson, we examined whether the lesson presented complete symbolic, verbal, and pictorial representations of a problem-solving procedure for addition of integers with different signs. In particular, we evaluated whether or not the lesson included symbolic, verbal, and visual representations for the first step (i.e., determining the value of the first number), the second step (i.e., adding the value of the second number), and the third step (i.e., using the resulting number as the final answer). To assess the use of an inductive method in each lesson, we determined whether or not the lesson progressed from familiar examples to a formal statement of the rule for addition of integers with different signs.

All three of the Japanese books systematically built connections among symbolic, verbal, and pictorial representations for each of three steps in solving the problem. In explaining how to add two numbers with different signs, one Japanese book (Kodaira, 1992) began by describing a water tank analogy in words. The book (p. 27) stated that "when the water level changes twice in succession, we can express

the changes, starting with the first change as: (the first change) + (the second change)." In relating this analogy to addition of two numbers with different signs, the book (p. 28) described the situation in words: "If the first change is –3 cm and the second change is +8 cm, then the total change is $(–3) + (+8)$, and this is +5 cm." Then the book presented the problem in symbolic form as "$(–3) + (+8) = +5$." Next to this was a pictorial representation of the problem consisting of three labeled frames, as shown in Figure 2a. Each step in the problem was represented, starting with negative 3, adding positive 8, and ending with positive 5. At the end of a series of examples, the book presented a rule for addition of numbers with different signs (p. 30):

In seeking the sum of two numbers with different signs, consider only their absolute values and subtract the smaller absolute value from the larger. Then assign to the sum the sign of the number with the larger absolute value. If the absolute values are equal, then the sum is 0.

Thus, the lesson was organized inductively, beginning with a familiar analogy and ending with a formal statement of the solution rule.

A second Japanese book (Fujita & Maehara, 1992) began its discussion of addition of different-signed integers by describing a walk along a road (p. 17):

Imagine that you are walking along a road which runs east and west in a straight line…. You first walk 3 meters to the east and then walk 5 meters to the west. Moving to the east will be used as the positive numbers and moving to the west will be used as the negative numbers.

Then, the book describes the computation in words and symbols (p. 17): "Two movements and their results will be expressed as follows, when positive and negative numbers are used…. The first movement is +3 m, the second movement is –5 m, the result is –2 m." On the right, the book presented a number line with an arrow from 0 to 3 corresponding to the first movement, from 3 to –2 corresponding to the second movement, and from 0 to –2 corresponding to the answer. This illustration is summarized in Figure 2b. Next, the example was expressed in symbolic form (p. 18):

When moving twice in succession, the results…are expressed as follows by adding two numbers: (the first movement) + (the second movement). When the results are expressed like this, the calculation for the example is as follows: $(+3) + (–5)$. The answer is –2, and so the computation is expressed as follows: $(+3) + (–5) = –2$.

Finally, after presenting several examples in verbal, visual, and symbolic forms, the section ended with a statement of the general principle (p. 20): "The sum of numbers with different signs: You can subtract the smaller absolute value from the larger one and assign to the sum the sign of the number with the larger absolute value. When the absolute values are equal, the sum is 0." As in the other Japanese book, this lesson was organized inductively—beginning with a familiar situation of walking east and west along a road

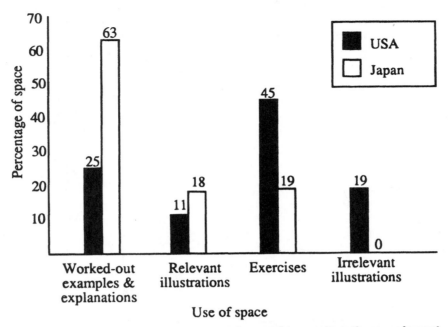

Figure 1. **Proportion of page space devoted to explanations, relevant illustrations, exercises, and irrelevant illustrations in Japan and the United States**

400 and ending with a formal statement of the procedure for addition of numbers with different signs.

The third book (Fukumori et al., 1992, pp. 18-19) also used verbal, visual, and symbolic representations to explain what to do "when you add a positive and negative number."
405 The book connected symbols, words, and pictures as follows: "(–7) + 5 means to get a number that is 5 larger than –7. A number 5 larger than –7 is the number –2, which is 2 smaller than 0, as you can see on the number line below." Directly below was an illustration of a number line with an
410 arrow from –7 to –2, and below that was the symbolic form of the problem, "(–7) + 5 = –2." After presenting several other examples of the same form in the same way, the section ended with a statement of general principle: "Addition of a negative and positive number means subtraction of the
415 negative number from the positive number... 3 + (–5) = 3 –5 = –2." Again, as in the other Japanese books, instruction moved from the familiar statement of a problem in words and pictures to a formal statement of the solution procedure as a rule.
420 In contrast, only one of the four U.S. books contained symbolic, verbal, and pictorial representations of example problems involving addition of integers with different signs. For example, one U.S. textbook (Willoughby, Bereiter, Hilton, & Rubinstein, 1991) began by presenting word prob-
425 lems about familiar analogies such as a thermometer: "The temperature is –4C. If it goes up 3C, what will it be?" For each word problem, the book stated the problem in symbolic form but did not give an answer, such as "–4 + 3 = ?" Thus, the book presented only the first two steps in the problem—
430 namely, starting at negative 4 and adding positive 3; it failed to describe the third step—namely, ending at negative 1. The

book also failed to connect the verbal and symbolic representation of the problem to a pictorial representation. In the next section of the chapter, entitled "Adding and Subtracting
435 Signed Numbers," the book (p. 263) listed rules such as: "To add 2 signed numbers, if the signs are different, subtract the smaller absolute value from the larger and use the sign of the one with the larger absolute value." Then, the book provided exercises such as "(–8) + (+7) = n" along with instructions to
440 use the above rule. This is a deductive approach because it begins with stating a rule and then tells the learner to apply the rule to exercise problems.

In another U.S. textbook (Rucker, Dilley, Lowry, & Ockenga, 1988), the section on "Integers" began by repre-
445 senting positive and negative integers as beakers containing positive and negative charges. Then, in the section on "Adding Integers," the book presented several examples. For each, there was a picture of one beaker containing positive or negative charges being poured into another beaker con-
450 taining positive or negative charges and the resulting beaker; below the picture was a symbolic representation of the problem. For example, Figure 3a shows a beaker containing one positive charge being poured into a beaker containing 5 negative charges, and the result is a beaker containing 4 free
455 negative charges. Directly under this picture was the equation, "–5 + +1 = –4." This lesson used symbols and pictures to present all three steps in the procedure—starting with negative 5, adding positive 1, and ending with negative 4— but failed to connect them to words. There was no verbal
460 description other than the general statement, "To understand how to add integers, you can think about putting charges together." The book then moved directly to exercises without ever presenting the solution rule.

2a. Excerpt from Japanese textbook that includes verbal, visual, and symbolic representations for each of three problem-solving steps.

We have a tank for storing water. If we put in or take out water, the water level in the tank goes up or down. If we express a change which raises the water level with a positive number, then we can express a change which lowers the water level with a negative number. If the water level rises 5 cm, the change in the water level is +5 cm. If the water level decreases 3 cm, the change in the water level is -3 cm...When the water level changes twice in succession we can express the change as:...

If the first change is: -3 cm
and the second change is: +8 cm
then the total change is: (-3) + (+8)
and this is +5 cm.   (-3) + (+8) = +5

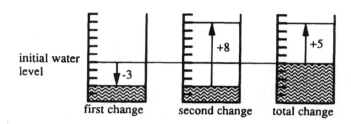

first change   second change   total change

initial water level

2b. Excerpt from Japanese textbook that includes verbal, visual, and symbolic representations for each of three problem-solving steps.

When you walk from A...you first walk 3 m to the east and then 5 m to the west. The two movements...will be expressed using positive and negative numbers. The first movement is +3 m, the second movement is -5 m, the result is -2 m... The calculation is expressed as follows: (+3) + (-5) = -2.

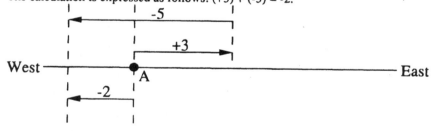

Figure 2. **Representations used in Japanese textbooks to teach addition of numbers with different signs.**
Note. 2a is adapted from Kodaira (1992); 2b is adapted from Fujita and Maehara (1992).

Another book (Fennell, Reys, Reys, & Webb, 1988) used a creative analogy about annihilation of matter and antimatter to explain addition of signed integers (p. 428):

In a galaxy totally different from our own, a scientist named Dr. Zarkov discovered antimatter. When he puts antimatter together with antimatter nothing happens. For example, if he puts 4 cups of antiwater together with 3 cups of antiwater, he gets 7 cups of antimatter. Strange as it may seem, however, when he puts equal amounts of matter and antimatter together, they both disappear. For example, if he puts 2 telephones and 2 antitelephones together, he is left with nothing. In his latest experiment, Dr. Zarkov added 2 antibricks to a box containing 5 bricks. There was a blinding flash of light. When the smoke cleared, he was left with 3 bricks.

There was no illustration for the bricks example, although there was an illustration depicting 2 light and 2 dark telephones being placed together, and then disappearing in a "poof." Later in the section, the bricks example was represented symbolically as, "2 antibricks + 5 bricks = 3 bricks," and as, "-2 + 5 = 3." In this case, the book described the three steps in the addition of signed integers within the context of an interesting situation and related them to a symbolic representation but failed to relate them to a pictorial representation. In addition, the book failed to state the solution rule in a formal way, but it asked the students to do so as an exercise (p. 429): "State rules for adding a positive integer and a negative integer."

Finally, the fourth U.S. book (Bolster et al., 1988) used a hockey analogy to explain addition of signed integers in a section entitled "Adding Integers: Different Signs." The section (p. 356) started by describing a hockey-scoring procedure: "Angelo's hockey coach uses a plus/minus system to rate the performance of the players. If a player is on the ice when his team scores, he gets 1. If he is on the ice when the other team scores, he gets −1. For his first 10 games, Angelo's plus rating was 4, and his minus rating was −7. What was his overall rating?" Next the book stated the problem symbolically: "Find 4 + (−7)." Finally, the book used a captioned number line illustration as shown in Figure 3b to represent the three steps in solving the problem. The caption described the steps: "Starting at zero, move 4 units to the right. From there, move 7 units to the left. His overall rating was −3." Although very short, this lesson makes connections among symbolic, verbal, and visual representations of all three steps in the example problem. Unlike the Japanese book which included many complete examples, however, this book presented only one complete example. Finally, the lesson ended with a statement of the solution rule (p. 357): "To add two integers with different signs, consider the distance each integer is from zero. Subtract the shorter distance from the longer distance. In your answer, use the sign of the number farther from zero." Like the Japanese book, this textbook used an inductive approach, moving from familiar examples to a formal statement of the rule.

In summary, the books differed in their use of multiple representations to explain how to add a negative and positive integer and in their inclusion of a statement of the solution rule. The Japanese books presented complete explanations of at least two examples of addition of a positive and negative integer; in these examples, all three steps in the procedure were presented symbolically, verbally, and pictorially, and the solution rule was clearly stated at the end of the explanation. In contrast, one U.S. textbook presented a complete explanation of one example and a statement of the rule, one presented an explanation that lacked a pictorial representation and a statement of the rule, one presented an explanation that lacked a verbal representation and a statement of the rule, and one presented an explanation that lacked a pictorial representation and lacked portions of the symbolic and verbal representations. Overall, all of the Japanese books presented multiple representations of example problems and presented material in inductive order, whereas most of the U.S. books did not employ these meaningful instructional methods.

The lesson was better integrated into the Japanese books than into the U.S. books, and the U.S. books were much longer than the Japanese books. Research on text structure has highlighted the importance of organizing topics in a simple and coherent structure (Britton, Woodward, &

Binkley, 1993; Jonassen, Beissner, & Yacci, 1993). The Japanese books, averaging less than 200 pages in length, contained an average of 7 chapters with each one divided into two or three coherent sections, whereas the U.S. textbooks, averaging 475 pages in length, contained an average of 12 chapters with each including approximately a dozen loosely related topics. For example, each of the Japanese books contained an entire chapter, entitled "Positive and Negative Numbers," devoted exclusively to signed numbers. The chapter consisted of three related sections involving an introduction to signed numbers, addition/subtraction of signed numbers, and multiplication/division of signed numbers. In contrast, lessons on addition and subtraction of signed numbers were presented as short fragments within more diverse chapters throughout most of the U.S. books. In three U.S. books, material on addition and subtraction of signed numbers was in the same chapter as solving equations and coordinate graphing of equations; in another, it was taught in a chapter that included units of measure, mixed numbers, and improper fractions. Overall, compared to the U.S. textbooks, the Japanese textbooks were more compact, presented a clearer structure, and covered fewer topics in more depth.

Conclusion

If textbooks serve as a sort of national curriculum, then international comparisons of textbook lessons can provide a partial picture of not only what is taught but also how it is taught across nations. Two competing methods for teaching students how to solve mathematics problems are drill and practice—in which page space is devoted to unexplained exercises involving symbol manipulation—and cognitive modeling—in which page space is devoted to presenting and connecting multiple representations of step-by-step problem-solving processes through worked-out examples. The drill-and-practice approach follows from a view of learning as knowledge acquisition that emphasizes the *product of problem solving*—that is, getting the right answer; in contrast, the cognitive modeling approach follows from a view of learning as knowledge construction, which emphasizes *the process of problem solving*—that is, how to get the right answer (Mayer, 1989).

In this study, we are concerned with how much space in Japanese and U.S. mathematics textbooks is devoted to unexplained exercises consisting of symbol manipulation and how much space is devoted to building and connecting multiple representations for problem solving through worked-out example problems. Building on the exposure hypothesis, which originally focused on the allocation of instructional time (Mayer, Tajika, & Stanley, 1991; Stevenson & Stigler, 1992), the amount of space in mathematics textbooks that is devoted to meaningful explanation of problem-solving strategies may be an important determinant of students' mathematical problem-solving competence.

If textbook page space is viewed as a limited resource, then the allocation of that space reflects the priorities of the cultures that produced them. In Japan, the major use of page space is to explain mathematical procedures and concepts in

3a. Excerpt from U.S. textbook that includes visual and symbolic representations for some of three problem-solving steps.

Example. -5 + +1 = ?

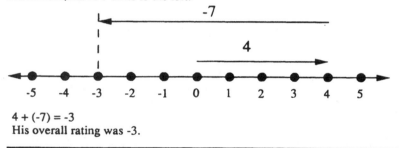

-5 + +1 = -4

3b. Excerpt from U.S. textbook that includes verbal, visual, and symbolic representations for each of three problem-solving steps.

Find 4 + (-7)

Starting at zero, move 4 units to the right.
From there, move 7 units to the left.

4 + (-7) = -3
His overall rating was -3.

Figure 3. **Representations used in the U.S. textbooks to teach addition of numbers with different signs.**
Note. 3a is adapted from Rucker, Dilley, Lowry, and Ockenga (1988); 3b is adapted from Bolster et al. (1988).

600 words, symbols, and graphics, with an emphasis on worked-out examples and concrete analogies. In U.S. books, where the use of page space for explanation is minimized relative to Japanese books, the major use of page space is to present unexplained exercises in symbolic form for the stu-
605 dents to solve on their own. These lessons are supplemented with attention-grabbing graphics that, unlike those in the Japanese books, are interesting but irrelevant. Japanese textbooks devote over 80% of their space, and U.S. books devote less than 40% of their space to instruction in the process
610 of problem solving (i.e., words, pictures, and symbols that explain how to add and subtract signed numbers), whereas U.S. books devote over 60% of their space, and Japanese books devote less than 20% of their space to hands-on exer-

cises without guidance and interesting-but-irrelevant illustra-
615 tions. A further analysis of lessons provides converging evidence: All three of the Japanese books and only one of the four U.S. books presented worked-out examples that explained how to solve problems in words, symbols, and pictures.
620   In Japan, the textbooks provide worked-out examples that model successful problem-solving strategies for students; in the U.S., textbooks are more likely to provide lots of exercises for students to solve on their own without much guidance. In Japan, the textbooks provide concrete analogies
625 that help the student relate the concepts of addition and subtraction of signed numbers to a familiar situation; in the U.S., textbooks may give rules without much explanation. In

Japan, the textbooks devote space to explaining mathematical ideas in words, whereas U.S. textbooks devote relatively more space to manipulating symbols.

The picture that emerges from our study of mathematics textbooks is that cognitive modeling of problem-solving processes is emphasized more in Japan than in the United States, whereas drill and practice on the product of problem solving is emphasized more in the United States than in Japan. Japanese textbooks seem to assume the learner is a cognitively active problem solver who seeks to understand the step-by-step process for solving a class of problems. In contrast, U.S. textbooks seem to assume the learner is a behaviorally active knowledge acquisition machine who learns best from hands-on activity in solving problems with minimal guidance and who needs to be stimulated by interesting decorative illustrations.

Our study is limited and should be interpreted as part of a converging set of research results. First, our data source involves only three Japanese and four U.S. books. Although we chose books that are widely used, we did not exhaustively review other books and supplemental materials, such as workbooks. Second, we examined only one lesson—amounting to a few pages in each of the books in our sample. Although the material is a typical component of the mathematics curriculum in both nations, we did not review other lessons. Furthermore, our subsequent analysis was even more restrictive, examining only addition of signed numbers with different signs. Finally, we focused on properties of the lessons that are related to problem-solving instruction, rather than other aspects of the text such as its readability. Ultimately, the practical goal of this study is to provide suggestions for the improvement of textbooks aimed at mathematical problem solving. The following suggestions need to be subjected to research study: (a) present a few basic topics in depth, organized into coherent lessons, rather than a huge collection of fragments; (b) embed the lesson within a familiar situational context so that verbal, visual, and symbolic representations are interconnected; (c) use worked-out examples to emphasize the process of problem solving; (d) present a verbal statement of the solution rule after presenting familiar worked-out examples. Finally, it should be noted that additional research is needed to determine not only how to design effective textbooks but also how to use them successfully in classrooms (Driscoll, Moallem, Dick, & Kirby, 1994).

References

Armbruster, B., & Ostertag, J. (1993). Questions in elementary science and social studies textbooks. In B. K. Britton, A. Woodward, & M. Binkley (Eds.), *Learning from textbooks: Theory and practice* (pp. 69-94). Hillsdale, NJ: Erlbaum.

Bolster, L. C., Crown, W., Hamada, R., Hansen, V., Lindquist, M. M., McNerney, C., et al. (1988). *Invitation to mathematics* (7th grade). Glenview, IL: Scott, Foresman & Co.

Britton, B. K., Woodward, A., & Binkley, M. (Eds.) (1993). *Learning from textbooks: Theory and practice*. Hillsdale, NJ: Erlbaum.

Chambliss, M. J., & Calfee, R. C. (1989). Designing science textbooks to enhance student understanding. *Educational Psychologist, 24,* 307-322.

Driscoll, M. P., Moallem, M., Dick, W., & Kirby, E. (1994). How does the textbook contribute to learning in a middle school science class? *Contemporary Educational Psychology, 19,* 79-100.

Fennell, F., Reys, B. J., Reys, R. E., & Webb, A. W. (1988). *Mathematics unlimited* (7th grade). New York: Holt, Rinehart, & Winston.

Fujita, H., & Maehara, S. (Eds.) (1992). *New math* (in Japanese). Tokyo: Shoseki.

Fukumori, N., Kikuchi, H., Miwa, T., Iijima, Y., Igarashi, K., Iwai, S., et al. (1992). *Math 1* (in Japanese). Osaka, Japan: Keirinkan.

Garner, R. (1992). Learning from school texts. *Educational Psychologist, 27,* 53-63.

Garner, R. Brown, R., Sanders, S., & Menke, D. J. (1992). "Seductive details" and learning from text. In K. A. Renninger, S. Hidi, & A. Krapp (Eds.), *The role of interest in learning and development* (pp. 239-254). Hillsdale, NJ: Erlbaum.

Glynn, S. M., Andre, T., & Britton, B. K. (1986). The design of instructional text. *Educational Psychologist, 21,* 245-251.

Grouws, D. A. (Ed.) (1992). *Handbook of research on mathematics teaching and learning.* New York: Macmillan.

Hiebert, J. (Ed.) (1986). *Conceptual antiprocedural knowledge: The case of mathematics.* Hillsdale, NJ: Erlbaum.

Jonassen, D. H., Beissner, K., & Yacci, M. (1993). *Structural knowledge.* Hillsdale, NJ: Erlbaum.

Kodaira, K. (Ed.) (1992). *Japanese grade 7 mathematics* (H. Nagata, Trans.). Chicago: University of Chicago. (Original work published 1984)

Levin, J. R., & Mayer, R. E. (1993). Understanding illustrations in text. In B. Britton, A. Woodward, & M. Binkley (Eds.), *Learning from textbooks: Theory and practice* (pp. 95-113). Hillsdale, NJ: Erlbaum.

Mayer, R. E. (1987). *Educational psychology: A cognitive approach.* New York: Harper Collins.

Mayer, R. E. (1989). Cognition and instruction in mathematics. *Journal of Educational Psychology, 81,* 452-456.

Mayer, R. E. (1992). *Thinking, problem solving, cognition* (2nd ed.). New York: Freeman.

Mayer, R. E. (1993). Illustrations that instruct. In R. Glaser (Ed.), *Advances in instructional psychology* (Vol. 4, pp. 253-284). Hillsdale, NJ: Erlbaum.

Mayer, R. E., Tajika, H., & Stanley, C. (1991). Mathematical problem solving in Japan and the United States: A controlled comparison. *Journal of Educational Psychology, 83,* 69-72.

McKnight, C. C., Crosswhite, F. J., Dossey, J. A., Kifer, E., Swafford, J. O., Trayers, K. J., & Cooney, T. J. (1987). *The underachieving curriculum: Assessing U.S. school mathematics from an international perspective.* Champaign, IL: Stipes.

Okamoto, Y. (1989, April). *An analysis of addition and subtraction word problems in textbooks: An across national comparison.* Paper presented at the Annual Meeting of the American Educational Research Association, San Francisco.

Robitaille, D. F., & Garden, R. A. (1989). *The IEA study of mathematics II: Contexts and outcomes of school mathematics.* Oxford, England: Pergamon.

Rucker, W. E., Dilley, C. A., Lowry, D. W., & Ockenga, E. G. (1988). *Heath mathematics* (7th grade). Lexington, MA: D. C. Heath.

Stevenson, H. W., & Bartsch, K. (1991). An analysis of Japanese and American textbooks in mathematics. In R. Leetsma & H. Walberg (Eds.), *Japanese educational productivity.* Ann Arbor: Center for Japanese Studies.

Stevenson, H. W., Lee, S-Y., Chen, C., Stigler, J. W., Hsu, C-C., & Kitamura, S. (1990). Contexts of achievement: A study of American, Chinese, and Japanese children. *Monographs of the Society for Research in Child Development, 55,* (1-2, Serial No. 221).

Stevenson, H. W., & Stigler, J. W. (1992). *The learning gap.* New York: Summit.

Stevenson, H. W., Stigler, J. W., Lee, S-Y., Kitamura, S., Kimura, S., & Kato, T. (1986). Achievement in mathematics. In H. Stevenson, H. Azuma, & K. Hakuta (Eds.), *Child development and education in Japan* (pp. 201-216). New York: Freeman.

Stigler, J. W., Lee, S-Y., & Stevenson, H. W. (1990). *Mathematical knowledge of Japanese, Chinese, and American elementary school children.* Reston, VA: National Council of Teachers of Mathematics.

Wade, S. E. (1992). How interest affects learning from text. In K. A. Renninger, Hidi, & A. Krapp (Eds.), *The role of interest in learning and development* (pp. 254-277). Hillsdale, NJ: Erlbaum.

Willoughby, S. S., Bereiter, C., Hilton, P., & Rubinstein, J. H. (1991). *Real math* (7th grade). La Salle, IL: Open Court.

Note: This project was supported by a grant from the Pacific Rim Research Program. Hidetsugu Tadika translated two of the Japanese textbook lessons into English.

The Authors: Richard E. Mayer is a Professor of Psychology and Education, Department of Psychology, University of California, Santa Barbara, CA 93106. His specializations are educational and cognitive psychology. Valerie Sims is a Ph.D. Candidate, Department of Psychology, University of California, Santa Barbara, CA 93106. Her specializations are cognitive and developmental psychology. Hidetsugu Tajika is an Associate Professor, Department of Psychology, Aichi University of Education, Kariya, Aichi 448 Japan. His specializations are memory and cognitive processes.

Exercise for Article 8

Factual Questions

1. The researchers explicitly state their research hypothesis for this study in which line(s)?

2. The lessons examined in this study ranged from a low of how many pages to a high of how many pages?

3. On the average, what percentage of the page space in Japanese textbooks is devoted to explanations of problem-solving procedures? What is the corresponding percentage for U.S. textbooks?

4. Which country's textbooks cover fewer topics?

5. According to the authors, which country's textbooks assume that students are "behaviorally active knowledge acquisition machines"?

6. The researchers note the need for research on how to use textbooks effectively in which lines?

Questions for Discussion

7. In lines 42–45, the researchers state that this study "contributes to an emerging research base on cross-national comparisons of textbooks" and cite three references for this statement. Would it have been appropriate for them to discuss this research base in more detail? Explain.

8. In lines 57–60, the researchers state that examining the content and teaching methods in textbooks "provides a partial account of how mathematics is taught...." Although it is partial, is it important? What else might be examined to get a fuller account? Explain.

9. The researchers examined only one type of lesson in only five textbooks. Is this an important limitation? Is the study of value despite this limitation? Explain.

10. The researchers state that the selected textbooks were "typical." How did they determine this? How would you determine it?

11. The researchers used two "independent raters." Why did they bother to use two raters? What does "independent" mean?

12. Beginning in line 177, the researchers describe their *quantitative* analysis. Beginning in line 313, they describe their *qualitative* analysis as a supplement to the quantitative one. In your opinion, which analysis yielded more important information about the differences between the two sets of textbooks? Explain.

13. Have these researchers demonstrated that differences between the two nations' textbooks are the *cause* of the differences in the mathematics achievement of the students in the two nations? Explain.

14. This study is an example of content analysis (also known as documentary analysis) in which the contents of documents are analyzed. Are there advantages and disadvantages to using content analysis as a research method for collecting information on problems in education? Explain.

Quality Ratings

Directions: Indicate your level of agreement with each of the following statements by circling a number from 5 for strongly agree (SA) to 1 for strongly disagree (SD). If you believe an item is not applicable to this research article, leave it blank. Be prepared to explain your ratings.

A. The introduction establishes the importance of the study.

SA   5   4   3   2   1   SD

B. The literature review establishes the context for the study.

SA   5   4   3   2   1   SD

C. The research purpose, question, or hypothesis is clearly stated.

SA   5   4   3   2   1   SD

D. The method of sampling is sound.

SA   5   4   3   2   1   SD

E. Relevant demographics (for example, age, gender, and ethnicity) are described.

SA   5   4   3   2   1   SD

F. Measurement procedures are adequate.

SA   5   4   3   2   1   SD

G. All procedures have been described in sufficient detail to permit a replication of the study.

SA   5   4   3   2   1   SD

H. The participants have been adequately protected from potential harm.

SA   5   4   3   2   1   SD

I. The results are clearly described.

SA   5   4   3   2   1   SD

J. The discussion/conclusion is appropriate.

SA   5   4   3   2   1   SD

K. Despite any flaws, the report is worthy of publication.

SA   5   4   3   2   1   SD

Article 9

Literature Preferences of Fourth-Graders

MARY ANN HARKRADER
Pierce Elementary School

RICHARD MOORE
Miami University

ABSTRACT. This study is an attempt to determine the literature preferences of fourth-grade boys and girls. The purpose of the study is to assist teachers in promoting reading by selecting literature that these children prefer to read. A fictitious-annotated-titles survey was used to determine reading preferences in ten fiction and eleven nonfiction categories, and to determine the effect of gender of main characters on reading preference. A sample stratified by type of school district was randomly selected from the elementary schools in Ohio. The final sample included 211 girls and 194 boys. Both boys and girls were found to prefer fiction more strongly than nonfiction. The girls preferred fiction more strongly than the boys, and the boys preferred nonfiction more strongly than the girls. The boys preferred male main characters more strongly than the girls. The girls preferred female main characters more strongly than the boys.

From *Reading Research and Instruction*, 36, 325–339. Copyright © 1997 by The College Reading Association. Reprinted with permission.

This study has been concerned with the literature preferences of a sample of fourth-grade boys and girls. Like other survey studies of intermediate age students, this research found that there are gender differences in the literature preferences of boys and girls and like these similar studies this
5 research found that some literature was preferred by both boys and girls. Recognizing that children's preferences in literature often overlap will make it easier for educators to select literature that both boys and girls will enjoy (Feely,
10 1982; Wolfson, Manning, & Manning, 1984; Haynes & Richgels, 1992).

Two reasons for investigating the literature preferences of children have been provided by Huck and Kuhn (1968). First, high interest materials enable a child to become ab-
15 sorbed in a book and he/she will engage in reading for longer periods of time. Second, knowing the literature preferences of children will enable the teacher to expand the interest of the children and anticipate new areas of interest. Wolfson, Manning, and Manning (1984) believed that
20 achievement was related to the interest in literature and a good reading program will provide books written at different reading levels in all interest areas to accommodate the preferences of children. The purpose of the present study is to investigate the literature interest of fourth-grade students.
25 This study also investigates the effect of the gender of main characters on the reading selections made by boys and girls.

In the last decade, important changes have occurred in the theory and practice of classroom reading instruction. The
30 emphasis has been on incorporating children's literature into the curricula and providing children authentic literary experiences (Huck, 1994: Hickman, Cullinan, & Hepler, Eds.). With the stress on using authentic literature for a variety of purposes, many teachers have moved, or are moving to literature-based and whole language learning (Goodman, 1986,
35 1988; Malloch, Malloch, & Francis, 1994; Hickman, Cullinan, & Hepler, Eds.).

Some indication of how much literature-based and whole language learning has been implemented in public and private schools can be found in the September 1992 *National
40 Assessment of Educational Progress* reading assessment report. The assessment was given to a nationally representative sample of fourth-, eighth-, and twelfth-grade students in public and private schools. This data yielded some interesting facts about instruction. About 49% of the fourth-grade
45 students were being taught reading using a combination of the basal text and trade books, and another 15% were reading complete literature works for all reading instruction. More than half of the students participated in silent reading almost daily, reading books of their choice (NAEP, 1993). It
50 is important that teachers and librarians know what children prefer to read so informed selections can be made when reading material is purchased (Saccardi, 1993/94).

To identify the literature preferences of children, the reading record, library withdrawal, observation, paired com-
55 parisons, interview, book list, and questionnaire (survey) have all been used extensively in the past (Purves & Beach, 1972). These various methods are useful in determining literature preference in different settings and with various samples of children (Purves & Beach, 1972).

60 It has been thought that children's literature choices begin about age eight (Downen, 1972). This is the time when children begin to identify with role models of their own sex. Childress (1985) discovered that in her school library, differences were evident at the kindergarten and first-grade
65 levels.

Feely (1982) replicated her 1972 study of middle grade students' reading and media interest (watching movies or television). Students used a 50-item title and annotation list, and indicated their interests by marking either read, watch,
70 read and watch, or neither. This is the same instrument used by Feely in her 1972 study. The sample for the 1982 study was all fourth- and fifth-grade students in Hackensack, NJ (urban) and Randolph Township, NJ (suburban).

She found that boys and girls had different interest patterns. One large difference noted between the two studies
75

was girls' increased interest in sports, which has always been a top choice of boys. Boys' interest in reading informational books continues to be a strong second. This reading, watching inventory indicates the literature of high interest for both boys and girls to be fantasy, science fiction, and humor.

Fisher (1988) investigated whether sex, race, grade, and teacher influences the reading preferences of children in the third, fourth, and fifth grades in an urban school. He used a reading preference survey developed by Bundy (1982). This survey contained 44 fictitious book titles and a fictitious description of each book. The 44 titles represented eleven different interest categories. The survey items were read to the children, and they were to mark their preference on a four point Likert scale. Boys preferred science and sports books, and the girls' preferences were biography, crafts, jokes, fairy tales, and animals. Mysteries were a high preference by both boys and girls.

A paired comparison reading preference inventory was prepared by Summers and Lukasevich (1983) and administered to students in grades five, six, and seven, in Ontario and British Columbia, Canada. They used fourteen reading themes in a paired-comparisons reading preference inventory. Theme preferences that ranked high for both boys and girls in all three grades were mystery, adventure, and sports. The girls in fifth and sixth grade preferred animal stories but this preference was replaced by the romance theme when they reached seventh grade. Boys in fifth grade preferred fantasy and science and this interest remained through seventh grade.

Haynes and Richgels (1992) used a regionally balanced sample of fourth-grade children for a literature preference study. A fictitious annotated titles inventory was constructed using 26 literature categories. Girls in this study ranked fantasy and items about growing up highest. This is similar to the findings of Wolfson, Manning, and Manning (1984). Boys' highest ranked items were adventure, space, science, and sports, which was consistent with Summers and Lukasevich (1983); Wolfson, Manning, and Manning (1984); and Fisher (1988). Realistic and historical fiction, and biography items were preferences of both boys and girls.

There has been some investigation of the literature preferences of boys and girls on the basis of gender of the main character. Johnson, Peer and Baldwin (1984) sampled classrooms from all regions of the country. Their study confirmed previous findings that young males tended to read and preferred to read about male main characters. This trend decreased as the grade level increased. Also, it was found that these girls and boys preferred male main characters equally. A recent study by Lowther (1993) also found that children enjoyed reading about main characters of their gender.

Design and Procedure

A fictitious-annotated-titles survey was created. Each of the titles and annotations was constructed to approximate literature found in the library. The survey consisted of 21 categories selected from Huck and Kuhn (1986) and previous research studies. There were ten fiction and eleven nonfiction categories in the survey:

Fiction	Nonfiction
(4) adjustment	(4) animals
(2) adventure	(2) art/hobbies
(2) animals	(4) biography/autobiography
(2) fairy tales	(2) earth science
(2) folk tales	(2) how-to science experiments
(2) friendship	(2) human body
(4) historical fiction	(2) people in other countries
(2) mystery	(2) plants
(2) science fiction	(2) space
(2) sports	(2) sports
	(2) weather

The numbers in parentheses indicate the number of items for each category. Four survey items were created for three of the categories to provide boys and girls a choice of male and female main characters. The fiction animal category contained two dog and two horse stories and the sports category included four different sports. Selection of items for each category and soundness of the items were validated by colleagues including a classroom teacher and a children's literature professor. In addition, adjustments were made on the basis of a field test of the survey with three fourth-grade classes. Finally, the items were placed in random order in the survey.

Method

Subjects

This study was conducted in fourth-grade classrooms in seventeen randomly selected elementary schools in the state of Ohio. A stratified sample of thirty-four schools was selected from the 2,063 elementary schools in Ohio. The strata represented the large cities, small cities, and rural local districts. Letters explaining the research study were sent to a fourth-grade teacher in each of the randomly selected elementary schools. Twenty-two fourth-grade teachers responded to this letter. Eighteen teachers were willing to participate and four were not. One teacher did not return the survey answer sheets. A total of 405 students participated in the survey—211 girls and 194 boys.

Administration of the Survey

The directions for administration asked the teachers to read each item in the same manner to prevent influencing the students' choices. Teachers were to read the following to the students: "Today you are going to give your opinion on books that could be in the library, but they are not. I will read to you a number, a book title, and the information. Please circle one of the five choices on your answer sheet. Here are the choices and what each one means."

yes, will read	you would read this book
maybe read	maybe you would read this book
?	you are not sure if you would read this book
probably not read	you would probably not read this book
not read	you would not read this book

Results

165   Each child's response for each item was given a value of 5, 4, 3, 2, or 1. A five represented a response of "yes will read" and the numbers descended corresponding to the decreasing desire of the student to read that item. Response distributions were then compared using a chi square test.

170   Since the value of 3 indicates uncertainty about a desire to read a title, and it is between preference and non-preference, a mean above 3 is taken as a preference for a title or category, and a mean below 3 is taken as preferring to not read the title or category.

175   Items that had more than one response circled on the response sheet were entered as blank, and response sheets with 75% or more of the responses the same were also entered as blanks.

    Both the fourth-grade boys and the fourth-grade girls in
180 this sample preferred fiction more strongly than nonfiction. Both boys and girls indicated a preference for reading fiction. This is indicated by means which are above 3. (See Table 1.)

Table 1
Boys' and Girls' Preferences for Fiction or Nonfiction

| Gender | Number of | | Mean | | Chi Square |
	Items	Responses	Fiction	Nonfiction	
Boys	52	9406	3.42	3.24	34.13*
Girls	52	10420	3.71	2.92	774.11*

*Significant at the .05 level. The chi squares compared the distribution of responses of the two categories for each gender.

    The literature preferences of the boys and girls in the
185 sample were compared and it was found that the girls in this study preferred to read fiction more strongly than the boys. However, it was found that the boys preferred to read nonfiction more strongly than the girls. The boys' mean for nonfiction was above 3, and the girls' mean was below 3. (See
190 Table 2.)

    There was a significant difference in the fiction preferences of these fourth-grade boys and girls. (See Table 3.) The girls indicated a stronger preference than the boys did for six fiction categories: friendship, fairy tales, animal sto-
195 ries, mystery, adjustment, and historical fiction. The boys did not have a strong preference for the friendship and fairy tale categories as indicated by a mean less than 3. The girls indicated a preference for every category with a mean above 3 in every instance. The boys indicated a stronger preference
200 for two fiction categories: sports and science fiction. No significant difference was found in the literature preferences of this sample of fourth grade boys and girls in the two fiction categories of adventure and folk tales.

    There were statistically significant differences in the
205 nonfiction preferences of these fourth-grade boys and girls. (See Table 4.) The boys preferred the following categories: sports (how-to), space, earth science, science (how-to), weather, and animals more strongly than the girls. The girls indicated a statistically stronger preference than the boys for
210 the nonfiction category of art and hobbies. The girls did not indicate a preference for the categories of sports (how-to),

space, weather, and plants. The boys did not indicate a preference for the categories of art and hobbies, plants, and people and lands. While neither the boys nor the girls indicated
215 a preference for the category of plants, the boys were statistically more favorable toward this category.

    This study found that the boys had a stronger preference than girls for a male main character. (See Table 5.) It was also found that the girls had a stronger preference for a fe-
220 male main character. It is important to note that the mean in each case was above 3. This indicates that there was a preference to read stories having a main character of the opposite gender even though the preference is stronger for same-gender main characters.

Discussion

Fiction

225   The boys and girls in this study were found to have a stronger preference for fiction when comparing their fiction to nonfiction responses. Watson (1985) had students record the books they read for one month and found that both boys and girls had a strong preference for fiction.

230   When comparing the boys' and girls' responses, it was found that girls have a stronger preference for fiction than boys. Haynes and Richgels (1992) also found that fourth-grade girls consistently preferred fiction in a study using a fictitious annotated titles inventory. The results of this study
235 are similar. It also found that boys have a stronger preference than girls for nonfiction, and the girls did not exhibit a preference for nonfiction.

    This research found significant differences in the preferences of boys and girls in eight of the traditional fiction
240 categories. Girls displayed a stronger preference than boys for four categories: animal stories, mystery, adjustment, and historical fiction. The categories of friendship and fairy tales were strongly preferred by the girls, and the boys were found not to prefer them. Fisher (1988), using a reading preference
245 survey, found that girls had a strong preference for mysteries, animal stories, and fairy tales. Summers and Lukasevich (1983) and Watson (1985) also found that girls had strong preferences for mysteries. Summers and Lukasevich (1983) used a paired comparison reading preference inventory for
250 their study, and Watson (1985) used a reading record for her study.

    In this study, the boys displayed a stronger preference than the girls for the fiction categories of sports and science fiction. Summers and Lukasevich (1983) and Haynes and
255 Richgels (1992) also found that boys strongly preferred sports and science fiction. No significant difference was found in this study between the boys' and girls' preferences for the categories of adventure and folk tales. The findings for the category of adventure are different from the studies
260 by Summers and Lukasevich (1983); Haynes and Richgels (1992); and Wolfson, Manning, and Manning (1984), who found that boys strongly preferred the category of adventure.

Nonfiction

    This study indicates that boys have a strong preference for nonfiction. The girls did not display a strong preference
265 for nonfiction. A significant difference was found in eight of

Table 2
Fiction and Nonfiction Preferences of Boys and Girls

		Boys		Girls		
Category	No. of Items	Responses	Mean	Responses	Mean	Chi Square
Fiction	26	4705	3.42	5222	3.71	121.65*
Nonfiction	26	4701	3.24	5198	2.92	179.01*

*Significant at the .05 level. The chi squares compared the distribution of responses of the two groups across the two categories.

Table 3
Literature Preferences of Boys and Girls for Fiction Categories

		Boys		Girls		
Category	No. of Items	Responses	Mean	Responses	Mean	Chi Square
Friendship	2	362	2.99	401	4.00	86.17*
Fairy Tales	2	359	2.89	400	3.87	83.60*
Animal Stories	4	722	3.29	805	3.79	53.58*
Mystery	2	361	3.80	404	4.26	28.20*
Adjustment	4	727	3.18	805	3.54	25.65*
Hist. Fiction	4	725	3.44	801	3.52	25.10*
Sports	2	360	3.54	402	3.21	14.57*
Science Fiction	2	362	3.86	401	3.67	10.90*
Adventure	2	365	3.82	401	3.89	6.00
Folk Tales	2	362	3.65	402	3.66	2.66

*Significant at the .05 level. The chi squares compared the distribution of responses of the two groups across the ten response categories.

Table 4
Literature Preferences of Boys and Girls for Nonfiction Categories

		Boys		Girls		
Category	No. of Items	Responses	Mean	Responses	Mean	Chi Square
Sports (How)	4	726	3.59	798	2.61	145.64*
Space	2	361	3.38	399	2.54	66.61*
Earth Science	2	361	3.66	402	3.03	52.58*
Science (How)	2	363	3.63	400	3.20	25.33*
Art & Hobbies	2	357	2.94	400	3.41	24.20*
Weather	2	359	3.00	397	2.63	23.10*
Plants	2	364	2.80	403	2.42	20.38*
Animals	2	364	3.40	402	3.06	14.82*
Biography/Autobio.	4	722	3.00	800	3.03	10.70
People/Lands	2	361	2.91	400	3.06	8.73
Human Body	2	363	3.25	397	3.08	4.42

*Significant at the .05 level. The chi squares compared the distribution of responses of the two groups across the eleven response categories.

Table 5
Main Character Preferences in Literature

		Boys		Girls		
Category	No. of Items	Responses	Mean	Responses	Mean	Chi Square
Male main	11	1993	3.51	2207	3.33	38.86*
Female main	11	1991	3.27	2208	3.81	149.26*

*Significant at the .05 level. The chi square compared the distribution of responses of the two groups across the two response categories.

the traditional nonfiction categories. Boys displayed a very strong preference for the how-to sports and space categories. The girls were found not to prefer either of these categories. Fisher (1988) and Haynes and Richgels (1992) found that
270 boys had a strong preference for sports. Haynes and Rich-

gels' (1992) research also found boys had a strong preference for the category of space. The girls in this study did not show a strong interest in sports. This does not support the findings of Feely (1982).
275   The boys in this study displayed a stronger preference

than the girls for three of the other nonfiction categories: earth science, how-to science experiments, and animals. The boys also were found to prefer the category of weather and the girls were found to reject the category of weather. Watson (1985) found that boys read more science and animal stories than girls. The studies of Fisher (1988); Haynes and Richgels (1992); and Summers and Lukasevich (1983) found the broad category of science strongly preferred by boys.

This study found a significant difference in the girls' preferences for the nonfiction category art and hobbies. Wolfson, Manning, and Manning (1984) found that girls preferred the art and hobby category. This study also found a significant difference in the category of plants. Neither the boys nor the girls were found to have an interest in this category, but the boys showed significantly more interest than the girls. The literature categories where no statistically significant differences were found between the boys' and girls' preferences were biography, people and other lands, and the human body.

Main Character

This study also examined the boys' and girls' gender preferences for the main characters of the literature they preferred. It was found that boys displayed a stronger preference for male main characters than girls. Girls were found to prefer female main characters more strongly than the boys. These findings support the studies of Johnson, Peer, and Baldwin (1984) and Lowther (1993) who found that boys and girls prefer to read stories with main characters of their gender.

The purpose of this research is to assist teachers and school librarians who select and purchase books for children to be used in a school setting. Since new literature for children is being published daily, librarians and teachers must make choices as to what will be purchased and made available for children to read in their school libraries and classrooms. Knowledge of the kinds of literature boys and girls are interested in reading can assist them when making these decisions.

Literature is also being used in the content areas of science, social studies, and math, making it important to keep up with the literature available and preferred by students. Many science concepts are being introduced and taught using literature. Social studies is frequently being integrated into reading instruction using historical fiction. Mathematics is a topic in children's literature that is often used in the classroom. Literature is frequently the link that connects all subject areas for the students. Therefore, it is important for educators to know the literature preferred by the children in order to make their educational experiences more meaningful.

When "trade books" become part of the instructional reading material, many questions arise. How does the teacher guide children to make sound selections? When literature is used for instruction, teachers and librarians need to develop strategies for choosing books for the classroom and library (Hiebert, Mervar, & Person, 1990). They can only make wise selections when acquiring reading material for

the school classrooms and libraries if they are knowledgeable about their children's preferences (Saccardi, 1993/94). The results of this study and others suggest the following:

1. There are gender differences in the literature preferences of boys and girls, although both prefer fiction over nonfiction.
2. Reading selections intended to interest girls should include fiction categories of mystery, friendship, adventure, fairy tales, and animal stories. Nonfiction categories for girls should include art and hobbies.
3. Reading selections intended to interest boys should include fiction categories of science fiction, mystery, and adventure. Nonfiction categories for boys should include earth science, how-to science experiments, and sports.
4. Boys and girls have interests that overlap, and some areas are of considerable interest to both.
5. Reading selections intended to interest both boys and girls should include the fiction categories of mystery and adventure, and perhaps science fiction. Nonfiction reading selections for both boys and girls should include the categories of earth science and how-to science experiments, and perhaps art and hobbies.
6. Boys and girls have stronger preferences for literature having same-gender main characters, but they also like to read stories with opposite-gender main characters.

References

Childress, G. T. (1985). Gender gap in the library: Different choices for girls and boys. *Top of the News, 42* (1), 69–73.

Dowen, T. W. (1972). Personal reading interests as expressed by children in grades three, four, and five in selected Florida Public Schools. *Dissertation Abstracts International, 32,* 6464A–6465A.

Feely, J. T. (1982). Content interest and media preferences of middle graders: Differences in a decade. *Reading World, 22* (1), 11–16.

Fisher, P. J. L. (1988, Fall). The reading preferences of third, fourth, and fifth graders. *Reading Horizons,* 62–70.

Goodman, K. (1986). *What's whole in whole language?* Portsmouth, NH: Heinemann Educational Books.

Haynes, C., & Richgels, D. J. (1992). Fourth graders' literature preferences. *Journal of Educational Research, 85,* 208–219.

Hiebert, E. H., Mervar, K. B., & Person, D. (1990). Research directions: Children's selection of trade books in libraries and classrooms. *Language Arts Language, 67,* 758–763.

Huck, C. S. (1994). The use and abuse of children's literature. In J. Hickman, S. Hepler & B. E. Cullinan (Eds.), *Children's literature in the classroom: Extending Charlotte's web* (pp. 1–15). Norwood, MA: Christopher-Gordon Publishers, Inc.

Huck, C. S., & Kuhn, D. Y. (1968). *Children's literature in the elementary school.* New York: Holt, Rinehart, and Winston, Inc.

Johnson, D. M., Peer, G. G., & Baldwin, R. S. (1984). Protagonist preferences among juvenile and adolescent readers. *Journal of Educational Research, 77,* 147–150.

Klein, M. L. (1988). *Teaching reading comprehension and vocabulary: A Guide for teachers.* Englewood Cliffs, NJ: Prentice Hall Inc.

Lowther, D. L., & Sullivan, H. J. (1993). *Reading preferences of American Indian and Anglo children for ethnicity, gender, and story setting.* New Orleans, LA: In Proceedings of Selected Research and Development Presentations at the convention of the Association for Educational Communications and Technology sponsored by the Research and Theory Division. (ERIC Document Reproduction Service No. ED 362 183).

Malloch, J., Malloch, I., & Francis, N. (1994). Planning for literature across the curriculum. In J. Hickman, S. Hepler, & B. E. Cullinan (Eds.), *Children's literature in the classroom: Extending Charlotte's web* (pp. 135–151). Norwood, MA: Christopher-Gordon Publishers, Inc.

NAEP data offer good news, bad news (1993, October/November). *Reading Today, 11,* 1, 11.

O'Neil, J. (1994, June). Rewriting the book on literature: Changes sought in how literature is taught, what students read. *ASCD Curriculum Update,* 1–8.

Osmont, P. (1987). Teacher inquiry in the classroom: Reading and gender set. *Language Arts, 64,* 758–761.

Purves, A. C., & Beach, R. (1972). *Literature and the reader.* Urbana, IL: National Council of Teachers of English.

Saccardi, M. (1993/94). Children speak: Our students' reactions to books can tell us what to teach. *Reading Teacher, 47* (4), 318–324.

Summers, E. G., & Lukasevich, A. (1983). Reading preferences of intermediate-grade children in relation to sex, community, and maturation (grade level): A Canadian perspective. *Reading Research Quarterly, 18,* 347–360.

Watson, M. (1985). *Differences in book choices for reading pleasure between second-through fifth-grade boys and girls.* (ERIC Document Reproduction Service No. ED 259 304)

Wheeler, M. A. (1984). Fourth grade boys' literacy from a mother's point of view. *Language Arts, 61,* 607.

Wolfson, B. J., Manning, G., & Manning, M. (1984, December). Revisiting what children say their reading interests are. *Reading World, 24* (2), 4–10.

Appendix
Fiction Items

Mystery
1. *The Mystery of the Hidden Jewels*—While visiting their grandparents two boys explore an abandoned house and find a sack of jewels under a broken board in the floor.
2. *The Voice in the Box*—Amy turns detective when on her way home from school she hears a voice coming from a box sitting on a porch.

Animal Stories
3. *The Adventures of Sam and Ginger*—These two dogs find adventure and trouble while traveling together through the fields and woods in eastern United States.
4. *King*—The story of a horse who is found roaming free, captured, and later becomes a winner in riding competition.
5. *Who Will Care for Dusty?*—The story of a dog who is left to roam the streets of a large city when its owner has to go to an old people's home. Will he find a new owner who will look after him?
6. *A Foal for Star*—Life changes on the range for the young mare as she feeds, protects, and cares for her new foal.

Friendship
7. *Waiting for Tomorrow*—Tomorrow Tom is moving to a small town and leaving his friend Chris behind. Tom is afraid he will have a difficult time making friends in the small town that is to become his new home.
8. *The Winner Is*—Two girls who are good friends become fierce competitors in gymnastics. They discover a way to remain friends after going head to head in a state-wide competition.

Sports
9. *The All-Star Catcher*—Sally was chosen to be the catcher for the All-Star team. Many problems await this honor.
10. *A Three Point Player*—Jason, the star player on the basketball team, becomes resentful when Jean, from France, shows his skills.

Historical Fiction
11. *A Friend with a Friend*—Rachel, a girl whose father is a station master for the Underground Railroad, finds that helping others can lead to death.
12. *Waiting for Pa*—Jeb and Jacob are expected to protect the family while their father is fighting the British. They suspect Indians are in the territory.
13. *Habib of Ancient Egypt*—An apprentice stonecutter gives you a view of life during the time the great pyramids were built.
14. *Hidden in the Barn*—Two young girls in German-controlled Denmark help a wounded British soldier during World War II.

Folk Tales/Myth
15. *The Golden Bird*—Hans, a poor, weak boy meets a golden bird while fetching firewood. The bird becomes his friend and grants him three wishes. What will he wish for?
16. *The Brightest Star*—A Greek myth of long ago tells how the sun was born.

Science Fiction
17. *The Coming of the Loo People*—Sarah discovers a family from a distant planet that has landed here on earth. Trying to keep the fact that the family is from a different planet becomes difficult for Sarah.
18. *A Journey in Time*—Joe and Josh investigate Professor Pabulum's time machine. Soon they find themselves in the northern hemisphere during the Ice Age.

Fairy Tales
19. *The Fiddler's Beautiful Music*—A plain, ordinary Princess is locked in the castle tower and can only be freed by the music of a magic fiddle.
20. *A Magic Feather*—Trond, the forest gnome, finds a feather one morning when gathering berries for breakfast and sticks it in his hat. He soon finds that this is not an ordinary feather.

Other Worlds
21. *The Dark Worlds*—On a planet light years away from earth, the people known as the Vetters fight for independence. Their leader uses his unusual powers to win the war.
22. *The Hole in the Tree*—You enter the hole and find yourself in another world and another time.

Adventure
23. *A Raft on the Wabash*—Two boys build a raft, leave the comforts of home, and set sail down the river for the Gulf of Mexico.
24. *Courage on White Mountain*—When backpacking with their scout troop, two girls become trapped on a ledge after a rock slide. Andrea, their friend, risks all to help them.

Realistic Fiction
25. *It's a New Year*—Jeremy wants to be a good student. Some of his friends do not care about school. He must make some difficult decisions.
26. *A Pot of Gold*—During a visit to Grandmother's house, Becky begins to understand why being different is good.
27. *Grandfather's Treasure Chest*—John finds Grandfather's old army footlocker in the attic. Each item inside represents an experience in Grandfather's life. Grandfather tells of these experiences.
28. *The President*—Jenny has been elected class president. She finds it difficult to be fair because her friends expect her to do what they want her to do.

Nonfiction Items

Animals
1. *Wings and Talons*—Learn how birds of prey get their food and protect themselves from their enemies.
2. *Ooze*—A lot of animals like to muck in the mud. Find out how they use mud in all sorts of ways.

How-to Science Experiments
3. *Water Wonders*—Directions and explanations are clearly given for conducting experiments that show the wonder of water.
4. *Science Investigations*—Pictures and clear directions are given for a wide variety of science experiments that can be done using items found in your home.

People in Other Lands
5. *A Family in South Africa*—A child tells about family life, school, religion, and sports in this African nation today.
6. *The New Ways*—Young people who live in Russia tell about the old customs and their day to day lives now in this eastern European country.

Plants
7. *The Travelers*—Learn how seeds from plants travel, find fertile soil, and produce plants just like they came from.
8. *A Fungi*—Find out about these interesting small plants that are found close to the ground. They do not sprout from a seed.

Earth Science
9. *The Changing Earth*—How many forces change the planet Earth? Learn what they are and how they change it.
10. *Earthquake*—What happens to the earth when it quakes? What causes it to quake? Why can't scientists tell when an earthquake will happen?

Human Body
11. *Your Lungs and How They Work*—Learn how these two sacs in your chest fill with air and what they have to do with other parts of your body.
12. *A New You Coming Every Day*—What happens in your body when you cut your finger? Find out how your body cells divide, grow, and change daily.

Space

13. *Probing Space: Unmanned Explorations*—Where did they go and what did they find?
14. *Using Satellites*—Find out how satellites help us communicate, predict the weather, study the earth, and do experiments in space.

Hobbies and Crafts

15. *Look Who's in the Kitchen*—A simple how-to cookbook with great meals and snacks to fix for family and friends.
16. *Models to be Made*—Drawings and directions on how to build airplanes, cars, gliders, rockets, ships, trains, and trucks.
17. *Paper and Printing*—Directions, diagrams, and pictures help you create many interesting projects using paper. Some projects include block printing, origami, kites, and cutout eggs.
18. *Making Things from Nature*—Easy to make projects from toys to terrariums using things found in the park, woods, or your backyard.

Sports

19. *The Hoops*—Four specific basketball skills that are needed to play the game are explained. Tips are also given for beginning players.
20. *Playing Better Soccer*—Ways to improve your offensive and defensive skills on the field are explained. Pictures and diagrams are also included.
21. *Baseball: The Game*—Have the winning edge in the field and at the plate. Get tips on fielding and hitting the baseball.
22. *Fishing*—Find out what equipment you use for fishing in streams and lakes. Also learn when and where to fish.

Weather

23. *Watching the Weather*—A simple introduction telling why we have weather happenings such as clouds, snow, rain, and sleet.
24. *Stormy Weather: Why It Happens*—Simple explanations of the causes and effects of thunderstorms, hurricanes, blizzards, and tornadoes.

History

25. *Fossils*—A book that tells how fossils were formed. Pictures can help you identify fossils found.
26. *Pompeii*—A fascinating description of life in this city when Mt. Vesuvius, a volcano, destroyed it over 1,500 years ago.
27. *Life at Home*—What was life like for Americans who fought in their own ways here in the U.S.A. during World War II.

Biographies

28. *Deborah Sampson*—A woman who disguised herself as a man and joined the Continental Army.
29. *Doctor*—The life story of Elizabeth Blackwell, the first woman doctor.
30. *Charles Goodyear*—Experience the story of Goodyear's many failures and finally success in making tires.
31. *Wilderness Scout*—The life of Daniel Boone, a guide for many people who traveled west over the Appalachian Mountains.

Exercise for Article 9

Factual Questions

1. The 21 categories of books were selected from what?

2. How were the items validated and refined?

3. What strata were used in the sampling of schools?

4. How many of the 34 teachers were willing to participate?

5. How did the researchers handle the problem created when students marked more than one choice for an item?

6. What was the mean score for boys on "Friendship"? What was the corresponding mean for girls?

7. The difference between boys and girls on "Sports" was statistically significant at what probability level?

Questions for Discussion

8. Given that a number of researchers have already examined children's literature preferences, was this study needed?

9. The researchers state that "response sheets with 75% or more of the responses the same were also entered as blanks." Thus, for example, if a student marked "yes, will read" for 75% of the items, his or her answer sheet was not used in the data analysis. Do you think this was a good idea? Why? Why not?

10. What is your opinion on using a "fictitious annotated titles inventory"? Would it have been better or worse to use annotations of books that actually exist? Explain.

11. In the Appendix at the end of the article, the researchers provide the fictitious titles and annotations. Is this Appendix an important part of the article? Explain.

12. For "Sports," the researchers used one annotation with a girl and one annotation with a boy. (See items 9 and 10 under "Fiction Items" in the Appendix to the article.) Was this a good idea? Explain.

13. Both boys and girls had a mean below 3.00 for "Plants." (See Table 4.) If you were a school librarian, would this cause you *not* to purchase books dealing with plants? Explain.

14. The researchers state that "teachers and librarians need to develop strategies for choosing books for the classroom and library." If you are an elementary school teacher or librarian, has this study helped to formulate a strategy? Explain.

15. To what population(s), if any, would you generalize the results of this study?

16. With hindsight, are there any changes you would make in the research methodology if you were planning another study on the same topic? Explain.

Quality Ratings

Directions: Indicate your level of agreement with each of the following statements by circling a number from 5 for strongly agree (SA) to 1 for strongly disagree (SD). If you believe an item is not applicable to this research article, leave it blank. Be prepared to explain your ratings.

A. The introduction establishes the importance of the study.

SA   5   4   3   2   1   SD

B. The literature review establishes the context for the study.

SA   5   4   3   2   1   SD

C. The research purpose, question, or hypothesis is clearly stated.

SA   5   4   3   2   1   SD

D. The method of sampling is sound.

SA   5   4   3   2   1   SD

E. Relevant demographics (for example, age, gender, and ethnicity) are described.

SA   5   4   3   2   1   SD

F. Measurement procedures are adequate.

SA   5   4   3   2   1   SD

G. All procedures have been described in sufficient detail to permit a replication of the study.

SA   5   4   3   2   1   SD

H. The participants have been adequately protected from potential harm.

SA   5   4   3   2   1   SD

I. The results are clearly described.

SA   5   4   3   2   1   SD

J. The discussion/conclusion is appropriate.

SA   5   4   3   2   1   SD

K. Despite any flaws, the report is worthy of publication.

SA   5   4   3   2   1   SD

Article 10

Russian and American College Students' Attitudes, Perceptions, and Tendencies Towards Cheating

ROBERT A. LUPTON
Central Washington University

KENNETH J. CHAPMAN
California State University, Chico

SUMMARY. The literature reports that cheating is endemic throughout the USA. However, lacking are international comparative studies that have researched cheating differences at the post-secondary business education level. This study investigates the differences between Russian and American business college students concerning their attitudes, perceptions and tendencies towards academic dishonesty. The study found significant differences between Russian and American college students' behaviours and beliefs about cheating. These findings are important for business educators called to teach abroad or in classes that are increasingly multinational in composition.

From *Educational Research, 44*, 17–27. Copyright © 2002 by Routledge Journals, Taylor & Francis, Ltd. Reprinted with permission.

Introduction

The Chinese have been concerned about cheating for longer than most civilizations have been in existence. Over 2,000 years ago, prospective Chinese civil servants were given entrance exams in individual cubicles to prevent
5 cheating, and searched for crib notes as they entered the cubicles. The penalty for being caught at cheating in ancient China was not a failing grade or expulsion, but death, which was applicable to both the examinees and examiners (Brickman, 1961). Today, while we do not execute students
10 and their professors when cheating is discovered, it appears we may not be doing enough to deter cheating in our classes (e.g., Collison, 1990; McCabe & Trevino, 1996; Paldy, 1996).

Cheating among U.S. college students is well documented
15 in a plethora of published reports, with a preponderance of U.S. studies reporting cheating incidences in excess of 70% (e.g., Baird, 1980; Collison, 1990; Davis et al., 1992; Gail & Borin, 1988; Jendrek, 1989; Lord and Chiodo, 1995; McCabe & Trevino, 1996; Oaks, 1975; Stern & Havlicek,
20 1986; Stevens & Stevens, 1987). Indeed, U.S. academicians have addressed the issues of cheating for the past century, publishing over 200 journal articles and reports (Payne & Nantz, 1994).[1] The U.S. literature can be divided into five primary areas: (a) reporting the incidences and types of

25 cheating (Baird, 1980; McCabe & Bowers, 1994, 1996), (b) reporting the behavioural and situational causes of cheating (Bunn, Caudill, & Gropper, 1992; LaBeff et al., 1990), (c) reporting the reactions of academicians towards cheating (Jendrek, 1989; Roberts, 1986), (d) discussing the preven-
30 tion and control of cheating (Ackerman, 1971; Hardy, 1981–1982), and (e) presenting statistical research methodologies used to measure academic misconduct (Frary, Tideman, & Nicholaus, 1997; Frary, Tideman, & Watts, 1977).

The U.S. studies on cheating behaviours are disturbing
35 since they indicate a widespread, insidious problem. Cheating devalues the educational experience in a number of ways. First, cheating behaviours may lead to inequitable grades and a misrepresentation of what a student may actually have learned and can use after graduation. Additionally,
40 successful cheating behaviours in college may carry over as a way of life after college. That is, students may believe that if they can get away with cheating now, they can get away with cheating later. Obviously, academic dishonesty is not to be taken lightly, yet cheating seems to be prevalent, at least
45 in the USA. This study investigated if the academic dishonesty problem crosses national boundaries. The researchers investigated if students' attitudes, beliefs, and cheating tendencies vary by country—specifically, as part of an ongoing research agenda (Lupton, Chapman, & Weiss, 2000); the
50 researchers report differences between Russian and American students.

The international literature provides mostly anecdotal evidence of academic dishonesty and has few *comparative* research efforts. International studies and reports have
55 looked at college students in Australia (Maslen, 1996; Waugh & Godfrey, 1994), Canada (Black, 1962; Chidley, 1997; Genereux & McLeod, 1995; Harpp & Hogan, 1993, 1998; Jenkinson, 1996), the UK (Baty, 1997; Bushby, 1997; Franklyn-Stokes & Newstead, 1995; Mackenzie & Smith,
60 1995; Newstead, Franklyn-Stokes, & Armstead, 1996), Palestine (Surkes, 1994), Poland (Curry, 1997) and Russia (Poltorak, 1995), and high school students in Austria (Hanisch, 1990), Germany (Rost & Wild, 1990) and Italy (*TES*, 1996).

Poltorak (1995), the only major Russian study, measured
65 attitudes about and tendencies towards cheating at four Russian post-secondary technical universities. The research

---

[1] For a comprehensive review of the cheating literature, see Lupton's (1999) published dissertation.

found cheating to be widespread, with over 80% of the students cheating at least once during college and with many of those incidences occurring during examinations. The most common types of cheating were: using crib sheets during examinations, looking at someone's examination, using unauthorized lecture notes during examinations, using someone's finished homework to copy from, and purchasing term papers and plagiarizing. Moreover, male college students were reported to have higher incidences of cheating than female students.

Only a handful of studies have investigated cross-national differences related to academic dishonesty (Curtis, 1996; Davis et al., 1994; Diekhoff et al., 1999; Evans, Craig, & Mietzel, 1993; Lupton et al., 2000; Waugh et al., 1995). Davis et al. (1994) reported that a majority of Australian and U.S. college students cheated more in high school than they did in college. The study is unique in that cheating is linked to grade-oriented and learning-oriented attitudes. It appears that Australian college students are more likely to attend school for the sake of learning, whereas U.S. students tend to be much more focused on grades. Thus, what motivates Australian college students to cheat is different from that of U.S. college students. Diekhoff et al. (1999) found that Japanese college students, as compared to U.S. students, report higher levels of cheating tendencies, have a greater propensity to neutralize the severity of cheating through rationale justification, and are not as disturbed when observing in-class cheating. Interestingly, U.S. and Japanese students agreed guilt is the most effective deterrent to cheating. Finally, Lupton et al. (2000) found significantly different levels of cheating between Polish and U.S. business students. The Polish students reported much higher frequencies of cheating than their American counterparts and were more likely to feel it was not so bad to cheat on one exam or tell someone in a later section about an exam. The Polish students were also more inclined than the American students to feel it was the responsibility of the instructor to create an environment that reduces the likelihood that cheating could occur.

Although cross-national comparative studies are appearing more often in academic literature, it is quite apparent that a major chasm in our knowledge still exists regarding cross-national attitudes, perceptions and tendencies towards cheating at the post-secondary education level. Moreover, to date, no cross-national study has been conducted comparing Russian and U.S. business college students. Russian universities have been known to produce top students, particularly in computer programming (*Chronicle of Higher Education*, 2000). However, like many institutions in Russia, education has been the recipient of severe swings in its support and funding over the years. Some reports indicate the post-secondary educational system is in serious disrepair, where bribes for entrance and grades are commonplace and learning is minimal (Dolshenko, 1999). Additionally, the value of an education seems to be in question, with only 53% of Russia's citizens believing that higher education is important (ibid.). It seemed likely that given some of the problems being experienced in the Russian higher education system, where the value of learning and education may be in a weak-

ened state, cheating could be commonplace. Substantial differences in academic honesty may also be found due to Russia being a more collective society compared to the USA, which is more individualistic in culture (Ryan et al., 1991).

Building on the research conducted in the USA, the researchers present a cross-national study that compares attitudes, perceptions, and tendencies of college business students in Russia and the USA. The research begins to *fill in* the gap in our knowledge about cross-national differences in attitudes, beliefs, and tendencies towards cheating.

Methodology

Method and sample

Undergraduate business students from the USA and Russia were asked to participate in the study. Questionnaires were administered in the classes. Given the sensitive nature of the questions, respondents were repeatedly told, orally and in writing, that their responses would be anonymous and confidential. The respondents were asked to answer as many questions as possible, as long as they felt comfortable with the particular question.

The American student sample was collected from Colorado State University, a mid-sized university located in the western USA, and the Russian sample was collected from Novgorod State University and the Norman School College. Colorado State University is located in Fort Collins, Colorado, a city of about 120,000 residents. Both Novgorod State University and the Norman School College are located in Novgorod, Russia, which has approximately 200,000 inhabitants. A total of 443 usable surveys were collected in the USA and 174 in Russia. Nearly 50% of the American students and 64% of the Russian students were male. In both regions, 90% of the sample was between the ages of 17 and 25, with an average age of 21 years. The average American grade-point average (GPA) was 3.02 and 4.27 for the Russian students (U.S. GPA, A = 4.0; Russian GPA, A = 5.0). Fifty-two percent of the American sample was juniors and 45.8% seniors. In contrast, 56.1% of the Russian survey respondents was freshmen, while sophomores and graduate students accounted for 20.5% and 17.5% respectively.

The survey instrument

Identical self-report questionnaires were used to collect the data in both countries. The survey was translated into Russian and translated back into English. To evaluate the attitudes, perceptions, and tendencies towards academic cheating, a 29-question survey instrument was developed consisting of a series of dichotomous (yes/no) and scalar questions, as well as a question that asked students to assess what proportion of their peers they believe cheat. Most of the yes/no questions specifically asked the students about cheating behaviours (e.g., "Have you cheated during college?" "Have you received information about an exam from students in earlier sections of the class?"). In addition, students were asked to respond to a series of statements using a seven-point scale anchored with Strongly disagree to Strongly agree. These scalar questions asked students about their attitudes and beliefs about cheating (e.g., "Cheating on one exam is really not that bad. I believe telling someone in

Table 1

Percentage of American or Russian Business Students Responding "Yes" to Questions About Cheating

	Percentage responding "yes"	
	American students $n = 443$	Russian students $n = 174$
Cheated at some point during college	55.4	64.2***
Cheated in current class	2.9	38.1*
Know student who has cheated on an exam at the university	77.3	80.9**
Know student who has cheated on an exam in current class	6.3	66.9*
Seen a student cheat on an exam at the university	61.3	72.4**
Seen a student cheat on an exam in current class	5.6	63.2*
Used exam answers from a prior term to study for a current exam	88.7	48.6*
Given student in a later section information about an exam	68.5	91.9*
Received exam information from a student in an earlier section	73.9	84.3**
Scenario A: John cheated by giving Jane his past exams	5.2	49.1*
Scenario A: Jane cheated by using John's past exams	9.7	63.9*
Scenario B: Jane cheated by using John's articles	77.5	66.9**

*χ^2 = test of differences between nationalities significant at $p < 0.000$.
**χ^2 = test of differences between nationalities significant at $p < 0.01$.
***χ^2 = test of differences between nationalities significant at $p < 0.05$.

a later section about an exam you just took is OK"). Students were also given two scenarios and asked to decide whether cheating had occurred. Each scenario was intentionally left rather vague. Having the scenarios be rather ambiguous meant that the student could not easily conclude that cheating had or had not occurred. In this fashion, students were left more to their own personal interpretations of trying to decide if cheating had or had not occurred. The first scenario (scenario A) was:

John Doe took Marketing 400 in the fall semester. His friend, Jane, took Marketing 400 in the spring semester. John gave Jane all his prior work from the course. Jane found John's answers to prior exams and uses these to prepare for tests in the course.

Students were then asked to decide if John and Jane had cheated. The next scenario (scenario B) was:

Jane also discovered that John had received good grades on some written assignments for the class. Many of these assignments required John to go to the library to look up articles about various topics. Jane decides to forgo the library work and uses John's articles for her papers in the class.

After reading scenario B, students were asked to decide if Jane had cheated. Finally, to account for possible confounds and explore individual level differences, the survey also included some basic demographic questions.

Results

American and Russian business students' positions on cheating behaviours

American and Russian business students had significantly different positions on their self-reported cheating behaviours, on the degree to which they knew or saw others cheat, and on their perception of whether or not cheating had occurred in the two case scenarios.

Table 1 highlights the significant differences in self-reported cheating behaviour between the American and Russian business students. A larger share of the Russian students reported cheating at some point. While about 55% of the

American students reported they had cheated at some point during college, nearly 64% of the Russian students reported having cheated. Russian students also were much more likely to report cheating in the class in which the data were collected. In fact, only 2.9% of the American students acknowledged cheating in the class where the data were collected, whereas 38.1% of the Russian students admitted to cheating in the class. Additionally, Russian students were more likely to have reported that they knew or had seen a student who had cheated. The percentage of students who had given or received information about an exam that had been administered in an earlier section was higher with Russian students. Nearly 92% of the Russian students admitted to conveying exam information to their peers in a later section, while 68.5% of the American students admitted doing so. American students, however, reported a greater incidence of using examinations from a prior term to study for current exams.

American and Russian business students also had very different impressions of whether or not cheating had occurred in the scenarios. In scenario A, the Russian students were much more likely to believe that John and Jane had cheated. For example, only 5.2% of the American students felt John had cheated by giving Jane his past exams, while 49.1% of the Russian students felt the same. Additionally, 9.7% of the American students compared to 63.9% of the Russian students felt Jane had cheated by using John's past exams. However, in scenario B, a larger share of the American students felt Jane had cheated by using John's articles. These statistically significant and quite large differences in interpretations of the scenarios suggest that American and Russian business students have extremely different perspectives of what is or is not cheating.

American and Russian business students' differences in beliefs about cheating

Table 2 reveals that American and Russian business students have significantly different beliefs about cheating. Students were asked to assess what proportion of their peers

Table 2
American and Russian Business Students' Beliefs About Cheating

	Overall mean	American students $n = 443$	Russian students $n = 174$
Percentage of students believed to cheat on exams	36.53	24.18	69.59*
Most students cheat on exams	3.45	2.80	5.12*
Most students cheat on out-of-class assignments	4.09	3.88	4.64*
Cheating on one exam is not so bad	2.90	2.34	4.36*
OK to tell someone in later section about an exam	4.71	4.07	6.36*
Giving someone your past exams is cheating	2.26	2.02	2.87*
Using an exam from a prior semester is cheating	2.65	2.23	3.02*
Instructor must make sure students do not cheat	3.68	3.88	3.18*
Instructor discussing issues tied to cheating reduces amount of cheating	3.92	4.27	3.01*

Note: The first item in the table is a percentage (e.g., 36.53%). All other items are mean ratings using a seven-point scale, where 1 = Strongly disagree and 7 = Strongly agree.

*t = test of mean differences between nationalities significant at $p < 0.000$.

they believed to cheat. Russian students felt that about 69% of their colleagues cheat on exams, while American students stated that they felt only about 24% of their fellow students cheat. In a series of Strongly disagree/Strongly agree belief statements, the Russian students were more likely than the American students to believe that most students cheat on exams and out-of-class assignments, that cheating on one exam is not so bad, and that it is OK to tell someone in a later section about an exam just completed. However, as revealed earlier, the Russian students seem to have a different position on what is or is not cheating. The American students did not believe that giving someone past exams or using exams from a prior semester was cheating, while the Russian students were more neutral on the matter.

Finally, the students in each country were asked if they believed the instructor is responsible for ensuring that cheating does not occur, and if by discussing cheating-related issues (e.g., ethics, penalties, responsibilities), the instructor can reduce cheating incidents. The Russian students were less likely than the American students to feel that it is the instructor's responsibility to prevent cheating in the classroom and were less likely to believe that the instructor merely discussing cheating-related issues would reduce cheating.

Analysis of possible confounds

Although a number of differences were found based on nationality, it is possible that these differences may be due to some other issue. Past literature has suggested that a number of idiosyncratic variables could influence the likelihood of someone cheating (e.g., Alschuler & Blimling, 1995; Bunn et al., 1992; Johnson & Gormly, 1971; Kelly & Worrell, 1978; McCabe & Trevino, 1996; Stern & Havlicek, 1986; Stevens & Stevens, 1987). Therefore, analyses were conducted to check if expected grade in the course, overall grade-point average, college class, gender, or age were having any effects on the findings and, in particular, if these factors interacted with nationality. Of focal concern was the extent to which these factors were influencing the number of students that had reported cheating. Neither expected grade in the course, overall grade-point average, college class and

gender, nor age interacted with country. This effectively eliminates the possibility that they are confounds for the differences found due to nationality

Conclusion

This is the first study to compare the attitudes, beliefs, and tendencies towards academic dishonesty of American and Russian business college students. The study reveals that American and Russian business students hold vastly different attitudes, perceptions, and tendencies towards cheating. It was surprising to find that Russian students reported much higher frequencies of cheating than their American counterparts. This raises the question: Do Russian students cheat more often than American students? In fact, we believe these higher self-reported cheating behaviours likely reflect that the Russian students have very different attitudes, beliefs, and definitions regarding cheating when compared to the American students. On the other hand, a few of the questions and the answers given were unequivocal. The Russian students were much more likely to feel it was not so bad to cheat on one exam or tell someone in a later section about an exam. This may indicate that the Russians do not take academic dishonesty as seriously as the Americans and/or are more motivated to cheat. Of course, the interpretation of why the differences exist between the Russian and American students is multidimensional, involving cultural nuances, societal values, teaching and educational philosophies, just to name a few. A true understanding of why these differences exist, however, is beyond the scope of this paper, but certainly worthy of future research endeavours.

Yet, educators hosting foreign students locally and teaching abroad need to understand the nuances and attitudes of different student populations and the association with classroom management. The better understanding we have of if and how international students' attitudes, perceptions, and tendencies towards academic dishonesty differ among countries, the greater the instructors' ability to communicate with expatriate students and take actions to prevent cheating. Students from all countries continue to enroll in colleges and universities around the world. Of the 1.5 million students who study abroad, nearly one-third of these (481,280) stud-

ied in the USA (*Chronicle of Higher Education,* 1998). Universities also continue to send faculty abroad to teach around the world. Organizations such as the International Institute
330 of Education (IIE), the Council for International Educational Exchange (CIEE), and the Agency for International Development (AID) encourage global education and resource exchanges abroad (Barron, 1993; Garavalia, 1997). Post-secondary business education has been introduced to the
335 former Soviet Union republics and to East Asia, bringing American faculty and resources to these regions (Fogel, 1994; Kerr, 1996; Kyj, Kyj, & Marshall, 1995; Petkus, 1995). As the student body becomes more international and educators increasingly teach abroad, research of this nature
340 becomes vital for effective classroom management.

Effective classroom management and teaching are influenced by the predominant norms within a country or region. Certainly part of the challenge that emerges for faculty members is to assist students in understanding what is or is
345 not academic misconduct. Especially when teaching abroad or in courses with a large multinational composition, the instructor needs to clearly articulate to the students, orally and in writing, what behaviours are or are not considered academic misconduct. Instructors should educate students on
350 the virtues of not engaging in cheating and the penalties for cheating, with the hope that this will reduce incidents of academic dishonesty. It should be noted, however, that while the American students felt neutral about the likelihood that discussing cheating-related issues might reduce the degree of
355 cheating in the course, the Russian students slightly disagreed. Additionally, the Russian students were more inclined than the American students to feel it was not the responsibility of the instructor to create an environment that reduces the likelihood that cheating could occur (e.g., devel-
360 oping multiple versions of the same examination, cleaning off desktops before examinations, arranging multiple proctors to oversee the test period, not allowing bathroom breaks).

To this end, more research needs to be undertaken in or-
365 der to fully understand how students view cheating. In particular, a cross-national study that compares data from a variety of diverse countries would greatly illuminate the magnitude of differences that may exist between countries. This research is the first step in highlighting and better under-
370 standing these differences.

References

Ackerman, P. D. (1971). The efforts of honor grading on students' test scores. *American Educational Research Journal, 8,* 321–33.

Alschuler, A. S., & Blimling, G. S. (1995). Curbing epidemic cheating through systematic change. *College Teaching, 43,* 4, 23–125.

Baird, J. S., Jr. (1980). Current trends in college cheating. *Psychology in the Schools, 17,* 4, 515–22.

Barron, C. (1993). An Eastern education. *Europe, 11,* 331, 1–2.

Baty, P. (1997). Prospering cheats on the up. *Times Higher Education Supplement, 50,* 3.

Black, D. B. (1962). The falsification of reported examination marks in a senior university education course. *Journal of Education Sociology, 35,* 346–54.

Brickman, W.W. (1961). Ethics, examinations, and education. *School and Society, 89,* 412–15.

Bunn, D. N., Caudill, S. B., & Gropper, D. M. (1992). Crime in the classroom: An economic analysis of undergraduate student cheating behavior. *Journal of Economic Education, 23,* 197–207.

Bushby, R. (1997). Internet essays cause degrees of concern. *Times Educational Supplement, 42,* 42, 3.

Chidley, J. (1997). Tales out of school. *Maclean's,* 76–9.

Chronicle of Higher Education. (1998). *Almanac issue, 45,* 1, 24.

Chronicle of Higher Education. (2000). Russian universities educate world's top student programmers. *Chronicle of Higher Education, 47,* 8, A43–4.

Collison, M. (1990). Apparent rise in students' cheating has college officials worried. *Chronicle of Higher Education, 36,* 34–5.

Curry, A. (1997). Psst, got the answer? Many say yes. *Christian Science Monitor, 89,* 157, 7.

Curtis, J. (1996). Cheating—let's face it. *International Schools Journal, 15,* 2, 37–44.

Davis, S. F., Grover, C. A., Becker, A. H., & McGregor, L. N. (1992). Academic dishonesty: Prevalence determinants, techniques, and punishments. *Teaching of Psychology, 19,* 1, 16–20.

Davis, S. F., Noble, L. M., Zak, E. N., & Dreyer, K. K. (1994). A comparison of cheating and learning: Grade orientation in American and Australian college students. *College Student Journal, 28,* 353–6.

Diekhoff, G. M., Labeff, E. E., Shinohara, K., & Yasukawa, H. (1999). College cheating in Japan and the United States. *Research in Higher Education, 40,* 3, 343–53.

Dolshenko, L. (1999). The college student today: A social portrait and attitudes toward schooling. *Russian Social Science Review, 40,* 5, 73–83.

Evans, E. D., Craig, D., & Mietzel, G. (1993). Adolescents' cognitions and attributions for academic cheating: A cross-national study. *Journal of Psychology, 127,* 6, 585–602.

Fogel, D. S. (1994). *Managing in Emerging Market Economies.* Boulder, CO: Westview Press.

Franklyn-Stokes, A., & Newstead, S. E. (1995). Undergraduate cheating: Who does what and why? *Studies in Higher Education, 20,* 2, 159–72.

Frary, R. B., Tideman, T. N., & Nicholaus, T. (1997). Comparison of two indices of answer copying and development of a spliced index. *Educational and Psychological Measurement, 57,* 1, 20–32.

Frary, R. B., Tideman, T. N., & Watts, T. M. (1977). Indices of cheating on multiple-choice tests. *Journal of Educational Statistics, 2,* 4, 235–56.

Gail, T., & Borin, N. (1988). Cheating in academe. *Journal of Education for Business, 63,* 4, 153–7.

Garavalia, B. J. (1997). International education: How it is defined by US students and foreign students. *Clearing House, 70,* 4, 215–23.

Genereux, R. L., & Mcleod, B. A. (1995). Circumstances surrounding cheating: A questionnaire study for college students. *Research in Higher Education, 36,* 6, 687–704.

Hanisch, G. (1990). *Cheating: Results of questioning Viennese pupils.* Vienna: Ludwig Boltzmann Institute fur Schulentwicklung und International Vergleichende Schulforschung.

Hardy, R. J. (1981–1982). Preventing academic dishonesty: Some important tips for political science professors. *Teaching Political Science, 9,* 68–77.

Harpp, D. N., & Hogan, S. J. (1993). Detection and prevention of cheating on multiple-choice exams. *Journal of Chemical Education, 70,* 4, 306–10.

Harpp, D. N., & Hogan, S. J. (1998). The case of the ultimate identical twin. *Journal of Chemical Education, 75,* 4, 482–5.

Jendrek, M. P. (1989). Faculty reaction to academic dishonesty. *Journal of College Student Development, 30,* 3, 401–6.

Jenkinson, M. (1996). If you can't beat 'em, cheat. *Alberta Report, 23,* 42, 36–7.

Johnson, C. D., & Gormly, J. (1971). Achievement, sociability and task importance in relation to academic cheating. *Psychological Reports, 28,* 302.

Kelly, J. A., & Worrell, L. (1978). Personality characteristics, parent behaviors, and sex of the subject in relation to cheating. *Journal of Research in Personality, 12,* 179–88.

Kerr, W. A. (1996). Marketing education for Russian marketing educators. *Journal of Marketing Education, 19,* 3, 39–49.

Kyj, L. S., Kyj, M. J., & Marshall, P. S. (1995). Internationalization of American business programs: Case study Ukraine. *Business Horizon, 38,* 55–9.

Labeff, E. E., Clark, R. E., Haines, V. J., & Dickhoff, G. M. (1990). Situational ethics and college student cheating. *Sociological Inquiry, 60,* 2, 190–8.

Lord, T., & Chiodo, D. (1995). A look at student cheating in college science classes. *Journal of Science and Technology, 4,* 4, 317–24.

Lupton, R. A. (1999). Measuring business students' attitudes, perceptions, and tendencies about cheating in Central Europe and the USA. *ProQuest* (dissertation).

Lupton, R. A., Chapman, K., & Weiss, J. (2000). American and Slovakian university business students' attitudes, perceptions, and tendencies toward academic cheating. *Journal of Education for Business, 75,* 4, 231–41.

McCabe, D. L., & Bowers, W. J. (1994). Academic dishonesty among males in college: A thirty-year perspective. *Journal of College Student Development, 35,* 1, 5–10.

McCabe, D. L., & Bowers, W. J. (1996). The relationship between student cheating and college fraternity or sorority membership. *NASPA Journal, 33,* 4, 280–91.

McCabe, D. L., & Trevino, L. K. (1996). What we know about cheating in college. *Change, 28,* 1, 29–33.

Mackenzie, R., & Smith, A. (1995). Do medical students cheat? *Student BMJ, 3,* 212.

Maslen, G. (1996). Cheats with pagers and cordless radio cribs. *Times Educational Supplement, 4186,* 16.

Newstead, S. E., Franklyn-Stokes, A., & Armstead, P. (1996). Individual differences in student cheating. *Journal of Educational Psychology, 88,* 2, 229–41.

Oaks, H. (1975). Cheating attitudes and practices at two state colleges. *Improving College and University Teaching, 23,* 4, 232–5.

Paldy, L. G. (1996). The problems that won't go away: Addressing the causes of cheating. *Journal of College Science Teaching, 26*, 1, 4–7.

Payne, S. L., & Nantz, K. S. (1994). Social accounts and metaphors about cheating. *College Teaching, 42*, 3, 90–6.

Petkus, E., Jr. (1995). Open for remodeling: Boise State helps prepare Vietnam's MBA faculty of the future. *Change, 27*, 64–7.

Poltorak, Y. (1995). Cheating behavior among students of four Moscow institutes. *Higher Education, 30*, 2, 225–46.

Roberts, R. N. (1986). Public university response to academic dishonesty: Disciplinary or academic? *Journal of Law and Education, 15*, 4, 371–84.

Rost, D. H., & Wild, K. P. (1990). Academic cheating and avoidance of achievement: Components and conceptions. *Zeitschrift fur Pedagogische Psychologie, 4*, 13–27.

Ryan, R. M., Chirkov, V. I., Little, T. D., Sheldon, K. M., Timoshina, E., & Deci, E. L. (1991). The American dream in Russia: Extrinsic aspirations and well-being in two cultures. *Personality and Social Psychology Bulletin, 25*, 12, 1509–24.

Stern, E. B., & Havlicek, L. (1986). Academic misconduct: Results of faculty and undergraduate student surveys. *Journal of Allied Health, 5*, 129–42.

Stevens, G. E., & Stevens, F. W. (1987). Ethical inclinations of tomorrow's managers revisited: How and why students cheat. *Journal of Education for Business, 63*, 24–9.

Surkes, S. (1994). Cheat at exams and risk going to prison. *Times Educational Supplement, 4068*, 18.

Times Educational Supplement. (1996). In brief: Italy. *Times Educ. Suppl., 4187, 16*, 27 September.

Waugh, R. F., & Godfrey, J. R. (1994). Measuring students' perceptions about cheating. *Educational Research and Perspectives, 21*, 2, 28–37.

Waugh, R. F., Godfrey, J. R., Evans, E. D., & Craig, D. (1995). Measuring students' perceptions about cheating in six countries. *Australian Journal of Psychology, 47*, 2, 73–82.

Acknowledgment: The authors wish to thank Dr. Susanne E. Jalbert, Jalbert Consulting, for administering and collecting the Russian surveys.

Address correspondence to: Dr. Robert A. Lupton, Department of Administrative Management and Business Education, Central Washington University, Ellensburg, WA 98926. Phone: (509) 963-2611. E-mail: luptonr@cwu.edu. Dr. Kenneth J. Chapman, Department of Finance and Marketing, College of Business, California State University, Chico, CA 95929. Phone: (530) 898-4820. E-mail: kchapman@csuchico.edu

Exercise for Article 10

Factual Questions

1. According to the literature review, did the only major Russian study find cheating to be widespread?

2. How many usable surveys were collected in Russia?

3. What percentage of the American students reported having seen a student cheat on an exam at the university? What was the corresponding percentage for Russian students?

4. Is the difference referred to in question 3 above statistically significant? If so, at what probability level is it significant?

5. Students responded to statements such as "most students cheat on exams" on a seven-point scale. What does a seven (7) represent?

6. Which group of students more strongly believed that it is the instructor's responsibility to prevent cheating in the classroom?
   A. American students   B. Russian students

Questions for Discussion

7. Do you think that the historical material in lines 1–9 is interesting? Does it help establish the context for the current study? Explain.

8. Do you think that the results of this study help establish that differences in cheating are caused by the fact that Russia is a more collective society than the United States? Explain. (See lines 125–128.)

9. The researchers report that students were repeatedly told, orally and in writing, that their responses would be anonymous and confidential. In your opinion, is this sufficient to ensure that all students would answer with complete honesty regarding their cheating behavior? Explain. (See lines 137–140.)

10. None of the American students were freshmen while 56.1% of the Russian students were. Is this important information? Explain. (See lines 158–161.)

11. The researchers state that each scenario was intentionally left rather vague so that students could not easily conclude that cheating had occurred. What is your opinion on the use of scenarios to gather information about attitudes toward cheating? (See lines 181–184.)

12. Do you agree with the researchers' call for future research? Explain. (See lines 364–370.)

Quality Ratings

Directions: Indicate your level of agreement with each of the following statements by circling a number from 5 for strongly agree (SA) to 1 for strongly disagree (SD). If you believe an item is not applicable to this research article, leave it blank. Be prepared to explain your ratings.

A. The introduction establishes the importance of the study.

   SA   5   4   3   2   1   SD

B. The literature review establishes the context for the study.

   SA   5   4   3   2   1   SD

C. The research purpose, question, or hypothesis is clearly stated.

   SA   5   4   3   2   1   SD

D. The method of sampling is sound.

   SA   5   4   3   2   1   SD

E. Relevant demographics (for example, age, gender, and ethnicity) are described.

   SA   5   4   3   2   1   SD

F. Measurement procedures are adequate.

SA   5   4   3   2   1   SD

G. All procedures have been described in sufficient detail to permit a replication of the study.

SA   5   4   3   2   1   SD

H. The participants have been adequately protected from potential harm.

SA   5   4   3   2   1   SD

I. The results are clearly described.

SA   5   4   3   2   1   SD

J. The discussion/conclusion is appropriate.

SA   5   4   3   2   1   SD

K. Despite any flaws, the report is worthy of publication.

SA   5   4   3   2   1   SD

Article 11

A National Assessment of Secondary School Principals' Perceptions of Violence in Schools

JAMES H. PRICE
University of Toledo

SHERRY A. EVERETT
Harvard School of Public Health

ABSTRACT: The purpose of this investigation was to examine the perceptions of secondary school principals regarding violence and weapons in public and private schools in the United States. Student weapon carrying was most often reported in larger schools, schools with higher levels of violence in the school's neighborhood, and in schools with a higher percentage of low-socioeconomic (SES) students. Perceived as major etiological factors of violence were lack of parental supervision at home, lack of family involvement with school, and exposure to violence in the mass media. Perceived as the major reasons students in the principals' own school committed acts of violence were that the student was provoked by others or was jealous of a girlfriend/boyfriend. Just over one-third of schools had already implemented some type of violence prevention program, and another reported they were planning to implement some type of violence prevention program. The most common barriers reported by the remaining principals were believing there was no need for a program in their school, being unsure which programs were needed, and being unsure of which programs were best.

From *Health Education & Behavior, 24,* 218-229. Copyright © 1997 by Society for Public Health Education and Sage Publications, Inc. Reprinted with permission of Sage Publications, Inc.

The mass media have given the impression that adults need to be personally concerned about violence against them by youths. The following figures are often cited: between 1983 and 1992, the aggravated assault rate of juveniles in-
5 creased by 73%, forcible rape by 38%, robbery by 33%, and murder by 23%.[1] The perpetrators of these crimes were predominantly adolescents.[1,2] Yet it should be noted that only 5% of all juvenile arrests were for the aforementioned violent offenses. Contrary to popular perceptions, teenagers are
10 three times as likely as adults over 20 years of age to be victims of violent crime.[1]

The number of children and youths who have been victimized by the epidemic of violence has reached an unprecedented level. In 1992, 1.55 million violent crimes were
15 committed against youths 12 to 17 years old.[2] Youths 12 to 17 years of age accounted for one-tenth the U.S. population but were the victims of almost one-quarter of the 6.62 million rapes, robberies, and assaults committed in 1992. One of every 13 youths was a victim of a violent crime, com-
20 pared to 1 of every 72 adults 35 years of age or older in 1992.[2]

A series of studies has examined violence and weapons issues associated with American youths. A study of inner-city youths (ages 14–23) by Schubiner et al. found that
25 78% expressed fear of being the victim of a violent act, 42% had seen someone shot or knifed, and 22% had actually seen someone killed.[3] This study found that 29% of the youths had carried a knife and 18% reported carrying a gun in the preceding 3 months. Price et al. conducted a survey of Mid-
30 west inner-city high school students' perceptions of guns and found that almost half of the students knew someone who took a gun to school and three-fourths had personally known someone who had been shot.[4] Almost 50% of the students believed there should be gun detectors in every
35 school doorway. Webster et al. examined perceptions regarding weapon carrying among inner-city junior high school students in Washington, D.C.[5] Forty-seven percent of the males had carried knives, and 25% had carried guns. Gun carrying appeared to be part of highly aggressive delin-
40 quency rather than simply a defensive reaction to a dangerous environment.

The National School Boards Association's study, *Violence in the Schools: How America's School Boards Are Safeguarding Our Children,* found that 78% of school dis-
45 tricts reported student assaults on other students, and 61% reported students bringing weapons to school.[6] This same study found that 60% of urban school systems reported student assaults on teachers.

The MetLife study, *Violence in America's Public*
50 *Schools,* assessed the perceptions of students and teachers regarding public school violence.[7] Students most often perceived the reasons for acts of violence as gang or group membership (35% agreed) and lack of parental supervision at home (35% agreed). One in four students reported having
55 been a victim of violence in or around school. Students reported that schools most often addressed the violence problem through disciplinary measures and, much less often, through educational interventions. Teachers in this survey were more likely to report being victims of violence if they
60 taught in the inner city (20%) rather than in small towns (9%) or rural (9%) settings. Almost one in five teachers reported that the level of violence had increased in the past year in their school.

The majority of published studies on violence and weap-
65 ons in the schools have examined the perceptions of students. Few studies have examined the perceptions of school administrators, prime movers in curriculum change, regard-

ing violence in America's schools. Thus, the purpose of this study was to examine the perceptions of secondary school principals regarding violence and weapons in public and private secondary schools. More specifically, the following questions were examined: (1) What is the prevalence of weapon carrying and weapon-related injuries in secondary schools? (2) How prevalent are problems known to be risk factors of violence in schools? (3) What are perceived to be the etiological factors of violence? (4) What provokes violent acts in students? (5) What are the types and prevalence of violence prevention programs in schools? (6) What prompted those schools with violence prevention programs to implement them? and (7) What are the perceived barriers principals face in implementing violence prevention programs?

Method

Subjects

From the membership list of the National Association of Secondary Principals (NASP), the national organization created a computerized random sample of 1,000 principals. A stratification sampling strategy based on a nationally representative sample of secondary schools by location of school was not possible because the proportion of secondary schools in urban, suburban, and rural communities could not be determined (personal communication, National Center for Educational Statistics, 1994). NASP provided mailing labels to the researchers. The nationally representative sample included members from all of the states including Alaska and Hawaii and represented both public and private schools.

Instrument

A survey instrument was developed for this investigation based on a comprehensive review of the literature; it was then sent to a panel of published authorities ($n = 5$) for content validity. Minor wording changes were incorporated in several items based on the experts' recommendations. The resulting instrument comprised 21 items, including 2 items on the prevalence of weapon carrying and injuries in school, 4 items on the prevalence and types of interventions that have been or are planned to be implemented, 1 item on barriers principals face, if any, in implementing violence prevention programs, 2 items on the perception of the role various factors play in contributing to violence among students, and 6 items on the prevalence of risk factors for violence (i.e., socioeconomic [SES] status of students, in-school drug and alcohol use, gang activity, dropping out, etc.). Demographic characteristics of the responding principal were described with the remaining 6 items. The response format was primarily closed, using either a 7-point Likert-type scale or "check all that apply."

Procedure

During the spring of 1994, the principals were surveyed with a three-wave approach to maximize the response rate. First, a cover letter, a copy of the survey, and a preaddressed, stamped envelope were sent to each participant. Two weeks following the initial mailing, a cover letter, a second copy of the survey, and a postage-paid, self-addressed envelope were mailed to the entire sample. Four weeks after the initial mailing, a postcard reminder was mailed to all subjects urging those who had not replied to do so. Surveys were not coded in any way to ensure confidentiality and anonymity.

Results

Subjects

Of the 1,000 principals, 567 returned a completed questionnaire, and 17 returned an unusable questionnaire (i.e., wrong address, incomplete, or ineligible), resulting in a response rate of 58%. The sample was 91% White, 7% African American, and 2% other, and was primarily non-Hispanic (77%; 21% left the ethnicity item unanswered). Respondents' mean age was 47.4 years ($SD = 6.7$). Respondents' highest level of education varied, with 1% reporting bachelor's, 67% reporting master's, 20% reporting educational specialist, and 12% reporting doctoral degrees. The respondents reported having been a principal for a mean of 9.5 years ($SD = 7.0$) and having taught prior to becoming a principal a mean of 12.3 years ($SD = 6.2$).

The majority of schools were found in small towns or rural areas (64%), whereas 22% were in suburban and 14% were in inner-city or urban areas. Two-thirds of the principals (66%) rated the level of violence in the neighborhood immediately surrounding their schools as low (1 or 2 on a 7-point Likert-type scale), whereas only 5% rated the level of violence as high (rated as a 6 or 7 on the 7-point scale). The mean number of students attending the principals' schools was 763 ($SD = 593$). Principals reported that their student population was predominantly White ($M = 79\%$, $SD = 27.4\%$), 12% African American ($SD = 21.7\%$), and 9% other ($SD = 18.4\%$). They also reported that 36% ($SD = 22.1\%$) of their students lived in a family that would be classified as poor.

Weapon Carrying and Weapon-Related Injuries

Principals were queried as to the number of students found carrying a weapon on school property and the number who were injured as a result of weapons during their previous school year (1992–1993). The mean number of students carrying a knife was 1.9 ($SD = 3.8$, range = 0–70). Firearms and other weapons were carried by an average of less than one student (range from 0–10 and 0–21, respectively). The mean number of injuries was less than one for firearms, knives, and other types of weapons. The range of injuries was 0–5 for firearms, 0–8 for knives, and 0–12 for other weapons.

Multiple regression was used to identify factors that would predict the number of students who were found carrying weapons (either firearms, knives, or some other weapon). A hierarchical model was used such that the number of low-SES students was entered first. To test the effect of other factors beyond SES, the size of the school, the level of violence in the neighborhood immediately surrounding the school, the percentage of African American students, and the school's location were then added to the model using a forward selection procedure. Weapon carrying was higher in

Table 1
Principals' Perceived Problems in Their Schools in the Previous Year

	Major problem		Moderate problem		No problem[a]	
	n	%	*n*	%	*n*	%
School absences	153	27	287	51	115	20
Verbal insults	138	24	281	50	137	24
Students with educational difficulties	136	24	343	60	60	11
Threats to students	64	11	288	51	203	36
Stealing	58	10	311	55	188	33
School dropout	57	10	225	40	271	48
Suspension rate	44	8	295	52	215	38
In-school fighting	28	5	248	44	279	49
Vandalism	22	4	233	41	299	54
Gang activity	19	3	110	19	424	75
In-school drug use	11	2	160	28	382	67
In-school alcohol use	11	2	128	23	412	73
Student arrests	8	2	107	19	435	77
Threats to teachers	7	1	107	19	440	77
Student weapon carrying	3	1	66	12	481	85

Note: *N* = 567.
a. Measured on a 7-point scale: 1 or 2 = no problem; 3, 4, or 5 = moderate problem; 6 or 7 = major problem.

schools with a higher percentage of low-SES students in the school (r^2 = .02), larger schools (r^2 = .18), and schools with higher levels of violence around the school (r^2 = .02), F = 49.3, df = 3, 523, p < .001, R^2 = .22. Because 90% of the schools reported no injuries resulting from either a firearm, knife, or other weapon, regression analysis was not used to identify the characteristics of those schools most at risk for student injuries.

Prevalence of Violence Risk Factors

Table 1 presents the prevalence of violence risk factors in the respondents' schools. The principals responded to each item on a 7-point Likert-type scale ranging from 1 (*not a problem*) to 7 (*major problem*). School absences (27%), verbal insults (24%), and students with educational difficulties (24%) were most commonly perceived as major problems. Several acts of violent behavior were rated as moderate risks such as threats to students (51%), in-school fighting (44%), vandalism (41%), gang activity (19%), threats to teachers (19%), and student weapon carrying (12%).

A risk factor subscale was created by summing the responses to each of the 15 risk factor items (possible scores ranged from 15 to 105). The range of scores was from 16 to 78, with a mean risk factor subscale score of 42.4 (*SD* = 14.3). A hierarchical multiple regression procedure was used to identify characteristics of schools most at risk for violence based on the principals' responses to the risk factor items. The percentage of low-SES students was entered first. Then, to test the effects of other factors beyond SES, the percentage of African American students, the level of violence in the school's neighborhood, and the school's location (effect coding was used) were added to the model using a forward selection procedure. The percentage of low-SES students (r^2 = .09) and the level of violence in the school's neighborhood (r^2 = .18) were significant positive predictors of the risk level of the school, F = 39.0, df = 5, 487, p < .001, R^2 = .27.

Perceived Etiology of Violence

Principals were provided with a list of factors to which they responded on a 7-point Likert-type scale their perception of whether the factor plays a minor role or major role in contributing to violence in schools (Table 2).

More than half of the principals believed that the primary etiological factors for violence included lack of parental supervision at home (63%), lack of family involvement with school (59%), and exposure to violence in the mass media (54%). Fewer believed that poverty (14%), lack of consistently enforced rules and penalties for violence in school (10%), racial conflicts between students (9%), and the absence of violence prevention units in the school curriculum (3%) played a major role in the etiology of violence.

Perceived Factors Provoking Violent Acts

Principals were asked about the role various factors played in provoking acts of violence among students who attend their school (Table 2). Being provoked by others (41%) and jealousy of a boyfriend/girlfriend (37%) were seen as the factors most likely to play a major role in provoking acts of violence, whereas wanting another person's private things (7%), desire to hurt someone else (3%), and prevalence of students carrying weapons in school (1%) were least likely to be seen as playing a major role.

Types and Prevalence of Intervention Programs

Three questions addressed violence prevention programs. First, respondents were specifically asked whether their school had implemented any violence prevention programs. Just over one-third (38%) reported they had already implemented a violence prevention program, 21% reported they were planning on implementing such a program, and 38% reported they did not plan on implementing a violence prevention program. The two remaining items dealt specifically with interventions to "limit weapon activity" (noneducational) and educational interventions to address violence. For those who had implemented noneducational interventions to

Table 2
Principals' Perceptions of the Etiology of Violence in Schools and Why Their Students Commit Acts of Violence

	Major role[a]		Moderate role		Minor role[a]	
	n	%	*n*	%	*n*	%
Etiology of violence in schools						
Lack of parental supervision at home	357	63	164	29	30	5
Lack of family involvement with the school	333	59	182	32	35	6
Exposure to violence in the mass media	305	54	203	36	41	7
Lack of future life goals	168	30	272	48	101	18
Boredom or a lack of motivation to learn	163	29	300	53	84	15
Gang or peer pressure	150	27	217	38	175	31
Involvement with drugs/alcohol	132	23	241	43	172	30
Students' lack of academic success	120	21	307	54	121	21
Violent behavior is prevalent in the community, and students have learned these patterns of behavior	118	21	193	34	230	40
Poverty	81	14	232	41	230	41
Lack of consistently enforcing rules and penalties for violence in school	57	10	149	26	333	59
Racial conflicts between students	51	9	208	37	281	50
Absence of violence prevention units in the school curriculum	19	3	218	38	300	53
Why students in *their* school commit acts of violence						
They are provoked by others	233	41	239	42	61	11
Jealousy of boyfriend/girlfriend	207	37	245	43	85	15
It makes them feel important or powerful	138	24	294	52	100	18
It impresses their friends	125	22	296	52	111	30
Prejudice or hate another group of students	71	13	200	35	261	46
Involvement with drugs/alcohol	69	12	227	40	236	42
Perception that a "tough fighter" reputation will protect them	63	11	235	41	232	41
Requirement to belong to a gang/peer group	63	11	152	27	314	55
They want another person's private things (i.e., jacket/sneakers)	39	7	141	25	348	61
Desire to hurt someone else	19	3	160	28	347	61
Prevalence of students carrying weapons in school	6	1	62	11	458	81

Note: $N = 567$ (between 30 and 41 principals did not respond to each item).
a. Measured on a 7-point scale: 1 or 2 = minor role; 3, 4, or 5 = moderate role; 6 or 7 = major role.

limit weapon activity (61%), random or scheduled locker searches, crisis management services, increased lighting, search dogs, and police/guards around school were seen as the most effective interventions (see Table 3). Nearly three in four schools (72%) reported implementing some type of educational violence prevention program. The most frequently reported educational interventions were conflict resolution (mediation), crisis intervention, and peer education (see Table 4). It appears that while a number of programs had been implemented by schools, both educational and noneducational, the interventions may not necessarily have been viewed specifically as violence prevention programs, and this may account for the discrepancy between the responses to the more general question about the status of violence prevention programs and the responses to specific interventions.

A multiple logistic regression procedure was used to identify schools most likely to report having implemented what they considered specifically a violence prevention program. Variables entered into the model were the percentage of low-SES students, the percentage of African American students, level of violence in the school's neighborhood, and the school's location. Results indicate that urban/inner-city schools were 5.9 times (95% confidence interval [CI] = .90, 38.9) more likely than small town/rural schools, and schools with high amounts of neighborhood crime (rated as a 6 or 7 on the 7-point Likert-type scale) were 9.4 times (95% CI = .89, 98.7) more likely than schools with low amounts of neighborhood crime (rated as a 1 or 2 on the 7-point Likert-type scale), to report having implemented a violence prevention program. Percentage of low-SES students and percentage of African American students did not significantly predict whether a violence prevention program had been implemented.

To identify if weapon carrying had any relationship to violence prevention programs, a one-way analysis of variance was used. Schools that had implemented what the principal considered to be a violence prevention program reported significantly more incidences of weapon carrying on school property ($M = 4.3$, $SD = 6.9$) than schools that planned to implement such a program ($M = 2.9$, $SD = 2.9$) and schools that had no intentions of implementing a violence prevention program ($M = 1.5$, $SD = 2.7$), $F = 16.5$, $df = 2, 549$, $p < .01$.

Table 3
Noneducational Interventions Implemented to Limit Weapon Activity and Perceived Effectiveness of Interventions

Intervention	n	%	Very Effective[a]	
			n	%
Dress code	184	32	56	10
Random or scheduled locker searches	159	28	60	11
Crisis management services	117	21	47	14
Increased lighting in the school and/or school grounds	116	20	48	14
Search dogs	96	17	46	13
Police/guards in or around school	88	16	58	17
Limited number of entrances into school building	84	15	33	10
Identification cards (student or staff)	78	14	25	7
Body searches for weapons	63	11	34	10
Metal detectors	59	10	19	5
Hidden/nonintrusive surveillance cameras	37	7	14	4
School-ground barriers	39	7	15	4
Other	38	7	22	6

Note: $N = 567$.
a. Measured on a 7-point scale where 6 or 7 = *very effective* (the percentage is based on the 346 schools that had implemented a program to limit weapon activity [61%]).

Finally, a one-way ANOVA identified significant differences in the level of risk for violence in schools by whether a specific violence prevention program had been implemented. Significantly higher risk factor estimates were found in schools that had implemented a violence prevention program ($M = 45.6$, $SD = 14.0$) than in schools that had not implemented such a program ($M = 37.3$, $SD = 13.0$). Also, the level of risk was higher in schools that reportedly planned to implement a violence prevention program ($M = 46.2$, $SD = 14.5$) than in those that had no such intentions, $F = 23.1$, $df = 2, 507$, $p < .001$.

Table 4
Educational Programs That Have Been Implemented to Address Violence in the Schools

Program	n	%[a]
Conflict resolution (mediation)	258	63
Crisis intervention	239	59
Peer education programs	211	52
Guest speakers discussing violence	196	48
Alternatives to fighting	154	38
Problem solving	148	36
Information about students' risks of being involved in a violent act	144	35
Anger management	115	28
Precursors to fights or acts of violence	87	21
Impulse control	40	10
Other	27	7

Note: $N = 406$ (72%) of 567 schools.
a. Percentage based on 406 schools.

Prompts and Barriers to Program Implementation

Principals who reported that they had already implemented or were planning to implement a violence prevention program were queried as to what prompted them to plan or to implement a program (Table 5). The majority (71%) reported that they had personally seen the need, followed by teacher (42%) and administration (40%) requests. Only 16% reported having received pressure from the community to do so.

Principals who reported their school did not plan to implement a violence prevention program identified from a list of options what barriers, if any, they have faced in implementing violence prevention programs. More than half (57%) of the principals who had no plans to implement a violence prevention program reported that there were no barriers, and 42% reported there was no need for a violence prevention program in their school. Other barriers included being unsure what programs were needed (24%) or being unsure which programs are best (18%). Five percent or less reported the high cost, unavailable trained personnel, lack of parental/community support, lack of administrative support, and/or "other" as barriers to implementing programs.

Table 5
What Prompted Schools to Implement or Plan to Implement Violence Prevention Programs

Item	n	%[a]
I have personally seen the need	238	71
Teacher requests	142	42
Administration requests	135	40
Parent requests	111	33
School staff/personnel requests	85	25
School board mandate/request	79	24
Student requests	76	23
Pressure from the community	53	16
Other	66	20

Note: Of the schools, 218 have implemented a program and 117 plan to implement a program (total $N = 335$).
a. Percentage based on 335 schools.

Discussion

The purpose of this investigation was to examine the perceptions of secondary school principals regarding weapons and violence in public and private schools in the United States. Consistent with other investigations of student weapon carrying,[8,9,10] larger schools, schools located in violent neighborhoods, and schools with more socioeconom-

ically disadvantaged students were significantly more likely to have a greater number of students carrying weapons to
325 school. The majority of principals reported no or only one weapon-related injury during the year preceding the survey. Given the low number of inner-city or urban schools represented in this study (14%), it is not surprising that the results do not match investigations that queried students (rather than
330 principals) about weapon carrying and injuries and focused specifically on inner-city schools. This may represent a lack of awareness by principals regarding these issues.

Risk factors for violent behavior and weapon carrying have been established as violence in the mass media, urban
335 living, African American race, gang membership, deviant behavior, exposure to violence, and history of aggression.[4,5,8-12] In many cases, principals' estimates of the most salient risk factors predicting violence were not in concert with the literature. For example, lack of future life goals,
340 gang or peer pressure, involvement with drugs or alcohol, students' lack of academic success, prevalence of violent behavior in the community, and poverty were seen as playing a major role in the etiology of violence by less than one-third of the principals.

345 Overall, principals who responded to the survey reported low rates of problems identified as risk factors to future violent behavior (i.e., students with educational difficulties, vandalism, in-school drug or alcohol use, stealing, threats to teachers or students, weapon carrying, etc.). This may ex-
350 plain why etiological factors of violence were underestimated and why two in five schools reported no plans to implement a violence prevention program.

Schools with a higher prevalence of risk factors were significantly more likely to have implemented or planned to
355 implement a violence prevention program. Thus, it appears as though most of the programs may have been implemented as a curative response to an unfavorable situation rather than as primary prevention. School administrators and educators need to receive further information regarding the cost-effec-
360 tiveness of primary prevention (to keep a violent environment from developing) compared to secondary prevention (to correct an existing violent school environment) or tertiary prevention (after students/teachers have already been seriously injured or killed).

365 Although the majority of principals reported no barriers to implementing a violence prevention program, the most common barriers, reported by those principals who reported some barriers, were perceptions that no violence prevention programs were needed, being unsure which programs are
370 needed, and unsure which programs are best. Clearly, an educational campaign is needed in order to counsel principals and other school administrators as to which programs are appropriate and efficacious in schools. Some have suggested school-based clinics,[13] peer education programs,[14]
375 and conflict resolutions.[15] However, others have suggested that these school-based approaches will be unsuccessful without careful consideration and amelioration of environmental influences of violence such as poverty, lack of perceived opportunity to succeed, and community and family
380 disintegration.[16-19]

Implications for Practice

The number of youths who have been victimized by violence has reached an unprecedented level, with 1 of every 13 youths being victimized by violence in 1992.[2] School admin-
385 istrators are in a unique position to influence school curricula and/or programs that may affect violence and weapon-related activities among adolescents. The results of this investigation suggest that schools with a high number of students from low-SES families and schools situated in vio-
390 lent neighborhoods are most at risk for violence given principals' reports of higher weapon-carrying activity and greater numbers and severity of factors shown to be risk factors for violent activity in schools (e.g., school absences, verbal insults, students with educational difficulties, vandal-
395 ism, in-school drug or alcohol use, etc.). It is noteworthy that the schools' proportion of African American students was not associated with risks for violent behavior or weapon-carrying activity when socioeconomic status was controlled for in statistical analyses.

400 Principals who reported higher levels of risk in and around their schools were most likely to have implemented a violence prevention program, whereas principals in schools with lower levels of risk were less likely to have implemented a program or report plans to do so. This implies that
405 principals take a traditional role of curative rather than preventive orientation toward violence and weapon-related activity. It appears that school administrators need further information regarding the cost-effectiveness of primary prevention compared to secondary or tertiary prevention in
410 schools. Further, schools that had implemented a violence prevention program were most likely to have done so because the principal had personally seen the need. Teacher and administration requests played a more minor role. Only 16% of principals reported they had received pressure from
415 the community to implement a violence prevention program. Thus, community groups may not perceive violence in their schools as a serious problem, or they may feel powerless in influencing change in the schools' curricula.

Some limitations of this investigation should be considered when interpreting the results. First, the response rate
420 was 58%. Whether nonrespondents hold the same views and represent similar demographic and background characteristics is unknown. Second, the survey instrument was monothematic and thus may have resulted in a response set bias by some respondents. Third, the results may underestimate
425 the prevalence of weapon-related activity and acts of violence. Inner-city and urban school principals were underrepresented and rural or small-town principals were overrepresented in the sample. Nationally, 25% of schools (elementary and secondary schools combined) are located in
430 urban areas and 51% are in rural or small-town districts (the information on location of just secondary schools could not be identified).[20] In this study, while not directly comparable, 14% of the principals of secondary schools reported their school was located in an inner-city or urban area, whereas
435 64% reported their school was in a rural area or small town. It is possible that the principals in the responding schools may have been unaware of weapon carrying or weapon-

related acts of violence in their schools and thus underreported these events. Further investigations might use a second reporter such as a school counselor or drug or education educator to examine the possibility of underreporting within a school.

440

References

1. Allen-Hagen B, Sickmund M: *Juveniles and Violence: Juvenile Offending and Victimization* (Fact Sheet No.3). Washington, DC, U.S. Department of Justice, Office of Juvenile Justice and Delinquency Prevention, July 1993.
2. Moone J: *Juvenile Victimization: 1987-1992* (Fact Sheet No. 17). Washington, DC, U.S. Department of Justice, Office of Juvenile Justice and Delinquency Prevention, June 1994.
3. Schubiner H, Scott R, Tzelpis A, Podany E, Konduri K: Exposure to violence among inner-city youth. *J Adolesc Health Care* 11:376, 1990.
4. Price JH, Desmond SM, Smith D: Inner city adolescents' perceptions of guns—A preliminary investigation. *J Sch Health* 61:255-259, 1991.
5. Webster DW, Gainer PS, Champion HR: Weapon carrying among inner-city junior high school students: Defensive behavior vs. aggressive delinquency. *Am J Public Health* 83:1604-1608, 1993.
6. National School Boards Association: *Violence in the Schools—How America's School Boards Are Safeguarding Our Children.* Alexandria, VA, National School Boards Association, 1993.
7. Louis Harris and Associates: *The American Teacher 1993—Violence in America's Public Schools.* New York, Louis Harris and Associates, Inc., 1993.
8. Fingerhut LA, Ingram DD, Feldman JJ: Firearm and nonfirearm homicide among persons 15 through 19 years of age. *JAMA* 267:3048-3053, 1992.
9. Callahan CM, Rivara FP: Urban high school youth and handguns. *JAMA* 267:3038-3042,1992.
10. Sheley JF, McGee ZT, Wright JD: Gun-related violence in and around inner-city schools. *Am J Dis Child* 146:677-682, 1992.
11. Davies J: The impact of the mass media upon the health of early adolescents. *J Health Educ* (suppl.):S28-S30, 1993.
12. Black MM, Ricardo IB: Drug use, drug trafficking, and weapon carrying among low-income, African-American, early adolescent boys. *Pediatrics* 93:1065-1072, 1994.
13. Ross JW: School-based clinics: An opportunity for social workers to address youth violence. *Health Social Work* 19:82-83, 1994.
14. Giuliano JD: A peer education program to promote the use of conflict resolution skills among at-risk school age males. *Public Health Rep* 109:158-161, 1994.
15. Christoffel KK: Toward reducing pediatric injuries from firearms: Charting a legislative and regulatory course. *Pediatrics* 88:294-305, 1991.
16. Ruttenberg H: The limited promise of public health methodologies to prevent youth violence. *Yale Law J* 103:1885-1912, 1994.
17. Webster DW: The uncovering case for school-based conflict resolution programs for adolescents. *Health Affairs* 12:126-141, 1993.
18. Novello AC, Shosky J, Froehlke R: From the surgeon general, US Public Health Service. *JAMA* 267:3007, 1992.
19. Committee on Adolescence: Firearms and adolescents. *Pediatrics* 89:784-787, 1992.
20. National Center for Educational Statistics: *Assigning Type of Local Codes to the 1987-1988 CCD Public School Universe* (ID No. CS89-194). Washington, DC, National Center for Educational Statistics, 1989.

Address correspondence to: James H. Price, PhD, MPH, Department of Health Promotion and Human Performance, University of Toledo, Toledo, OH 43606; phone: (419) 530-2743; fax: (419) 530-4759; e-mail: jprice@utnet.utoledo.edu.

About the authors: James H. Price is a professor in the Department of Health Promotion and Human Performance, University of Toledo, Toledo, OH. Sherry A. Everett is a postdoctoral student at Harvard School of Public Health, Boston.

Acknowledgment: This study was funded by a grant from the Center for Educational Research and Service, College of Education and Allied Professions, University of Toledo.

Exercise for Article 11

Factual Questions

1. What is the explicitly stated purpose of this study?

2. Did the researchers stratify to obtain a sample with the correct proportions of principals of urban, suburban, and rural schools?

3. What did the researchers do to establish the content validity of their survey instrument?

4. Was the second mailing sent to the entire sample *or* only to those who did not respond to the first mailing?

5. On the average, how long had respondents been principals?

6. What was the range for the question on how many students had been found carrying a knife during the previous school year?

7. What percentage of the principals believed that a primary etiological factor for violence was a lack of parental supervision at home?

Questions for Discussion

8. Although the survey was conducted in 1994, it was not published until 1997. Is this "publication lag" a problem? Explain.

9. The researchers state that to ensure confidentiality and anonymity, the surveys were not coded in any way. Is this important? Explain.

10. The researchers report a response rate of 58%. Is this the rate you would have expected if you had conducted this survey? In your opinion, is it an adequate rate of return? Explain.

11. Some researchers offer rewards and incentives in order to increase the response rates to their surveys. Do you think that it would be appropriate to do this in a survey of principals? Explain.

12. The researchers indicate that schools that had implemented a violence prevention program had significantly more weapon carrying on school property than those that did not implement such a program. Is this evidence that prevention programs cause more weapon carrying?

13. In the Discussion section, the researchers note that there was a low number of inner-city and urban schools represented in this study (14%). Is this an important problem? Explain.

14. What is your reaction to the suggestions offered by the researchers in the last two sentences of this article?

15. Do you believe that principals are the best source of information about the prevalence of violence in their schools? If no, what other sources might supplement the information they provide in order to get a better picture of the extent of the problem?

16. To what population(s), if any, would you be willing to generalize the results of this study?

17. With hindsight, what change(s), if any, would you make in the research methodology used in this study?

Quality Ratings

Directions: Indicate your level of agreement with each of the following statements by circling a number from 5 for strongly agree (SA) to 1 for strongly disagree (SD). If you believe an item is not applicable to this research article, leave it blank. Be prepared to explain your ratings.

A. The introduction establishes the importance of the study.

    SA   5   4   3   2   1   SD

B. The literature review establishes the context for the study.

    SA   5   4   3   2   1   SD

C. The research purpose, question, or hypothesis is clearly stated.

    SA   5   4   3   2   1   SD

D. The method of sampling is sound.

    SA   5   4   3   2   1   SD

E. Relevant demographics (for example, age, gender, and ethnicity) are described.

    SA   5   4   3   2   1   SD

F. Measurement procedures are adequate.

    SA   5   4   3   2   1   SD

G. All procedures have been described in sufficient detail to permit a replication of the study.

    SA   5   4   3   2   1   SD

H. The participants have been adequately protected from potential harm.

    SA   5   4   3   2   1   SD

I. The results are clearly described.

    SA   5   4   3   2   1   SD

J. The discussion/conclusion is appropriate.

    SA   5   4   3   2   1   SD

K. Despite any flaws, the report is worthy of publication.

    SA   5   4   3   2   1   SD

Article 12

Symptoms of Anxiety Disorders and Teacher-Reported School Functioning of Normal Children

PETER MURIS
Maastricht University, The Netherlands

COR MEESTERS
Maastricht University, The Netherlands

SUMMARY. Correlations between scores on the Spence Children's Anxiety Scale, a questionnaire for measuring symptoms of anxiety disorders and a report of school functioning by teachers, were computed for 317 primary school children and 13 teachers in The Netherlands. Analysis showed a small but significant negative correlation between scores for total anxiety and school functioning ($r = -.20$, $p < .001$). The finding is consistent with the notion that high symptoms indicating anxiety disorders in children are accompanied by less optimal functioning in school.

From *Psychological Reports*, *91*, 588–590. Copyright © 2002 by Psychological Reports. Reprinted with permission.

Anxiety disorders are among the most common types of psychopathology in children (Bernstein, Borchardt, & Perwien, 1996). It is also well known that subclinical manifestations of these disorders are highly prevalent among youths of
5 all ages (e.g., Bell-Dolan, Last, & Strauss, 1990). Despite this high prevalence rate, only a small proportion of children with anxiety disorders seeks treatment (Spence, 2001). This is probably because anxiety is a so-called internalizing problem, which causes relatively little burden to others in the
10 children's environment. Although it is generally assumed that anxiety disorders can potentially interfere significantly with children's functioning in a wide range of domains, relatively few studies have actually addressed this issue (but see Strauss, Frame, & Forehand, 1987). The present investiga-
15 tion examined the relation between magnitude of children's symptoms indicating anxiety disorders and school functioning as perceived by their teachers.

Primary school children (154 boys and 163 girls, aged 10 to 12 years) completed a shortened version of the Children's
20 Anxiety Scale (Spence, 1998), a 20-item 4-point rating scale with anchors of 0 = never and 3 = always for measuring symptoms of social phobia, panic disorder, separation anxiety disorder, and generalized anxiety disorder. Examples of items are "I feel afraid that I will make a fool of myself in
25 front of people," "All of a sudden I feel really scared for no reason at all," "I feel scared if I have to sleep on my own," and "I worry that something bad will happen." Subscale scores and a total anxiety score can be computed by summing across relevant items. In addition, children's teachers

30 ($n = 13$) completed the Pyramid Test (Smits, 1983), a sociometric ranking procedure on which the teacher ranks all children in class on four 9-point "normal distribution"-based scales representing the following aspects of school functioning: learning attitude, relation with teacher, relation with
35 peers, and self-esteem.

All assessment scales were reliable, with Cronbach's alphas between .74 (separation anxiety disorder) and .88 (total score) for the Spence Children's Anxiety Scale, and .77 for the total score of school functioning. Various correlations
40 between scores on the Spence scale and school functioning (see Table 1) were significant. For example, the correlation between the Total Anxiety and General School Functioning scores was $-.20$ ($p < .001$). Furthermore, anxiety scores appeared particularly associated with two specific domains of
45 school functioning, *viz.*, Relation with Peers and Self-Esteem. Finally, the most substantial connection emerged between Social Phobia symptoms and children's Relation with Peers ($r = -.29$, $p < .001$). In all cases, correlations were negative, indicating that higher symptoms of anxiety
50 disorder were accompanied by lower school functioning.

Although this study was cross-sectional in nature so one cannot draw causal conclusions, the data indicate that teachers perceive some impairment in the school functioning of children with more intense symptoms related to anxiety dis-
55 orders. At the same time, it should be acknowledged that correlations between such anxiety symptoms and school functioning were rather low. None accounted for more than 9% of the common variance. This seems to indicate that children's problems with anxiety in most cases remain
60 largely hidden. If one is willing to implement early intervention programs for childhood anxiety disorders in the schools (see Dadds, Spence, Holland, Barrett, & Laurens, 1997), screening by means of self-report anxiety measures seems potentially useful.

References

Bell-Dolan, D. J., Last, C. G., & Strauss, C. C. (1990). Symptoms of anxiety disorders in normal children. *Journal of the American Academy of Child and Adolescent Psychiatry*, *29*, 759–765.

Bernstein, G. A., Borchardt, C. M., & Perwien, A. R. (1996). Anxiety disorders in children and adolescents: A review of the past 10 years. *Journal of the American Academy of Child and Adolescent Psychiatry*, *35*, 1110–1119.

Table 1
Correlations (Corrected for Sex) Between Scores on Spence Children's Anxiety Scale and School Functioning As Ranked by Teachers

Spence Children's Anxiety Scale	M	SD	Teacher-Reported School Functioning				
			General Functioning	Learning Attitude	Relation with Teacher	Relation with Peers	Self-Esteem
Total anxiety	10.4	7.5	−.20**	−.10	−.06	−.27**	−.18*
Social phobia	3.3	2.7	−.26**	−.16*	−.10	−.29**	−.24**
Panic disorder	2.2	2.3	−.09	−.02	−.03	−.15*	−.07
Separation anxiety disorder	1.5	2.0	−.14*	−.07	−.02	−.19**	−.14*
Generalized anxiety disorder	3.3	2.7	−.11*	−.05	−.02	−.17*	−.08

* $p < .05$, ** $p < .05/25$ (i.e., Bonferroni correction).

Dadds, M. R., Spence, S. H., Holland, D. E., Barrett, P. M., & Laurens, K. R. (1997). Prevention and early intervention for anxiety disorders: A controlled trial. *Journal of Consulting and Clinical Psychology, 65,* 627–635.

Smits, J. A. E. (1983). *Piramide Techniek (PT), een methode voor het beoordelen van leerlingen door leidsters en leerkrachten.* Nijmegen: Berkhout.

Spence, S. H. (1998). A measure of anxiety symptoms among children. *Behaviour Research and Therapy, 36,* 545–566.

Spence, S. H. (2001). Prevention strategies. In M. W. Vasey & M. R. Dadds (Eds.), *The developmental psychopathology of anxiety.* New York: Oxford University Press., pp. 325–351.

Strauss, C. C., Frame, C. L., & Forehand, R. (1987). Psychosocial impairment associated with anxiety in children. *Journal of Clinical Child Psychology, 16,* 235–239.

Address correspondence to: Dr. Peter Muris, Department of Medical, Clinical, and Experimental Psychology, Maastricht University, P.O. Box 616, 6200 MD Maastricht, The Netherlands. E-mail: p.muris@dep.unimaas.nl

Exercise for Article 12

Factual Questions

1. The researchers speculate that anxiety is a so-called internalizing problem that causes what?

2. What was the age range of the students in this study?

3. Who performs the ranking on the Pyramid Test?

4. Was the relationship between Total Anxiety and General School Functioning direct (i.e., positive) or inverse (i.e., negative)?

5. The strongest relationship was found between which two variables?

6. What was the value of the correlation coefficient for the relationship between Social Phobia and Learning Attitude?

7. How many of the correlation coefficients are statistically significant at the .001 level?

Questions for Discussion

8. In the second paragraph, the researchers present sample items from the Children's Anxiety Scale. To what extent do the sample items help you understand what the scale measures?

9. In the third paragraph, the researchers report that all Cronbach's alphas were between .74 and .88. If you have studied measurement, what does this mean?

10. Are you surprised that all the coefficients in this report are negative? Explain.

11. If you were conducting a study on the same topic, what changes, if any, would you make in the research methodology?

Quality Ratings

Directions: Indicate your level of agreement with each of the following statements by circling a number from 5 for strongly agree (SA) to 1 for strongly disagree (SD). If you believe an item is not applicable to this research article, leave it blank. Be prepared to explain your ratings.

A. The introduction establishes the importance of the study.

SA   5   4   3   2   1   SD

B. The literature review establishes the context for the study.

SA   5   4   3   2   1   SD

C. The research purpose, question, or hypothesis is clearly stated.

SA   5   4   3   2   1   SD

D. The method of sampling is sound.

SA   5   4   3   2   1   SD

E. Relevant demographics (for example, age, gender, and ethnicity) are described.

SA   5   4   3   2   1   SD

F. Measurement procedures are adequate.

SA   5   4   3   2   1   SD

G. All procedures have been described in sufficient detail to permit a replication of the study.

SA   5   4   3   2   1   SD

H. The participants have been adequately protected from
    potential harm.

        SA   5   4   3   2   1   SD

I. The results are clearly described.

        SA   5   4   3   2   1   SD

J. The discussion/conclusion is appropriate.

        SA   5   4   3   2   1   SD

K. Despite any flaws, the report is worthy of publication.

        SA   5   4   3   2   1   SD

Article 13

The Significance of Language and Cultural Education on Secondary Achievement: A Survey of Chinese-American and Korean-American Students

STEVEN K. LEE
California State University, Dominguez Hills

ABSTRACT. This study attempted to answer the question: What is the significance of language and cultural orientation on academic achievement? This study examined the relationship between the students' level of interest in maintaining their heritage language and culture and their achievement in school. The subjects for this study were 105 U.S.-born, Chinese-American and Korean-American students attending public high schools in Southern California. The study found that those who valued the acculturation process (adapting to the mainstream culture while preserving their language and culture) had superior academic achievement levels to those who were most interested in the assimilation process and who adopted the values and lifestyles of the dominant culture. In light of the implementation of the "English Only" policy in California's public schools, this study has important implications in public education—that curriculum and instruction should focus on helping language and cultural minority students to develop and maintain their heritage while exposing them to new ideas.

From *Bilingual Research Journal*, 26, 213–224. Copyright © 2002 by National Association for Bilingual Education. Reprinted with permission.

There is a prevalent stereotype in the American society that Asian-American students are high achievers; hence, the term "model minority" is often used in reference to Asian-Americans. Such use emerged during the 1960s in the midst of the civil rights movement (Osajima, 1988; Sue & Kitano, 1973). It was coined as a hegemonic device, attempting to divert attention away from the racial and ethnic tension of the period and laud the economic success of Asian-Americans outside of the movement. Thus, the term was not really used to recognize the important contribution of Asian-Americans to American society. On the contrary, the model minority stereotype was propagated by the media to subdue growing demands from the African-American and other minority groups for equal rights. The media often cited Asian-Americans as an example of a model group that achieved educational and social prosperity in the absence of government assistance or intervention in schools and in employment, and who were able to seek educational and employment opportunities—thereby delegitimizing the issue of ra-

cial inequality and suppressing public outcry for rectification and improvements in educational and social systems of the United States.

According to many scholars (e.g., Caplan, Choy, & Whitmore, 1991; Hsu, 1971; Kitano, 1969; Mordkowitz & Ginsberg, 1987; Sung, 1987) Asian-Americans are more successful in school because their culture emphasizes the value of education. In addition, the family oriented nature of Asian cultures, in which academic success is equated with upholding the family honor, is seen as facilitating conditions for educational success. Suzuki (1980), one of the first to examine educational achievement from a historical cultural perspective, posited that academic success of Asian-Americans was a reaction to social stratification that existed in the United States: Exclusion of Asian-Americans from social participation forced parents to push for education for their children to overcome the social and political barriers. More recent studies (e.g., Hirschman & Wong, 1986; Mark & Chih, 1982; Sue & Okazaki, 1990) seem to support Suzuki's theory that perception of education as a key to social mobility is a contributing factor in academic achievement of Asian-Americans. Stacey Lee (1996) found that among the different Asian-American student groups, the group that held the highest regard for education as the most essential for social mobility had superior academic achievement than those groups who did not see school as the key to upward mobility in the society. Whereas the former group felt obligated to do their best in school, the latter group placed little interest in education.

In explaining the difference in academic achievement among minority groups, Ogbu (1989) distinguished between voluntary and involuntary minorities. According to this theory, voluntary immigrants do better in school because they accept the host culture. This theory also posits that voluntary immigrants believe that their future is determined by their ability to overcome social and economic hurdles through academic success. Studies by Mark and Chih (1982) and Lee (1996) seem to support this theory: They found that parents of Asian-American students often reminded their children to excel in school to overcome racial prejudice and discrimination. In other words, Asian-Americans perceived education as the most important form of empowerment for social mobility. Considering that a relatively high percentage (5.3%) of Asian-Americans enter colleges and universities, Asian-American parents seem to have a great influence on their children's educational interests. Involuntary immigrants are thought to reject the dominant culture because they perceive the mainstream culture to be a threat to their own identity. Thus, according to this theory, involuntary immigrants may regard school success as giving up their culture at the expense of assimilating to the dominant culture with which school is associated.

Although it is true that Asian-Americans are generally more successful in education than other minority groups—measured in terms of SAT scores and the percentage of Asian-Americans who have completed or are currently enrolled in higher education—there is growing evidence to suggest that not all Asian-American students are doing well in school. Rumbaut and Ima (1988) found that among the Southeast Asian students, the Khmer and the Lao had a grade point average (GPA) below that of the majority (white) students, whereas the GPA of the Vietnamese and Chinese-Vietnamese students was well above the average of the majority students. More recent studies (e.g., Trueba, Cheng, & Ima, 1993) seem to point in the direction that there is a need to clarify conceptual findings by examining intragroup differences within the Asian-American population. That is, academic achievement of Asian-Americans can no longer be predicted based simply on the notion that all Asian-Americans share a common culture. The implicit message is that the socio- and psycho-cultural dynamics of Asian-American students are as complex as any other ethnic group's. As such, studies related to educational achievement of Asian-American students must go beyond the rudimentary task of developing a conceptual framework based on collective descriptions.

In explaining inter-group differences in academic achievement, Ogbu (1989) classifies all Asian-Americans as belonging to one group. That is, according to Ogbu's framework, fifth-generation Asian-Americans are no different from recent immigrants—both belong to the voluntary immigrant group. Although this framework provides an interesting and dichotomous view of the relationship between culture and academic achievement, it fails to consider intragroup and individual differences. That is, why are some groups within the Asian-American population, presumably who came to the United States voluntarily to seek improved livelihood, doing better than others? And why do some Asian-American students excel while others barely make it through high school?

Caudill and De Vox (1956) were among the first to examine educational achievement of Asian-Americans from a cultural perspective. Based on their research on Japanese-Americans, they reported that Japanese-Americans are more successful because their cultural characteristics are those highly regarded by the mainstream society. Kitano (1969) and Caplan, Choy, and Whitmore (1991) concluded that Asian-Americans are more successful in the schools because of compatibility of their culture with middle-class American culture. Although these postulations provide interesting perspectives, they seem to reinforce the "model minority" stereotype by assuming that all Asian-Americans share similar cultural backgrounds. For example, what does Hmong culture have in common with Korean or Japanese culture? Or, do middle-class Americans really hold high regard for Cambodian culture? Studies based on the stereotypical treatment of Asian-Americans as a homogeneous group ignore the importance of adaptive strategies and other psychological and social variables that may influence the learning experiences of Asian-American students.

Gibson (1988) observed that among Punjabi students, there was a positive correlation between their arrival in the United States and school success: The longer the students have been in the United States, the better their performance. Gibson's studies clearly suggest that appropriate behavior cannot be the most important determinant factor of academic achievement. That is, assimilation is more likely for those students who have been exposed longer to the dominant culture than for those who have recently arrived in the United States, so that there may be more cultural similarities between mainstream students and those students who have been in the United States longer than with the newcomers. Considering this, theories based on behavior and cultural compatibility do not adequately explain the educational achievement of Asian-American students. For example, if we were to accept the notion that Asian-American students do better in school than other minority students because there is "cultural match" with the mainstream culture, it predicates not only that Asian-American students share the same culture, but also that there is no heuristic process within the Asian and Asian-American culture.

The purpose of this study was to examine the significance of language and cultural identity on academic achievement of Chinese-American and Korean-American students in secondary schools. This study was motivated by the emergence of studies that indicate that there is variation in academic achievement among Asian-American students. This study attempted to answer the question: Is there a correlation between the students' level of interest in and awareness of cultural heritage and the level of academic achievement? This study investigated the possibility that educational achievement may be related to the students' involvement, interest, and awareness of their ancestral culture.

Method

Subjects

Subjects for this study were 105 male and female students of Chinese ($n = 57$) and Korean ($n = 48$) heritage enrolled in two high schools in an upper-middle-class community of Orange County, California. All the subjects, between the ages of 15 and 17, were enrolled in regular classes. Both schools offered courses in Chinese and Korean as foreign language classes. The two groups represented the largest minority group (approximately 20%) in the community. All subjects were born in the United States.

Instrument

The questionnaire, consisting of 10 closed-ended questions, was pretested on 23 high school students for clarification and appropriateness of the questions contained in the survey. The randomly selected students each received a questionnaire to be completed prior to beginning their class. Questions surveyed the subjects' background, interest, awareness, and views on cultural identity. They included:

1. Have you attended a Chinese or Korean language/culture school for more than one year while you were in middle or high school?
2. Do you know much about the history/culture of China or Korea?
3. Have you studied Chinese or Korean for more than one year at your high school?
4. Do you regularly attend (at least once a month) Chinese- or Korean-related cultural events/activities, including religious functions?
5. Do you speak Chinese or Korean in the home and/or with relatives/friends?
6. Are you interested in learning more about your cultural heritage?
7. Do you feel it is important for you to maintain your cultural identity?
8. Do you feel your culture/heritage contributes to the American culture/heritage?
9. Do you feel there should be diverse cultures represented in the United States?
10. Do you feel people should have a greater interest in their own ethnic culture/heritage than in the mainstream culture?

In addition to the questionnaire, Asian-American students were observed and interviewed during lunchtime for a total of approximately 20 hours.

Procedures

A research assistant distributed and collected the questionnaires. The research assistant also provided instructions prior to administering the questionnaire. The investigator personally observed and interviewed the students. Interviews were recorded on a cassette tape with the subjects' permission.

Results

Responding "yes" to the questions on the survey indicated orientation toward acculturation, an additive process of adapting to the mainstream culture while preserving the heritage culture. Conversely, responding "no" on the survey suggested orientation toward assimilation, toward adopting the values, behaviors, beliefs, and lifestyles of the dominant culture. The subjects' GPAs in relation to the number of affirmative responses were used to establish a correlation.

Although there was a wide range, 0 to 10, the majority of the subjects (about two-thirds) responded affirmatively to six to nine questions. The grade point average (GPA) ranged from 2.98 to 3.81 with a mean of 3.54. With the exception of two subjects who responded affirmatively to three questions, and who had a GPA of 2.98, there was a pattern in the relationship between the number of affirmative responses and the subjects' GPA; the subjects' GPA increased as the number of affirmative responses increased. Using the Pearson product-moment correlation coefficient (r) to find the strength of the relationship at the critical value of .05, 96 degrees of freedom (df), the correlation (r) was .94. Thus, the statistical analysis indicated that there was a strong correlation between the students' GPAs and the extent to which the subjects showed an interest in their cultural heritage. The level of significance for a two-tailed test at this level for a sample size of 105 is .201. Hence, the results revealed that students who had a greater awareness for and interest in developing biculturalism had superior grade point averages than their counterparts who had less interest in their heritage. The correlation was very significant, statistically.

Table 1
GPA in Relation to Number of Affirmative Responses

Subjects ($n = 105$)	No. of "Yes" Responses	GPA ($M = 3.54$)
2	0	3.17
2	3	2.98
6	4	3.19
10	5	3.25
17	6	3.27
23	7	3.58
19	8	3.76
17	9	3.78
9	10	3.81

It is interesting to note that only 38% indicated that they knew much about the history/culture of China or Korea. This is in sharp contrast to the 86% who responded that they were interested in learning more about their cultural heritage. This strongly suggests that Asian-American students were not receiving an adequate amount of exposure to Asian history and culture in and outside the home. Also, while 81% of the subjects indicated that they have attended a Chinese or Korean language/culture school for at least a year, only 25% responded that they have studied Chinese or Korean at a high school. Thus, it seems most Chinese-American and Korean-American students are receiving educational language and cultural lessons at community-based private schools rather than at the public high schools. Considering the fact that both schools offered instructions in Chinese and Korean, the disparity between the two seems to suggest that the public schools may not be offering the kinds of instruction and experience students expect from the language classes.

Also worth noting is the great disparity between the percentage of subjects who indicated the importance of maintaining cultural identity (90%) and the percentage who thought their heritage contributed to American culture (41%). It seems the majority of the subjects perceived cultural heritage to be more important for personal identification than for actual contribution to United States culture. When subjects were asked this question during interviews, many thought that most Americans of different racial, ethnic, and/or cultural backgrounds did not recognize Chinese or Korean culture as part of U.S. culture. Therefore, it appears that for many, cultural contribution is based on their perception of the level of acceptance by other Americans. This was supported by 93% of the respondents, who indicated that cultural diversity should exist in the United States (see Table 2).

Table 2
Percentage of Affirmative Responses

Question	Percentage
1. Attended Chinese or Korean community school	81%
2. Knowledge about Chinese of Korean history/ culture	38%
3. Studied Chinese or Korean at high school	25%
4. Attended Chinese- or Korean-related cultural activity	90%
5. Speak Chinese or Korean at home/with relatives/ friends	78%
6. Interested in learning more about cultural heritage	86%
7. Important to maintain cultural identity	90%
8. Cultural heritage contributes to American Culture	41%
9. Cultural diversity should exist in the United States	93%
10. Greater interest for own culture than mainstream culture	60%

Discussion

As one of the fastest growing minority groups in the United States, Asian-Americans are expected to account for 10% of the total population of the United States by 2040 (González, 1990). In California, Asian-American students already outnumber African-American students. Yet the model minority stereotype seems to have desensitized the need for inclusion of Asian-Americans on discussions of race and education; Asian-Americans are often treated as outsiders needing no special consideration. The results of this study seem to suggest that there are indeed intra-group and individual differences in academic achievement within the Chinese-American and Korean-American student populations. The study found that there was a strong correlation between the students' cultural interest/identity and their academic achievement.

Suzuki (1980) stated that Asian-American students receive favorable evaluations from their teachers due to compatibility between the Asian culture and the teachers' expectations. That is, certain Asian cultural characteristics, such as obedience, conformity, and respect for authority, were viewed favorably by teachers. In fact, Suzuki claimed that teachers may assign good grades to Asian-American students based on behavior rather than on academic performance. Both Goldstein (1985) and Lee (1996) reported that teachers' evaluation of Asian-American students was often based on observable characteristics and not on actual academic achievement. According to E. Lee and M. Lee (1980), acculturation vis-à-vis assimilation plays an important factor

in academic achievement of Asian-American students because it allows them to exhibit those behaviors favored by teachers. Although these studies are helpful in understanding how behavior can influence teachers' assessment of students, they seem to discredit the achievement of Asian-American students by generating yet another overly simplified proposition—that behavior is what sets Asian-American students apart from other students. These findings do not substantiate (a) why some Asian-Americans fail while other Asian-Americans are successful, (b) why Asian-Americans generally score higher than other minority students on standardized tests in which observable behavior has no influence on the outcome, and (c) why grades based on behavior are Asian-American specific.

The results of this study have revealed that there are indeed intra-group differences among U.S.-born Chinese-American and Korean-American students. Those students who had had greater experience and interest in developing bilingualism and biculturalism enjoyed higher academic achievement than those who were less interested in their cultural heritage. Thus, this study not only invalidated the deeply rooted stereotype that Asian-Americans belong to a group that adheres to common cultural values and practices, but also that personal interest in bilingualism and biculturalism is related to academic achievement. The results revealed a positive correlation between the students' language and cultural identity and their academic achievement.

This study was an attempt to examine educational achievement of Chinese-Americans and Korean-Americans from an intra-cultural perspective. That is, rather than attempting to devise an overly simplified concept based on collective treatment of Asian-Americans as a group, this study examined the issue of educational attainment from a psychocultural perspective of Chinese-Americans and Korean-Americans as individuals. This study has found that among Chinese-American and Korean-American students, the cultural interests and experiences of Asian-American students vary, and that these differences may influence their academic performance. Thus, the implication from this study is that the educational community must recognize the significant contribution of education programs that promote heritage language and culture for language- and cultural-minority students.

There is no doubt that inclusion of Asian and Asian-American experiences, as well as the recognition of the importance of their presence in schools, will empower Asian-American students to participate in the learning process. It is hypothesized that those students who had greater interest in their language and cultural identity had superior academic achievement than their counterparts because they had greater motivation for a diversified learning experience and interest. That is, these students had superior cognitive, meta-cognitive, and socioaffective strategies to help them do better in school. Hence, rather than emulating their peers to conform to the norm of the dominant culture (cultural compensatory strategy), these students were interested in empowering themselves by developing awareness and pride in their heritage while undergoing personal experiences in the

mainstream culture (cultural enrichment strategy). Thus, in this dichotomy, students who utilize the cultural enrichment strategy draw upon the positive qualities of at least two cultures from which to adapt to the learning needs of the class-
365 room. On the contrary, students applying the cultural compensatory strategy are at a disadvantaged position because their primary interest is to assimilate to the mainstream culture at the expense of losing their heritage. Thus, cultural compensatory strategy tends to devalue one's ancestral cul-
370 ture while placing a high priority in adopting the mainstream culture.

As diversity within the Asian-American community increases, so is the likelihood that students will come to school with varying interests in their cultural heritage. In 1992, ap-
375 proximately 41% of Asian-Americans were foreign born (Wong, 1992). By the year 2000, this percentage is projected to increase to about 50%. The increasing presence of Asian-American students in our schools will inevitably demand that institutions of learning prepare themselves to be able to
380 provide facilitative instruction in which bilingualism and biculturalism are encouraged and promoted for all students, including Asian-American students. This study has shown that the issue of language and culture in academic achievement is more than a collective interpretation of similarities
385 and differences between two cultures: It is about accepting and supporting the students' language and culture while allowing them the opportunity to experience diversity in thinking and practice. To this end, bilingual education programs in which the students' first language and culture are valued,
390 respected, and encouraged—while students are exposed to a new language and culture—are invaluable to students' eventual success in school.

References

Caplan, N., Choy, M. H., & Whitmore, J. K. (1991). *Children of the boat people: A study of educational success.* Ann Arbor, MI: University of Michigan Press.

Caudill, W., & De Vox, G. (1956). Achievement, culture and personality: The case of the Japanese Americans. *American Anthropologist, 58,* 1102–1127.

Gibson, M. (1988). *Accommodation without assimilation: Sikh immigrants in an American high school.* Ithaca, NY: Cornell University Press.

Goldstein, B. (1985). *Schooling for cultural transitions: Hmong girls and boys in American high schools.* Unpublished doctoral dissertation, University of Wisconsin, Madison.

González, R. (1990). When minority becomes majority: The challenging face of English classrooms. *English Journal, 79*(1), 16–23.

Hirschman, C., & Wong, M. G. (1986). The extraordinary educational attainment of Asian Americans: A search for historical evidence and explanations. *Social Forces, 65*(1), 1–27.

Hsu, F. L. K. (1971). *The challenge of the American dream: The Chinese in the United States.* Belmont, CA: Wadsworth.

Kitano, H. H. L. (1969). *Japanese Americans: The evolution of a subculture.* Englewood Cliffs, NJ: Prentice-Hall.

Lee, E., & Lee, M. (1980). *A study of classroom behaviors of Chinese American children and immigrant Chinese children in contrast to those of Black American children and White American children in an urban head start program.* Unpublished doctoral dissertation, University of San Francisco.

Lee, S. J. (1996). *Unraveling the model minority stereotype.* New York, NY: Teachers College Press.

Mark, D. M. L., & Chih, G. (1982). *A place called America.* Dubuque, IA: Kendall Hunt.

Mordkowitz, E. R., & Ginsberg, H. P. (1987). Early academic socialization of successful Asian-American college students. *Quarterly Newsletter of the Laboratory of Comparative Human Cognition, 9,* 85–91.

Ogbu, J. U. (1989). The individual in collective adaptation: A framework for focusing on academic underperformance and dropping out among involuntary minorities. In L. Weis, E. Farrar, & H. G. Petrie (Eds.), *Dropouts from school: Issues, dilemmas, and solutions* (pp. 181–204). Albany: State University of New York Press.

Osajima, K. (1988). Asian Americans as the model minority: An analysis of the popular press image in the 1960s and 1980s. In G. Y. Okihiro, S. Hune, A. A. Hansen, &

J. M. Liu (Eds.), *Reflections on shattered windows: Promises and prospects for Asian American studies* (pp. 165–174). Pullman: Washington State University Press.

Rumbaut, R. G., & Ima, K. (1988). *The adaptation of Southwest Asian refugee youth: A comparative study.* Washington, DC: U.S. Office of Refugee Settlement.

Sue, S., & Kitano, H. H. L. (1973). Stereotypes as a measure of success. *Journal of Social Issues, 29*(2), 83–98.

Sue, S., & Okazaki, S. (1990). Asian-American educational achievements: A phenomenon in search of an explanation. *American Psychologist, 45*(8), 913–920.

Sung, B. L. (1987). *The adjustment experience of Chinese immigrant children in New York City.* New York: Center for Migration Studies.

Suzuki, R. H. (1980). Education and the socialization of Asian Americans: A revisionist analysis of the "model minority" thesis. In R. Endo, S. Sue, & N. N. Wagner (Eds.), *Asian-Americans: Social and psychological perspectives, Vol. 2* (pp. 155–175). Ben Lomond, CA: Science and Behavior Books.

Trueba, H. T., & Ima, K. (1993). *Myth or reality: Adaptive strategies of Asian Americans in California.* Washington, DC: The Farmer Press.

Wong, G. (1992). *California State University Asian Language BCLAD Consortium proposal.* Long Beach, CA: California State University Asian Language BCLAD Consortium.

Exercise for Article 13

Factual Questions

1. According to the literature review, Ogbu classifies Asian-Americans as belonging to how many groups?

2. How many of the subjects in this study were of Korean ancestry?

3. Responding "yes" to the questions on the survey indicated orientation toward
   A. acculturation.   B. assimilation.

4. In this report, what is the symbol for correlation?

5. What is the value of the correlation coefficient for the relationship between GPA and affirmative responses to the survey?

6. What was the GPA of the nine subjects who responded "yes" to all 10 survey questions?

7. Among all subjects, what percentage responded in the affirmative to studying Chinese or Korean at high school?

Questions for Discussion

8. The researcher states: "In addition to the questionnaire, Asian-American students were observed and interviewed during lunchtime for a total of approximately 20 hours." In your opinion, is this an important part of the study? Explain. (See lines 202–204.)

9. Would you characterize the correlation coefficient reported in this study as being "very strong"? Explain. (See lines 227–239.)

10. The researcher states that the correlation coefficient in this study was very statistically significant. However, he does not indicate the probability level at which it was significant. In your opinion, is this an important omission? Explain. (See lines 230–239.)

11. In your opinion, does the correlation coefficient of .94 lend support to the possibility that acculturation *causes* higher achievement as indicated by students' GPAs? Does it indicate *proof of causation*? Explain.

12. In your opinion, to what extent do you think the results of this study support this implication stated by the researcher: "…the educational community must recognize the significant contribution of education programs that promote heritage language and culture for language- and cultural-minority students"? (See lines 341–345.)

Quality Ratings

Directions: Indicate your level of agreement with each of the following statements by circling a number from 5 for strongly agree (SA) to 1 for strongly disagree (SD). If you believe an item is not applicable to this research article, leave it blank. Be prepared to explain your ratings.

A. The introduction establishes the importance of the study.

    SA   5   4   3   2   1   SD

B. The literature review establishes the context for the study.

    SA   5   4   3   2   1   SD

C. The research purpose, question, or hypothesis is clearly stated.

    SA   5   4   3   2   1   SD

D. The method of sampling is sound.

    SA   5   4   3   2   1   SD

E. Relevant demographics (for example, age, gender, and ethnicity) are described.

    SA   5   4   3   2   1   SD

F. Measurement procedures are adequate.

    SA   5   4   3   2   1   SD

G. All procedures have been described in sufficient detail to permit a replication of the study.

    SA   5   4   3   2   1   SD

H. The participants have been adequately protected from potential harm.

    SA   5   4   3   2   1   SD

I. The results are clearly described.

    SA   5   4   3   2   1   SD

J. The discussion/conclusion is appropriate.

    SA   5   4   3   2   1   SD

K. Despite any flaws, the report is worthy of publication.

    SA   5   4   3   2   1   SD

Article 14

The Effects of Computer-Assisted Instruction on First-Grade Students' Vocabulary Development

CHARLOTTE BOLING
The University of West Florida

SARAH H. MARTIN
Eastern Kentucky University

MICHAEL A. MARTIN
Eastern Kentucky University

ABSTRACT. The purpose of the present study was to determine the effect of computer-assisted instruction on first-grade students' vocabulary development. Students participating in this study were randomly divided into experimental and control groups. The students in both groups were involved in DEAR (Drop Everything And Read) as part of their instruction in a balanced literacy program. During their normal DEAR time, the control group used a book and tape to explore stories. The experimental group explored stories using computerized storyboards. The results of the study show a significant difference for both groups on pre- and posttests. However, the mean difference demonstrates a much larger gain for students in the experimental group.

From *Reading Improvement*, 39, 79–88. Copyright © 2002 by Project Innovation, Inc. Reprinted with permission.

What can teachers do to ensure that the children they teach will develop into successful readers? This is a question that has puzzled the educational community for years. Most educators have their individual opinion as to how the reading
5 process occurs. Morrow and Tracey (1997) state that some educators believe in a behaviorist approach, where reading is taught in a skills-based environment through a prescribed curriculum. Others believe in a more constructivist approach, where a relationship between the context and child
10 must be developed where students build knowledge and gain skills through immersion in a literature-rich environment (Czubaj, 1997; Daniels & Zemelman, 1999). Whatever one believes, these approaches to reading instruction—behaviorist or constructivist—continue to be the subject of
15 debates in our classrooms and communities.

The core beliefs that teachers possess have a great impact on students learning to read. Teachers' personal beliefs concerning the processes involved in learning to read greatly influence their instructional choices. A teacher's beliefs are
20 based on his or her personal knowledge, experiences with instructional techniques, and the way students respond to the instructional strategies in classroom situations (Dillon, 2000; Howard, McGee, Purcell, & Schwartz, 2000; Kinzer and Leu, 1999). Therefore, while teachers maintain their core
25 beliefs about how children best learn to read, they are continuously striving to find the technique(s) that will have the greatest impact on their students.

Since the early 1920s, educators have used a multisensory approach to teaching reading by combining reading,
30 writing, and speaking in a natural context and not through deliberate teaching (Chall, 1992). This has been particularly useful in the teaching of vocabulary. It stands to reason then that the most active vocabulary growth occurs in the early years of life. A child learns to connect an object with the
35 sight, sound, smell, taste, and feel associated with the object. This experience is followed by certain sounds made to represent the object. Thus, communication begins and the concept associated with the object develops into vocabulary. For example, a child understands the physical properties of an
40 apple. He knows how the object looks, tastes, feels, smells, and sounds. A loving parent then builds vocabulary in a natural context by adding the word associated to this object—apple. Then, this label is connected to the experience. "You are eating an apple."
45 As the vocabulary increases, children realize words are used in many contexts. Children must then reach beyond the actual word and activate their schema of the context in which the word is used to understand the meaning. For example, the word "mouse" can have different meanings, such
50 as a small rodent or a computer device. A child needs to experience words being used in different contexts to understand the complexity of our language. The more children experience vocabulary in context, the sooner they will begin to realize that it is the concept of the word in question in the
55 given context that provides meaning.

As a child progresses through the various aspects of literacy development (listening, speaking, reading, and writing), his/her communication skills become more interdependent upon vocabulary development. Vocabulary devel-
60 opment involves understanding the "labeling" that goes with the "concept" that makes the word meaningful. It is acquired through direct experience, multiple exposure, context, association, and comprehension. As students become comfortable with new vocabulary words, they are more likely to use
65 the words when communicating.

Elements of our "Technological Age" often influence the instructional decisions that teachers make in the classroom. One such decision is the role that computers will play in the reading development of the children one teaches. Computer-
70 based teaching and learning have produced positive effects in the classroom. Students seem to be motivated by learning

through this medium (Forcier, 1999). Therefore, it is essential that today's teachers change as our society changes (Hoffman & Pearson, 2000). Children who enter today's primary classrooms have been processing multisensory concepts for most of their young lives. Home computers, interactive games, television, the Internet, and software companies capitalize on this multisensory concept.

Software companies have developed many programs for beginning reading that appeal to the senses and interests of the young child who is learning to read. This multimedia concept stimulates the learner with sight, sound, and action while integrating skills necessary for language development. Instructional technology offers virtual multisensory perception that should provide meaningful instruction.

Teacher-centered instruction is one approach to the use of instructional technology in the classroom (Forcier, 1999). The teacher-centered approach is similar to the direct-instruction approach in that the teacher is directing the children through the learning in order to achieve the goals of the lesson. One category of the teacher-centered approach is computer-assisted instruction. When using computer-assisted instruction, the teacher organizes the learning situation. He/she selects the targeted learning goal, situates the learning environment, and then allows exploratory time as students engage in learning. The teacher then monitors the learning activities and modifies the instructional level as needed to meet the various needs of the children involved.

Classroom teachers have the unique opportunity to infuse a variety of technological components with multisensory learning while situating the learning situation. One area where this is especially true is in the teaching of reading to young children. The research study being reported employed a teacher-centered, computer-assisted instructional technique that situated progressive reading material in an attempt to answer the following question:

Will a computerized multisensory approach to the teaching of reading increase first graders' vocabulary development?

Review of Literature

Many software programs offer "read alongs" and "edutainment" that assist students as they learn letter sounds, vocabulary concepts, comprehension, and to enjoy literature. Interactive multimedia allows the printed word to take on sight, sound, and action, which visually and mentally stimulates the individual.

One such program is DaisyQuest I and II (Mitchell, Chad & Stacy, 1984–2000). An in-depth study investigated the phonological awareness in pre-school children utilizing this software (Brinkman & Torgesen, 1994). Each child in the treatment group interacted with a computerized story concerning "Daisy the friendly dragon." A computer, monitor, mouse, and standard headphone were provided to allow the child, as he/she listened to the story, to discover clues revealing where the dragon was hiding. The clues were revealed by correctly answering at least four correct answers in a row. The skills assessed were rhyming words, beginning sounds, ending sounds, middle sounds, and whether a word contained a given number of sounds. This study revealed that children in the treatment group responded at a higher and faster rate of reading readiness than children in the control group. Not only did the children in the treatment group gain knowledge to aid in their ability to read, these preschoolers had fun!

In another study, two literacy teachers (one a Reading Recovery teacher, the other a Title I reading teacher) wrote simple, predictable texts using the multimedia software HyperStudio (Wagner, 1978). These teachers created "talking books" for their students, with a focus on high-frequency words with graphics and animation to offer sight, sound, and movement. Students enjoyed experiencing the stories as the computer "read" the story to them as the cursor (pointing finger) touched each word. This process came full circle by the end of the school year, as these students were writing and reading their own stories. Students were then encouraged to use invented spelling, graphics, and sounds while they created their own stories using the Kid Pix Software program (Hickman, 1984–2000). "The computer serves as a motivational tool in their journey to literacy" (Eisenwine & Hunt, 2000, p. 456).

There are many reasons why computer-assisted reading instruction has been effective. The computer provides immediate responses and practice for the child learning a skill. Struggling readers interface with the computer and practice a skill without embarrassing situations in the classroom. Interaction with a multisensory format provides motivation and a positive attitude toward reading and learning (Case & Truscott, 1999; Forcier, 1999).

A word of caution accompanies much of the literature, warning educators to focus on the targeted instructional goals and not be "enchanted" by the entertainment that makes software packages so appealing (Case & Truscott, 1999; Sherry, 1996). While this multisensory approach is highly motivating for young readers, the instructional purpose is to enable them to become better readers. Educators should choose the types of software and technological resources carefully in order to maximize learning without being entangled in the "bells and whistles."

The benefits of using instructional technology include "an intrinsic need to learn technology…motivation increases engagement time…students move beyond knowledge and comprehension and into application and analysis…and students develop computer literacy by applying various computer skills as part of the learning process" (Dockstader, 1999, p. 73). As Ray and Wepner (2000) suggest, the question as to whether or not technology is the valuable educational resource we think it is may be a moot point since it is such an integral part of our lives. However, the question concerning the most productive methods of using technology in the classroom still needs to be addressed. Therefore, the purpose of this study was to investigate the effects of computer-assisted instruction on first-grade students' vocabulary development. Specifically, this study investigated the impact of the WiggleWorks program (CAST & Scholastic, 1994–1996) on first-grade students' vocabulary development.

Method

Sample

185   A first-grade classroom at a mid-Atlantic elementary school was selected for this research project. The subjects were 21 first-grade students. There were 10 boys and 11 girls involved in this study. The ethnic background of this class was as follows: 13 Caucasian students, six African
190 American students, one Hispanic student, and one Pakistani student. Students were from a lower socioeconomic status and had limited exposure to educational experiences outside the school. The subjects were assigned to either the control or experimental group by using a table of random numbers
195 and applying those numbers to the students. Ten students were assigned to the control group and 11 to the experimental group.

Computer-Assisted Program

    The WiggleWorks (1994–1996) software program was used in this study. Co-developed by CAST and Scholastic,
200 Inc., this program offers a literacy curriculum based on a combination of speech, sounds, graphics, text, and customizable access features. The software program features 72 trade books, audiocassettes, and a variety of computer-based activities. Students use the trade books and audiocassettes to
205 read independently with or without the support of the audiocassette. Using the software program, students may listen to a story, read along with a story, or read a story silently. As they read, students are encouraged to review the suggested vocabulary words by selecting My Words. Students may
210 listen to a pronunciation of the word by clicking on it or hear the word contextually in the story. Students may add new words to their vocabulary list by clicking on the selected word and the plus sign or remove words by clicking on the subtraction sign. Students may read and reread the story as
215 they wish. Students may also create word families or practice spelling using a magnetic alphabet.

    After listening to or reading a story, students have the option of composing their own stories. WiggleWorks provides a story starter, cloze-structured text, or free writing to
220 help young students write their story. After composing a story, students may illustrate personal stories using basic drawing tools, stamps of the story characters, and/or story event backgrounds. Students may share their stories with others by recording their stories or printing the story and
225 creating a book. These functions are available in a Read Aloud, Read, Write, My Book, and Magnet Board menu available to the individual user.

    WiggleWorks is a managed instructional system. The management functions allow the teacher the opportunity to
230 customize the computer-assisted instruction for each child. For instance, in Read Aloud, the settings can be adjusted so that the story is read to the student using a word-by-word, line-by-line, or whole-page approach. The management system also keeps a running log of individual and class activi-
235 ties. The Portfolio Management feature provides a reading record for each child (tracks the stories read, date and time individual stories were read, etc.), including reading and writing samples. The WiggleWorks software program pro-

240 vides a multimedia approach to literacy while supporting traditional methods with the accompanying trade books and audiocassettes.

Variables

    The research project tested the independent variable of computer-assisted instruction on reading vocabulary devel-
245 opment. Eleven students received the treatment monitored by one of the researchers. The dependent variable was a pre- and post-vocabulary test. The test was an independent word list administered by the researcher to the experimental and control groups at the beginning and end of each session.

Measurement

    The instrument used to determine the effect of computer-
250 assisted instruction on vocabulary was a pre- and posttest designed by one of the researchers. Six high-frequency vocabulary words from each of the seven stories were selected by the researcher and placed on an independent list. The independent list of words served as the pre- and post-
255 vocabulary test for each. All results were compared to determine the effect the treatment had on these subjects.

Procedure

    As a part of the regular curriculum, all students received reading vocabulary instruction. The teacher utilized the reading instructional curriculum adopted by the county, which
260 consisted of reading textbooks, related materials, and charts provided by the publishing company. Students participated in daily reading instruction. Each student in the class was randomly assigned into two groups: a control group and an experimental group. In an attempt to limit extraneous learn-
265 ing, both groups continued to receive regular reading instruction by the researcher/teacher. The regular reading curriculum had a 20-min time block, where students participated in a DEAR (Drop Everything And Read) program. The researchers used this block of time to implement this
270 research project.

    Seven predetermined stories were used for this research project. The stories were available on book and tape as well as on interactive, computerized storyboards. The control group experienced the story in a variety of ways. First, they
275 listened to the assigned story as the teacher/researcher read the story to them. Next, students listened to the story on tape and read along with an accompanying book. Last, students were provided with an assortment of literature: library books, classroom literature, or the students' personal books
280 to read at their leisure after the predetermined book and tape assignment had been completed. During that 20-min time span, the 10 students in the experimental group visited the media computer lab and explored the same story using the computerized storyboard. A computer, monitor, mouse, and
285 headphone were provided for each subject. During the first session, the teacher/researcher explained the working mechanics of the computer laboratory and answered any questions from the students. Then, the lessons began as students listened to enjoy the story. Next, the students revisited and
290 identified words unknown to them by clicking on the word. The computerized storyboards served as a remediator. These

subjects saw the printed word highlighted and heard it as the word was produced in sound. Students were required to listen to the story once while reading along.

After completing those requirements, students could listen to and/or read any story previously read or any story at a lower level. Students were introduced to a new Wiggle-Works story every other day. During this project, students experimented with seven different stories that became progressively more challenging. The ability levels of the stories ranged from kindergarten to second grade. The project continued for 6 weeks.

Results

The results were analyzed using a paired-samples t test. An alpha level of .05 was set incorporating a two-tailed significance level. The analyses showed significant positive changes for both groups. The mean scores confirm that students using computerized storyboards demonstrate significant gains in their ability to recall a greater amount of new vocabulary words (see Table 1). The pre- and posttest were analyzed using a paired-samples t test. The results demonstrate a statistically significant difference ($p < .002$) in the experimental (computer) group. A significant difference ($p < .01$) was also found (see Table 2) in the control group (Book/Tape).

Table 1
Means and Standard Deviations

Group	Pretest		Posttest	
	M	SD	M	SD
Computer	3.7	4.37	16.9	13.17
Book/Tape	1.8	2.68	5.45	6.07

The mean scores of the pre- and post-vocabulary tests indicate a significant gain in the experimental (computer storyboard) group (MeanPre = 3.7; MeanPost = 16.9). A further analysis involving the reading ability of the individual students demonstrated that students with higher reading ability scored higher in the experimental and control groups than average-ability or low-ability students. Those students who were performing successfully in their reading scored significantly higher than those students who were performing at a lower level.

Table 2
Paired-Samples t Test

Group	df	t	p
Computer	9	4.18	0.002
Book/Tape	10	3.17	0.010

Discussion

The stories selected for this project were progressively more challenging so as to meet the needs of as many young readers as possible. Students with greater reading ability scored higher on the pretests and showed greater improvement on the posttests. These students seemed to possess a greater command of reading and technological skills required in maneuvering the storyboards.

Students with less reading ability did not gain as much from the experience. While they seemed to enjoy the stories, they were greatly challenged by the pre- and posttest. These students would have been more successful with stories developmentally appropriate for their reading ability. Overall, the ability level of the students in the classroom seemed to mirror their performance in the computer-based reading instruction. Strong readers worked somewhat independently, average-ability students were at an instructional level with reading and technology skills, while students with less reading ability needed assistance with reading and technology. Students in the experimental group (computer storyboards) were greatly motivated by the use of computers. They enjoyed the interactive, multisensory aspect of learning. This was evidenced by the students' request to spend more time listening to stories on the computers. Multisensory teaching seemed to make their learning fun.

Implications and Significance

This research project was designed to investigate the effects of computer-assisted instruction on first-grade students' vocabulary development. With the integration of sights, colors, sounds, actions, plus the printed word, vocabulary lessons took on a new meaning. Students recognized the word on sight, remembered the word through association and phonemes, and quite a few could use the word as a part of their spoken and written vocabulary. Students were able to recognize the words in isolation and in text.

Overall, implications of this research project are that a 20-min DEAR time using computerized storyboards directly results in improved vocabulary development among first-grade students. Learning new vocabulary words took place at a faster pace with greater accuracy than with the direct teaching format. "Technology brings to your classroom the capability of connecting dynamic, interactive vocabulary learning with reading, writing, spelling, and content learning" (Fox & Mitchell, 2000, p. 66).

Computerized classroom instruction does not imply inflated test scores or a magic potion for teaching. It is a motivating medium that enhances good teaching. The infusion of technology and literacy is a lifelong learning gift we create for our students.

Recommendations

Computer-assisted instruction has a positive influence on students' motivation, interest, and learning. This research project validates the effect that computer-assisted instruction has on first graders' vocabulary development during a crucial time when they are learning to read. To improve upon this study, a concentrated effort should be made to determine the developmental reading level of each student. Students could then receive more individualized instruction at their appropriate reading level. Additionally, teachers/researchers need to move students from dependent direct instruction to more independent learning. A natural follow-up to this study could be to see if this move to more independent learning is facilitated by differing uses of technology in the classroom.

References

Brinkman, D., & Torgeson, J. (1994). Computer administered instruction in phonological awareness: Evaluation of the DaisyQuest program. *The Journal of Research and Development in Education, 27*(2), 126–137.

Case, C., & Truscott, D. M. (1999). The lure of bells and whistles: Choosing the best software to support reading instruction. *Reading and Writing Quarterly, 15*(4), p. 361.

Chall, J. (1992). The new reading debates: Evidence from science, art, and ideology. *Teachers College Record, 94*(2), 315.

Czubaj, C. (1997). Whole language literature reading instruction. *Education, 117*(4), 538.

Daniels, H., & Zemelman, S. (1999). Whole language works: Sixty years of research. *Educational Research, 57*(2), 32.

Dillon, D. R. (2000). Identifying beliefs and knowledge, uncovering tensions, and solving problems. *Kids' insight: Reconsidering how to meet the literacy needs of all students* (pp. 72–79). Newark, DE: International Reading Association.

Dockstader, J. (1999). Teachers of the 21st century know the what, why, and how of technology integration. *T.H.E. Journal, 26*(6), 73–74.

Eisenwine, M. J., & Hunt, D. A. (2000). Using a computer in literacy groups with emergent readers. *The Reading Teacher, 53*(6), 456.

Forcier, R. C. (1999). Computer applications in education. *The computer as an educational tool* (pp. 60–93). Upper Saddle, NJ: Prentice-Hall, Inc.

Fox, B. J., & Mitchell, M. J. (2000). Using technology to support word recognition, spelling, and vocabulary acquisition. In R. Thurlow, W. J. Valmont, & S. B. Wepner (Eds.). *Linking Literacy and Technology.* Newark, DL: International Reading Association, Inc.

Hickman, C. (1984–2000). Kid Pix. Deluxe Version. [Unpublished computer software]. Available: http://www.pixelpoppin.com/kidpix/index.html

Hoffman, J., & Pearson, P. D. (2000). Reading teacher education in the next millennium: What your grandmother's teacher didn't know that your granddaughter's teacher should. *Reading Research Quarterly, 35*(1), 28–44.

Howard, B. C., McGee, S., Purcell, S., & Schwartz, N. (2000). The experience of constructivism: Transforming teacher epistemology. *Journal of Research on Computing in Education, 32*(4), 455–465.

Kinzer, C. K., & Leu, D. J. (1999). *Effective Literacy Instruction.* Upper Saddle River, NJ: Prentice-Hall, Inc.

Mitchell, C., & S. (1984–2000). DaisyQuest. [Unpublished computer software]. Available: http://www.greatwave.com/html/daisys.html

Morrow, L. M., & Tracey, D. H. (1997). Strategies used for phonics instruction in early childhood classrooms. *The Reading Teacher, 50*(8), 644.

Ray, L. C., & Wepner, S. B. (2000). Using technology for reading development. In R. Thurlow, W. J. Valmont, & S. B. Wepner (Eds.). *Linking Literacy and Technology.* Newark, DL: International Reading Association, Inc.

Sherry, L. (1996). Issues in distance learning. *International Journal of Educational Telecommunications, 1*(4), 337–365.

Wagner, R. (1978). HyperStudio. [Unpublished computer software]. Available: http://www.hyperstudio.com/

WiggleWorks [Computer Software]. (1994–1996). New York: CAST and Scholastic, Inc.

Exercise for Article 14

Factual Questions

1. What is the research question explored by this study?

2. What "caution" is mentioned in the Review of Literature?

3. How many students participated in this study?

4. Who designed the instrument used in this study?

5. What is the value of the posttest mean for the book/tape group?

6. Were the gains by the experimental group statistically significant? If yes, at what probability level?

Questions for Discussion

7. The first five paragraphs provide a general background for the study. The use of computers is introduced in the sixth paragraph. In your opinion, how important are the first five paragraphs in establishing a context for the study?

8. The researchers state that the students were assigned at random to one of the two groups. How important is this? Would it be better to use a different method for assigning students? Explain. (See lines 193–197.)

9. In your opinion, is the Procedure described in sufficient detail? Explain. (See lines 257–302.)

10. Has this study convinced you of the superiority of computer-assisted instruction for improving vocabulary development? Explain.

11. If you were conducting a study on the same topic, what changes in the research methodology, if any, would you make?

Quality Ratings

Directions: Indicate your level of agreement with each of the following statements by circling a number from 5 for strongly agree (SA) to 1 for strongly disagree (SD). If you believe an item is not applicable to this research article, leave it blank. Be prepared to explain your ratings.

A. The introduction establishes the importance of the study.

   SA   5   4   3   2   1   SD

B. The literature review establishes the context for the study.

   SA   5   4   3   2   1   SD

C. The research purpose, question, or hypothesis is clearly stated.

   SA   5   4   3   2   1   SD

D. The method of sampling is sound.

   SA   5   4   3   2   1   SD

E. Relevant demographics (for example, age, gender, and ethnicity) are described.

   SA   5   4   3   2   1   SD

F. Measurement procedures are adequate.

   SA   5   4   3   2   1   SD

G. All procedures have been described in sufficient detail to permit a replication of the study.

   SA   5   4   3   2   1   SD

H. The participants have been adequately protected from potential harm.

SA   5   4   3   2   1   SD

I. The results are clearly described.

SA   5   4   3   2   1   SD

J. The discussion/conclusion is appropriate.

SA   5   4   3   2   1   SD

K. Despite any flaws, the report is worthy of publication.

SA   5   4   3   2   1   SD

Article 15

The Effect of a Computer Simulation Activity versus a Hands-on Activity on Product Creativity in Technology Education

KURT Y. MICHAEL
Central Shenandoah Valley Regional Governor's School, Virginia

Computer use in the classroom has become a popular method of instruction for many technology educators. This may be due to the fact that software programs have advanced beyond the early days of drill and practice instruc-
5 tion. With the introduction of the graphical user interface, increased processing speed, and affordability, computer use in education has finally come of age. Software designers are now able to design multidimensional educational programs that include high-quality graphics, stereo sound, and real
10 time interaction (Bilan, 1992). One area of noticeable improvement is computer simulations.

Computer simulations are software programs that either replicate or mimic real world phenomena. If implemented correctly, computer simulations can help students learn
15 about technological events and processes that may otherwise be unattainable due to cost, feasibility, or safety. Studies have shown that computer simulators can:

1. Be equally as effective as real life, hands-on laboratory experiences in teaching students scientific concepts
20   (Choi & Gennaro, 1987).
2. Enhance the learning achievement levels of students (Betz, 1996).
3. Enhance the problem-solving skills of students (Gokhale, 1996).
25 4. Foster peer interaction (Bilan, 1992).

The educational benefits of computer simulations for learning are promising. Some researchers even suspect that computer simulations may enhance creativity (e.g., Betz, 1996; Gokhale, 1996; Harkow, 1996); however, after an
30 extensive review of literature, no empirical research has been found to support this claim. For this reason, the following study was conducted to compare the effect of a computer simulation activity versus a traditional hands-on activity on students' product creativity.

Background

Product Creativity in Technology Education

35 Historically, technology educators have chosen the crea-
tion of products or projects as a means to teach technological concepts (Knoll, 1997). Olson (1973), in describing the important role projects play in the industrial arts/technology classroom, remarked, "The project represents human crea-
40 tive achievement with materials and ideas and results in an experience of self-fulfillment" (p. 21). Lewis (1999) reiterated this belief by stating, "Technology is in essence a manifestation of human creativity. Thus, an important way in which students can come to understand it would be by en-
45 gaging in acts of technological creation" (p. 46). The result of technological creation is the creative product.

The creative product embodies the very essence of technology. The American Association for the Advancement of Science (Johnson, 1989) stated, "Technology is best de-
50 scribed as a process, but is most commonly known by its products and their effects on society" (p. 1). A product can be described as a physical object, article, patent, theoretical system, an equation, or new technique (Brogden & Sprecher, 1964). A creative product is one that possesses some degree
55 of unusualness (originality) and usefulness (Moss, 1966). When given the opportunity for self-expression, a student's project becomes nothing less than a creative product.

The creative product can be viewed as a physical representation of a person's "true" creative ability encapsulating
60 both the creative person and process (Besemer & O'Quin, 1993). By examining the literature related to the creative person and process, technology educators may gain a deeper understanding of the creative product itself.

The Creative Person

Inventors such as Edison and Ford have been recognized
65 as being highly creative. Why some people reach a level of creative genius while others do not is still unknown. However, Maslow (1962), after studying several of his subjects, determined that all people are creative, not in the sense of creating great works, but rather, creative in a universal sense
70 that attributes a portion of creative talent to every person. In trying to understand and predict a person's creative ability, two factors have often been considered: intelligence and personality.

Intelligence

A frequently asked question among educators is "What is
75 the relationship between creativity and intelligence?" Re-

search has shown that there is no direct correlation between creativity and intelligence quotient (I.Q.) (Edmunds, 1990; Hayes, 1990; Moss, 1966; Torrance, 1963). Edmunds (1990) conducted a study to determine whether there was a relation-
80 ship between creativity and I.Q. Two hundred and eighty-one randomly selected students, grades eight to eleven, from three different schools in New Brunswick, Canada, participated. The instruments used to collect data were the *Torrance Test of Creative Thinking* and the *Otis-Lennon School*
85 *Ability Test*, used to test intellectual ability. Based on a Pearson product moment analysis, results showed that I.Q. scores did not significantly correlate with creativity scores. The findings were consistent with the literature dealing with creativity and intelligence.
90   On a practical level, findings similar to the one above may explain why I.Q. measures have proven to be unsuccessful in predicting creative performance. Hayes (1990) pointed out that creative performance may be better predicted by isolating and investigating personality traits.

Personality Traits
95   Researchers have shown that there are certain personality traits associated with creative people (e.g., DeVore, Horton, & Lawson, 1989; Hayes, 1990; Runco, Nemiro, & Walberg, 1998; Stein, 1974). Runco, Nemiro, and Walberg (1998) identified and conducted a survey investigating personality
100 traits associated with the creative person. The survey was mailed to 400 individuals who had submitted papers and/or published articles related to creativity. The researchers asked participants to rate, in order of importance, various traits that they believed affected creative achievement. The survey
105 contained 16 creative achievement clusters consisting of 141 items. One hundred and forty-three surveys were returned reflecting a response of 35.8%. Results demonstrated that intrinsic motivation, problem finding, and questioning skills were considered the most important traits in predicting and
110 identifying creative achievement. Though personality traits play an important part in understanding creative ability, an equally important area of creativity theory lies in the identification of the creative process itself.

The Creative Process
      Creativity is a process (Hayes, 1990; Stein, 1974; Taylor,
115 1959; Torrance, 1963) that has been represented using various models. Wallas (1926) offered one of the earliest explanations of the creative process. His model consisted of four stages that are briefly described below:

1. Preparation: This is the first stage in which an individ-
120   ual identifies then investigates a problem from many different angles.
2. Incubation: At this stage the individual stops all conscious work related to the problem.
3. Illumination: This stage is characterized by a sudden or
125   immediate solution to the problem.
4. Verification: This is the last stage at which time the solution is tested.

Wallas' model has served as a foundation upon which other models have been built. Some researchers have added

130 the communication stage to the creative process (e.g., Stein, 1974; Taylor, 1959; Torrance, 1966). The communication stage is the final stage of the creative process. At this stage, the new idea confined to one's mind is transformed into a verbal or nonverbal product. The product is then shared
135 within a social context in order that others may react to and possibly accept or reject it. A more comprehensive description of the creative process is captured within a definition offered by Torrance (1966):

> Creativity is a process of becoming sensitive to prob-
140 > lems, deficiencies, gaps in knowledge, missing elements, disharmonies, and so on; identifying the difficult; searching for solutions, making guesses or formulating hypotheses about the deficiencies, testing and re-testing these hypotheses and possibly modifying and re-testing
145 > them, and finally communicating the results (p. 8).

Torrance's definition resembles what some have referred to as problem solving. For example, technology educators Savage and Sterry (1990), generalizing from the work of several scholars, identified six steps to the problem-solving
150 process:

- Defining the problem: Analyzing, gathering information, and establishing limitations that will isolate and identify the need or opportunity.
- Developing alternative solutions: Using principles,
155 ideation, and brainstorming to develop alternate ways to meet the opportunity or solve the problem.
- Selecting a solution: Selecting the most plausible solution by identifying, modifying, and/or combining ideas from the group of possible solutions.
160 - Implementing and evaluating the solution: Modeling, operating, and assessing the effectiveness of the selected solution.
- Redesigning the solution: Incorporating improvements into the design of the solution that address
165 needs identified during the evaluation phase.
- Interpreting the solution: Synthesizing and communicating the characteristics and operating parameters of the solution (p. 15).

By closely comparing Torrance's (1966) definition of
170 creativity with that of Savage and Sterry's (1990) problem-solving process, one can easily see similarities between the descriptions. Guilford (1976), a leading expert in the study of creativity, made a similar comparison between steps of the creative process offered by Wallas (1926) with those of
175 the problem-solving process proposed by the noted educational philosopher, John Dewey. In doing so, Guilford simply concluded that "Problem solving is creative; there is no other kind" (p. 98).
      Hinton (1968) combined the creative process and prob-
180 lem-solving process into what is now known as creative problem solving. He believed that creativity would be better understood if placed within a problem-solving structure. Creative problem solving is a subset of problem solving based on the assumption that not all problems require a crea-
185 tive solution. He surmised that when a problem is solved

with a learned response, no creativity has been expressed. However, when a simple problem is solved with an insightful response, a small measure of creativity has been expressed; when a complex problem is solved with a novel solution, genuine creativity has occurred.

Genuine creativity is the result of the creative process that manifests itself into a creative product. Understanding the creative process as well as the creative person may play an important role in realizing the true nature of the creative product. Though researchers have not reached a consensus as to what attributes make up the creative product (Besemer & Treffingger, 1981; Joram, Woodruff, Bryson, & Lindsay, 1992; Stein, 1974), identifying and evaluating the creative product has been a concern of some researchers. Notable is the work of Moss (1966) and Duenk (1966).

Evaluating the Creative Product in Industrial Arts/ Technology Education

Moss (1966) and Duenk (1966) have arguably conducted the most extensive research establishing criteria for evaluating creative products within industrial arts/technology education. Moss (1966), in examining the criterion problem, concluded that unusualness (originality) and usefulness were the defining characteristics of the creative product produced by industrial arts students. A description of his model is presented below:

1. Unusualness: To be creative, a product must possess some degree of unusualness [or originality]. The quality of unusualness may, theoretically, be measured in terms of probability of occurrence; the less the probability of its occurrence, the more unusual the product (Moss, 1966, p. 7).

2. Usefulness: While some degree of unusualness is a necessary requirement for creative products, it is not a sufficient condition. To be creative, an industrial arts student's product must also satisfy the minimal principle requirements of the problem situation; to some degree it must "work" or be potentially "workable." Completely ineffective, irrelevant solutions to teacher-imposed or student-initiated problems are not creative (Moss, 1966, p. 7).

3. Combining Unusualness and Usefulness: When a product possesses some degree of both unusualness and usefulness, it is creative. But, because these two criterion qualities are considered variables, the degree of creativity among products will also vary. The extent of each product's departure from the typical and its value as a problem solution will, in combination, determine the degree of creativity of each product. Giving the two qualities equal weight, as the unusualness and/or usefulness of a product increases so does its rated creativity; similarly, as the product approaches the conventional and/or uselessness its rated creativity decreases (Moss, 1966, p. 8).

In establishing the construct validity of his theoretical model, Moss (1966) submitted his work for review to 57 industrial arts educators, two measurement specialists, and six educational psychologists. Results of the review found the proposed model was compatible with existing theory and practice of both creativity and industrial arts. No one disagreed with the major premise of using unusualness and usefulness as defining characteristics for evaluating the creative products of industrial arts students.

To date, little additional research has been conducted to establish criteria for evaluating the creative products of industrial arts and/or technology education students. If technology is best known by its creative products, then technology educators are obligated to identify characteristics that make a product more or less creative. Furthermore, educators must find ways to objectively measure these attributes and then teach students in a manner that enhances the creativity of their products. A possible approach to enhancing product creativity is by incorporating computer simulation technology into the classroom. However, no research has been done in this area to measure the true effect of computer simulation on product creativity. For that reason, other studies addressing computer use in general and product creativity will be explored.

Studies Related to Computers and the Creative Product

A study conducted by Joram, Woodruff, Bryson, and Lindsay (1992) found that average students produced their most creative work using word processors as compared to students using pencil and paper. The researchers hypothesized that word processing would hinder product creativity due to constant evaluation and editing of their work. To test the hypotheses, average and above-average eighth-grade writers were randomly assigned to one of two groups. The first group was asked to compose using word processors while the second group was asked to compose using pencil and paper. After collecting the compositions, both the word-processed and handwritten texts were typed so that they would be in the same format for the evaluators. Based on the results, the researchers concluded that word processing enhances the creative abilities of average writers. The researchers attributed this to the prospect that word processing may allow the average writer to generate a number of ideas, knowing that only a few of them will be usable and the rest can be easily erased. However, the researchers also found that word processing had a negative effect on the creativity of above-average writers. These mixed results suggest that the use of word processing may not be appropriate for all students relative to creativity.

Similar to word processing, computer graphics programs may also help students improve the creativeness of their products. In a study conducted by Howe (1992), two advanced undergraduate classes in graphics design were assigned to one of two treatments. The first treatment group was instructed to use a computer graphic program to complete a design project whereas the other group was asked to use conventional graphic design equipment to design their product. Upon completion of the assignment, both groups' projects were collected and photocopied so that they would be in the same format before being evaluated. Based on the results, the researcher concluded that students using computer graphics technology surpassed the conventional method in product creativity. The researchers attributed this to the prospect that computer graphics programs may enable graphic designers to generate an abundance of ideas, then capture the most creative ones and incorporate them into their designs. However, due to a lack of random assignment, results of the study should be generalized with caution.

Like word processing and computer graphics, simulation technology is a type of computer application that allows users to freely manipulate and edit virtual objects. Thus, it was surmised that computer simulation may enhance creativity. This notion led to the development of the study reported herein.

Purpose of the Study

This study compared the effect of a computer simulation activity versus a traditional hands-on activity on students' product creativity. A creative product was defined as one that possesses some measure of both unusualness (originality) and usefulness. The following hypothesis and sub-hypotheses were examined.

Major Research Hypothesis

There is no difference in product *creativity* between the computer simulation and traditional hands-on groups.

Research Sub-Hypotheses

1. There is no difference in product *originality* between the computer simulation and traditional hands-on groups.
2. There is no difference in product *usefulness* between the computer simulation and traditional hands-on groups.

Method

Subjects

The subjects selected for this study were seventh-grade technology education students from three different middle schools located in Northern Virginia, a middle-to-upper-income suburb outside of Washington, D.C. The school system's middle school technology education programs provide learning situations that allow the students to explore technology through problem-solving activities. The three participating schools were chosen because of the teachers' willingness to participate in the study.

Materials

Kits of *Classic Lego Bricks*™ were used with the hands-on group. The demonstration version of *Gryphon Bricks*™ (Gryphon Software Corporation, 1996) was used with the simulation group. This software allows students to assemble and disassemble computer-generated Lego-type bricks in a virtual environment on the screen of the computer. Subjects in the computer simulation group were each assigned to a Macintosh computer on which the *Gryphon Bricks* software was installed. Each subject in the hands-on treatment group was given a container of Lego bricks identical to those available virtually in the Gryphon software.

Test Instrument

Products were evaluated based on a theoretical model proposed by Moss (1966). Moss used the combination of *unusualness* (or originality) and *usefulness* as criteria for determining product creativity. However, Moss' actual in-strument was not used in this study due to low inter-rater reliability. Instead, a portion of the *Creative Product Semantic Scale* or *CPSS* (Besemer & O'Quin, 1989) was used to determine product creativity. Sub-scales "Original" and "Useful" from the *CPSS* were chosen to be consistent with Moss' theoretical model.

The *CPSS* has proven to be a reliable instrument in evaluating a variety of creative products based on objective, analytical measures of creativity (Besemer & O'Quin, 1986, 1987, 1989, 1993). This was accomplished by the use of a bipolar, semantic differential scale. In general, semantic differential scales are good for measuring mental concepts or images (Alreck, 1995). Because creativity is a mental concept, the semantic differential naturally lends itself to measuring the creative product. Furthermore, the *CPSS* is flexible enough to allow researchers to pick various subscales based on the theoretical construct being investigated, like the use of the "Original" and "Useful" subscales in this study. In support of this, Besemer and O'Quin (1986) stated, "... the subscale structure of the total scale lends itself to administration of relevant portions of the instrument rather than the whole" (p. 125).

The *CPSS* was used in a study conducted by Howe (1992). His reliability analysis, based on Cronbach's alpha coefficient, yielded good to high reliability across all sub-scales of the *CPSS*. Important to this study were the high reliability results for subscales "Original" (.93) and "Useful" (.92). These high reliability coefficients are consistent with earlier studies conducted by Besemer and O'Quin (1986, 1987, 1989).

The Pilot Study

A pilot study was conducted in which a seventh-grade technology education class from a Southwest Virginia middle school was selected. The pilot study consisted of 16 subjects who were randomly assigned to either a hands-on treatment group or a simulation treatment group. As a result of the pilot study, the time allocated for the students to assemble their creative products was reduced from 30 minutes to 25 minutes since most of them had finished within the shorter time. Precedence for limiting the time needed to complete a creative task was found in Torrance's (1966) work in which 30 minutes was the time limit for a variety of approaches to measuring creativity.

Procedure

One class from each of the three participating schools was selected for the study. Fifty-eight subjects participated, 21 females and 37 males, with an average age of 12.4 years. Subjects were given identification numbers, then randomly assigned to either the hands-on or the computer simulation treatment group. The random assignment helped ensure the equivalence of groups and controlled for extraneous variables such as students' prior experience with open-ended problem-solving activities, use of Lego blocks and/or computer simulation programs, and other extraneous variables that may have confounded the results. The independent variable in this study was the instructional activity and the dependent variable was the subjects' creative product scores as

400 determined by the combination of the "Original" and "Useful" subscales from the *CPSS* (Besemer & O'Quin, 1989).

Subjects in both the hands-on and the simulation groups were asked to construct a "creature" that they believed would be found on a Lego planet. The "creature" scenario 405 was chosen because it was an open-ended problem and possessed the greatest potential for imaginative student expression. The only difference in treatment between the two groups was that the hands-on group used real Lego bricks in constructing their products whereas the simulation treatment 410 group used a computer simulator. Treatments were administered simultaneously and overall treatment time was the same for both groups. The hands-on treatment group met in its regular classroom whereas the simulation treatment group met in a computer lab. The classroom teacher at each school 415 proctored the hands-on treatment group and the researcher proctored the simulation treatment group.

The subjects in the hands-on treatment group were given five minutes to sort their bricks by color while subjects in the simulation treatment group watched a five-minute in-420 structional video explaining how to use the simulation software. By having the students sort their bricks for five minutes, the overall treatment time was the same for both groups, thus eliminating a variable that may otherwise influence the results. Then, the subjects in both groups were 425 given the following scenario:

Pretend you are a toy designer working for the Lego Company. Your job is to create a "creature" using Lego bricks that will be used in a toy set called Lego Planet. What types of creatures might be found on a Lego 430 planet? Use your creativity and make a creature that is *original* in appearance yet *useful* to the toy manufacturer.

One more thing: The creature you construct must be able to fit within a five-inch cubed box. That means you must stay within the limits of your green base plate and make 435 your creature no higher than 13 bricks.

You will have 25 minutes to complete this activity. If you finish early, spend more time thinking about how you can make your creature more creative. You must remain in your seat the whole time. If there are no ques-440 tions, you may begin.

When the time was up, the subjects were asked to stop working. The hands-on treatment group's products were labeled, collected, and then reproduced in the computer simulation software by the researcher. This was done so that 445 the raters could not distinguish from which treatment group the products were created. Finally, the images of the products from both groups were printed using a color printer.

Product Evaluation

To evaluate the students' solutions, two raters were recruited: a middle school art teacher and a middle school sci-450 ence teacher. The teachers were chosen because of their willingness to participate in the study and had a combined total of 36 years of teaching experience. To help establish inter-rater reliability, a rater training session was conducted during the pilot study. The same teacher-raters used in the

455 pilot study were used in the final study. The training session provided the teacher-raters with instructions on how to use the rating instrument and allowed them to practice rating sample products. During the session, disagreements on product ratings were discussed and rules were developed by 460 the raters to increase consistency. The pilot study confirmed that there was good inter-rater reliability across all the scales and thus the experimental procedures proceeded as designed. No significant difference in creativity, originality, or usefulness was found between the two treatment groups during the 465 pilot study.

For the actual study, the teacher–raters were each given the printed images of the products from each of the 58 subjects and were instructed to independently rate them using the "Original" and "Useful" subscales of the *CPSS* (Besemer 470 & O'Quin, 1989). Three weeks were allowed for the rating process.

Findings

Once the ratings from the two raters had been obtained, an inter-rater reliability analysis, based on Cronbach's alpha coefficient, was conducted. Analysis yielded moderate to 475 good inter-rater reliability (.74 to .88) across all the scales. The stated hypotheses were then tested using one-way analysis of variance (ANOVA).

- No difference in product *Creativity* scores was found between the computer simulation group ($M = 41.7$, 480 $SD = 7.67$) and the hands-on group ($M = 42.0$, $SD = 5.58$). Therefore, the null hypothesis was not rejected, $F(5,52) = 0.54$, $p = 0.75$.
- No difference in product *Originality* scores was found between the computer simulation group ($M = 485 20.59$, $SD = 4.44$) and the hands-on group ($M = 21.10$, $SD = 3.10$). Thus, the null hypothesis was not rejected, $F(5,52) = 1.07$, $p = 0.39$.
- No difference in product *Usefulness* scores between the computer simulation group ($M = 21.15$, $SD = 490 4.17$) and the traditional hands-on group ($M = 20.90$, $SD = 3.20$). Once again, the researcher failed to reject the null hypothesis, $F(5,52) = 0.49$, $p = 0.78$.

Conclusion

Though there are only a few empirical studies to support their claims, some researchers believe that computers in 495 general may improve student product creativity by allowing students to generate an abundance of ideas, capture the most creative ones, and incorporate them into their product (Howe, 1992; Joram, Woodruff, Bryson, & Lindsay, 1992). Similarly, some researchers speculate that the use of com-500 puter simulations may enhance product creativity as well (Betz, 1996; Gokhale, 1996; Harkow, 1996). However, based on the results of this study, the use of computer simulation to enhance product creativity was not supported. The creativity, usefulness, or originality of the resulting products 505 appears to be the same whether students use a computer simulation of Lego blocks or whether they manipulated the actual blocks.

Because the simulation activity in this study was nearly identical to the hands-on task, one might conclude that product creativity may be more reliant upon the individual's creative cognitive ability rather than the tools or means by which the product was created. This would stand to reason based on Besemer and O'Quin's (1993) belief that the creative product is unique in that it combines both the creative person and process into a tangible object representing the "true" measure of a person's creative ability. With this in mind, when studying a computer simulation's effect on student product creativity, researchers may want to focus more attention on the creative person's traits and the cognitive process used to create the product rather than focusing on the tool or means by which the product was created. This approach to understanding student product creativity may lend itself more to qualitative rather than quantitative research.

If quantitative research is to continue in this area of study, researchers may wish to consider using a different theoretical model and instrument for measuring the creative product. For example, if replicating this experiment, rather than using only the two subscales of the *Creative Product Semantic Scale* (Bessemer & O'Quin, 1989), the complete instrument might be used, yielding additional dimensions of creativity. Additional research regarding the various types of simulation programs is needed, along with the different effects they might have on student creativity in designing products. The use of computer simulations in technology education programs appears to be increasing with little research to support their effectiveness or viable use.

References

Alreck, T. L., & Settle, B. R. (1995). *The survey research handbook* (2nd Ed.). Chicago: Irwin Inc.

Besemer, S. P., & O'Quin, K. (1993). Assessing creative products: Progress and potentials. In S. G. Isaksen (Ed.), *Nurturing and developing creativity: The emergence of a discipline* (pp. 331–349). Norwood, New Jersey: Ablex Publishing Corp.

Besemer, S. P., & O'Quin, K. (1989). The development, reliability, and validity of the revised creative product semantic scale. *Creativity Research Journal, 2*, 268–279.

Besemer, S. P., & O'Quin, K. (1987). Creative product analysis: Testing a model by developing a judging instrument. In S. G. Isaksen, *Frontiers of creativity research: Beyond the basics.* (pp. 341–357). Buffalo, NY: Bearly Ltd.

Besemer, S. P., & O'Quin, K. (1986). Analysis of creative products: Refinement and test of a judging instrument. *Journal of Creative Behavior, 20*(2), 115–126.

Besemer, S. P., & Treffinger, D. (1981). Analysis of creative products: Review and synthesis. *Journal of Creative Behavior, 15*, 158–178.

Betz, J. A. (1996). Computer games: Increase learning in an interactive multidisciplinary environment. *Journal of Technology Systems, 24*(2), 195–205.

Bilan, B. (1992). *Computer simulations: An Integrated tool.* Paper presented at the SAGE/6th Canadian Symposium, The University of Calgary.

Brogden, H., & Sprecher, T. (1964). Criteria of creativity, In C. W. Taylor. *Creativity, progress and potential.* New York: McGraw Hill.

Choi, B., & Gennaro, E. (1987). The effectiveness of using computer simulated experiments on junior high students' understanding of the volume displacement concept. *Journal of Research in Science Teaching, 24*(6), 539–552.

DeVore, P., Horton, A., & Lawson, A. (1989). *Creativity, design, and technology.* Worcester, Massachusetts: Davis Publications, Inc.

Duenk, L. G. (1966). *A study of the concurrent validity of the Minnesota Test of Creative Thinking, Abbr. Form VII, for eighth-grade industrial arts students.* Minneapolis: Minnesota University. (Report No. BR-5-0113).

Edmunds, A. L. (1990). Relationships among adolescent creativity, cognitive development, intelligence, and age. *Canadian Journal of Special Education, 6*(1), 61–71.

Gokhale, A. A. (1996). Effectiveness of computer simulation for enhancing higher order thinking. *Journal of Industrial Teacher Education, 33*(4), 36–46.

Gryphon Software Corporation (1996). *Gryphon Bricks Demo* (Version 1.0) [Computer Software]. Glendale, CA: Knowledge Adventure. [On-line] Available: http://www.kidsdomain.com/down/mac/bricksdemo.html

Guilford, J. (1976). Intellectual factors in productive thinking. In R. Mooney & T. Rayik (Eds.), *Explorations in creativity.* New York: Harper & Row.

Harkow, R. M. (1996). *Increasing creative thinking skills in second and third grade gifted students using imagery, computers, and creative problem solving.* Unpublished master's thesis, NOVA Southeastern University.

Hayes, J. R. (1990). *Cognitive processes in creativity.* (Paper No. 18). University of California, Berkeley.

Hinton, B. L. (1968, Spring). A model for the study of creative problem solving. *Journal of Creative Behavior, 2*(2), 133–142.

Howe, R. (1992). Uncovering the creative dimensions of computer-graphic design products. *Creativity Research Journal, 5*(3), 233–243.

Johnson, J. R. (1989). *Project 2061: Technology* (Association for the Advancement of Science Publication 89-06S). Washington, DC: American Association for the Advancement of Science.

Joram, E., Woodruff, E., Bryson, M., & Lindsay, P. (1992). The effects of revising with a word processor on writing composition. *Research in the Teaching of English, 26*(2), 167–192.

Knoll, M. (1997). The project method: Its vocational education origin and international development. *Journal of Industrial Teacher Education, 34*(3), 59–80.

Lewis, T. (1999). Research in technology education: Some areas of need. *Journal of Technology Education, 10*(2), 41–56.

Maslow, A. (1962). *Toward a psychology of being.* Princeton, NJ: Van Nostrand.

Moss, J. (1966). *Measuring creative abilities in junior high school industrial arts.* Washington, DC: American Council on Industrial Arts Teacher Education.

Olson, D. W. (1973). *Tecnol-o-gee.* Raleigh: North Carolina University School of Education, Office of Publications.

Runco, R. A., Nemiro, J., & Walberg, H. J. (1998). Personal explicit theories of creativity. *Journal of Creative Behavior, 32*(1), 1–17.

Savage, E., & Sterry, L. (1990). *A conceptual framework for technology education.* Reston, VA: International Technology Education Association.

Stein, M. (1974). *Stimulating creativity: Vol. 1. Individual procedures.* New York: Academic Press.

Taylor, I. A. (1959). The nature of the creative process. In P. Smith (Ed.), *Creativity: An examination of the creative process* (pp. 51–82). New York: Hastings House Publishers.

Torrance, E. P. (1966). *Torrance test on creative thinking: Norms-technical manual* (Research Edition). Lexington, MA: Personal Press.

Torrance, E. P. (1963). Creativity. In F. W. Hubbard (Ed.), *What research says to the teacher* (Number 28). Washington, DC: Department of Classroom Teachers American Educational Research Association of the National Education Association.

Wallas, G. (1926). *The art of thought.* New York: Harcourt, Brace and Company.

About the author: Kurt Y. Michael is a technology education teacher at Central Shenandoah Valley Regional Governor's School, Fishersville, Virginia. E-mail: michael@csvrgs.k12.va.us

Exercise for Article 15

Factual Questions

1. According to Moss (1966), a creative product is one that possesses what two things?

2. What two factors does the researcher mention as being often considered when trying to understand and predict creative ability?

3. The researcher cites a study in which the effects of word processors on creativity were evaluated. Were the results of this study conclusive? Explain.

4. The subjects were drawn from how many different middle schools?

5. *CPSS* stands for what words?

6. What does the researcher identify as "the independent variable in this study"?

7. ANOVA stands for what words?

8. What was the mean *Originality* score of the hands-on group?

Questions for Discussion

9. The researcher cites a reference published in 1926. Do you think this helps provide a historical context for this study? Do you think that providing a historical context is important? Explain. (See lines 116–136.)

10. The literature review is longer than those in the other research articles in this book. Do you think it is about the right length given the nature of this study? Explain.

11. The major research hypothesis and the research sub-hypotheses predict "no difference." Is this what you would have predicted in hypotheses if you had conducted the study? Explain. (See lines 315–320.)

12. In your opinion, are the materials used in this study described in sufficient detail? Explain. (See lines 330–340.)

13. To what extent does the fact that the researcher conducted a pilot study increase your overall evaluation of the study? (See lines 375–386.)

14. The researcher assigned students at random to the two groups. Do you agree with him that this was a desirable way to assign the students? Explain. (See lines 390–397.)

15. The researcher describes the inter-rater reliability as moderate to good. Do you agree? Explain. (See lines 474–475.)

16. Despite the findings of no differences between the groups, do you think that additional quantitative research should be conducted on this topic? Explain. (Consider the researcher's discussion of this issue in lines 508–537 before answering this question.)

Quality Ratings

Directions: Indicate your level of agreement with each of the following statements by circling a number from 5 for strongly agree (SA) to 1 for strongly disagree (SD). If you believe an item is not applicable to this research article, leave it blank. Be prepared to explain your ratings.

A. The introduction establishes the importance of the study.

    SA   5   4   3   2   1   SD

B. The literature review establishes the context for the study.

    SA   5   4   3   2   1   SD

C. The research purpose, question, or hypothesis is clearly stated.

    SA   5   4   3   2   1   SD

D. The method of sampling is sound.

    SA   5   4   3   2   1   SD

E. Relevant demographics (for example, age, gender, and ethnicity) are described.

    SA   5   4   3   2   1   SD

F. Measurement procedures are adequate.

    SA   5   4   3   2   1   SD

G. All procedures have been described in sufficient detail to permit a replication of the study.

    SA   5   4   3   2   1   SD

H. The participants have been adequately protected from potential harm.

    SA   5   4   3   2   1   SD

I. The results are clearly described.

    SA   5   4   3   2   1   SD

J. The discussion/conclusion is appropriate.

    SA   5   4   3   2   1   SD

K. Despite any flaws, the report is worthy of publication.

    SA   5   4   3   2   1   SD

Article 16

Using Virtual Reality to Teach Disability Awareness

JAYNE PIVIK
University of Ottawa

IAN MACFARLANE
Nortel Networks

JOAN MCCOMAS
University of Ottawa

MARC LAFLAMME
University of Ottawa

ABSTRACT. A desktop virtual reality (VR) program was designed and evaluated to teach children about the accessibility and attitudinal barriers encountered by their peers with mobility impairments. Within this software, children sitting in a virtual wheelchair experience obstacles such as stairs, narrow doors, objects too high to reach, and attitudinal barriers such as inappropriate comments. Using a collaborative research methodology, 15 youth with mobility impairments assisted in developing and beta-testing the software. The effectiveness of the program was then evaluated with 60 children in grades 4–6 using a controlled pretest/posttest design. The results indicated that the program was effective for increasing children's knowledge of accessibility barriers. Attitudes, grade level, familiarity with individuals with a disability, and gender were also investigated.

From *Journal of Educational Computing Research, 26*, 203–218. Copyright © 2002 by Baywood Publishing Company, Inc. Reprinted with permission.

Inclusive education of children with disabilities in public education institutions is now common in developed countries. In Canada, this means that 373,824 children with special needs between the ages of 5–14 years attend regular classes [1]. Inclusive education is considered by most as a positive experience for both children with and without disabilities and an important social policy toward ensuring full participation and accessibility for individuals with disabilities [2]. Theoretically, inclusive education allows children with disabilities the opportunity for "free and appropriate public education" as determined by the Education of the Handicapped Act (EHA) in the United States in 1975.

However, in reality, children with disabilities often have to contend with structural, physical, and attitudinal barriers for the 30 hours per week they spend at school. Examples of structural barriers include steep ramps, uncut sidewalk curbs, heavy doors, and one-inch thresholds [3,4]. Stairs, narrow bathrooms, revolving doors, and turnstiles also have been reported as impediments that limit access and inclusion for individuals who use wheelchairs [5]. In addition to structural barriers, children with disabilities have to manage the physical limitations inherent to their disability. For example, a child with spina bifida may have to contend with poor upper extremity function (limiting fine motor skills such as writing), poor hand–eye coordination, potential neurological deficits, and difficulties with organizational skills [6].

Perhaps the most difficult type of barrier encountered by children with disabilities is negative attitudes expressed by their peers [7]. Attitudinal barriers experienced in educational integration, such as rejection and stereotyping [8, 9] or covert and overt bullying [10], can further isolate children with a disability and impact on their feelings of social acceptance and self-esteem. Social isolation has been linked to difficulty with future peer relations [4] and lower academic and cognitive development [11].

In order to increase social awareness, understanding, and acceptance toward children with disabilities by their nondisabled peers, disability awareness programs have been developed. Current methods of disability awareness programs for school children include: 1) simulating a disability (e.g., sitting in a wheelchair or wearing a blindfold), 2) providing information about disabilities, 3) live and video presentations/testimonials by individuals with disabilities, 4) pairing disabled and nondisabled children together in a buddy system, 5) group discussions about disability, and 6) a combination of the above methods [7]. Along with disability awareness, Roberts and Smith [12] recommend providing children without a disability with knowledge and practical skills that assist with social interactions with their disabled peers. Logic dictates that one of the most effective ways to impart knowledge about the realities for children with disabilities is to try to simulate the experience of the disability. In other words, to provide an opportunity where the child without a disability literally experiences different situations, viewpoints, perceptions, and interactions from the perspective of a child with a disability.

Simulation has been the cornerstone of virtual reality (VR), and in fact, the first uses of VR involved the simulation of military experiences as noted by Kozak, Hancock, Arthur, and Chrysler [13]. VR is defined as a three-dimensional, participatory, computer-based simulation that occurs in real time and is often multisensory [14]. In other words, VR responds to the user's actions, has real-time 3-D graphics, and provides a sense of immersion. There are many advantages to using VR for simulation. For example, VR provides a safe environment for practicing a skill, such

as learning to cross street intersections [15–17]. Simulations using VR may also be less costly than real-world simulations [18] and provide the user the opportunity for repetitive prac-
70 tice [19, 20]. Experiences that are not available in the real world can be simulated in a virtual environment, such as moving through a cellular structure or visiting historical sites that are presently nonexistent or too far away to be accessible. Past experience has shown us that children using VR
75 find it very interesting and stimulating, thus motivating the training experience [21]. Finally, desktop VR can provide a simulation that can be made widely accessible through dissemination via the Internet.

The purpose of this project was to develop and evaluate a
80 desktop VR program designed to teach children about the accessibility and attitudinal barriers faced by children with mobility impairments. Desktop VR utilizes a personal computer, where the virtual environment is displayed on a conventional computer monitor and movement within the envi-
85 ronment is effected through either a mouse, keyboard, or joystick. Although less immersive than systems that use head-mounted display units, desktop VR systems have the advantages of being less expensive, more portable, and easier to use. The developed program, titled *Barriers: The*
90 *Awareness Challenge*, used desktop VR to simulate the experiences of a child in a wheelchair in an environment familiar to most children—an elementary school. The specific objectives of this project were to examine the effectiveness of using a disability simulation with virtual reality to: 1)
95 increase children's knowledge of accessibility and attitudinal barriers that impact individuals with disabilities and 2) promote more positive attitudes toward children with disabilities.

Method

There were four phases to The Barriers Project. The first
100 was to utilize a collaborative research methodology, where youth with mobility impairments (our Disability Awareness Consultants) identified the barriers that would comprise the content of the software. The second phase was to develop the software, which involved organizing the barriers into a
105 script or storyboard, building the virtual environment, and then beta-testing it with our consultants. The third phase of the project involved evaluating the software to examine the impact of the program on youth without disabilities. The final phase involved disseminating information about the
110 program and providing free access to the software via the Internet.

Collaborative Software Development

In order to ensure that the software reflected the current status of accessibility and inclusion within an elementary school setting, a collaborative research methodology was
115 used. Fifteen Disability Awareness Consultants assisted in the content development and testing of the software. The consultants (aged 9–16 years) attended eight different schools on a full-time basis and had either cerebral palsy (*n* = 11) or spina bifida (*n* = 5). Their mobility impairments
120 ranged from difficulty walking (on uneven surfaces and/or for long periods of time) to constant use of an electric

wheelchair for independent mobility. The barriers to full inclusion in their schools and the proposed solutions to these barriers were identified by these consultants during three
125 focus group meetings. The final list of barriers and proposed solutions was then prioritized by the focus group participants, where each person was given seven stickers and was asked to place one or more of the stickers on the barrier(s) they felt were necessary to include in the software. The bar-
130 riers with the greatest number of stickers became the basis for the script or storyboard of the software program. Using this script, a virtual elementary school was developed, which includes the exterior of a school, an outside playground, hallways, a classroom, a library, and two washrooms (one
135 inaccessible). The children using the program were told that they were to travel in a "virtual wheelchair" and seek out all of the "building" and "bad attitude" barriers in the school. There are 24 barriers in the program, which include building barriers such as narrow hallways, crowded classrooms, a
140 ramp that is too steep, a locker hook that is too high, and inaccessible bathroom fixtures. The attitudinal barriers include comments from virtual students such as "Hey, look at the kid in the wheelchair!" or "Ha! Ha! You can't play here!"

145 The program presents a gaming style interface with a first-person point of view during navigation through the world. The user moves within the virtual school using the cursor keys and can activate events such as opening doors or using the elevator by pressing the left button of the mouse.
150 Two message areas are used: a task message area and an information message area. The task messages instruct the child to complete specific tasks such as performing an action or going to a specific location. The information message center gives feedback to the child when barriers are identi-
155 fied. A "wheelchair damage" display is used to encourage children to be careful as they navigate through the world and is activated when they bump into walls, objects, or people. As each barrier is correctly identified, the score is updated. A number of icons (such as a coat, key, and book) also are
160 displayed. The icons are added and removed as the student completes specific tasks. At the end of the program, a results section is displayed listing all the barriers and each one is labeled as to whether it was found or not during the program.

165 The program was developed in VRML 2.0 (Virtual Reality Modeling Language) using CosmoWorlds. The Cosmo-Player 2.1 plug-in (for Netscape Navigator and Microsoft Internet Explorer) was used as the 3D viewer. The virtual school that was developed used the scripting capabilities of
170 VRML to control interactions with the virtual objects and people in the school. Fields, events, proximity nodes, and collision sensors are used extensively throughout the virtual world. Each barrier, whether it is structural or attitudinal, is activated by a proximity node. A number of fields are used
175 to record the state of the world in relation to the location of the wheelchair and the interactions that have taken place. The child identifies a structural barrier by moving close to the barrier and clicking on the "Barrier" button that floats just in front of the virtual wheelchair. For example, when

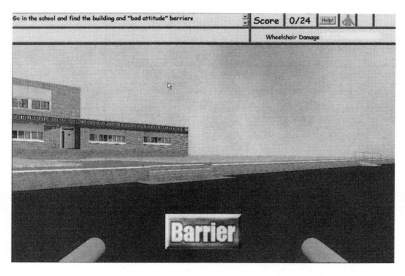

Figure 1. When first entering the world, the user is placed in the parking lot facing the school.

180 first entering the world, the user is placed in the parking lot facing the school (Figure 1).

A proximity node surrounds the front steps that lead up to the school. A number of fields indicate where the wheelchair is and which barriers have been found. For the front 185 steps, the "atSidewalkSteps" field is initially "false" and the "SidewalkStepsIDed" field (which records whether the steps have been identified as a barrier or not) is set to "false." If the "Barrier" button is clicked when the wheelchair is not at any of the barriers, an audio clip that indicates an incorrect 190 choice is played. When the child navigates closer to the steps, the virtual wheelchair collides with the proximity node that surrounds the steps. This collision triggers an event that sets the "atSidewalkSteps" field to "true." Now, if the "Barrier" button is clicked, a number of events occur: 1) the 195 number of correct barriers found is incremented, 2) an appropriate message is displayed in the information message area (in this case, it informs the child that wheelchairs cannot go up stairs), 3) the "SidewalkStepsIDed" field is set to "true," which is used in the results section to indicate which 200 barriers were found and which were not found, 4) the proximity sensor is permanently disabled, and 5) an HTML page that corresponds to the current running total of the number of barriers found is loaded in the score frame. If the child navigates out of the proximity node without identifying the 205 barrier, the value of the "atSidewalkSteps" field is toggled back to "false."

Attitudinal barriers are identified by clicking on the "Barrier" button after hearing an audio "bad attitude" comment. The script works in a manner similar to the structural 210 barriers, except that an audio node is triggered when a collision with the corresponding proximity node occurs. For example, when the child enters the classroom, a collision with a proximity node that is located just inside the door is triggered. This event triggers a sound node to play an audio clip 215 "It's the kid in the wheelchair" (said in a nasty, sarcastic tone indicating "a bad attitude"). While the wheelchair remains in the proximity node, the child can identify the attitudinal barrier (Figure 2). However, if the child moves far-

ther into the classroom, they will leave the proximity node 220 and will be unable to identify the barrier unless they move back in (which will re-trigger the playing of the audio clip).

There are three distinct areas of the virtual world: outside the school, inside the school, and the results section. The transition between the areas is accomplished by using a 225 touch sensor to trigger an event that uses a switch node to change to the next "level." The touch sensor for the transition from the outside to the inside is the automatic door opener, and the one that triggers the loading of the results is on the computer in the library. Once you have left an area, 230 you cannot go back. The switch node is used so that the entire program can be implemented in a single VRML file that interacts with the HTML frames in which the world is loaded. The single file was necessary so that the running score for the entire world could be maintained without the 235 need for applications, CGIs, or servlets running on a server. This permits schools and other users with slow Internet connections to download the entire set of files once and then run them locally on their machine whenever they want. Six of the Disability Awareness Consultants returned to the Reha-240 bilitation Sciences Virtual Reality Lab at the University of Ottawa to beta-test the program for content validity and general usability. Modifications to the software were made based on their feedback.

Evaluation of the Software
Study Design

In order to evaluate the effectiveness of The Barriers 245 software, a controlled pretest/posttest design was used. Using random assignment, half of the sample was given the VR intervention and the other half received an alternate desktop VR program—similar in length and based in a school setting, but without disability awareness information—in order 250 to control for computer practice effects. The control program titled "Wheels," developed by R. J. Cooper & Associates, is an excellent desktop VR program designed to teach children how to use electric wheelchairs. Hence, the viewpoint of the

Figure 2. While the wheelchair remains in the proximity node, the child can identify the attitudinal barrier.

control program also is from the first-person perspective at wheelchair height. As well, the control program also simulates wheelchair usage such as orienting oneself properly to enter doorways. The main difference between the two virtual environments is the presence of barriers (physical and attitudinal) in the intervention program. The hypotheses were that children receiving the Barriers Program would at posttest have: 1) a greater knowledge of barriers than the control group and 2) more positive attitudes toward peers with a disability compared to the control group.

Participants

Sixty youth (aged 9–11 years) participated in the study. All were from a local urban school and attended either grade 4 ($n = 20$), grade 5 ($n = 19$), or grade 6 ($n = 21$). There were 24 males and 36 females in the sample. Half of the sample ($n = 30$) received the Barriers intervention and the other half received the control program. Both programs took one-half hour to complete. Each child was tested individually and completed the program one time.

Measures

Two questionnaires were administered to the entire sample one week before and one week after the VR intervention. The Knowledge Questionnaire consisted of simply asking all the children to write out as many "building" and "people" barriers they could think of that might impact on children who use wheelchairs or crutches at school. Barriers were defined as "things that stop a person from doing what everybody else can do or cause people to be treated differently because of a disability." The building barrier example that was given was "smooth elevator buttons for people who are blind," and the people barrier example given was "someone who has a 'bad attitude' toward those who are different." Although this questionnaire was not a standardized measure, it was a simple, effective method for determining the youth's current knowledge of accessibility and attitudes within a school setting. For each accurate statement, the youth received one point.

The attitude measure used was the Children's Social Distance from Handicapped Persons Scale, a scale developed specifically for school settings, which has shown to be a quick, reliable measure of affective attitudes toward peers with a disability ($r = .78$) [22]. Concern over the word "handicapped" was allayed through conversations with experts in attitude measurement who indicated that the word "handicapped" is better understood by children than the word "disabled" (Hazzard; Rosenbaum, personal communications, 1999). An example item of this measure is, "It would be okay if a handicapped kid sat next to me in class," to which the child could respond with "yes," "maybe yes," "maybe no," or "no." Scores on this scale range from 0–30, with higher scores indicating more positive affective attitudes. The children also were asked to indicate whether they knew someone who was handicapped, to indicate what that handicap was, whether the person was a friend, an acquaintance or a family member, and finally, how much they liked this person.

Results

Knowledge

The self-report Knowledge Scale was used to ascertain knowledge of both building or structural barriers and people or attitude barriers for both groups using ANOVAs (group membership × time). Overall knowledge of barriers was examined by adding both the structural and attitude barriers together. Table 1 describes the building and attitudinal barriers for both groups before and after the intervention.

Table 1
Mean (SD) Knowledge Scores Before and After VR Intervention

	Time	
Group	Before	After
Barriers		
Building	2.9 (1.9)	6.4 (3.9)
Attitude	2.2 (1.8)	3.2 (2.6)
Total	5.2 (3.3)	9.6 (6.0)
Control		
Building	2.5 (1.7)	3.4 (2.6)
Attitude	2.5 (1.4)	2.9 (2.1)
Total	5.0 (2.7)	6.4 (4.2)

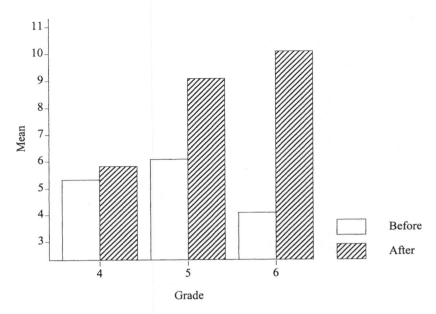

Figure 3. Pre- and postknowledge of barriers by grade for intervention group.

These results indicate that prior to the VR intervention, both the control group and the intervention group reported similar levels of knowledge within their school setting; however, following the intervention, the youth in the Barriers group reported a significantly greater number of barriers than the control group, $F(1,57) = 5.35$, $p < .05$. When broken down by type (building or attitude barriers), there was a significant difference in post-reported barriers between the two groups for the building barriers, $F(1,56) = 11.27$, $p = .001$, with the Barriers group reporting more barriers.

There were no differences between groups for knowledge of attitudinal barriers, which was not unexpected since only 4 of the 24 barriers in the program were "bad attitude" barriers. Gender was also not a significant factor for knowledge of barriers. There was a significant difference for children receiving the Barriers intervention by grade level on the total barriers reported following the VR intervention, $F(2,57) = 3.26$, $p < .05$, with grades 5 and 6 showing the greatest learning curve (see Figure 3).

Attitude and Previous Experience

No differences were found between the two groups or within groups for affective attitude measured with the Children's Social Distance from Handicapped Persons Scale [22]. However, there was a significant difference between males and females on the post-attitude scale, $F(1,57) = 4.68$, $p < .05$, with males reporting higher affective attitudes than females. Previous experience of knowing someone with a disability has been shown to impact on attitude scores. In this study, neither knowledge nor attitude scores showed differences for children who knew: 1) someone with a disability, 2) the type of disability of that person, 3) whether that person was a friend, an acquaintance, or a family member, or 4) how much they liked that person. Interestingly, 54

of the 60 children reported they knew someone with a disability.

Discussion

Based on the results of this study, *Barriers: The Awareness Challenge* software was effective for increasing the knowledge of barriers within a familiar setting for children in grades 4, 5, and 6. Building barriers were remembered most often, with grades 5 and 6 showing the greatest change. It is unclear whether the older children remembered more of the program at the posttest or whether their greater change in scores reflected previous findings that older children are more knowledgeable about disabilities [22] and are more accepting of their peers with a disability [23]. Regardless, sensitizing individuals to the difficulties associated with accessibility in public buildings remains an important component to disability awareness promotion. Rowley-Kelly provides an excellent checklist of potential accessibility barriers that school administrators can use to evaluate their structural resources for all different types of disabilities [24]. Examples include the need for wider aisles for access by people who use wheelchairs, tactile markings for individuals with visual impairments, flashing lights for fire alarms for individuals who are hearing impaired, and pictorial signage for those who have difficulty reading.

Although it has been 25 years since the precedent-setting Education of Handicapped Act, our children's schools are still riddled with accessibility barriers that serve to further isolate them from full participation and inclusion. More resources need to be allocated to improve accessibility in schools and attention paid to making adjustments to existing provisions [25, 26]. Another recommendation for school resource allocation that arose from the focus groups with our Disability Awareness Consultants was the necessity for ensuring that teachers and support staff have disability aware-

380 ness training. This suggestion has been reinforced in the literature and specifically recommends that teachers be provided with training, sufficient materials, and on-site assistance [27, 28].

The lack of differences in attitude scores between the
385 control and experimental groups was in all likelihood a function of the very high attitude scores of all the students participating in the study. On both the pretest and posttest scores, both groups had attitude scores just under 90%; thus, either the measure was not sensitive enough and/or a ceiling
390 effect occurred. Other factors that have been shown to impact the effectiveness of disability awareness programs include gender, where females report more positive attitudes, and familiarity, where knowing someone with a disability positively influences knowledge of and attitudes toward per-
395 sons with disabilities [29]. In our study, gender did not differentiate the two groups on knowledge of barriers or attitude before the VR intervention; however, males did report a significantly higher posttest attitude score. This result is inconsistent with the literature [30, 31]. One possible explana-
400 tion is that males were more familiar with the interactive gaming aspect of the VR program, as indicated by their higher game scores during the program ($M = 16.5$, $S.D. = 4.56$) vs. females ($M = 14.39$, $S.D. = 3.57$). This gaming familiarity may have allowed the males to focus on the edu-
405 cational material being presented vs. maneuverability and orientation.

Regarding familiarity with disability issues, the high attitude scores were most likely influenced by the great number of children in the study who knew someone with a disability
410 [29]; in this case, 90% of the total sample. As such, knowledge and attitude scores showed no differences for children who knew someone with a disability, the type of disability of that person, whether that person was a friend, acquaintance or family member, or how much they liked them. However,
415 in evaluating the effectiveness of the software, even though most of the study sample knew someone with a disability, and, as a group had very positive attitudes, they were still able to learn about accessibility barriers. This is important since increased knowledge about disabilities is believed to
420 be necessary for creating a lasting influence on positive attitudes [32].

The authors realize that no simulation program will ever be able to truly describe the experiences and perceptions associated with having a disability. The concern expressed
425 by French is that simulation programs trivialize the cumulative social and psychological effects of a disability and that they do not address the environmental and social barriers associated with a disability [33]. On the other hand, a lack of knowledge and understanding about issues related to a dis-
430 ability has been shown to lead to discrimination and isolation in schools [8,24]. The Barriers Project was designed with these concerns and issues in mind. The collaboration of youth with disabilities in the design of the program provided assurances of content validity as well as support for the con-
435 cept of using VR to impart knowledge to their peers. As well, the focus of the program is not based on simulating a sense of the physical limitations associated with a disability,

but rather on the environmental and social barriers encountered by persons with a disability. Utilizing the social–
440 political model of disability, the Barriers Project revolved around the impact of the environment (both physical and social) on the experiences of a person using a wheelchair [2]. Every effort was made to accurately design a program that simulates maneuverability in a wheelchair in order to high-
445 light structural barriers such as narrow aisles, doorways, washroom stalls, and crowded classrooms. Although this provided a sense of frustration for the children tested on the program, it served to provide a sense of environmental constraints as well as to highlight the capabilities of their peers
450 who use a wheelchair.

The program also attempted to provide facilitated learning by using a problem-solving approach. In designing an environment that required active exploration for solutions, we anticipated that the children would remember more bar-
455 riers—a recommendation suggested by previous researchers [34–36]. However, during the beta-testing phase, when the entire VR school was open to exploration, we found that the children missed many areas important to the learning objective. It appeared that in providing a totally unstructured envi-
460 ronment, the children focused on exploration vs. barrier identification. Thus, the program was modified to be semi-structured (i.e., where the children were directed to different areas, such as the library, where they could search and identify the barriers specific to that location). Overall, this was
465 found to be an effective strategy based on the results and the anecdotal comments reported by the students testing the program. The anecdotal comments included that: 1) it gave them a better understanding of the accessibility barriers that are all around them that they had not previously noticed, 2)
470 "bad attitudes" are just as difficult as, if not more difficult than, building barriers, 3) the VR program was good at simulating maneuverability in a wheelchair and could be extremely frustrating at times, 4) they had a new appreciation of the capabilities of people who use wheelchairs, and
475 5) the program was very motivating and they were interested in trying it again.

Limitations and Recommendations

The most obvious limitation of this study is the lack of effect of attitudinal change. This was probably due to positive attitudes of the students toward peers with a disability
480 before the intervention as well as the relatively few attitudinal barriers in the program. The school that agreed to be in the study is one of eight schools out of 128 that is identified as "accessible" by the school board. From a structural point of view, however, the school had all the accessibility barriers
485 that were identified in the program. As part of the "accessible distinction," it is likely that there is a greater incidence of children with disabilities in this school (however, there were no children who used wheelchairs or crutches in the three classes tested), and, thus, greater disability awareness. For
490 future studies, we would recommend controlling for place effects by testing the program in settings with and without previous awareness and sensitivity training.

Another likely influence that impacted on attitudinal scores was the small percentage of attitudinal barriers presented in the program (four of twenty-four). Poor attitudes were depicted as nasty or sarcastic comments by virtual students. The use of these students or avatars in the program use up a considerable amount of memory, which in turn slows down the program. For ease of use, we decided to include as few avatars as possible. However, as both the hardware and software capabilities improve in the future, more avatars can be used to depict attitudinal barriers. The content of the attitudinal barriers also posed difficulties. Many of the statements that our Disability Awareness Consultants proposed (such as the word "crip") were not included for fear of promoting or teaching negative attitudes. For that reason, this program could serve as a jump start for discussing negative attitudes toward people who are different.

VR was chosen as a teaching medium for a number of reasons: 1) it provided first-person simulation effects, 2) allowed us to control the environment (e.g., define and place barriers where we chose), 3) is accessible to many individuals if distributed over the Internet, and 4) has shown to be an enjoyable experience for children. However, since this is the first VR program that provides disability awareness, we would recommend future studies compare it to traditional forms of disability awareness training such as real-world wheelchair simulation, presentations, testimonials, and videos.

As well, since this project is the first of its kind to use VR to promote disability awareness, in this case, for mobility impairments, it would be interesting to develop and test the effectiveness of VR for simulating other types of disabilities. It also would be interesting to give the user the opportunity to make modifications that would erase barriers within the virtual environment. For example, the user could widen aisles or lower drinking fountains in order to make them more accessible.

Even in a school whose students had very positive attitudes about peers with disabilities, they were still able to learn about structural barriers in their environment that negatively impact the lives of individuals with disabilities. Hence, *Barriers: The Awareness Challenge* was considered successful in teaching about the environmental conditions faced by individuals with mobility limitations and, thus, was made available free of charge via the Internet at http://www.health.uottawa.ca/vrlab. We hope that along with children utilizing the program, teachers, staff, and parents also try the software. Along with raising awareness about structural and attitudinal barriers, we hope this program will serve to initiate further discussions about disabilities, highlight how environmental constraints and attitudes impact society's views toward their members with a disability, and provide a forum that emphasizes the capabilities of individuals who have disabilities.

References

1. Statistics Canada, *1991 Canadian Census*, Statistics Canada, Ottawa, Ontario, 1992.

2. M. Law and W. Dunn, Perspectives on Understanding and Changing the Environments of Children with Disabilities, *Physical & Occupational Therapy in Pediatrics*, 13:3, pp. 10–17, 1993.

3. M. Law, Changing Disabling Environments through Participatory Research, *Canadian Journal of Rehabilitation*, 7:1, pp. 22–23, 1993.

4. S. R. Asher and A. R. Taylor, Social Outcomes of Mainstreaming: Sociometric Assessment and Beyond, in *Social Development of Exceptional Children*, P. Strain (ed.), Aspen Systems, Rockville, Maryland, pp. 1–18, 1982.

5. S. B. Baker and M. A. Rogosky-Grassi, Access to the School, in *Teaching the Student with Spina Bifida*, L. Fern, F. Rowley-Kelly, and D. H. Reigel (eds.), Paul H. Brooks Publishing, Baltimore, pp. 31–70, 1993.

6. M. Rogosky-Grassi, Working with Perceptual-Motor Skills, in *Teaching the Student with Spina Bifida*, L. Fern, F. Rowley-Kelly, and D. H. Reigel (eds.), Paul H. Brooks Publishing, Baltimore, pp. 193–209, 1993.

7. J. Donaldson, Changing Attitudes toward Handicapped Persons: A Review and Analyses of Research, *Exceptional Children*, 46:7, pp. 504–513, 1980.

8. J. Gottlieb, Attitudes toward Retarded Children: Effects of Labeling and Academic Performance, *American Journal of Mental Deficiency*, 78, pp. 15–19, 1980.

9. J. Gottlieb, L. Cohen, and L. Goldstein, Social Contact and Personal Adjustment as Variables Relating to Attitudes toward EMR Children, *Training School Bulletin*, 71, pp. 9–16, 1974.

10. A. Llewellyn, The Abuse of Children with Physical Disabilities in Mainstream Schooling, *Developmental Medicine and Child Neurology*, 37, pp. 740–743, 1995.

11. H. Gardner, Relations with Other Selves, in *Developmental Psychology* (2nd Edition), M. H. Bornstein and M. Lamb (eds.), Lawrence Erlbaum Associates, Hillsdale, New Jersey, pp. 72–98, 1982.

12. C. Roberts and P. Smith, Attitudes and Behavior of Children toward Peers with Disabilities, *International Journal of Disability, Development and Education*, 46:1, pp. 35–50, 1999.

13. J. J. Kozak, P. A. Hancock, E. J. Arthur, and S. T. Chrysler, Transfer of Training from Virtual Reality, *Ergonomics*, 36, pp. 777–784, 1993.

14. K. Pimentel and K. Teixeira, *Virtual Reality: Through the New Looking Glass*, McGraw-Hill, Toronto, 1995.

15. D. P. Inman and K. Loge, Teaching Motorized Wheelchair Operation in Virtual Reality, in *Proceedings of the 1995 CSUN Virtual Reality Conference*, California State University, Northridge, 1995.

16. D. Strickland, L. M. Marcus, G. B. Mesibov, and K. Hogan, Brief Report: Two Case Studies using Virtual Reality as a Learning Tool for Autistic Children, *Journal of Autism and Developmental Disorders*, 26:6, pp. 651–659, 1996.

17. F. D. Rusch, R. E. Cimera, D. L. Shelden, U. Thakkar, D. A. Chapman, Y. H. Khan, D. D. Moore, and J. S. LeBoy, Crossing Streets: A K–12 Virtual Reality Application for Understanding Knowledge Acquisition, in *Proceedings of the IEEE Virtual Reality Annual International Symposium*, IEEE Press, New York, 1997.

18. J. W. Regian, W. L. Shebilske, and J. M. Monk, Virtual Reality: An Instructional Medium for Visual-Spatial Tasks, *Journal of Communication*, 42, pp. 136–149, 1992.

19. P. N. Wilson, N. Foreman, and D. Stanton, Virtual Reality, Disability and Rehabilitation, *Disability and Rehabilitation*, 19:6, pp. 213–220, 1997.

20. B. R. Lowery and F. G. Knirk, Micro-Computer Video Games and Spatial Visualization Acquisition, *Journal of Educational Technology Systems*, 11, pp. 155–166, 1982.

21. J. McComas, J. Pivik, and M. Laflamme, Children's Transfer of Spatial Learning from Virtual Reality to Real Environments, *CyberPsychology & Behavior*, 1:2, pp. 115–122, 1998.

22. A. Hazzard, Children's Experience with Knowledge of and Attitude toward Disabled Persons, *Journal of Special Education*, 17:2, pp. 131–139, 1983.

23. G. Royal and M. Roberts, Students' Perceptions of and Attitudes toward Disabilities: A Comparison of Twenty Conditions, *Journal of Clinical Child Psychology*, 16:2, pp. 122–132–1987.

24. F. Rowley-Kelly, Social Acceptance and Disability Awareness, in *Teaching the Student with Spina Bifida*, L. Fern, F. Rowley-Kelly, and D. H. Reigel (eds.), Paul H. Brooks Publishing, Baltimore, Maryland, pp. 245–250, 1993.

25. S. B. Baker and M. A. Rogosky-Grassi, Access to the School, in *Teaching the Student with Spina Bifida*, L. Fern, F. Rowley-Kelly, and D. H. Reigel (eds.), Paul H. Brooks Publishing, Baltimore, Maryland, pp. 31–70, 1993.

26. G. Clunies-Ross and K. O'Meara, Changing the Attitudes of Students toward Peers with Disabilities, *Australian Psychologist*, 24:2, pp. 273–284, 1989.

27. A. Hazzard and B. Baker, Enhancing Children's Attitudes toward Disabled Peers Using a Multi-Media Intervention, *Journal of Applied Developmental Psychology*, 3, pp. 247–262, 1982.

28. W. Henderson, Recommendations of Program Presenters about the Design and Implementation of Disability Awareness Programs for Elementary Students, doctoral dissertation, University of Massachusetts, 1987, *Dissertation Abstracts International*, 48:09, p. 153, 1988.

29. P. L. Rosenbaum, R. W. Armstrong, and S. M. King, Determinants of Children's Attitudes toward Disability: A Review of Evidence, *Children's Health Care*, 17:1, pp. 32–39, 1988.

30. Y. Leyser, C. Cumblad, and D. Strickman, Direct Intervention to Modify Attitudes toward the Handicapped by Community Volunteers: The Learning about Handicaps Programme, *Educational Review*, 38:3, pp. 229–236, 1986.

31.   A. Tripp, R. French, and C. Sherrill, Contact Theory and Attitudes of Children in Physical Education and Programs toward Peers with Disabilities, *Adapted Physical Activity Quarterly, 12*, pp. 323–332, 1995.

32.   M. Karniski, The Effect of Increased Knowledge of Body Systems and Functions on Attitudes toward the Disabled, *Rehabilitation Counseling Bulletin, 22*, pp. 16–20, 1978.

33.   S. French, Simulation Exercises in Disability Awareness Training: A Critique, in *Beyond Disability: Towards an Enabling Society*, G. Hales (ed.), The Open University, Bristol, Pennsylvania, pp. 114–123, 1996.

34.   K. Diamond, Factors in Preschool Children's Social Problem-Solving Strategies for Peers With and Without Disabilities, *Early Childhood Research Quarterly, 9*:2, pp. 195–205, 1994.

35.   J. Kilburn, Changing Attitudes, *Teaching Exceptional Children, 16*, pp. 124–127, 1984.

36.   S. Thurston, R. Wideman, M. Wideman, and P. Willet, Promoting Positive Attitudes on the Disabled, *History and Social Science Teacher, 21*, pp. 39–43, 1985.

Acknowledgments: This project was funded by Human Resources Development Canada and Nortel Networks. The authors would like to thank our Disability Awareness Consultants, The Ottawa Children's Treatment Centre, The Canadian Paraplegic Association, Jason Odin, and Corpus Christi School for their assistance in this project.

Address correspondence to: Dr. Jayne Pivik, School of Rehabilitation Sciences, University of Ottawa, 451 Smyth Road, Ottawa, Ontario, Canada K1H 8M5

Exercise for Article 16

Factual Questions

1.   How is VR defined in this article?

2.   What was the age range of the Disability Awareness Consultants?

3.   What type of assignment was used to place students into the two programs?

4.   How many students received the Barriers intervention treatment?

5.   What was the mean post-reported (i.e., after intervention) building barriers score for the Barriers group? What was the corresponding mean for the control group?

6.   Was the difference between the two means in your answer to question 5 statistically significant? If yes, at what probability level?

7.   Was there a difference between the Barriers group and the Wheels group on the Children's Social Distance from Handicapped Persons Scale?

Questions for Discussion

8.   In lines 27–29, the researchers indicate that negative attitudes expressed by their peers may be the most difficult type of barrier encountered by children with disabilities. Would you recommend this program to educators who are looking for a tool to help reduce negative attitudes? Explain.

9.   The control group also received a VR program (i.e., "Wheels"). Do you think it would be worthwhile to conduct another study in which the control group did not receive a program? Explain. (See lines 244–253.)

10.   In your opinion, is the control program ("Wheels") described in sufficient detail? Explain.

11.   When scores are very high (near the top of a scale) at the beginning of an experiment, there is little room for improvement. Thus, it is not possible to obtain large increases. This problem is called the "ceiling effect," which the researchers refer to in lines 389–390. Were you previously aware of this type of problem in conducting research? How important do you think it was in this study?

12.   If you were conducting a study on the same topic, what changes in the research methodology, if any, would you make?

Quality Ratings

Directions: Indicate your level of agreement with each of the following statements by circling a number from 5 for strongly agree (SA) to 1 for strongly disagree (SD). If you believe an item is not applicable to this research article, leave it blank. Be prepared to explain your ratings.

A.   The introduction establishes the importance of the study.

SA   5   4   3   2   1   SD

B.   The literature review establishes the context for the study.

SA   5   4   3   2   1   SD

C.   The research purpose, question, or hypothesis is clearly stated.

SA   5   4   3   2   1   SD

D.   The method of sampling is sound.

SA   5   4   3   2   1   SD

E.   Relevant demographics (for example, age, gender, and ethnicity) are described.

SA   5   4   3   2   1   SD

F.   Measurement procedures are adequate.

SA   5   4   3   2   1   SD

G.   All procedures have been described in sufficient detail to permit a replication of the study.

SA   5   4   3   2   1   SD

H. The participants have been adequately protected from potential harm.

SA   5   4   3   2   1   SD

I. The results are clearly described.

SA   5   4   3   2   1   SD

J. The discussion/conclusion is appropriate.

SA   5   4   3   2   1   SD

K. Despite any flaws, the report is worthy of publication.

SA   5   4   3   2   1   SD

Article 17

Using a Psychoeducational Approach to Increase the Self-Esteem of Adolescents at High Risk for Dropping Out

DON WELLS
Louisiana Tech University

JEROME TOBACYK
Louisiana Tech University

MARK MILLER
Louisiana Tech University

ROBERT CLANTON
Louisiana Tech University

ABSTRACT. The effectiveness of an ecologically oriented approach in changing the self-concepts of 80 high-risk adolescents was investigated. Participants were administered a self-esteem scale before and after an eight-week psychoeducational program designed for dropout prevention. Results indicated significant reductions in dropout rates and increased self-esteem among participants.

From *Adolescence*, 37, 431–434. Copyright © 2002 by Libra Publishers, Inc. Reprinted with permission.

Over 10% of white adolescents, 15% of African American adolescents, and 35% of Hispanic adolescents drop out of school (U.S. Department of Commerce, 1995). In addition, Kelly (1963) contends that many young adolescents continue to attend school even though they have mentally dropped out.

There are numerous reasons why adolescents drop out of school, including lack of interest in school, low grades, misconduct, low reading and math abilities, financial problems, personality problems, parental influence, family background, and other socioeconomic factors (Browne & Rife, 1991; Buhrmester, 1990; Horowitz, 1992; Kupersmidt & Coie, 1990; Sarigiani et al., 1990; Zarb, 1984). Finally deciding to drop out, however, appears to be a decision made over time. Many adolescents, by the time they do drop out, have lost all confidence in their ability to succeed in school (Nunn & Parish, 1992) and have developed feelings of inferiority (Cairns, Cairns, & Neckerman, 1989). This study addresses the issue of feelings of inferiority and low self-esteem in adolescents. Specifically, it describes the changes in self-esteem of high-risk students who participated in an eight-week residential program designed to reduce dropout rates.

Method

An eight-week summer program was designed and implemented to prevent high-risk adolescents from dropping out of school. Identified by their high school counselors as being at high risk for dropping out, participants were provided a total immersion curriculum that included academic and vocational instruction, as well as personal counseling services. They were housed on a southern university campus for the entire eight weeks, including weekends. Five days a week, participants received four hours of academic instruction by master's level schoolteachers and four hours of vocational instruction. Each evening they received 1–4 hours of individual and/or group counseling by counseling psychology graduate students.

Participants

The participants were 80 economically disadvantaged adolescents who were at high risk for dropping out. They ranged from 14 to 16 years of age. There were 32 females and 48 males.

Instrument

The Coopersmith Self-Esteem Inventory–School Form (Coopersmith, 1986) was administered to measure the participants' self-esteem. This 58-item measure consists of five subscales: General Self, Social Self–Peers, Home–Parents, School–Academic, and Total Self. A pretest was administered to participants upon entry into the program, and a posttest administration was completed eight weeks later, just prior to leaving the program.

Results

Table 1 provides the results of the two administrations of the Coopersmith Self-Esteem Inventory–School Form for participants in the program. Significant differences were found between pretest and posttest self-esteem total scores (i.e., Total Self) ($t = 3.24$, $p < .003$), as well as between Home–Parents subscale scores ($t = 4.22$, $p < .001$).

A follow-up study of participants' school retention rates was conducted over the two years directly after participation in the dropout prevention program. The first year after intervention yielded a dropout rate of zero. Following the second year, the dropout rate of participants was 6%. For a control group of similar individuals not receiving intervention, the dropout rate was 21.2% for the same time period.

Discussion

The psychoeducational theory providing the foundation of the program involved removing adolescents from their

Table 1
Self-Esteem Scores for 80 At-Risk Adolescents

| | Pretest | | Posttest | | | |
	M	SD	M	SD	t	p
General Self	32.2	7.8	31.8	8.0	−1.52	ns
Social Self–Peers	10.7	3.7	10.5	4.1	−0.83	ns
Home–Parents	9.5	4.3	11.2	4.1	4.22	< .001
School–Academic	8.9	3.5	9.1	3.8	1.98	ns
Total Self	61.3	14.9	62.6	15.3	3.24	< .003

Maximum possible scores: General Self, 52; Social Self–Peers, 16; Home–Parents, 16; School–Academic, 16; and Total Self, 100.

current home environments. Therapists and educators were then afforded the opportunity of presenting an alternative to
65 their current course, that is, potentially dropping out of school. In addition to increasing academic abilities and providing prevocational training, the program offered participants the opportunity to consult with counselors on a daily basis, all of which most likely contributed to the success of
70 the program in reducing dropout rates.

Underlying these changes, however, were apparent changes in self-esteem. Curiously, the subscale on which scores most significantly changed during the program was Home–Parents, the area from which they were intentionally
75 removed for the eight-week program. During that time, these adolescents apparently experienced perceptional changes they related to their homes and families.

Significant changes in self-concept cannot fully account for the dramatic reduction in the dropout rates of partici-
80 pants. Given, however, that increasing the self-esteem of these high-risk dropouts was a central focus of the therapeutic milieu, further investigations may reveal the specific relationships between increases in self-esteem and reductions in dropout rates.

References

Browne, C. S., & Rife, J. C. (1991). Social, personality, and gender differences in at-risk and not-at-risk sixth-grade students. *Journal of Early Adolescence, 11,* 482–495.

Buhrmester, D. (1990). Intimacy of friendships, interpersonal competence, and adjustment during preadolescence and adolescence. *Child Development, 61,* 1101–1111.

Cairns, R. B., Cairns, B. D., & Neckerman, H. J. (1989). Early school dropout: Configuration and determinants. *Child Development, 60,* 1436–1452.

Coopersmith, S. (1986). *Self-Esteem Inventory.* Palo Alto, CA: Consulting Psychologist Press.

Horowitz, T. R. (1992). Dropout—Mertonian or reproduction scheme? *Adolescence, 27,* 451–459.

Kelly, E. C. (1963). The dropout–Our greatest challenge. *Educational Leadership, 20,* 294–296.

Kupersmidt, J. B., & Coie, J. D. (1990). Preadolescent peer status, aggression, and school adjustment as predictors of externalizing problems in adolescence. *Child Development, 61,* 1350–1362.

Nunn, G. D., & Parish, T. S. (1992). The psychosocial characteristics of at-risk high school students. *Adolescence, 27,* 435–440.

Sarigiani, P. A., Wilson, J. L., Peterson, A. C., & Viocay, J. R. (1990). Self-image and educational plans of adolescents from two contrasting communities. *Journal of Early Adolescence, 10,* 37–45.

U.S. Department of Commerce, Bureau of the Census. (1995). *Statistical abstract of the United States, 1995.* Washington, DC: U.S. Government Printing Office.

Zarb, J. M. (1984). A comparison of remedial failure and successful secondary school students across self-perception and past and present school performance variables. *Adolescence, 19,* 335–348.

Address correspondence to: Don Wells, Department of Psychology and Behavioral Sciences, Louisiana Tech University, P.O. Box 10048, Ruston, LA 71272.

Exercise for Article 17

Factual Questions

1. In the literature review, the researchers state that "There are numerous reasons why adolescents drop out of school," followed by a list of reasons. How many references are cited for this portion of the literature review?

2. Where were students "housed" during the program?

3. Who conducted the counseling in the evenings?

4. The difference between the pretest and posttest means on the Home–Parents subscale scores was statistically significant. At what probability level was it significant?

5. What was the pretest mean on the Home–Parents subscale?

6. On the Home–Parents subscale, the posttest mean is how many points higher than the pretest mean?

7. What was the dropout rate for the control group?

Questions for Discussion

8. The researchers mention that "many young adolescents continue to attend school even though they have mentally dropped out." In your opinion, is this an important point to make in the introduction to this particular study? If so, would you find it useful to have more information on this issue? (See lines 4–6.)

9. The program is described in lines 23–35. In your opinion, is it described in sufficient detail? Explain. The researchers state that the participants were "economically disadvantaged." Is this important to know? Explain.

10. Speculate on the meaning of the abbreviation "ns" in Table 1.

11. The researchers mention the dropout rate for a control group in lines 58–60. They state that the control group consisted of "similar individuals." Would it be helpful to know how the researchers determined their similarity? Explain.

12. The researchers use the term "curiously" in discussing one of the differences. Do you agree that it is "curious"? (See lines 72–77.)

13. If you were conducting a study on the same topic, what changes, if any, would you make in the research methodology?

Quality Ratings

Directions: Indicate your level of agreement with each of the following statements by circling a number from 5 for strongly agree (SA) to 1 for strongly disagree (SD). If you believe an item is not applicable to this research article, leave it blank. Be prepared to explain your ratings.

A. The introduction establishes the importance of the study.

SA   5   4   3   2   1   SD

B. The literature review establishes the context for the study.

SA   5   4   3   2   1   SD

C. The research purpose, question, or hypothesis is clearly stated.

SA   5   4   3   2   1   SD

D. The method of sampling is sound.

SA   5   4   3   2   1   SD

E. Relevant demographics (for example, age, gender, and ethnicity) are described.

SA   5   4   3   2   1   SD

F. Measurement procedures are adequate.

SA   5   4   3   2   1   SD

G. All procedures have been described in sufficient detail to permit a replication of the study.

SA   5   4   3   2   1   SD

H. The participants have been adequately protected from potential harm.

SA   5   4   3   2   1   SD

I. The results are clearly described.

SA   5   4   3   2   1   SD

J. The discussion/conclusion is appropriate.

SA   5   4   3   2   1   SD

K. Despite any flaws, the report is worthy of publication.

SA   5   4   3   2   1   SD

Article 18

Academic Achievement and Between-Class Transition Time for Self-Contained and Departmental Upper-Elementary Classes

CAROLE J. MCGRATH
Lincoln County Schools

JAMES O. RUST
Middle Tennessee State University

ABSTRACT. This study investigated the relationship between elementary school classroom organizational structure (i.e., self-contained versus departmental formats) and standardized achievement scores, transition time between classes, and instruction time. Participants included 103 fifth-grade and 94 sixth-grade students from one school district. Based on previous findings, students from self-contained classes were predicted to achieve significantly more than comparable students from departmentalized classes, take significantly less time to change classes, and spend more time in instruction. Results indicated that the self-contained group gained significantly more on Total Battery, Language, and Science subtests compared to the departmentalized group. Departmentalized classes took significantly longer to transition from subject to subject than did the self-contained classes. No differences were evident for instructional time. Findings were consistent for fifth and sixth grades. The results are limited because of using only one school district.

From *Journal of Instructional Psychology*, 29, 40–43. Copyright © 2002 by *Journal of Instructional Psychology*. Reprinted with permission.

Educators have debated elementary school organizational structure since the beginning of the twentieth century (Gibb & Matala, 1962; Lamme, 1976). One aspect of organizational structure involves the number of subject areas covered by each teacher. In the self-contained approach, the teacher acts as a generalist and carries responsibility for the curriculum all day. The other extreme is the departmentalized approach. Here, students change teachers for instruction in different subjects. Thus, teachers cover fewer subject areas (Roger & Palardy, 1987; Mac Iver & Epstein, 1992). Advocates for a self-contained organizational pattern argue that it promotes instruction that is children-centered rather than subject-centered. Self-contained classrooms allow the teacher and students the opportunity to become well acquainted. Moreover, self-contained teachers know their students' strengths, weaknesses, and personality traits, enabling better accommodation of the students' individual learning styles (Squires, Huitt, & Segars, 1983). Additionally, self-contained classes allow for greater flexibility in scheduling. Elkind (1988) argues that the time students spend gathering books and papers and moving to other departmental classes cuts into valuable instruction time.

On the other hand, some educators have found that departmentalized organizational approaches offer distinct advantages for the student (e.g., Culyer, 1984). Anderson (1962) presented a strong case for specialization when he reported that only 4 of 260 teachers considered themselves well prepared in all subject areas. Walker (1990) noted greater emphasis on curriculum matters in departmentalized elementary schools.

This paper is similar to one by Garner and Rust (1992), which found that fifth-grade students in self-contained rooms scored significantly higher on group achievement tests compared to their departmentalized peers. The present study added measures of transition time and actual instruction time.

Method

Participants

The participants included 197 students (103 fifth graders and 94 sixth graders) from two kindergarten–sixth-grade schools in rural Tennessee. There were 109 students from School A. Of these students, 58 fifth graders (30 boys and 28 girls) and 51 sixth graders (23 boys and 28 girls) attended departmentalized classes. School B's participants included 88 students. Of these students, 45 fifth graders (20 boys and 25 girls) and 43 sixth graders (21 boys and 22 girls) attended self-contained classrooms. All of the participants attended self-contained classrooms in the fourth grade. School A used departmentalized fifth- and sixth-grade classes. School B maintained self-contained classes through grade 6. The social class compositions of Schools A and B were similar, with 27% of the students at each school getting free or reduced-fee lunch.

Apparatus

The scale scores and normal curve equivalents of the norm-referenced component of the Tennessee Comprehensive Assessment Program (TCAP) were dependent variables. The primary aim of the instrument is to provide a measure of achievement of basic skills in reading, spelling, language, mathematics, study skills, science, and social studies. The Tennessee Department of Education considers the scale scores obtained on the TCAP useful for measuring growth of students or groups of students from year to year (Tennessee

Comprehensive Assessment Program, 1993). Scores range from 0 to 999. Parents, students, and teachers can monitor annual progress up the scale in each subject from 0 toward 999. McWherter and Smith (1993) refer to year-to-year scale score comparisons as value-added assessment. The TCAP also supplies traditional normal curve equivalents (NCEs), which have many of the characteristics of percentile ranks, but have the additional advantage of being based on an equal-interval scale. NCEs have a mean of 50 and a standard deviation of 10 (Bock & Wolfe, 1996).

Transition time was recorded by direct observation. Each group was observed for two full days, not consecutively, and not the same day of the week. Actual time was recorded and rounded to the nearest minute from the closing of one subject until the beginning of the next. Instruction time was recorded during the same days. Subject matter was noted. The first author made these observations.

Results

Normal curve equivalents (NCEs) and scale scores from the TCAP Total Battery and subtests (Reading, Language, Mathematics, Science, and Social Studies) were analyzed in six separate 2 (Grades: 5, 6) x 2 (Organizational Structure: Self-contained and Departmental) x 2 (Male, Female) analyses of variance. The mean gains were calculated by subtracting the difference between TCAP pretest scale scores from posttest scale scores (see Table 1). School A implemented a departmentalized organizational structure, and School B implemented a self-contained structure.

Table 1
Mean Value-Added Scores

	Departmentalized		Self-Contained	
Test	*5th*	*6th*	*5th*	*6th*
Total Battery	7.62	19.60	16.24	27.88
Reading	16.24	14.51	18.04	21.49
Language	2.15	12.87	20.00	18.94
Mathematics	4.98	30.90	9.49	44.47
Science	−5.60	8.16	13.28	28.22
Social Studies	23.82	5.53	21.62	19.93

Significant effects were found for gain scores using the TCAP scale scores. Self-contained students gained significantly more than departmentalized students in Total Battery, Language, and Science in fifth and sixth grades (see Table 1). No differences were found in Reading, Mathematics, or Social Studies. Inspection of Table 1 reveals wide differences in gain scores. One of the fifth-grade classes lost points in Science. All of the other groups improved compared to the previous year's scores. The gain scores found here are more variable and more modest than those presented in a longitudinal study of the TCAP (Bock & Wolfe, 1996).

In the NCE analyses, there were no significant main effects or interactions for organizational structure. Transition time was significantly more efficient in the self-contained classes compared to the departmentalized school (average transition time was 3.27 minutes for the self-contained groups compared to 4.55 minutes for the departmental

groups). However, there was no significant difference in actual instruction time. Departmentalized classes averaged 48 minutes of instruction time per hour while self-contained classes were engaged in instruction an average of 46 minutes. That difference was not significant. Anecdotal observations revealed that teachers in self-contained classes offered instruction in academically oriented areas that were not included in the study. Computer lab, creative writing, and journal writing are some examples.

Discussion

Implications for practice resulting from this study include some support for self-contained instruction for fifth- and sixth-grade children. As hypothesized, significantly higher gains were found in three academic areas. These findings support those of Garner and Rust (1992).

There were two additional measures in the present study: transition time and instruction time. Transition time findings agree with those of Culyer (1984) and Elkind (1988) that students spend more time transitioning from class to class in schools that follow a departmental structure compared to those organized in self-contained groups.

One would logically assume, as Culyer (1984) did, that the self-contained structure would increase time-on-task because of the reduced time required to organize materials and change classrooms. Elkind (1988) posited, also, that the extra time spent changing classes would cut into valuable instruction time. However, the present study did not find that to be the case. The present study found no meaningful differences between departmental and self-contained situations for instruction time. Despite the longer transition time, the departmental teachers allotted a similar amount of instructional time in the five major subject areas compared to self-contained teachers. The reason for the nonsignificant difference of instruction time appeared to be that the self-contained teachers included time for computer lab, creative writing, and art. The study included some support for self-contained instruction for these children. As hypothesized, significantly higher gains were found in Language, Science and Total Battery. However, no differences were evident in Reading, Mathematics, and Social Studies.

The study was limited by the small number of classes used in one small southern town. Observation lasted only two days for determining transition and instruction time. Future studies will need to expand this database to allow for generalization.

References

Anderson, R. C. (1962). The case for teacher specialization in the elementary school. *Elementary School Journal, 62,* 253–260.

Bock, R. D., & Wolfe, R. (1996). Audit and review of the Tennessee value-added assessment system (TVAAS): Preliminary report (Technical Report, pp. 1–35). Tennessee Office of Education Accountability, Comptroller of the Treasury, Nashville, TN.

Culyer, R. C. (1984). The case for self-contained classroom. *Clearing House, 57,* 417–419.

Elkind, D. (1988). Rotation at an early age. *Principal, 36,* 11–13.

Garner, S. S., & Rust, J. O. (1992). Comparison of fifth-grade achievement in departmentalized and self-contained rural schools. *Tennessee Educational Leadership, 19,* 32–37.

Gibb, E. G., & Matala, D. C. (1962). Studies on the use of special teachers of science and mathematics in grades 5 and 6. *School Science and Mathematics, 62,* 565–585.

Lamme, L. L. (1976). Self-contained to departmentalized: How reading habits changed. *Elementary School Journal, 76*, 208–218.

Mac Iver, D. J., & Epstein, J. L. (1992). Middle grades education. In M. Alkin (Ed.) *Encyclopedia of educational research* (6th ed., pp. 834–844). New York: MacMillan/American Educational Research Association.

McWherter, N., & Smith, C. E.(1993). *21st Century Schools Value Added Assessment.* Nashville: Tennessee Department of Education.

Roger, J. S., & Palardy, J. M. (1987). A survey of organizational patterns and grouping strategies used in elementary schools in the southeast. *Education, 108*, 113–118.

Squires, D. A., Huitt, W. G., & Segars, J. K. (1983). *Effective schools and classrooms: A research-based prospective.* (ASCD No. 611–83298). Alexandria, VA: Association for Supervision and Curriculum Development.

Tennessee Comprehensive Assessment Program: Guide to test interpretation. (1993). Monterey, CA: CTB, Macmillan/McGraw-Hill.

Walker, D. (1990). *Fundamentals of Curriculum.* San Diego, CA: Harcourt Brace Jovanovich.

Address correspondence to: James O. Rust, Box 533, MTSU Station, Murfreesboro, TN 37132. E-mail: jorust@mtsu.edu

Exercise for Article 18

Factual Questions

1. In the literature review, the results by Anderson (1962) were cited to support which type of organizational approach?

   A. Departmentalized organizational approach.
   B. Self-contained organizational approach.

2. How many of the participants in School A were girls? How many of the participants in School B were girls?

3. TCAP is an acronym for the name of what test?

4. What term do McWherter and Smith (1993) use to refer to year-to-year scale score comparisons?

5. The departmentalized sixth graders gained how many points on Language?

6. Which group lost points in Science?

7. Was the difference between the two averages for transition time significant?

Questions for Discussion

8. Is it important to know that the social class compositions of the two schools were similar? Explain. (See lines 48–51.)

9. Apparently, individual students were *not* assigned at random to attend one of the two schools (i.e., random assignment was not used). In your opinion, if it were possible to assign the students at random, would the study be improved? Why? Why not?

10. Observations of transition time were done on two different days of the week. Speculate on why the researchers used two days instead of one (e.g., both on Mondays).

11. Instruction time was determined by observations made by one of the researchers. In your opinion, would it be an important improvement to use more than one observer? Explain.

12. In your opinion, are the anecdotal observations described in lines 110–114 important? Explain.

13. The researchers indicate that their results provide "some support" for self-contained instruction. In your opinion, how strong is this support? Explain. (See lines 115–119.)

14. The researchers state that "The study was limited by the small number of classes used in one small southern town." Do you think that this is an important limitation? Explain.

Quality Ratings

Directions: Indicate your level of agreement with each of the following statements by circling a number from 5 for strongly agree (SA) to 1 for strongly disagree (SD). If you believe an item is not applicable to this research article, leave it blank. Be prepared to explain your ratings.

A. The introduction establishes the importance of the study.

   SA   5   4   3   2   1   SD

B. The literature review establishes the context for the study.

   SA   5   4   3   2   1   SD

C. The research purpose, question, or hypothesis is clearly stated.

   SA   5   4   3   2   1   SD

D. The method of sampling is sound.

   SA   5   4   3   2   1   SD

E. Relevant demographics (for example, age, gender, and ethnicity) are described.

   SA   5   4   3   2   1   SD

F. Measurement procedures are adequate.

   SA   5   4   3   2   1   SD

G. All procedures have been described in sufficient detail to permit a replication of the study.

   SA   5   4   3   2   1   SD

H. The participants have been adequately protected from potential harm.

   SA   5   4   3   2   1   SD

I. The results are clearly described.

   SA   5   4   3   2   1   SD

J.   The discussion/conclusion is appropriate.

SA   5   4   3   2   1   SD

K.   Despite any flaws, the report is worthy of publication.

SA   5   4   3   2   1   SD

Article 19

Effects of Wellness, Fitness, and Sport-Skills Programs on Body Image and Lifestyle Behaviors

ELISSA KOFF
Wellesley College

CONNIE L. BAUMAN
Wellesley College

ABSTRACT. One hundred forty college women participating in one of three types of physical education classes (wellness, fitness, sport skills) responded to questions about body image, body-self relations, and lifestyle behaviors at the onset and conclusion of a 6-wk. program. Pre-post changes for the wellness classes involved the largest number of domains and included increased satisfaction with body and physical appearance, more positive assessment of physical fitness and health, higher orientation toward fitness and health, and reports of positive changes in lifestyle behaviors. Pre-post changes for the fitness classes were mainly in the fitness domain, including a more positive assessment of fitness, a higher orientation toward fitness, and an increase in fitness-oriented activities; increased satisfaction with body and physical appearance was also reported. Participation in sport-skills classes produced only one pre-post change, an increase in fitness-oriented activities. Possible reasons for the success of the wellness classes are discussed. Results suggest that participation in wellness classes provides students with a positive, proactive, empowered attitude toward their own health and well-being.

From *Perceptual and Motor Skills*, *84*, 555–562. Copyright © 1997 by Perceptual and Motor Skills. Reprinted with permission. All rights reserved.

There has been much discussion about the most effective ways to help women develop more positive attitudes about their bodies and their physical appearance and to motivate lifestyle changes. Participation in exercise and sport activi-
5 ties has been shown to have positive physical and psychological benefits (e.g., Cooper, 1970; Evans & Rosenberg, 1992), but less attention has been paid to other types of personal experiences that might yield equivalent benefits such as participation in structured wellness programs. Wellness
10 programs offer certain advantages over exercise and sport activities such as consciously promoting the integration of emotional health and well-being with improved physical functioning by focusing simultaneously on improving fitness, promoting healthy nutritional habits, and developing
15 effective stress management techniques. More systematic study of the comparative benefits of these three approaches, exercise, sport activities, and wellness, is necessary. Accordingly, in the current study, the effects on psychological functioning and lifestyle behaviors of these different approaches
20 were evaluated. Included were measures of body image; evaluation of and attention to physical appearance, physical

fitness, and physical health; weight-related attitudes and behaviors; and three dimensions of lifestyle, fitness-oriented activities, healthy eating, and management of stress. Sub-
25 jects were students in one of three types of physical education classes at the same institution and were participating in the classes to fulfill a general physical education requirement. The majority of subjects selected their classes because of interest in the course content, although a small number
30 were constrained by the time the courses were offered.

The three types of classes were wellness, fitness, and sport skills. In the wellness classes, students learned fundamental principles of aerobic fitness, healthy eating behaviors, and management of stress. In addition to the formal
35 classroom learning, they were required to participate in a self-paced independent aerobic activity for 30 minutes at least three times a week with the goal of developing cardiovascular fitness. When questioned informally at the start of the classes, a number of women said they had enrolled in the
40 class because they wanted to learn to control their weight through exercise and healthy eating and also to acquire better strategies for managing stress. The fitness classes emphasized either the development of muscular strength and endurance (strength training classes) or improving cardio-
45 vascular fitness (step aerobics or running classes). Women enrolled in the fitness classes typically said they wanted to tone up their bodies and develop more lean body mass. The sport-skills classes (tennis and racquetball) emphasized skill development and game play, and participants in these classes
50 said they had enrolled either to learn a new sport or improve their current skill. All classes met twice a week for 60 to 70 minutes for a 6-wk. period (12 class sessions).

On the first and last day of classes, subjects completed a questionnaire containing measures of body image, physical
55 appearance, physical fitness, and physical health evaluation and orientation, weight-related concerns, and lifestyle assessment. Given the more holistic approach of wellness programs and their emphasis on integrating psychological and physical functioning, it was expected that participation in the
60 wellness program would be associated with a greater number of positive changes in a larger number of domains than the other two programs.

Method

Subjects

Subjects were 140 female college students, enrolled in

the three types of physical education classes already described; 95% were between the ages of 18 and 22 years.
Only those who were present on the first and last day of their
class were included in this study, which covered four 6-wk.
terms. They were divided as follows: wellness, $n = 33$, fitness, $n = 60$, and sport-skills classes, $n = 47$. Subjects were
students at a women's college; by self-definition, 60% were
Caucasian, 29% were Asian American, 6% were African
American, and 3% were Latina.

Procedure

Subjects were told that the study was concerned with attitudes and behaviors related to lifestyle habits, body-self
relations, and body image. They were informed that a questionnaire would be administered on the first (pretest) and last
(posttest) days of the class and that the purpose of the study
was to examine the effects of different types of physical
education classes on these attitudes and behaviors. Subjects
were tested in their classes, assured of confidentiality, and
asked to respond as accurately and honestly as possible. Participation was voluntary and was in no way associated with
receiving credit for the class; written informed consent was
obtained. On both occasions, subjects responded to the following measures in the order listed.

(1) *Lifestyle Assessment.*—This scale assesses three distinct aspects of lifestyle: fitness, eating, and management of
stress. Initially, the scale was developed to assess lifestyle
patterns of first-year college students (Bauman, 1992) and
has three subscales.

(a) *Fitness-oriented Activities.*—Subjects indicated how
much they agreed with 10 statements about fitness-oriented
activities on 5-point scales (1 = definitely disagree; 5 = definitely agree). Examples of statements are "I exercise aerobi-
cally three times per week (continuous vigorous exercise for
at least 20 minutes)" and "I climb the stairs rather than take
the elevator." Scores for this and the other two subscales are
means; higher scores indicate more participation in physical
fitness activities. Cronbach alpha was .79. This and all subsequent alphas are for Time 1 scores.

(b) *Healthy Eating.*—Subjects indicated how much they
agreed with 10 statements about behaviors associated with
healthy eating on 5-point scales (1 = definitely disagree, 5 =
definitely agree). Examples of statements are "I limit the
amount of fat, saturated fat, and cholesterol I eat" and "I eat
high-fiber foods (vegetables, fruits, whole grains) several
times a day." Higher scores indicate healthier eating. Cronbach alpha for this scale was .75.

(c) *Management of Stress.*—Subjects indicated how
much they agreed with each of 10 statements about time
management and control of stress on 5-point scales (1 =
definitely disagree, 5 = definitely agree). Examples of statements are "I am able to organize my time effectively" and "I
prepare in advance for potentially stressful situations."
Higher scores indicate more effective strategies for management of stress and time. Cronbach alpha was .71.

(2) *Multidimensional Body-Self Relations Questionnaire*
(Brown, Cash & Mikulka, 1990; Cash, 1990).—This 69-item
scale provides a multidimensional attitudinal assessment of

body image and weight-related variables. The scale consists
of three groups of subscales, the 54-item Body-Self Relations Questionnaire, the 9-item Body Areas Satisfaction
Scale, and six items assessing attitudes about weight.

(a) *Body-Self Relations Questionnaire.*—Subjects indicated how much they agreed with 54 items measuring attitudes toward three somatic domains: physical appearance,
physical fitness, and physical health on 5-point scales (1 =
definitely disagree, 5 = definitely agree). Within each of the
domains, separate items address either *evaluation,* or the
extent of liking, attainment, or satisfaction, or *orientation,*
the importance of and attention paid to the domain, and behaviors associated with maintaining or improving that domain. The scale yields seven subscales, indicated below with
an example of a component statement in parenthesis. Subscales are Appearance Evaluation ("I like the way I look
without my clothes"), Appearance Orientation ("I am always
trying to improve my physical appearance"), Fitness Evaluation ("I easily learn physical skills"), Fitness Orientation ("I
do things to improve my physical strength"), Health Evaluation ("I am a physically healthy person"), Health Orientation
("I have deliberately developed a healthy life style"), and
Illness Orientation ("I pay close attention to my body for any
signs of illness"). Scores are means, and higher scores indicate higher evaluation of or attention paid to the particular
domain. Cronbach alpha for the subscales ranged from .76 to
.90, with a mean of .82.

(b) *Body Areas Satisfaction Scale.*—Subjects indicated
how satisfied they were with nine body parts or aspects, e.g.,
face, weight, lower torso, on 5-point scales (1 = very dissat-
isfied, 5 = very satisfied). Scores are means and higher
scores indicate greater satisfaction. Cronbach alpha was .81.

(c) *Weight-related Attitudes.*—The six items assessing
weight attitudes ask about fat anxiety, weight vigilance, current dieting, and eating restraint, and how the subject and
others perceive her weight on 5-point scales, with higher
scores indicating greater concern. The first four items comprise a subscale yielding a mean score for weight preoccupation (Cash, Wood, Phelps, & Boyd, 1991). Cronbach alpha
was .75.

(3) *Figure Rating Scale.*—Stimuli were scales of nine
schematic drawings of females, ordered by increasing size
(Stunkard, Sorenson, & Schlusinger, 1983). Subjects rated
the figures according to how they thought they looked currently (think), how they felt they looked most of the time
(feel), and how they would like to look (ideal). Figure ratings also were used to construct three discrepancy measures:
feel minus think (FT), feel minus ideal (FI), and think minus
ideal (TI). Discrepancy scores such as "feel minus ideal" and
"think minus ideal" have been widely used as measures of
subjective dissatisfaction with the body (Thompson &
Altabe, 1991). The "feel minus think" measure has indicated
that subjects typically feel larger than they think they actually look (Thompson & Psaltis, 1988), which has been taken
as another measure of body dissatisfaction.

(4) Subjects reported their current weight and height,
which were used to construct a body mass index (BMI), a
measure of relative fatness (Bray, 1978).

Table 1

Mean Scores for All Measures at Pretest and Posttest for Wellness, Fitness, and Sport-Skills Classes[a]

Type of Class:	Wellness			Fitness			Sport-Skills		
Measure	Pretest	Posttest	p	Pretest	Posttest	p	Pretest	Posttest	p
Height	65.20	65.20		63.83	64.92		65.13	62.98	
Weight	141.48	141.55		129.80	130.68		133.87	134.43	
BMI	23.83	23.37		21.55	21.81		22.37	21.50	
Appearance Evaluation	2.89	3.10	.005	3.30	3.51	<.001	3.15	3.22	
Appearance Orientation	3.31	3.30		3.37	3.34		3.38	3.36	
Fitness Evaluation	3.20	3.43	.01	3.32	3.49	.01	3.60	3.56	
Fitness Orientation	2.98	3.40	<.001	3.22	3.44	<.001	3.27	3.28	
Health Evaluation	3.26	3.65	.004	3.80	3.92		3.74	3.78	
Health Orientation	3.30	3.72	<.001	3.48	3.54		3.36	3.47	
Illness Orientation	3.15	3.32		3.17	3.17		3.22	3.28	
Body Satisfaction	3.00	3.18	.007	3.24	3.40	<.001	3.24	3.30	
Weight Preoccupation	2.52	2.36		2.47	2.43		2.29	2.32	
Self-perceived Weight	3.85	3.64	.006	3.46	3.44		3.62	3.60	
Other-perceived Weight	3.58	3.45		3.12	3.07		3.32	3.26	
Fitness Activities	3.42	3.94	<.001	3.49	4.01	<.001	3.28	3.52	.001
Healthy Eating	3.47	3.88	<.001	3.69	3.73		3.61	3.69	
Stress Management	3.20	3.59	<.001	3.48	3.55		3.38	3.42	
Current Figure	4.48	4.58		3.85	3.76		4.09	4.04	
Felt Figure	4.94	4.79		4.26	4.03	.01	4.28	4.30	
Ideal Figure	3.42	3.55		3.20	3.14		3.29	3.33	
Feel Minus Think (FT)	.45	.21		.43	.29		.20	.26	
Think Minus Ideal (TI)	1.06	1.03		.64	.63		.84	.76	
Feel Minus Ideal (FI)	1.52	1.24		1.07	.91		1.00	.98	

[a]p values for paired *t* tests are exact; only values ≤ .01 are displayed.

Results and Discussion

The major purpose of this study was to assess whether participating in a particular type of physical education class resulted in reports of changes in lifestyle, attitudes toward physical appearance, fitness, and health, body satisfaction, and preoccupation with weight. The responses of 140 students present on the first and last days of their classes were compared using paired *t* tests; data for the three types of classes were examined separately. Mean scores for all measures are presented in Table 1. Given the number of dependent variables, the overall level of significance for the study was set at $p = .01$ (Bonferroni correction). We looked first at whether there were physical changes and then at whether there were changes in the attitudinal and behavioral variables from pretest to posttest.

Wellness Class.—There were no significant changes in height, weight, or BMI over the 6-wk. period. On the Body-Self Relations Questionnaire, significant changes occurred on five of the seven subscales, with scores increasing on Appearance Evaluation, Fitness Evaluation, Fitness Orientation, Health Evaluation, and Health Orientation. There also was a significant increase in body satisfaction. There was a significant decrease in self-classified weight, with subjects perceiving themselves to be thinner at posttest, but no significant changes in the figure ratings. There also were significant increases in fitness-oriented activities and healthy eating, and improved strategies for managing stress and time.

Fitness Class.—There were significant increases on three subscales of the Body-Self Relations Questionnaire: Appearance Evaluation, Fitness Evaluation, and Fitness Orientation as well as a significant increase in body satisfaction. There also was a significant increase in fitness-oriented ac-

tivities, but no other lifestyle changes. Interesting, on the figure-rating scales, the rating for how one felt most of the time decreased.

Sport-skills Class.—With the exception of an increase in fitness-oriented behaviors, there were no significant changes on any of the measures.

The results indicated positive effects of participating in wellness and fitness classes on lifestyle behaviors, body-self relations, and body image. Students in the sport-skills classes, who participated in programs focused exclusively on skill development and game play, did not report parallel benefits.

After participating in wellness classes for 6 wks., subjects reported increased satisfaction with body and physical appearance, perceived themselves to be more physically fit, reported being more actively involved in behaviors to enhance or maintain fitness, rated their physical health higher, and reported being more health conscious and oriented toward a healthy lifestyle. They also perceived themselves to be thinner. Finally, subjects reported changes in lifestyle behaviors, reflected in increases in fitness-oriented activities, healthier eating, and improved strategies for stress and time management.

Participating in fitness classes for 6 wks. also produced positive changes, but they were less extensive than those produced by the wellness classes. Fitness participants reported feeling more physically fit and being more actively involved in activities to enhance or maintain their fitness. They also reported increased satisfaction with body and physical appearance, reflected in part in their choice of a smaller "felt" figure. They reported that their fitness-oriented activities increased, although the other aspects of lifestyle we assessed were unaffected.

Interestingly, participating in sport-skills classes for 6
wks., while associated with an increase in fitness-oriented
245 activities, appeared to have little effect on other types of
behaviors that typically are associated with a healthier lifestyle. Contrary to popular belief, participating in a sport
alone did not improve perceptions of fitness or healthiness or
eventuate in healthier lifestyle behaviors.

250 The results of this study present a particularly strong case
for the positive physical and psychological benefits of a
wellness course. Examination of the wellness curriculum
offers some insights into why this program might have been
so successful. There were two aspects of the course that dis-
255 tinguished it from the other two courses we evaluated: a demand for accountability and a requirement for work outside
the classroom. In addition to the 70-min. theory class that
met twice a week, students were required to engage in a self-
paced independent aerobic activity of their own choosing. At
260 the first class meeting, each student was required to develop
specific goals and action plans for her aerobic fitness. She
was expected to participate in three exercise sessions per
week of at least 30 min. duration at an exercise intensity of
60% to 80% of maximum heart rate and to submit weekly
265 activity journals documenting progress toward her fitness
goals. In parallel fashion, students also were expected to
formulate goals and action plans for the course components
of nutrition and management of stress. All students met individually with their instructor to discuss ways to best
270 achieve their goals.

Although students take many courses during their college
careers, few actually provide them with knowledge and
skills that could enhance their quality of life. Data from this
study suggest that a structured wellness program could serve
275 such a function. It is striking that so many behavioral and
attitudinal changes occurred in the relatively short timeframe
of 6 wks.; clearly the next step is to look at adherence to
positive lifestyle changes over the longer term. Even in the
short term, however, it is apparent that students leave the
280 course with a positive, proactive, empowered attitude toward
their own health and well-being. A follow-up of three
months or a year would be informative.

References

BAUMAN, C. L. (1992) Lifestyle assessment of first-year incoming students. (Unpublished manuscript, Wellesley College, Wellesley, MA)
BRAY, G. A. (1978) Definition, measurement, and classification of the syndromes of
obesity. *International Journal of Obesity*, 2, 99-112.
BROWN, T. A., CASH, T. F., & MIKULKA, P. J. (1990) Attitudinal body-image
assessment: factor analysis of the Body-Self Relations Questionnaire. *Journal of
Personality Assessment*, 55, 135-144.
CASH, T. F. (1990) The Multidimensional Body-Self Relations Questionnaire. (Un-
published test manual, Old Dominion Univer., Norfolk, VA)
CASH, T. F., WOOD, K. C., PHELPS, K. D., & BOYD, K. (1991) New assessments
of weight-related body image derived from extant instruments. *Perceptual and Mo-
tor Skills*, 73, 234-241.
COOPER, K. (1970) *The new aerobics*. New York: Bantam.
EVANS, W., & ROSENBERG, I. H. (1992) *Biomarkers: The 10 keys to prolonging
vitality*. New York: Fireside, Simon & Schuster.
STUNKARD, A., SORENSON, T., & SCHLUSINGER, F. (1983) Use of the Danish
Adoption Registry for the study of obesity and thinness. In S. Kety, L. P. Rowland,
R. L. Sidman, & S. W. Matthysse (Eds.), *The genetics of neurological and psychiat-
ric disorders*. New York: Raven Press. Pp. 115-120.
THOMPSON, J. K., & ALTABE, M. A. (1991) Psychometric qualities of the figure
rating scale. *International Journal of Eating Disorders*, 10, 615-619.
THOMPSON, J. K., & PSALTIS, K. (1988) Multiple aspects and correlates of body
figure ratings: a replication and extension of Fallon and Rozin (1985). *International

Journal of Eating Disorders, 7, 813-817.

Acknowledgment: This research was funded by the Margaret Hamm Kelley Chair in Psychology (E. Koff) and a faculty grant from Wellesley College (C. L. Bauman). We thank Dr. Lawrence Baldwin, Melissa Allen, and
Elizabeth Andreason for their expert assistance.

Address reprint requests to: Elissa Koff, Department of Psychology,
Wellesley College, Wellesley, MA 02181.

Exercise for Article 19

Factual Questions

1. What reasons did a number of the women in the wellness class give for enrolling in the class?

2. If a student was present on the first day of class but
   absent on the last day, was she included in the study?

3. The students were told that the study had what purpose?

4. What do the authors mean by "discrepancy scores"?

5. Were there significant changes in the weight of students in the wellness class?

6. In which two of the three types of classes did students
   report a significant increase in body satisfaction?

7. The researchers characterize which finding as "contrary to popular belief"?

Questions for Discussion

8. The researchers state that "participation was voluntary
   and in no way associated with receiving credit for the
   class." Is this important to know? Explain.

9. The researchers state that Cronbach alpha was .75 for
   the Healthy Eating instrument. What kind of information does Cronbach alpha give you? Is .75 an acceptable level?

10. The researchers provide examples of the items con-
    tained in the various instruments. How important is
    this to you as a consumer of this research report?

11. Is there sufficient information about how all three
    classes were conducted for you to conduct a replication
    of this study? Explain.

12. Instead of assigning students at random to the three
    classes, each student selected a class. Is this an impor-
    tant limitation of the study? Explain.

13. In the Table of Contents of this book, this study is classified as an example of "quasi-experimental research." Why does it have this classification instead of "true experimental research"?

14. For students in the wellness class, there was a statistically significant difference on Fitness Evaluation, with the mean pretest score being 3.20 and the mean posttest score being 3.43. (See Table 1.) Keeping in mind that this variable was measured on a scale from 1 to 5, do you regard this as a "large" difference? Explain.

15. The authors suggest that a follow-up three months to a year later would be informative. Do you agree? Why? Why not?

16. To what population(s), if any, would you be willing to generalize the results of this study?

17. If you were conducting a study on the same topic, what changes in the research methodology, if any, would you make?

Quality Ratings

Directions: Indicate your level of agreement with each of the following statements by circling a number from 5 for strongly agree (SA) to 1 for strongly disagree (SD). If you believe an item is not applicable to this research article, leave it blank. Be prepared to explain your ratings.

A. The introduction establishes the importance of the study.

    SA 5 4 3 2 1 SD

B. The literature review establishes the context for the study.

    SA 5 4 3 2 1 SD

C. The research purpose, question, or hypothesis is clearly stated.

    SA 5 4 3 2 1 SD

D. The method of sampling is sound.

    SA 5 4 3 2 1 SD

E. Relevant demographics (for example, age, gender, and ethnicity) are described.

    SA 5 4 3 2 1 SD

F. Measurement procedures are adequate.

    SA 5 4 3 2 1 SD

G. All procedures have been described in sufficient detail to permit a replication of the study.

    SA 5 4 3 2 1 SD

H. The participants have been adequately protected from potential harm.

    SA 5 4 3 2 1 SD

I. The results are clearly described.

    SA 5 4 3 2 1 SD

J. The discussion/conclusion is appropriate.

    SA 5 4 3 2 1 SD

K. Despite any flaws, the report is worthy of publication.

    SA 5 4 3 2 1 SD

Article 20

The Use of Accelerated Reader
with Emergent Readers

MEGHAN J. CUDDEBACK
Albion Central School District

MARIA A. CEPRANO
Buffalo State College

Introduction

Accelerated Reader (AR) is a computer-based reading and management program that is designed for students in grades K–12. AR is developed and distributed by Advantage Learning Systems, a Wisconsin-based company. The goal of AR is to provide measurable reading practice time for each student participant. It purports to supplement any class-based reading curriculum by providing the teacher and each student in the class immediate feedback on how well reading material has been comprehended.

AR data measure three aspects of students' reading practice: quantity, quality, and challenge. Quantity is defined as the number of books read and the number of points earned. Quality is indicated by how well the students score on AR tests. Level of challenge refers to the relationship between the difficulty of books read and the students' tested reading ability ("Idaho Statewide Implementation," 1999).

Description and Rationale for AR

According to AR providers (Advantage Learning Systems, Inc., 1999) teachers in non-AR classrooms often are unable to measure comprehension of material students read independently without carrying on a one-on-one discussion with the student or evaluating journal entries or worksheets pertaining to books completed by the reader. The AR computer system provides more than 27,000 different books, both fiction and nonfiction at different reading levels or zones. Students having access to the system first choose a book in their reading zone and read the story. After reading the story at least once, the students take a computerized multiple-choice test, which usually contains 5, 10, or 20 questions. The test measures the students' knowledge and comprehension of the story. After the students complete the test, they are given immediate feedback regarding their score and questions that were answered incorrectly. The students then earn a number of points based on difficulty level and how many questions were answered correctly. The points accumulate to make the students eligible for a number of prizes (Carter, 1996). AR's management system allows teachers to create reports to track students' progress, number of books read, number of questions answered correctly, and number of points earned (Briggs & Clark, 1997).

According to AR providers, teachers can be fairly sure that students have read and basically comprehended the story with AR test products. AR provides continuous assessment and accountability for literature-based reading (Paul, Vanderzee, Rue, & Swanson, 1996).

Background

One of the occasional criticisms directed at the AR system, including its related assessments, has been that use of it fosters "lower-level" comprehension of what is read. Lower-level comprehension, sometimes referred to as "literal comprehension," generally is accepted as referring to the understanding of information explicitly stated in the text. As opposed to lower-level comprehension, higher-level comprehension requires understanding as well as a use of background knowledge to make critical judgments about the text (Leu & Kinzer, 1995). Both lower- and higher-level comprehension are subsumed under a general definition of comprehension—the awareness of that which is being read and the ability to initiate strategies that help when something is not being understood (Bossert & Schwantes, 1995–1996).

Another criticism directed at the AR system centers over its use of an extrinsic reward system to encourage wide reading. While it is agreed that AR helps schools earn higher standardized test scores, some literacy specialists are concerned that these higher scores may come at a great price. Briggs and Clark (1997) maintain that AR devalues reading by rewarding students with extrinsic motivators, such as points and prizes for their reading. Supported by a fair amount of research arising from behavioral conditioning ideology, Briggs and Clark hold that a tangible reward system inhibits the students' development of an intrinsic appreciation and/or love of reading. Students, particularly those who would be struggling readers, are apt to be conditioned to read only when they can garner extrinsic rewards.

As pertains to the above-noted criticisms, providers of the AR system maintain that they are unjustified. AR developers hold that literal comprehension is important. When educators promote higher-level over lower-level comprehension, students begin to see lower-level thinking as unimportant. Higher-order skills often reflect students' backgrounds rather than their achievement so that comprehension gleaned from text is biased for experience. AR tests are less subject to bias and, therefore, all students who read the book and understand it at a basic level receive the same score (Institute for Academic Excellence, April 1999).

85 Disputing claims on the inadvisability of providing extrinsic rewards, the Institute (November, 1997) points to an experimental study completed in 1994 by Cameron and Pierce indicating that extrinsic motivators, when properly administered, actually enhance intrinsic motivation by positively affecting attitude, behavior, and interest.

90 A fair amount of research provides insights on how AR affects children in selected age groups. A five-year longitudinal study by Peak and DeWalt (1993) concluded that AR students scored higher on reading measures and had better reading attitudes than their non-AR peers. Briggs and Clark

95 (1997) showed that AR students reported reading more hours per week and checking out more library books per grading period than the non-AR students, and Vollands, Topping, and Evans (1996) showed that sixth graders who used AR and Reading Renaissance (techniques on how to

100 use AR) acquired higher scores in reading comprehension and showed greater improvements in reading attitudes. A doctoral thesis by McKnight (1992) revealed that AR effectively motivates students and helps them acquire better reading habits (cited in Advantage Learning Systems, Inc.,

105 1999), while a study reported by Briggs and Clark (1997) concluded that the more students use AR effectively, the better chance they will have of passing the Texas Assessment of Academic Skills (TAAS). Finally, a study by Topping and Paul (1999) showed that the more students practice

110 reading, the better they become. Topping and Paul concurred that the easier reading becomes for students, the greater chance they will have of spending more time reading. As students increase their reading time, they may then obtain a love for reading. A review of the literature investigating the

115 effects of AR on emergent readers yielded little, if any, insights about its effectiveness.

Purpose

The purpose of this study was to determine if AR is beneficial to the reading development of young emergent readers' comprehension. More specifically, will AR improve

120 young struggling readers' comprehension skills and attitudes so that they can more easily become true independent readers?

Method

Subjects who received AR treatment were 12 of 36 students from a rural high-need school who, after completing

125 first grade, did not meet the district DRP benchmark (a score of at least 12) for promotion. The students receiving AR had been randomly assigned to one of three different summer school classrooms. Their instructor is the first author of this article.

130 Summer school encompassing the AR program ran over a 4-week period. The children attended school 4 days per week for 4 hours a day. The 12 children examined for effects received AR treatment for periods of approximately 30 to 40 minutes a day every day, with the exception of the last day

135 of each week, when they were expected to write about their favorite AR book using a story grammar guide provided by the teacher. Specifically, the guide asked students to write about or dictate for the teacher or aide (Crawley & Merritt, 2000) the following elements pertaining to the AR book that

140 was their favorite of the week: Title, Characters, Problem, Solution.

During the first 2 weeks of AR time, the children were required to read books within their reading zone (for this study, these were levels 1.0–1.9) and take at least one AR

145 test every day. During the second 2 weeks, the level of books provided was increased, with students having a choice of books that ranged up through 2.9. A motivational bulletin board located in the classroom encouraged students to read and accumulate points. Prizes were awarded to students each

150 week based on the number of points they had accumulated. When the students were not working with AR, they received direct instruction in phonics, sight words, use of context clues (mini-book making) and math.

Whether engaged in AR testing or writing, students were

155 allowed access to the books with which they were working so that they could locate the responses to questions presented. For some students, scaffolding was provided to help them with vocabulary difficulties they encountered while reading a particular book or taking a test.

160 Finally, to help determine the specific benefits of AR on attitudes, children were administered a short survey at the end of their 4-week program. In a series of three multiple-choice items, the survey asked: What did you like best?, …second best, and…least about learning how to read this

165 summer: …taking AR test?, …playing vowel games?, …making mini-books?, …or writing?

The answers were then tabulated for the final results.

Report of Findings: Literal Comprehension

Displayed [on the next page] is a chart of the 12 students' AR comprehension scores (% received out of 100%)

170 for each of the 4 weeks. The middle and end columns provide a comparison between achievements for the first 2 weeks when book levels available were levels 1.0–1.9 and weeks 3 and 4 when choice was provided from books ranging in between levels 1.0–2.9.

175 Using a 5-point gain or loss from week 1 to week 2, it can be noted that all but two children maintained or improved their literal understandings of stories read, with only one of the children performing below the 70% level of performance often used to determine adequate silent reading

180 performance on many publicized informal reading inventories (IRIs) (e.g., Ekwall/Schanker Reading Inventory, 1993).

When students were given a choice of materials with the option of choosing books that might well be above their reading zones, five students showed a decrease in their lit-

185 eral comprehension performances, though three of these students performed at adequate levels of silent reading comprehension performance, according to publicized IRIs.

Overall, the class mean increased from 81% to 83.9% from week 1 to week 2 and from 74.2% to 76.4% from week

190 3 to 4. While the conclusions drawn from this facet of the study are limited due to the time over which children's com-

			Comprehension Scores			
Students	Week 1	Week 2	Weeks 1 & 2	Week 3	Week 4	Weeks 3 & 4
Madison	70	86.7	Increase +16.7	60	86.7	Increase +20.7
Cody	86.7	88.6	Increase +2.6	68	83.3	Increase +15.3
Jacob	88	100	Increase +12.0	80	90	Increase +10.0
Calvin	66.7	76	Increase +9.3	46.7	66.7	Increase +20.0
Melissa	44	72	Increase +28.0	80	60	**Decrease −20.0**
Shaquille	80	90	Increase +10.0	80	64	**Decrease −16.0**
Dillan G.	86.7	86.7	Same	93.3	90	**Decrease −3.3**
Dillan S.	100	100	Same	93.3	68	**Decrease −25.3**
Caitlyn	83.3	80	**Decrease −3.3**	73.3	84	Increase +10.7
Ryan	85.7	62.9	**Decrease −22.8**	47.5	68	Increase +20.5
Richard	86	80	**Decrease −6.0**	75	70	**Decrease −5.0**
Samantha	85	84	**Decrease −1.0**	93.3	86.7	**Decrease −6.6**

*Names of subjects have been changed for confidentiality purposes.

prehension at different levels was evaluated, most students seem to benefit from their experiences with AR.

195 With regard to influence of extrinsic motivators utilized in conjunction with this aspect of the study, the instructor felt that they were not harmful. When AR was not in use, students appeared to have just as much enthusiasm as they did when AR was in use. AR was seen as giving some students a "jump start" into reading books for the first time.

Report of Findings: Higher-Level Comprehension

200 To determine if AR affected higher-level comprehension, students answered four questions pertaining to story grammar elements of their favorite book each week. They were given 45 minutes to answer these questions on paper. The following chart shows how many students correctly an-
205 swered each of the four aspects of story grammar week by week.

	Week 1	Week 2	Week 3	Week 4
Title	12	12	11	11
Characters	11	12	11	11
Problem	7	9	10	10
Solution	2	4	8	7
n	12	12	11	11
n = number of students				

In order to receive a correct answer, the student must have correctly identified the particular aspect of story grammar. A correct answer is as follows: 1) Title: the correct
210 title must be written, 2) Characters: the main characters must be written, 3) Problem: at least one problem must be identified from the story, and 4) Solution: the correct solution to the problem stated must be expressed.

As the chart shows, identification of title and characters
215 (literal comprehension) of the stories they had read posed no difficulty for most of the students. With regard to identifying the problem and solution within each story (higher-level comprehension), this skill, being relatively weak in comparison to identifying title and character during the initial week
220 of the study, was improved for several of the students by the final week of the study.

Case Studies

The written drafts comparing each of two children's understandings of story grammar components for the first week as compared to the final week are displayed below so that
225 qualitative improvements in performance might be observed. Both samples reflect great strides in ability to express understanding. It should be noted here that improvements shown below reflect efforts of the instructor to promote students' story grammar understanding as well as written/oral expres-
230 sion apart from the directives and materials provided by AR.

Madison:

First Week:
All Tutus should be pink. (Title)
Emily and little g (Characters)

235 *Final Week*:
More Spaghetti I Say. (Title)
Freddy and Minnis (Characters)
Minnis won't play with Freddy because she is eating spaghetti. (Problems)
240 She got sick. From eating spaghetti.
Now Freddy is going to play (?) with spaghetti too. (Solution)

Madison began the program by being able to write only the title and half the characters. As can be seen by the above example, after 4 weeks she improved tremendously and
245 wrote to all four aspects of the story quite well, though details could have been more clear with regard to the solution.

Calvin:

First Week:
(Note: Calvin simply copied the model provided by the teacher
250 in a demonstration lesson. When asked to write his own answers to the questions, Calvin merely copied the last sentence in the book.)

Final Week:
The title is up up and away (Title)
255 The characters is a boy and girl (Characters)
They get in a rocket
They get in the car
They go back home

131

As can be noted, Calvin went from copying and not showing any comprehension at all to writing the correct title, characters, and sequence of events (with some exclusions). The book he wrote about is a simple book that has no apparent problem and solution, yet his sequencing and organization of the story were accurate.

Children's Perceptions of Instructional Materials

The survey that was administered to the children during the final week of the program provides some merit for the activities. When students were asked what part of summer school helped them most to become better readers, the majority of students chose AR. Interestingly enough, the vowel games, although played widely and enjoyed by the students, received only one vote. Most of the students indicated that AR gave them more practice reading and therefore made them better readers. Furthermore, 100% of the students put AR as one of their top two choices when asked to indicate their favorite summer school activity.

Conclusion

The findings lead the authors to conclude that AR did contribute to students' reading comprehension improvement when utilized in conjunction with other materials and teaching procedures. AR by itself is very motivating and, as with many programs, can be made even more effective when coupled with instructional directives that promote comprehension improvement—both literal and higher level. AR does accomplish its goal of giving students more reading practice time and also goes beyond the goal by increasing comprehension knowledge.

It is our feeling that AR can be beneficial if teachers are trained on how to use the program correctly and also how to supplement the program to increase higher-level thinking skills.

Limitations and Recommendations

One limitation of this study was the shortness of its duration. Only 4 weeks of data were collected. A longer period of observation may have revealed results that would be considered more reliable.

A second limitation of this study arises from the fact that it was conducted with at-risk readers. Thus, the benefits of AR cannot be generalized to a normal population.

It is recommended that consideration be given to completing the study with a heterogeneous group of first graders approximately halfway through the regular school year. It is also recommended that the element of choice of books from a wider range of reading levels be studied, with more careful attention to experimental controls.

References

Advantage Learning Systems, Inc. (1999, October). *Research summary* (Issue No. LO331). Wisconsin Rapids, WI.

Bossert, T., & Schwantes, F. (1995–1996). Children's comprehension monitoring: Training children to use rereading to aid comprehension. *Reading Research and Instruction, 35*(2), 109–121.

Briggs, K., & Clark, C. (1997). *Reading programs for students in the lower elementary grades: What does the research say?* (Clearinghouse No. CS013213). Austin, Texas: Texas Center for Educational Research. (ERIC Document Reproduction Service No. ED 420 046)

Cameron, J., & Pierce, W. D. (1994). Reinforcement, reward, and intrinsic motivation: A meta-analysis. *Review of Educational Research, 64*(3), 363–423.

Carter, B. (1996). Hold the applause! *School Library Journal, 42*(10), 22–26.

Crawley, S., & Merritt, K. (2000). *Remediating reading difficulties* (Rev. ed.). Boston, MA: McGraw Hill.

Eisenberger, R., & Cameron, J. (1996). Detrimental effects of reward: Reality or myth? *Journal of the American Psychological Association, 51*(11), 1153–1166.

Ekwall, E. E., & Shanker, J. L. (1994) *Ekwall/Shanker Reading Inventory* (Third Edition 1993). Allyn and Bacon.

Fowler, D. (1998). Balanced reading instruction in practice. *Educational Leadership, 55*(6), 11–12.

Idaho Statewide Implementation of Reading Renaissance. (1999). Madison, WI: Institute for Academic Excellence.

Institute for Academic Excellence. (1997, November). *Toward a balanced approach to reading motivation: Resolving the intrinsic–extrinsic rewards debate.* Madison, WI. (ERIC Document Reproduction Service No. ED 421 687)

Institute for Academic Excellence. (1999, April). *The design of reading practice and literacy skills assessments* (Issue No. LO334). Madison, WI.

Institute for Academic Excellence. (1999, October). *ZPD guidelines: Helping students achieve optimum reading growth.* Madison, WI.

Leu, D., & Kinzer, C. (1995). *Effective reading instruction.* (Rev. ed.). Englewood Cliffs, NJ: Prentice-Hall.

Paul, T. (1996). *Patterns of reading practice.* Madison, WI: Institute for Academic Excellence.

Paul, T., Vanderzee, D., Rue, T., & Swanson, S. (1996). *Impact of the accelerated reader.* Atlanta, GA: Institute for Academic Excellence. (ERIC Document Reproduction Service No. ED 421 684)

Paul, T. (1998). *How accelerated reader quizzes are designed* (Clearinghouse No. CS 013256). Madison, WI: Institute for Academic Excellence. (ERIC Document Reproduction Service No. ED 421 690)

Peak, J., & DeWalt, M. (1993, February). Effects of the computerized accelerated reader program on reading achievement. Paper presented at the annual meeting of the Eastern Educational Research Association, Clearwater Beach, FL.

Sterl, A. A. (1996). Controversial issues relating to word perception. *The Reading Teacher, 50*(1), 10–13.

Topping, K., & Paul, T. (1999). Computer-assisted assessment of practice at reading: A large-scale survey using accelerated reader data. *Reading and Writing Quarterly, 15*(3), 213–231.

Vollands, S., Topping, K., & Evans, H. (1996, October). *Experimental evaluation of computer-assisted self-assessment of reading comprehension: Effects on reading achievement and attitude.* Paper presented at the National Reading Research Center Conference "Literacy and Technology for the 21st century," Atlanta, GA.

Exercise for Article 20

Factual Questions

1. In the AR system, how is quantity defined?

2. According to the researchers, one of the occasional criticisms of the AR system and its related assessments is that it fosters what?

3. How many subjects participated in this study?

4. How often were prizes awarded to students?

5. What was administered to determine the specific benefits of AR on attitudes?

6. From week 1 to week 2, Jacob's percentage points increased from 88 to what value?

Questions for Discussion

7. The researchers note the controversy on the use of extrinsic motivation, which is used in the AR system. What is your opinion on this controversy? Did the lit-

erature cited by the researchers on this topic influence your opinion? Explain. (See lines 59–89.)

8. Does the chart showing increases and decreases for individual children help you understand the results? Would you be just as informed if the researchers provided only means and standard deviations for each week? Explain.

9. Do the findings convince you that AR had a positive effect on higher-level comprehension? Explain.

10. In your opinion, how important are the case studies that are reported in lines 222–264 for understanding the effects of AR?

11. Do you agree with the researchers regarding generalizing the results? (See lines 294–296.)

12. To what extent would including a control group improve this study? (See lines 299–302.)

Quality Ratings

Directions: Indicate your level of agreement with each of the following statements by circling a number from 5 for strongly agree (SA) to 1 for strongly disagree (SD). If you believe an item is not applicable to this research article, leave it blank. Be prepared to explain your ratings.

A. The introduction establishes the importance of the study.

SA   5   4   3   2   1   SD

B. The literature review establishes the context for the study.

SA   5   4   3   2   1   SD

C. The research purpose, question, or hypothesis is clearly stated.

SA   5   4   3   2   1   SD

D. The method of sampling is sound.

SA   5   4   3   2   1   SD

E. Relevant demographics (for example, age, gender, and ethnicity) are described.

SA   5   4   3   2   1   SD

F. Measurement procedures are adequate.

SA   5   4   3   2   1   SD

G. All procedures have been described in sufficient detail to permit a replication of the study.

SA   5   4   3   2   1   SD

H. The participants have been adequately protected from potential harm.

SA   5   4   3   2   1   SD

I. The results are clearly described.

SA   5   4   3   2   1   SD

J. The discussion/conclusion is appropriate.

SA   5   4   3   2   1   SD

K. Despite any flaws, the report is worthy of publication.

SA   5   4   3   2   1   SD

Article 21

The Impact of Recycling Education on the Knowledge, Attitudes, and Behaviors of Grade School Children

JEFFREY M. SMITH
Northern Kentucky University

CHRISTINE RECHENBERG
Northern Kentucky University

LARRY CRUEY
Northern Kentucky University

SUE MAGNESS
Keep Cincinnati Beautiful

PEGGY SANDMAN
Keep Cincinnati Beautiful

ABSTRACT. A pretest-posttest design measuring the effects of a paper recycling education program on knowledge and behaviors of third, fourth, fifth, and sixth graders from private and public schools was employed. Results indicate that the program improved children's knowledge, attitudes, and behaviors toward paper recycling, with greater improvements occurring in private schools and with older grade school children.

From *Education, 118*, 262-266. Copyright © 1997 by Project Innovation. Reprinted with permission.

A number of school systems have instituted environmental education programs to increase environmental awareness among their students. The primary goals of these programs are to increase environmental knowledge, instill
5 proenvironmental attitudes, and encourage proenvironmental behaviors. Many of these programs operate under the general premise that if one changes global environmental attitudes and beliefs, this change will impact a large number of proenvironmental behaviors (Bell, Fisher, Baum, & Greene,
10 1996). Unfortunately, this premise has not always been supported by the research findings (Lipsey, 1977; Fortner & Teates, 1980). While the education programs seem to enhance awareness and change attitudes, specific behaviors are weak (Diamond & Loewy, 1991). One of the main reasons
15 for this is the lack of consistency between a general attitude and a specific behavior (Bell, Fisher, Baum, & Greene, 1996). As a general rule, attitude and behavior congruency occurs primarily when a specific attitude is closely linked to a specific behavior (Bell, Fisher, Baum, & Greene, 1996).
20 Other issues of interest for environmental educators are the characteristics of the target population and the pedagogical approach of the curriculum. It has been suggested that environmental awareness education is most effective on younger preadolescent children who do not have well-
25 established environmental habits (Asch & Shore, 1975). It is also possible that a more hands-on experiential approach may be more effective in changing attitudes and behaviors than a primarily knowledge-based presentation.

This study assessed the effectiveness of a short duration
30 recycling education program that attempted to link specific environmental knowledge and attitudes towards paper recycling with the paper recycling behavior of grade school children. It was expected that students would demonstrate improved recycling knowledge, more prorecycling attitudes,
35 and engage in more recycling behaviors after experiencing the education program. Three variables that may have an impact on the effectiveness of the education program were also explored. These variables were type of school (public or private), grade level at time of presentation, and classroom
40 presentation or field trip to a landfill.

Method

Participants

The sample consisted of 349 students in grades three through six attending public and private schools in the city of Cincinnati. The recycling education program was part of an ongoing education effort sponsored by Keeping Cincin-
45 nati Beautiful. The program was presented to students in response to an invitation by the school's science curriculum faculty. Two versions of the paper recycling education program were used. The first consisted of a classroom presentation which stressed basic knowledge of how paper is
50 recycled, the need for recycling, and some suggestions as to how students can reuse paper. Version two of the program was similar to the classroom presentation but the knowledge portion focused primarily on landfill composition and included a tour of a local landfill. The classroom presentation
55 was administered to 200 students. The landfill program was experienced by 149 students.

Materials

Two forms of the knowledge measures were developed based on the program's curriculum. One form assessed knowledge of paper production and recycling and the other
60 form assessed knowledge of landfill composition and recycling. The attitude questionnaire consisted of 6 statements pertaining to paper recycling. Students indicated their level of agreement with each statement by placing a mark on a five-point Likert scale with alternatives ranging from

65 strongly agree to strongly disagree. The most prorecycling answers were worth five points and the least prorecycling answers were valued at one point. The behavioral measure consisted of a self-report account of prorecycling behaviors that the student engaged in during the past week. Prorecy-

70 cling behaviors were operationally defined as a reduction in the use of a paper (writing on both sides of the paper), reusing paper for other purposes (scrap paper), or recycling paper.

Procedure

Data were collected from September 1994 through March

75 1995. Knowledge, attitude, and behavior surveys were administered two days before or immediately prior to the education program. The questionnaires were group administered with standardized instructions. Post-knowledge measures were administered immediately following the presentation.

80 Post-attitude and behavioral measures were obtained 7–14 days after the education program.

Scores on knowledge measures consisted of the percent correct. Scores on the attitude measures were computed based on the students' level of agreement with the 6 state-

85 ments concerning paper recycling and landfill composition. Scores on behavioral measures consisted of the total number of proenvironmental behaviors that the student engaged in during the past week. These scores ranged from 0–3.

Results

Dependent *t* tests were used to test for the impact of the

90 program on each of the dependent measures. Significant differences were found for each of the dependent measures, with greater knowledge, prorecycling attitudes, and behaviors recorded after the recycling program; see Table 1.

Table 1
Pre- and Post-Recycling Program Attitude, Knowledge, and Behavior Scores

	Recycling Program			
	Pre-	Post-		
Attitudes	25	26	$t(348) = 3.46$	$p < .001$
Knowledge	40.18%	73.87%	$t(348) = 31.17$	$p < .0001$
Behaviors	.78	.91	$t(348) = 3.31$	$p < .001$

Table 2
Attitude and Behavior Change Scores as a Function of Program Type

	Program Type			
	Classroom	Landfill	$F(1,347)$	p
Attitudes	24.9	26.7	21.74	.0001
Behavior	.68	1.07	50.91	.0001

Significant differences were found for program type with

95 more prorecycling attitudes and behavioral changes occurring as a result of the landfill visit compared to the classroom discussion; see Table 2.

Intercorrelations between change scores for attitudes, behavior, and knowledge were computed for each type of pro-

100 gram. For the classroom presentation, there was a significant correlation between knowledge and behavior ($r = .16$, $p < .05$). For the landfill field trip, there was significant correlation between attitude and behavior ($r = .19$, $p < .05$). This indicates that the academic classroom presentation may have

105 changed behavior by first changing knowledge, while the behavior change associated with the field trip may have resulted from an initial change in attitude. Knowledge comparisons between classroom presentations and landfill field trips cannot be directly made due to differences in the con-

110 tent of the knowledge items for the landfill and the classroom presentations, although attitude and behavioral measures were comparable for the different programs.

Significant differences were found as a function of grade level, with 5th and 6th graders having greater knowledge,

115 attitude, and behavioral changes than the 3rd and 4th graders; see Table 3.

Table 3
Attitude, Knowledge, and Behavior Change Scores as a Function of Grade Level

	Grade Level			
	3rd & 4th	5th & 6th	$F(1,347)$	p
Attitudes	24.8	26.6	26.97	.0001
Behavior	.66	1.05	51.59	.0001
Knowledge	47.42	67.26	178.96	.0001

Table 4
Attitude, Knowledge, and Behavior Change Scores as a Function of School Type

	School			
	Private	Public	$F(1.347)$	p
Attitudes	26.9	24.88	31.11	.0001
Behavior	1.01	.74	22.24	.0001
Knowledge	66.5	51.14	83.50	.0001

For school type, it was found that private school students had more knowledge, prorecycling attitudes and behaviors than public school students; see Table 4.

120 For private schools, attitude changes were found to be correlated with behavior change ($r = .20$, $p < .05$). This relationship was not found for public school students.

Discussion

As expected, the recycling education program signifi-cantly increased students' recycling, knowledge, created a

125 more positive attitude toward recycling, and increased the number of recycling behaviors. Given that the education program was of a relatively short duration and the large number of other influences on attitudes and behavior, the fact that a brief program produced significant differences is

130 promising. It appears that a well-constructed short-term education intervention that focuses on specific behavioral recommendations aimed at grade school children can impact behavior.

The program version differences would seem to indicate

135 that a good field trip illustrating the consequences of not recycling on landfills is a more effective way of increasing recycling behavior, while a classroom discussion lends itself more to increasing student knowledge.

The finding that older grade school children exhibit more

140 prorecycling attitude changes and behaviors than younger children indicates that there may be a critical period just prior to adolescence in which students are most amenable to the efforts of environmental educators. This would indicate

that environmental education efforts should target older grade school children for maximum benefit.

The fact that private school students exhibit more prorecycling attitudes and behaviors than public school students may reflect a broader socioeconomic difference. Although socioeconomic status was not recorded for the current sample, it appeared that the private school students tended to be more affluent and racially homogeneous.

Overall, these findings support the idea that environmental education that focuses on school-age children and closely links environmental knowledge with specific behaviors can be effective.

References

Asch, J., & Shore, B. M. (1975). Conservation behavior as the outcome of environmental education. *Journal of Environmental Education, 6*, 25-33.

Bell, Fisher, Baum, & Greene (1996). *Environmental Psychology* (4th ed., pp. 533-538). Fort Worth, TX: Harcourt Brace.

Cohen, M.R. (1973). Environmental information versus environmental attitudes. *The Journal of Environmental Education, 5*, 5-8.

Diamond, W.D. & Loewry, B.Z. (1991). Effects of probabilistic rewards on recycling attitudes and behavior. *Journal of Applied Social Psychology, 21*, 1590-1607.

Fortner, R., & Teates, T. (1980). Baseline studies for marine education: Experiences related to marine knowledge and attitudes. *Journal of Environmental Education, 11*, 11-19.

Howenstine, E. (1993). Market segmentation for recycling. *Environment and behavior, 25*, 86-102.

Lipsey, M. W. (1977). The personal antecedents and consequences of ecologically responsible behavior: A review. *JSAS Catalog of Selected Documents in Psychology, 7*, 70-71.

Exercise for Article 21

Factual Questions

1. What were the alternatives (i.e., choices) on the Likert scale?

2. What is the possible range of scores on the attitude measure (i.e., what is the lowest possible score and what is the highest possible score)?

3. What was the operational definition of prorecycling behavior?

4. According to Table 1, what was the average attitude score on the pretest?

5. Why did the researchers decide *not* to compare the knowledge scores for the two types of instructional programs?

6. On average, how many prorecycling behaviors did private school students report?

7. Did the researchers find a relationship between attitude changes and behavior for the public school students?

Questions for Discussion

8. The researchers measured prorecycling behaviors using the students' self-reports. In your opinion, is this a reliable way to measure such behavior? Are there other ways to measure it? Explain.

9. The researchers do not state how they decided which children would receive the classroom presentation and which ones would receive the landfill presentation. Would you be interested in having this information? Explain.

10. In your opinion, is the landfill program described in sufficient detail? Explain.

11. Does a correlation coefficient (r) of .16 represent a strong relationship? (See lines 100–102.) Explain.

12. Would the study be stronger if it had included a control group that did not receive any recycling program? Why? Why not?

13. Do you agree that this research is "promising"? (See lines 126–130.)

14. To what population(s), if any, would you be willing to generalize the results of this study?

Quality Ratings

Directions: Indicate your level of agreement with each of the following statements by circling a number from 5 for strongly agree (SA) to 1 for strongly disagree (SD). If you believe an item is not applicable to this research article, leave it blank. Be prepared to explain your ratings.

A. The introduction establishes the importance of the study.

SA 5 4 3 2 1 SD

B. The literature review establishes the context for the study.

SA 5 4 3 2 1 SD

C. The research purpose, question, or hypothesis is clearly stated.

SA 5 4 3 2 1 SD

D. The method of sampling is sound.

SA 5 4 3 2 1 SD

E. Relevant demographics (for example, age, gender, and ethnicity) are described.

SA 5 4 3 2 1 SD

F. Measurement procedures are adequate.

SA 5 4 3 2 1 SD

G. All procedures have been described in sufficient detail to permit a replication of the study.

SA   5   4   3   2   1   SD

H. The participants have been adequately protected from potential harm.

SA   5   4   3   2   1   SD

I. The results are clearly described.

SA   5   4   3   2   1   SD

J. The discussion/conclusion is appropriate.

SA   5   4   3   2   1   SD

K. Despite any flaws, the report is worthy of publication.

SA   5   4   3   2   1   SD

Article 22

The Effectiveness of Training Teachers to Identify and Intervene with Children of Alcoholics, Abuse, and Neglect

SUSAN J. HILLMAN
Saint Joseph College

ANTHONY J. SIRACUSA
Siracusa Associates

From *Journal of Alcohol and Drug Education*, *41*, 49–61. Copyright ©
1995 by the American Alcohol and Drug Information Foundation. Reprinted with permission.

Introduction

Schools are called upon to solve many of society's problems. Children of alcoholics (COAs) and children who suffer abuse and neglect (CANs) are one such problem where schools are being turned to for help. Schools are now faced
5 with significant numbers of these youngsters in their classrooms, and teachers have limited understanding of these students' characteristics, ways to work with them in the classroom, and any required legal responsibilities.

According to the National Institute on Alcohol Abuse
10 and Alcoholism, estimates indicate that one out of five children in classrooms is a child from an alcoholic family (as cited in Robinson, 1990). Many more children who are the offspring of parents who use drugs are coming into the classroom. The National Institute on Drug Abuse estimated in
15 1990 that six million women of childbearing age use illegal drugs, with at least a million using cocaine (Office of Inspector General, 1990). Therefore, having children in school from drug- or alcohol-involved families is common.

Prevalent, too, are the increasing numbers of children
20 who are abused or neglected. Sedlak (1990) reports that the revised Second National Incidence Study of Child Abuse and Neglect shows that there were 931,000 reported cases of child abuse and neglect across the country. This figure represents a 49% increase in all forms of abuse since the last
25 incidence study in 1980. Physical abuse increased by 35%, and sexual abuse was up by 178%.

Many situations involving abuse or neglect may occur within a family evidencing substance abuse (Milner & Chilamkurti, 1991). Hillbrand, Foster, and Hirt (1991) have as-
30 sociated alcohol abuse with an increased risk of physical and sexual victimization within the family. In a slightly earlier study, it was found that alcohol had been reported to be used in 60% of known child abuse cases (Scheitlin, 1990). Child neglect is even more prevalent in families where one or both
35 parents are abusing alcohol (O'Rourke, 1990).

These statistics reflect that in all classrooms across the country, children of alcoholics and children who have been abused and/or neglected will be present. The reactions of these children to their family environments will differ. Some
40 will be cooperative or perhaps be overachievers while trying to compensate for their home life; others will be disruptive or inattentive as they cope as best they can (Robinson, 1989). In reality, all are at high risk given that developmental difficulties including learning disabilities, and behavioral
45 and emotional problems are common. Molnar and Gliszczinski (1983) have reported that 25% of abused children and 64% of the neglected children in their study demonstrated a delay in motor development, while 39% of the abused children and 72% of the neglected children had problems in lan-
50 guage development.

Since the child protection and foster care systems are overburdened (Kinscherff & Kelly, 1991), these children's needs must be attended to as they remain living with parental alcoholism and abuse. What could or should teachers be
55 called upon to do?

Teachers are in a unique position to identify children who are from families who abuse alcohol and/or maltreat their children. Since teachers and other school staff generally have a long-term relationship with these children, the school
60 setting is an ecologically natural place in the child's environment to respond to a child's maltreatment. In cases of abuse and neglect, teachers not only have the opportunity to intervene, but they have a legal mandate to report suspected situations. However, teachers and school personnel do not
65 report cases of abuse at a frequency that would reflect the degree of contact they have with children.

In a study conducted by the American Association for Protecting Children (1988), findings indicate that 57% of the abuse and neglect cases reported in 1986 involved children
70 of school age. However, only 16.3% of the reports for those cases originated from school personnel. The revised incidence study (Sedlak, 1990) shows that teacher reporting was up to 24% for school-age children, still a low figure. In an effort to understand why teachers underreport abuse and
75 neglect, a National Teacher Survey (NTS) was conducted (as cited in Casey, 1990). The NTS was based on a national sample of 1,694 elementary and middle school teachers to which 575 teachers responded. Teachers reported that they received little pre- or inservice training on identifying, re-
80 porting, and intervening in suspected cases of abuse and

138

neglect. Sixty-six percent of the teachers who have received training believed that the training they received was not sufficient. Although 90% stated that they reported suspected cases, a high number in light of the American Association for Protecting Children research, these reports were typically made to the principal or school social worker. Only about 23% actually made a report to the local child protective service as mandated by law, a number consistent with findings of the national incidence study.

Several factors prevent teachers from becoming more involved in child maltreatment, according to the NTS respondents: lack of adequate knowledge about child abuse, ramifications of reporting such as fear of reprisals against the child or the teacher, predicted damage to the parent-teacher or teacher-student relationship, and perceived lack of community or school support in making the allegations. Although the NTS goes on to recommend that teachers need better training in this area and must learn how to work with victims of abuse who are in our classrooms, little systematic training goes on.

Therein lies the purpose of this study. Pre- and inservice teachers were given the opportunity to learn more about children who come from families who abuse alcohol, and children from families who abuse and neglect. The investigation sought to determine if, after a specialized training for educators, teacher knowledge increased to help them identify these children, whether they understood their legal obligations, and if they could articulate more ways that they would use to effectively work with these children in their classrooms.

In an effort to answer the aforementioned questions regarding teacher knowledge and practice in identifying children in this population, three studies were conducted. Study I involved assessing student teachers who had just completed their training to obtain baseline data on knowledge and practice without any targeted training. In the second study, preservice teachers were assessed on their knowledge and practice prior to and following a training workshop. Finally, Study III replicated Study II but was completed with experienced teachers.

In all three studies, indicators of COAs and CANs were categorized into four groups: physical, behavioral, psychological, and other. Physical indicators were those that were identified as observable and involved the child's appearance. Some examples included skin or bone injuries or lack of attention to physical care such as inappropriate clothing for cold weather.

Behavioral indicators were observable and involved actions by the child which fell outside the range of acceptability. For example, acting out or physically withdrawing from the class would fall under this category. Psychological indicators reflected the emotional, internal state of the child. A child being identified as hostile, angry, and/or having low self-esteem would reflect the use of psychological indicators. Within the present studies, respondents also used "other" indicators that did not fit easily within the parameters of the three categories of physical, behavioral, or psychological indicators. This "other" category included the child disclosing information concerning abuse, poor academic performance, or extensive knowledge of alcohol or sex.

Study I

Method

Subjects. Fifty-one student teachers from a private, urban college and a public, rural, state college were utilized in Study I. The majority of the preservice teachers had just completed their student teaching in an elementary school setting, but preschool, high school, and special education also were represented. Twenty-nine of the student teachers had no prior classroom experience, and twenty-two had assisted in day care centers or had served as teacher assistants in various school settings.

Instruments and Procedure. All subjects were administered the "Pre-service Teacher Survey" (PTS). The PTS sought information on the respondents' knowledge base concerning how to identify and intervene with COAs and CANs. Their predicted incidence of these children at risk within their student teaching classroom was obtained, in addition to preservice teacher demographics.

Results and Discussion

Findings indicate that 69% of the preservice teachers had suspicions of COAs and CANs in their student teaching classrooms. They identified suspected cases utilizing behavior indicators 57% of the time. The other categorical type of indicator used even with slightly greater frequency, 60% of the time, was one labeled "other." This category did not focus on the student teachers' ability to identify, but instead was based on the child self-disclosing information or the supervising teacher informing the preservice teacher. Physical and psychological indicators also were reported but with much less frequency.

When asked in general how they would identify COAs and CANs within future classrooms, the student teachers depended most consistently on behavior indicators such as "acting-out," "disruptive," "apprehensive of adult contact" (see Table 1). Physical indicators were most readily used when attempting to identify physically abused or neglected children. Psychological identifiers focusing on the emotional state of the child were rarely provided. Nearly all identifiers were negative. Little recognition of positive attributes which do exist within these populations was given.

The most common intervention which they would pursue was to report to a school official, counselor, or colleague (see Table 2). In fact, in cases of physical, sexual abuse and neglect, *all* student teachers stated that they would seek help from a school person. With COAs, the percentage drops to 65%, yet this is still a sizeable majority. Within this category of "Report to School Personnel," the most identified person was the principal and/or school counselor.

The second most common response was interventions, such as "provide a stable classroom," "build the child's self-esteem," "offer reading materials." One-third of the student teachers identified strategies that they could directly use with the student within their classrooms.

Reporting to outside authorities was the last categorical

intervention that was identified to any extent. Relating to CAN cases, approximately one-fourth of the preservice teachers said they would report to authorities. This proportion reflects the actual rate of teacher reporting behavior found in the National Teacher Survey. What is surprising is that when asked specifically about their legal obligation to report, 92.2% recognized that they must report physical abuse, 88.2% stated they would have to report sexual abuse, and 64.7% understood that they were to report neglect. Sixty-eight percent realized they were not legally mandated to report COA situations.

Table 1
Study I—Percentages of Student Teachers Identifying Indicators for COAs and CANs

	COA	Physical abuse	Sexual abuse	Neglect
Behavior indicators	65%	84%	73%	57%
Physical indicators	20%	88%	16%	61%
Psychological indicators	24%	6%	12%	10%
Other indicators	29%	16%	37%	12%
Any positive attributes	4%	4%	0%	4%

Table 2
Study I—Percentages of Student Teachers Mentioning Interventions They Would Utilize with COAs and CANs

	COA	Physical abuse	Sexual abuse	Neglect
Report to outside authorities	16%	27%	25%	22%
Report to school personnel	65%	100%	100%	100%
Go to parents	12%	6%	0%	0%
Classroom interventions	33%	33%	33%	41%

Study II

Method

Subjects. Subjects in Study II were 17 graduate students pursuing teacher certification. Many had prior classroom experience as an aide or parent volunteer. Student teaching sites ranged from urban inner-city schools to rural settings.

Instrument and Procedure. The PTS was administered within the second week of student teaching. A workshop then was conducted to train teachers to identify and intervene with COAs and CANs. The training workshop was based on a curriculum developed by the authors entitled *Children in Peril* (Hillman & Siracusa, 1992). The curriculum is composed of two modules. The first module trains educators in detecting and working with COAs. The second module focuses on teachers identifying and providing appropriate intervention strategies for CANs. The training lasted for approximately five hours.

Two months later, following the completion of the student teachers' practicum, a second copy of the PTS was administered. Chi square analyses were conducted in examining the pre- and post-test responses. It was predicted that following training the preservice teachers would increase their ability to identify COAs and CANs utilizing all categorical indicators—physical, behavioral, psychological, other. Moreover, it was hypothesized that the participants after training would propose intended interventions which

they would pursue, reflecting a variety of ways to work with these children within their classroom, and also in recognizing their legal obligation to report CAN cases.

Results and Discussion

These graduate-level student teachers were slightly weaker than the student teachers from Study I in listing indicators in initially identifying COAs and CANs (see Table 3). At the post-survey, their ability to identify indicators increased across all categories other than the psychological dimension with respect to neglect.

Several significant differences were found in the post-survey measure. With identifying physically abused children, psychological indicators were listed significantly more ($p = .0423$) than prior to training. Behavioral and physical indicators with identifying sexually abused children also were significant ($p = .0040$, $p = .0063$, respectively). In the case of identifying neglected children, other factors, such as the child self-disclosing or information from other sources, were mentioned significantly more ($p = .0307$). Caution must be taken, however, in generalizing these results due to the small number of subjects involved.

Pre-survey intervention patterns were similar to those found in Study I (see Table 4). The post-survey results reflect shifts moving toward a more comprehensive approach to intervention, especially classroom intervention. However, these shifts were not significant.

Discrepancy still is apparent, even post-training, between recognition of legal responsibility to report cases of CANs, but not mentioning reporting when asked about interventions they would implement.

Study III

Method

Subjects. Seventy experienced teachers took part in the first portion of Study III. These teachers were all from a low socioeconomic, rural school district in western Massachusetts. They taught primarily at the elementary level, including regular and special education appointments.

Forty-four of the seventy original teachers completed the post-survey portion of Study III. This reflects 63% of the original subjects.

Instrument and Procedure. The Inservice Teacher Survey (ITS) was an instrument similar to the PTS, with some demographic questions being different. It was given to teachers prior to the first module of the *Children in Peril* workshop.

The first module was presented in October and covered identification and intervention with COAs. The second module occurred in December and focused on CANs. Six months later, in June, a second copy of the ITS was dropped off to the schools to be completed. Forty-four were returned. As with Study II, chi square analyses were used to analyze the pre- and posttest responses. The predictions in this study also paralleled those in Study II. The experienced teachers would evidence an increase in their ability to identify COAs and CANs utilizing all categorical indicators—physical, behavioral, psychological, other. In addition, after training, the teachers would propose intended interventions reflecting

Table 3
Study II—Percentages of Student Teachers Identifying Indicators of COAs and CANs, Pre- and Post-Survey

	COA		Physical abuse		Sexual abuse		Neglect	
	Pre-	Post-	Pre-	Post-	Pre-	Post-	Pre-	Post-
Behavior indicators	65%	82%	65%	71%	41%	94%	53%	71%
Physical indicators	18%	24%	71%	94%	12%	59%	53%	76%
Psychological indicators	18%	41%	18%	47%	24%	29%	29%	18%
Other indicators	18%	35%	6%	12%	12%	41%	0%	29%
Any positive attributes	6%	29%	0%	6%	0%	0%	0%	0%

Table 4
Study II—Percentages of Student Teachers Mentioning Interventions They Would Utilize with COAs and CANs, Pre- and Post-Survey

	COA		Physical abuse		Sexual abuse		Neglect	
	Pre-	Post-	Pre-	Post-	Pre-	Post-	Pre-	Post-
Report to outside authorities	24%	18%	24%	65%	12%	59%	12%	59%
Report to school personnel	53%	94%	71%	71%	65%	71%	53%	71%
Go to parents	0%	12%	0%	12%	0%	0%	6%	0%
Classroom interventions	12%	47%	12%	41%	12%	41%	29%	29%

a variety of ways to work with these children within their classroom. Finally, they would recognize their legal obligation to report CAN cases.

Results and Discussion

285　Pre-survey scores on the ITS reflect a lower percentage (average of 47%) listing behavioral indicators (see Table 5), than either sample of preservice teachers (70% and 56% average respectively in Study I and Study II). Physical indicators with physical abuse and neglect were most often

290　cited, followed by behavioral indicators. Most post-survey percentages increased, with a couple of areas being noteworthy.

　One post-survey trend for COA identifiers reflects the positive attributes of this population. Some teachers appear

295　to have acquired a better understanding that children who are overachievers, who aim to please, who seek to placate may be, in fact, a COA.

　Psychological factors were significantly used to a greater extent to identify physically abused children ($p = .0187$), as

300　well as helping to identify the sexually abused child ($p = .0024$). Sexually abused children were also more readily identified through physical indicators ($p = .0251$).

　When working with COAs and CANs, teachers' most frequent response both pre- and post-survey was to bring

305　these situations to the attention of the school principal, nurse, and/or school counselor (see Table 6). Percentages were stable across the pre- and post-survey, reflecting more than half the teachers taking this direction. It is interesting to note, however, that although the majority will report to a

310　school official, this percentage is markedly less than the student teachers in either Study I or Study II.

　Beyond going to school officials, teachers having COAs in the classroom are most likely to next offer internal classroom interventions, such as "talking to the child" or "provid-

315　ing support." Although 20% more teachers in the post-survey mentioned classroom interventions for COAs, this finding was not significant. With CANs, reporting to an

external authority, such as Child Protective Services, was the next intervention listed on both the pre- and post-surveys. A

320　distressing trend, which did not seem to emerge so drastically in Study II, was the consistent lack of classroom interventions listed by the teachers for CANs. It is almost as if they relinquish their responsibility to provide for these children-at-risk, since an external agency would be involved.

325　Similar to the findings in Studies I and II, teachers here appear to understand their legal obligation to report CANs with 100% accuracy posttest. However, when asked what interventions they would use, one-third of the teachers do not list making a report.

Summary and Recommendations

330　The efficacy of the training has been in its ability to broaden identifiers of COAs and CANs for teachers. Specifically, significant findings have shown that teachers who received the training can now cite physical, behavioral, and psychological indicators more readily for sexually abused

335　children, and psychological indicators for physically abused children. A trend was found that teachers in Study III detailed an increase in positive attributes in COAs which were not present prior to training.

　Given that the training involved only five hours, the last-

340　ing effect of these changes a half year later should not be minimized. However, one must point to problem areas in the study which should be recognized. First, the attrition in Study III is a weakness. The pre-assessment was distributed to teachers prior to the training, and was subsequently col-

345　lected on the training day. The post-assessment occurred in June with the participants returning their survey to the principal's office. The attrition rate could be due to the multitude of competing tasks facing the teacher at the close of the school year. One problem with attrition, of course, is that

350　those who continue to participate may be more highly motivated. Although this is true, it should be noted that motivation aside, a broad range of knowledge levels still were reflected. In other words, teachers who indicated that they

Table 5
Study III—Percentages of Experienced Teachers Identifying Indicators of COAs and CANs, Pre- and Post-Survey

	COA		Physical abuse		Sexual abuse		Neglect	
	Pre-	Post-	Pre-	Post-	Pre-	Post-	Pre-	Post-
Behavior indicators	36%	55%	61%	57%	46%	66%	44%	59%
Physical indicators	26%	34%	79%	86%	7%	30%	84%	84%
Psychological indicators	10%	23%	9%	27%	6%	34%	6%	14%
Other indicators	26%	27%	20%	25%	23%	23%	19%	27%
Any positive attributes	7%	25%	0%	2%	0%	0%	1%	5%

Note: Pre-test *n* = 70; Post-test *n* = 44.

Table 6
Study III—Percentages of Inservice Teachers Mentioning Interventions They Would Utilize with COAs and CANs, Pre- and Post-Survey

	COA		Physical abuse		Sexual abuse		Neglect	
	Pre-	Post-	Pre-	Post-	Pre-	Post-	Pre-	Post-
Report to outside authorities	14%	14%	51%	50%	49%	55%	41%	48%
Report to school personnel	39%	45%	67%	59%	66%	61%	64%	59%
Go to parents	1%	7%	1%	2%	1%	5%	3%	7%
Classroom interventions	11%	30%	16%	16%	16%	14%	13%	18%

Note: Pre-test *n* = 70; Post-test *n* = 44.

were not sure of the indicators or what interventions they would pursue, even following the training, also returned their questionnaires. Thus, the respondents who participated in the post-assessment were not just those who were or became knowledgeable in this area. Second, this study must be seen as an examination of teachers' *intent* to intervene, and may not, in fact, translate into real behavior. The teachers are self-reporting what they would do. However, without a follow-up study observing teachers who have had the training, it cannot be determined whether the training actually translated into behavioral changes in working with COAs and CANs.

Given the implications of the aforementioned issues, the following recommendations are offered:

1. Specialized training should be provided to principals, school counselors, and nurses, since they are seen by teachers, especially beginning teachers, as the first responders to COA and CAN situations that come to the teacher's attention.

2. Training, when conducted, should encourage the development of identifiers beyond behavior indicators which the teacher seems to rely on most readily.

3. Ongoing training and support for alternative classroom interventions for teachers to work with this population should be emphasized. When possible, incorporating interventions into a child's IEP, especially when a child is experiencing a direct barrier to learning, should be followed.

4. When training occurs, follow-up studies should be pursued to determine the impact of this training on the behavior of teachers, going beyond their intent to intervene, but whether they actually implement these intentions in their classroom.

5. Additional research examining factors which impede the reporting of CAN cases should be undertaken. Teachers are able to learn about their legal responsibility to report CANs, but barriers still exist to reporting. Perhaps the additional barriers identified in the NTS study could be explored with recommendations for ways to eradicate them.

References

American Association for Protecting Children (1988). *Highlights of the official child neglect and abuse reporting, 1986.* Denver, CO.

Casey, K. (1990). Teachers and child abuse. *The APSAC Advisor, 3*(4), 6-7.

Hillbrand, M., Foster, H., & Hirt, M. (1991). Alcohol abuse, violence, and neurological impairment: A forensic study. *Journal of Interpersonal Violence, 6*(4), 411-422.

Hillman, S.J., & Siracusa, A.J. (1992). *Children in peril: A training curriculum for teachers to work with children of alcoholics and children of abuse and neglect.* Unpublished manuscript.

Kinscherff, R.T., & Kelly, S.J. (1991). Substance abuse: Intervention with substance abusing families. *The APSAC Advisor, 4*(4), 3-5.

Milner, J.S., & Chilamkurti, C. (1991). Physical child abuse perpetrator characteristics: A review of the literature. *Journal of Interpersonal Violence, 6*(3), 345-366.

Molnar, A., & Gliszczinski, C. (1983). Child abuse: A curriculum issue in teacher education. *Journal of Teacher Education, 60*(1), 105-109.

Office of Inspector General, Department of Health and Human Services (1990). *Crack Babies* (706-926 :30010). Washington, DC: U.S. Government Printing Office.

O'Rourke, K. (1990). Recapturing hope: Elementary school support groups for children of alcoholics. *Elementary School Guidance and Counseling, 25,* 107-115.

Robinson, B.E. (1990). The teacher's role in working with children of alcoholic parents. *Young Children, 5*(5), 68-72.

Robinson, B.E. (1989). *Working with children of alcoholics.* Lexington, MA: Lexington Books.

Scheitlin, K. (1990). Identifying and helping children of alcoholics. *Nurse Practitioner, 15*(2), 34-47.

Sedlak, A.J. (1990). *Technical amendment to the study findings - national incidence and prevalence of child abuse and neglect: 1988.* Rockville, MD: Westat, Inc.

Address correspondence to: Susan J. Hillman, Department of Child Study, Education and Special Education, St. Joseph College, 1678 Asylum, West Hartford, CT 06117.

Exercise for Article 22

Factual Questions

1. In which lines do the researchers first explicitly state "the purpose of this study"?

2. From what types of colleges were the subjects of Study I drawn?

3. In Study I, what percentage of the student teachers said they would seek help from a school person in cases of physical and sexual abuse and neglect?

4. In Study I, what percentage of the student teachers said they would go to the parents in cases of COA?

5. What reason do the researchers give for using caution in generalizing the results of Study II?

6. In Study III, what percentage of the original subjects completed the post-survey portion of this study?

7. In Study III, what was the most frequent intervention mentioned on both the pre- and post-survey?

8. According to the researchers, what is the "problem with attrition"?

Questions for Discussion

9. In the paragraph just before the heading "Study I," the researchers define and give examples of behavioral, psychological, and "other" indicators. In your opinion, are the definitions adequate? Are there enough examples? Explain.

10. In lines 151–157, the researchers describe the PTS. Do you think it is adequately described? Explain.

11. Is there sufficient information on the training workshop used in Studies II and III? Since you could read the book titled *Children in Peril* to obtain more detailed information, is it still desirable for the authors to provide detailed information in this article?

12. The researchers noted that the training lasted "only five hours." Do you think a future study in which the training is longer is warranted? Explain.

13. In the Summary and Recommendations section, the researchers note that they measured only the "teachers' *intent* to intervene." Do you regard this as a serious limitation of the study? Explain.

14. This study is classified as an example of "pre-experimental" research in the Table of Contents of this book. Do you agree that it is "experimental"? Explain. If yes, speculate on why it is classified as "pre-experimental" instead of "true experimental."

15. Suppose you were a member of a school board and a school psychologist recommended using the training described in this article in your school district. Assum-

ing the district had sufficient funds to pay for the training, would you vote to implement it in light of the data in this article? Why? Why not?

16. To what population(s), if any, would you be willing to generalize the results of this study? Explain.

Quality Ratings

Directions: Indicate your level of agreement with each of the following statements by circling a number from 5 for strongly agree (SA) to 1 for strongly disagree (SD). If you believe an item is not applicable to this research article, leave it blank. Be prepared to explain your ratings.

A. The introduction establishes the importance of the study.

SA   5   4   3   2   1   SD

B. The literature review establishes the context for the study.

SA   5   4   3   2   1   SD

C. The research purpose, question, or hypothesis is clearly stated.

SA   5   4   3   2   1   SD

D. The method of sampling is sound.

SA   5   4   3   2   1   SD

E. Relevant demographics (for example, age, gender, and ethnicity) are described.

SA   5   4   3   2   1   SD

F. Measurement procedures are adequate.

SA   5   4   3   2   1   SD

G. All procedures have been described in sufficient detail to permit a replication of the study.

SA   5   4   3   2   1   SD

H. The participants have been adequately protected from potential harm.

SA   5   4   3   2   1   SD

I. The results are clearly described.

SA   5   4   3   2   1   SD

J. The discussion/conclusion is appropriate.

SA   5   4   3   2   1   SD

K. Despite any flaws, the report is worthy of publication.

SA   5   4   3   2   1   SD

Article 23

Effects of Holding Students Accountable for Social Behaviors During Volleyball Games in Elementary Physical Education

CRAIG A. PATRICK
Pepper Ridge Elementary School

PHILLIP WARD
University of Nebraska—Lincoln

DARRELL W. CROUCH
Carlock Elementary School

ABSTRACT. This study investigated the effects of a semiformal accountability intervention (a modified version of the good behavior game) on the occurrence of appropriate and inappropriate social behaviors, and appropriate skill attempts during a 20-lesson volleyball unit. Participants were 67 students in Grades 4, 5, and 6. Following the collection of baseline data, students received intervention consisting of (a) differential awarding and removing of points for appropriate and inappropriate behavior, (b) public posting of team points, (c) the establishment of daily criteria, (d) a special activity for teams that met the criteria, and (e) an end-of-unit activity for teams that consistently met the criteria. A multiple baseline design across students showed that the intervention was effective in reducing inappropriate social behaviors and increasing appropriate social behaviors, but did not affect the number of correct volleyball skills performed. Results are discussed relative to task systems and social skills.

From *Journal of Teaching in Physical Education*, 17, 143–156. Copyright © 1998 by Human Kinetics Publishers, Inc. Reprinted with permission.

The promotion of socially responsible behavior in the form of moral character, conformity to social rules and norms, cooperation, and positive styles of social interaction has been a traditional and valued educational objective for American...public schools in almost every educational policy statement since 1848, being promoted with the same frequency as the development of academic skills. (Wentzel, 1991, p. 2)

Despite the implied equity between academic and social objectives in Wentzel's statement, there is a substantive difference between the number of studies that investigate academic outcomes and those that investigate social outcomes. Nonetheless, social skills are commonly investigated in several literatures, including classroom management, social competence, and fair play. In each literature, a shared objective for social skills is that students learn and apply the rules of a particular context. Because the contexts often differ, the type of social skill required varies (e.g., the skills needed to work together to complete a group assignment in a classroom are different from those needed to respond to point losses during volleyball games). Furthermore, the theoretical perspective through which social skills are viewed by a particular literature also influences the type and function of social skill observed (e.g., management versus fair play).

In the classroom management literature, the purpose of social skills is viewed primarily, but not exclusively, as contributing to classroom order by developing skills necessary to participate successfully in classroom events (Colvin & Sugai, 1988; Doyle & Carter, 1984; Soar & Soar, 1979). In physical education, several researchers have addressed the theme of what it takes to be a "member in good standing" in a class, often concurrent with their primary focus, and often from the perspective of preventative management (Hastie & Pickwell, 1996; Johnston, 1995; Oslin, 1996; O'Sullivan & Dyson, 1994). While the problem of inadequate social skills is acknowledged in physical education (e.g., Hellison, 1995; Sharpe, Brown, & Crider, 1995), there has been little effort to empirically examine efforts to remedy it.

In the social competence literature, the purpose of social skill development is to learn the rules not just of the classroom and the school, but to acquire skills that generalize beyond the classroom to other settings (e.g., home, after school, present and future work settings). It includes studies of moral citizenship and values education (Kohler & Fowler, 1985; Ostroky & Kaiser, 1995; Wentzel, 1991). In physical education, social competence studies have investigated self-responsibility for delinquency-prone youth (DeBusk & Hellison, 1989), moral development (Gibbons, Ebback, & Weiss, 1995; Romance, Weiss, & Brockover, 1986; Weiss & Bredemeier, 1986), and values education (Chen, 1996; Ennis, 1992; Wandzilak, Carroll, & Ansorge, 1988).

Though similar to investigations of social competence, the fair play literature is specific to physical education. Within the past decade, a small number of researchers have investigated social skills in the context of game play (Giebink & McKenzie, 1985; Grant, 1992; Sharpe, et al. 1995). Of particular interest are the studies conducted by Giebink and McKenzie (1985) and Sharpe et al. (1995). Giebink and McKenzie (1985), using a multitreatment reversal design (A–B–C–D–A), intervened on three behaviors during softball lessons: (a) compliment your teammates, (b) play fair, and (c) accept the consequences. The behaviors were assessed across baseline (A) and three experimental conditions: teacher instructions and praise for fair play behaviors (B), modeling of fair play behaviors (C), and a point system for fair play behaviors (D). All three interventions increased fair play behaviors and decreased inappropriate behaviors

60 when compared to baseline. The behaviors developed in softball, however, did not generalize to a new setting: recreational basketball games. Giebink and McKenzie (1985) then intervened in the recreation setting using a multitreatment reversal design (A–B–A–C) to compare baseline (A) with

65 the teacher instructions and praise for fair play behaviors (B) and the point system (C). In the recreational basketball setting, inappropriate social behaviors decreased in both experimental conditions compared to baseline levels; however, fair play behaviors did not improve in any condition.

70   Sharpe et al. (1995) used an intervention designed to teach conflict resolutions and leadership skills in physical education and reported that these behaviors generalized to regular classroom settings. The Sharpe et al. (1995) study is particularly significant because of evidence of generalization

75 of social skills to classroom settings, and because it provides an empirical validation of a social skills curriculum. At least three other social skills curricula have been developed to address the context-specific needs of children in sports: *Fair Play for Kids* (1990), *Sport Education* (Siedentop, 1994),

80 and *Teaching Responsibility Through Physical Activity* (Hellison, 1995).

    One conclusion from the above review is that unless planned for and taught by the teacher, appropriate social skills often remain underdeveloped. If one accepts that im-

85 proving social skills ought to be part of the functional curriculum, then teaching social skills becomes one of the tasks of teaching. Given this conclusion, the task system paradigm provides a useful framework to empirically investigate the improvement of social skills in education and physical edu-

90 cation in particular. Though originally derived from the classroom management literature, the task system framework has great utility as a tool for investigating dimensions of classroom life. The major task systems in physical education are instructional, managerial, and social (Siedentop,

95 1991; Tousignant & Siedentop, 1983). Within a task system, tasks are defined and maintained by the effectiveness of the accountability used by the teacher. When there is no accountability, or when it is ineffective, task accomplishment may be incomplete, or the task may be modified by the stu-

100 dent in such a manner as to change the intended outcome (Doyle, 1983). Holding students accountable for the accomplishment of social tasks is a key instructional procedure to ensure that such skills taught by the teacher are acquired by students.

105   This study was occasioned by a concern of the first author (an elementary school physical education teacher), who noted that during game play in volleyball (including applied tasks with modified rules), students in his classes were seldom encouraging and supportive of each other and that at

110 times some students behaved inappropriately. He wanted to find a proactive strategy designed not only to reduce the occurrences of inappropriate behaviors, but to increase the occurrence of encouraging and supportive behavior. After some discussion, we decided to modify an intervention

115 called the "good behavior game" (Barrish, Saunders, & Wolf, 1969) to meet the teacher's goals. The good behavior game is a group contingency that typically operates as fol-

lows: A class is divided into at least two groups, and when any member of the group misbehaves, a point is marked

120 against that group. At the end of a period of time, the group with the fewest points wins. Winning typically allowed the group members to engage in some special activity. In short, the group is held accountable for its members' inappropriate behavior. In our discussions, we decided to modify the good

125 behavior game to hold students accountable for both appropriate and inappropriate behaviors by adding points for appropriate behaviors and removing them for inappropriate behaviors. Furthermore, we decided that rather than have teams compete against each other, we would instead have

130 them compete against a daily criterion. Thus, any and all teams that met the criterion would "win."

    In classroom studies of social competence, an implied outcome of social skill improvement has often been improved academic performance (Wentzel, Weinberger, Ford,

135 & Feldman, 1990). One possible explanation for improved achievement in the classroom is that with fewer inappropriate social skills less disruption and distraction occurs, which improves the opportunity to learn. In the present study, in addition to assessing the effects of the intervention on social

140 skills, we were also interested in determining whether or not the number of successful forearm passes and overhead passes were affected as a result of the social skills intervention.

    Three experimental questions guided our investigation

145 during volleyball game play:

1. What is the effect of the modified good behavior game on the number of occurrences of inappropriate social behaviors?
2. What is the effect of the modified good behavior game
150 on the number of occurrences of appropriate social behaviors?
3. What is the effect of the modified good behavior game on the number of successful forearm passes and overhead passes?

Method

Participants and Setting

155   Participants in the study were the students enrolled in three intact physical education classes and their physical education teacher at a suburban elementary school: a fourth-grade class consisting of 21 students (12 boys, 9 girls), a fifth-grade class consisting of 25 students (11 boys, 14 girls),

160 and a sixth-grade class consisting of 21 students (11 boys, 10 girls). Parental consent for participation was obtained for all students. In addition, each student volunteered to participate in the study. The teacher was in his tenth year of teaching.

    Physical education classes were held daily for 20 min-

165 utes in Grade 4, and daily for 30 minutes in Grades 5 and 6. The lessons were conducted in half of the school gymnasium, in an area approximately the size of one basketball court (90 x 50 ft). During each of the 20 lessons in the volleyball unit, 10 minutes were allocated for game play with

170 modified rules. Students in each class were grouped into four teams of 5–6 students. The students remained in these

teams for the duration of the study. Teams typically played against each other on a rotated schedule.

Data Collection Procedures

Three classes of behavior were measured: (a) the number of appropriate social behaviors per class, (b) the number of inappropriate social behaviors per class, and (c) the number of correct forearm passes and sets per class. Appropriate and inappropriate social behaviors were further subdivided into three categories: physical acts, verbal statements, and gestures committed by students. The following list presents the behaviors, definitions, and examples of each category:

Appropriate Social Behaviors

- *Physical:* Physical contact between students that is supportive in nature or that is a response to good play (e.g., high five, pat on the back, handshake).
- *Verbal:* Statements made by students that are supportive in nature or that are a response to good play (e.g., "good job," "good try," and "way to go").
- *Gestures:* Gestures made by students that are supportive in nature or that are a response to good play (e.g., thumbs up, clapping hands following a good performance).

Inappropriate Social Behaviors

- *Physical:* Physical contact between students that is combative in nature (e.g., pushing, fighting), acts of vandalism (e.g., pulling net; slamming, kicking, or throwing the ball), acts of anger (e.g., leaving the game; nonparticipation).
- *Verbal:* Statements made by students that are discouraging or offensive in nature (e.g., "shut up," ridiculing others, arguing and/or shouting, laughing at others' mistakes).
- *Gestures:* Gestures made by students that are discouraging or offensive in nature (e.g., making faces in jest, clapping hands following a poor performance).
- *False acts:* Appropriate behaviors emitted in the absence of any play for the purpose of achieving points.

Volleyball Skills

- *Forearm pass:* With hands together, player contacts ball off the forearms, and lands inbounds.
- *Overhead pass:* With two hands, player contacts ball with fingers, and lands inbounds.

In coding an instance of an appropriate behavior, we made a judgment regarding an observed contingent relationship between the appropriate behavior and the events that preceded it. In addition, a separate subcategory labeled "false acts" was included to record instances where students used an appropriate behavior that was not contingent upon some success or effort by team members but occurred in the presence of the teacher merely to earn a point. For example, during a break in the game and as the teacher passes by, one student turns to another and says "well done."

Data were collected via videotape for a 5-minute block of the 10-minute game for all 20 lessons of the unit. "Interactions during game play" was selected as the unit of analysis because the teacher had observed the most inappropriate acts during this phase of the lesson. Two games occurred concurrently. Data collection was limited to 5 minutes of each game due to equipment limitations and also to standardize the observation interval. Data collected for appropriate and inappropriate social behaviors were limited to the sensitivity of the camera's microphone and the lens of the camera. Because of the need to capture the verbal comments of the students, the camera was placed to the side and at an angle to the court. As such, it was quite obtrusive. The school, however, was a regular site for student teachers who were supervised and videotaped by university personnel. The practice of videotaping was therefore a common event in the school and in these classes in particular. Students were informed that the camera would be used to help the teacher make judgments about their performance during the volleyball unit.

The forearm pass and overhead pass skills were selected because they represented the content of the instruction that preceded games for each class and were the most frequently used skills in the game. The physical education teacher for the class determined the criteria for correct performance of the volleyball skills.

Independent Variable

The independent variable consisted of five components. Each will be discussed in turn.

Differential Awarding and Removing of Points. During the 10 minutes of game play, the teacher moved between the two games and awarded points to teams when members demonstrated appropriate behaviors. Points were removed from the team score if the teacher observed instances of inappropriate behavior. A "false act" also resulted in a lost point.

Public Posting of Team Points. During scheduled breaks in the game, students recorded the points that were awarded for appropriate behavior and/or lost due to inappropriate behavior on a wall poster under their team name.

The Establishment of Daily Point Criteria. At the beginning of each class, the teacher established a criterion for each group to meet or exceed during the daily game. On the first day of the intervention, the teacher established a criterion that was 10 times that of the teams' baseline. With the exception of the first day of the intervention, teams were required to meet or exceed the previous day's performance, or a criterion established by the teacher in the case of an occasion where there were an exceptional number of points accrued on the previous day.

Daily Special Activity. Teams that met the daily criterion played an additional 3 minutes of game play each lesson. Teams that did not meet the criterion were not awarded the special game time. Any and all teams that met the criterion were awarded the special game time.

Special End-of-Unit Activity. A special end-of-unit lunchtime game was provided for the two (or more, if they were equal) teams in each class that met the daily criterion most often. Thus, though a team may have exceeded the criterion each day, in order to participate in this lunchtime

game, the criterion had to be consistently met over the dura-
280 tion of the unit of instruction.

Experimental Design and Procedure

A multiple baseline design across classes (Cooper, Heron, & Heward, 1987) was used to assess the efficacy of the modified good behavior game in holding students accountable for the targeted social behaviors. In single-subject
285 designs, judgments about internal validity are made on the basis of visual analysis of changes in the data as a consequence of changing experimental conditions (which includes the removal or introduction of a baseline). The multiple baseline design uses a time-lagged strategy to assess internal
290 validity when changes in the data path (level and trend) plotted on the first tier occur at the point of intervention, without changes occurring in the underlying tiers. This effect, when reproduced in Tier 2, and in particular in Tier 3, increases confidence that changes in the dependent variable are in fact
295 due to the presence of the independent variable (see Cooper et al., 1987, for a more detailed explanation).

Baseline. During baseline, students played the game of volleyball.

Intervention. On Day 1 of the intervention, the teacher
300 took 10–15 minutes to (a) explain the rules of the good behavior game, (b) have the students put the poster on the wall with their team names marked on it, (c) allow a short rehearsal where the teacher awarded points for good behavior, and (d) establish the daily criterion. Later during that lesson
305 and for the remainder of the unit, points were awarded or removed contingent upon the targeted behaviors during game play. Due to the time-lagged strategy of the multiple baseline design, Grade 5 received the intervention first, followed by Grade 4 and then Grade 6. We made the decision
310 to intervene in this order based on the stability and trend of the data paths of each class.

Interobserver Agreement

Judgments of correct and incorrect performance of volleyball skills made by the teacher were compared to those of a second trained observer (another physical education
315 teacher in the school) to determine the percentage of interobserver agreement. The second observer was not directly involved with the study's implementation and had been trained using direct observation and video recordings to a criterion of three sessions at 80% or higher prior to the start of the
320 study. Both observers coded the dependent variables from the videotape independent of each other. Interobserver agreement (IOA) was assessed on 50% of the sessions distributed across baseline and intervention phases (typically, every other day). The IOA percentages were calculated us-
325 ing a trial-by-trial method, by dividing the number of agreements by the number of agreements plus disagreements and multiplying by 100. Mean IOA percentages for social behaviors were: Grade 5, 85% (range = 73–93%); Grade 4, 85% (range = 74–97%), and Grade 6, 87% (range = 70–
330 98%).

Interobserver agreement was also conducted on 25% of the sessions (two baseline and three intervention sessions for each class) for the correct performance of the forearm pass and overhead pass. The means for correct volleyball skills
335 were calculated similarly for social behaviors (i.e., trial-by-trial) and were: Grade 5, 93% (range = 91–95%); Grade 4, 89% (range = 81–96%); and Grade 6, 92% (range = 90–95%).

While the IOA means for social behaviors in each grade
340 lie in the mid-80s, the range of the IOAs for each grade indicate there was at least one occasion per class (in Grade 4 there were two occasions) where IOA agreement scores were in the 70s. In contrast, the IOA means for the forearm pass and overhead pass were quite high with a small range.
345 The difference in variability in the ranges and level of agreement between the IOAs for social behaviors and volleyball skills may be an artifact of the difficulty of coding the less obvious social behaviors versus the more overt volleyball skills. This problem of lower reliability for social
350 skills has been reported elsewhere (Dugan et al., 1995).

Procedural Integrity

During both baseline and intervention, in order to standardize instruction, the teacher was instructed to (a) only stop a game to deal with managerial problems (e.g., arguments over the score fights) or to allow the points accrued
355 during the intervention to be posted on the wall chart, (b) restrict his feedback, and (c) maintain his monitoring (movement around the court perimeter) of games.

Results

Four primary dependent measures (inappropriate and appropriate social behaviors, and correct and incorrect skill
360 trials) were totaled for each day and plotted. In addition, the mean and range for each variable during baseline and intervention were calculated. Also of interest, and totaled for each day, were two secondary variables: the number of false acts and the days where teams reached their criterion level of
365 points.

The first question addressed in this study was "What is the effect of the modified good behavior game on the number of occurrences of inappropriate social behaviors?" As shown in Table 1, mean baseline measures were 25, 23, and
370 25 for Grades 5, 4, and 6, respectively. During intervention, the means dropped to 3, 2, and 1. Visual inspection of the graphed data in Figure 1 indicates that the change in level was immediate and was maintained throughout the intervention for each class.

375 The second question addressed in this study was "What is the effect of the modified good behavior game on the number of occurrences of appropriate social behaviors?" Mean baseline measures for appropriate behaviors were 12, 10, and 12 for Grades 5, 4, and 6 (see Table 1). When the
380 intervention was implemented, the means rose to 102, 121, and 135. Visual inspection of the graphed data in Figure 1 indicates that the change in level was immediate and increased throughout the study for Grades 5 and 4, and was relatively stable after Day 1 of the intervention for Grade 6.

385 There were few false acts observed. No false acts were observed in Grade 5. In Grade 4, on Day 16, four false acts were committed by the same student. In Grade 6, on Day 11, two acts (by different students) occurred, and on Day 16,

Table 1
Means and Ranges for Appropriate and Inappropriate Social Behaviors

	Appropriate behaviors				Inappropriate behaviors			
	Baseline		Intervention		Baseline		Intervention	
	M	Range	M	Range	M	Range	M	Range
Grade 5	12	8–16	102	35–184	25	21–30	3	1–6
Grade 4	10	2–16	121	53–196	23	15–43	2	0–4
Grade 6	12	6–20	135	100–153	25	8–41	1	0–2

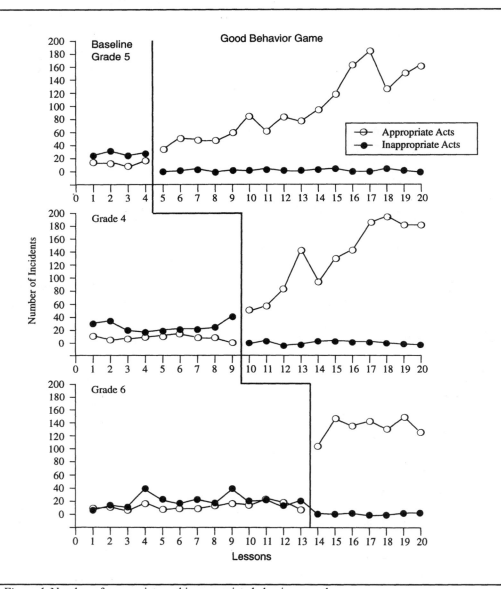

Figure 1. Number of appropriate and inappropriate behaviors per class.

one false act was observed. Data were collected on the num-
390 ber of days a team in any class did not meet its established
criterion. For Grades 5 and 6, there were no instances when
teams in either class failed to meet the criterion. In Grade 4,
there were two occasions (two separate teams) when the
criterion was not met.

395   The final question addressed in this study was "What is
the effect of the modified good behavior games on the num-

ber of successful forearm and overhead passes?" Figure 2
displays the number of correct and incorrect forearm passes
and overhead passes performed by members of each class.
400 The vertical dotted line indicates when the good behavior
game intervention occurred for each class. Changes in the
level or trend of the data at and following that point in time
would indicate that the intervention targeted on the social
behaviors influenced the volleyball skill performances as

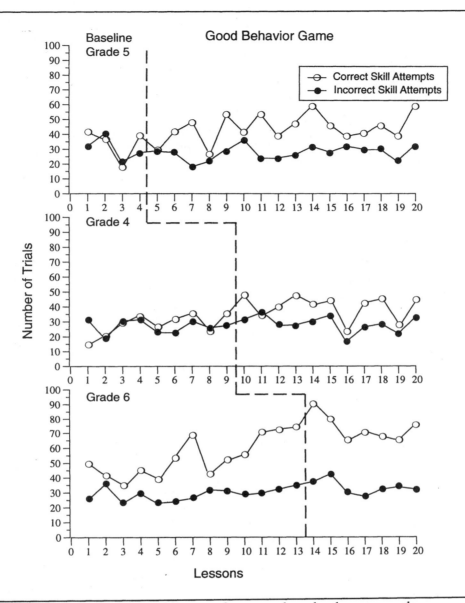

Figure 2. Number of correct and incorrect forearm and overhead passes per class.

405 well. Visual inspection of the graphed data in Figure 2 indicates that there were no concurrent changes for any of the classes at the time of the social skills intervention. Data paths for correct and incorrect volleyball skill performances maintained their trends.

Discussion

410   The results of this study show that the modified version of the good behavior game was effective in reducing inappropriate social behaviors and increasing appropriate social behaviors, but did not affect the quality of students' skill attempts. During the baseline in each class, more inappropri-
415 ate social behaviors occurred than appropriate social behaviors. This finding was also obtained by Giebink and McKenzie (1985) in both the softball and basketball settings they investigated. The finding is also consistent with the conclusions from the classroom management, social compe-

420 tence, and fair play research that suggest that appropriate social skills often remain underdeveloped unless planned for and taught by the teacher.

The good behavior game represents one strategy that can be used by teachers to teach social skills in physical educa-
425 tion. Focusing on the group rather than on specific individuals in the good behavior game allows those individuals who have fewer social skills to be in the presence of peers who can model correct behaviors and who are present at the time of an inappropriate behavior to discourage it. One possible
430 negative outcome of such contingencies is that an individual within the group may be unfairly punished by members for the inappropriate behavior if it prevents the group from achieving the daily criterion. In this study, there were only two occasions in the entire study where teams did not meet
435 their established criterion and therefore did not play in the

149

daily special event. Furthermore, no instances were observed where one member of a group was unfairly treated by other group members. One explanation for this may lie in how the criteria were established. Each teams' criterion was based on the previous day's score of that team (i.e., meet or exceed the previous day's performance) and was not a mean of the class or an arbitrary judgment made by the teacher.

Although students were not interviewed to assess their enjoyment and sense of the intervention, the teacher reported that during the intervention, the students seemed to relax and there was less pressure to do well. He suggested that this was because it was less likely that a student would be ridiculed if a bad play was made during the intervention, and because playing the game under the good behavior game conditions was fun.

The finding that volleyball skills remained unaffected by the intervention is interesting. Social competence studies suggest that social competence and achievement in classrooms may be causally related (Wentzel, 1991). If so, then improved volleyball skill performance during the intervention would have occurred concurrent with the introduction of the intervention. It did not, which suggests either (a) that the social and psychomotor response classes are unrelated (i.e., there is no causal link, as Wentzel suggests), or (b) that the baseline conditions in this study for social skills were not sufficiently "inappropriate" to influence the performance of volleyball skills. One explanation for this might be that the inappropriate behaviors deemed undesirable by the teacher and researchers did not functionally affect student achievement. Another explanation is that the intervention did not produce conditions that were positive enough to influence skill achievement. This seems quite unlikely given the level of appropriate social skills demonstrated. It is more likely that the positive environment did not influence the skill performance. Similar findings have been reported in classroom studies (Soar & Soar, 1979). Soar and Soar (l979), in their studies of classroom climates, found little difference in achievement gains in classrooms where the climate was either neutral or positive, but they found negative correlations in classrooms where the climate was negative.

The previous discussion notwithstanding, the development of social skills does not require the rationale of improved student learning. As Wentzel (1991) noted, the development of social skills and social competence as educational objectives was a component of "every educational policy statement since 1848" (p. 2). There are three challenges for researchers in the area of social skills training. First, strategies designed to improve social skill competence need to be empirically assessed. Second, such assessment should demonstrate that changes resulting from social skills training and interventions can be maintained in the setting. Third, researchers need to assess the generalization of social skills to new settings. In the present study, while the efficacy of a strategy designed to improve social skills was assessed, maintenance and generalization were not. In physical education, few studies have assessed the effects of maintenance and generalization of social skills. Giebink and McKenzie (1985) found that social skills training did not generalize from a softball setting to a basketball setting. Sharpe et al. (1995), however, did report generalization of conflict resolution skills from the gymnasium to classroom settings. These mixed findings, relative to the generalization of social skills in physical education, reflect a larger problem of generalizing social skills from one setting to another. In a review of social skills in preschool settings, the most extensively and rigorously studied setting for social skills, Chandler, Lubeck, and Fowler (1992) noted that "generalization and maintenance have been particularly difficult to obtain in applied research with peer interactions and young children" (p. 416). Future studies in physical education should try to assess the maintenance and generalization of social skills and, in particular, the generalization of social skills to classrooms and playgrounds, as well as to different units of instruction.

Framing social competence as skill development allows social skills to be viewed in the same manner as cognitive and psychomotor skills. In this study, doing so allowed social skill to be examined within the tasks systems or ecological paradigm (Doyle 1979, 1986). In this paradigm, a task, a social skill in the present case, can be treated as a dependent variable, and some form of accountability (e.g., teacher monitoring, public posting, peer mediation) can be used as an independent variable to assess and improve task accomplishment. The task systems framework has allowed researchers in physical education to investigate different dimensions of teaching and learning. For example, researchers have (a) examined the specific systems in operation in physical education (e.g., Silverman, Kulinna, & Crull, 1995; Tousignant & Siedentop, 1983); (b) examined the congruence between tasks stated by the teacher and the actual tasks performed by students (e.g., Jones, 1992; Lund, 1992); and (c) examined the ecology of the social system that operates in different physical education contexts, such as camp, dance, and sports settings (e.g., Hastie & Pickwell, 1996; Hastie & Saunders, 1990); and (d) most recently, used task accomplishment as a dependent variable and accountability as an independent variable to improve student achievement (Crouch, Ward, & Patrick, 1997; Ward, Smith, & Sharpe, 1997).

The present study's use of the good behavior game to increase socially appropriate behavior and reduce socially inappropriate behaviors extends the research on tasks and accountability in at least two ways. First, it assesses the efficacy of the good behavior game as a type of semiformal accountability. Second, the study represents an initial step toward expanding the empirical base of the task systems paradigm (specifically, tasks and accountability) into domains other than the psychomotor—in this case, the affective domain. In addition, the study represents one of a small number of studies that empirically validate strategies designed to improve social skill competence in physical education. We hope that additional research efforts along these lines will lead to other strategies that will focus on the affective domain in physical education.

References

Barrish, H.H., Saunders, M., & Wolf, M.M. (1969). Good behavior game: Effects of individual contingencies for group consequences on disruptive behavior in a classroom. *Journal of Applied Behavior Analysis, 2,* 119–124.

Chandler, L.K., Lubeck, R.C., & Fowler, S.A. (1992). Generalization and maintenance of preschool children's social skills: A critical review and analysis. *Journal of Applied Behavior Analysis, 25,* 415–428.

Chen, A. (1996). Validation of personal meaning in secondary physical education. *Research Quarterly for Exercise and Sport, 67* (Suppl.), A76.

Colvin, G., & Sugai, G. (1988). Proactive strategies for managing social behavior problems: An instructional approach. *Education and Treatment of Children, 11,* 341–348.

Cooper, J.O., Heron, T.E., & Heward, W.L. (1987). *Applied behavior analysis.* Columbus, OH: Merrill.

Crouch, D.W., Ward, P., & Patrick, C.A. (1997). The effects of peer-mediated accountability on task accomplishment during volleyball drills in elementary physical education. *Journal of Teaching in Physical Education, 17,* 26–39.

DeBusk, M., & Hellison, D. (1989). Implementing a physical education self-responsibility model for delinquency-prone youth. *Journal of Teaching in Physical Education, 8,* 104–112.

Doyle, W. (1979). Classroom tasks and student abilities. In P.L. Peterson & H.J. Walberg (Eds.), *Research on teaching: Concepts, findings, and implications* (pp. 183–205). Berkeley, CA: McCutchan.

Doyle, W. (1983). Academic work. *Review of Educational Research, 53,* 159–199.

Doyle, W. (1986). Classroom organization and management. In M.C. Wittrock (Ed.), *Handbook of research on teaching* (3rd ed., pp. 392–431). New York: Macmillan.

Doyle, W., & Carter, K. (1984). Academic tasks in classrooms. *Curriculum Inquiry, 14,* 129–149.

Dugan, E., Kamps, D., Leonard, B., Watkins, N., Rheinberger, A., & Stackaus, J. (1995). Effects of cooperative learning groups during social studies for students with autism and fourth-grade peers. *Journal of Applied Behavior Analysis, 28,* 175–188.

Ennis, C.D. (1992). The influence of value orientations in curriculum decision making. *Quest, 44,* 317–329.

Fair Play for Kids. (1990). Ottawa, ON, Canada: Commission for Fair Play.

Gibbons, S.L., Ebback, V., & Weiss, M.R. (1995). Fair Play for Kids: Effects on the moral development of children in physical education. *Research Quarterly for Exercise and Sport, 66,* 247–255.

Giebink, M.P., & McKenzie, T.L. (1985). Teaching sportsmanship in physical education and recreation: An analysis of interventions and generalization effects. *Journal of Teaching in Physical Education, 4,* 167–177.

Grant, B.C. (1992). Integrating sport into the physical education curriculum in New Zealand secondary schools. *Quest, 44,* 304–316.

Hastie, P.A., & Pickwell, A. (1996). Take your partners: A description of a student social system in a secondary school dance class. *Journal of Teaching in Physical Education, 15,* 171–187.

Hastie, P.A., & Saunders, J.E. (1990). A study of monitoring in secondary school physical education classes. *Journal of Classroom Interaction, 25,* 47–54.

Hellison, D. (1995) *Teaching responsibility through physical activity.* Champaign, IL: Human Kinetics.

Jones, D.L. (1992). Analysis of task structures in elementary physical education classes. *Journal of Teaching in Physical Education, 11,* 411–425.

Johnston, B.D. (1995). Withitness: Real or fictional? *The Physical Educator, 52,* 22–28

Kohler, F.W., & Fowler, S.A. (1985). Training prosocial behaviors to young children: An analysis of reciprocity with untrained peers. *Journal of Applied Behavior Analysis, 18,* 187–200.

Lund, J. (1992). Assessment and accountability in secondary physical education. *Quest, 44,* 352–360.

Oslin, J.L. (1996). Routines as organizing features in middle school education. *Journal of Teaching in Physical Education, 15,* 319–337.

Ostroky, M.M., & Kaiser, A.P (1995). The effects of a peer-mediated intervention on the social communicative interactions between children with and without special needs. *Journal of Behavioral Education, 5,* 151–171.

O'Sullivan, M., & Dyson, B. (1994). Rules, routines, and expectations of 11 high school physical education teachers. *Journal of Teaching in Physical Education, 13,* 361–374.

Romance, T.J., Weiss, M.R., & Brockover, J. (1986). A program to promote moral development through elementary school physical education. *Journal of Teaching in Physical Education, 5,* 126–136.

Sharpe, T., Brown, M., & Crider, K. (1995). The effects of a sportsmanship curriculum intervention on generalized positive social behavior of urban elementary school students. *Journal of Applied Behavior Analysis, 28,* 401–416.

Siedentop, D. (1991). *Developing teaching skills in physical education* (3rd ed.). Palo Alto, CA: Mayfield.

Siedentop, D. (1994). *Sport education.* Champaign, IL: Human Kinetics.

Silverman, S., Kulinna, P.H., & Crull, G. (1995). Skill-related task structures, explicitness, and accountability: Relationships with student achievement. *Research Quarterly for Exercise and Sport, 66,* 32–40.

Soar, R., & Soar, R. (1979). Emotional climate and management. In P.L. Peterson & H.J. Walberg (Eds.), *Research on teaching: Concepts, findings, and implications* (pp. 97–118). Berkeley, CA: McCutchan.

Tousignant, M., & Siedentop, D. (1983). A qualitative analysis of task structures in required secondary physical education classes. *Journal of Teaching in Physical Education, 1,* 47–57.

Wandzilak, T., Carroll, T., & Ansorge, C.J. (1988). Values development through physical activity. *Journal of Teaching in Physical Education, 8,* 13–23.

Ward, P., Smith, S., & Sharpe, T. (1997). The effects of accountability on task accomplishment in collegiate football. *Journal of Teaching in Physical Education, 17,* 40–51.

Weiss, M.R., & Bredemeier, B.J. (1986). Moral development. In V. Seefeldt (Ed.), *Physical activity and well-being* (pp. 373–390). Reston, VA: American Alliance for Health, Physical Education, Recreation, and Dance.

Wentzel, K.R. (1991). Social competence at school: Relation between social responsibility and academic achievement. *Review of Educational Research, 61,* 1–24.

Wentzel, K.R., Weinberger, D.A., Ford, M.E., & Feldman, S.S. (1990). Academic achievement in preadolescence: The role of motivational, affective, and self-regulatory processes. *Journal of Applied Developmental Psychology, 11,* 179–193.

About the Authors: Craig Patrick is with the Pepper Ridge Elementary School, Bloomington, IL 61701. Phillip Ward is with the Department of Health and Human Performance, 247 Mabel Lee Hall, University of Nebraska-Lincoln, Lincoln, NE 68588-0229. Darrell Crouch is with the Carlock Elementary School in Carlock, IL 61725.

Acknowledgments: Special thanks to Mary O'Sullivan and Bill Murphy for their comments on the manuscript.

Exercise for Article 23

Factual Questions

1. Which body of literature is specific to physical education?

2. Did all the parents grant consent for their children to participate in this evaluation?

3. How are "false acts" defined?

4. What did the students do during the *baseline*?

5. IOA stands for what words?

6. What was the mean number of inappropriate behaviors observed among the fifth graders during the baseline?

7. According to the researchers, what is the first of the "three challenges for researchers" working in the area of social skills training?

Questions for Discussion

8. In your opinion, are the definitions of appropriate and inappropriate social behaviors adequate? (See lines 182–205.) Given these definitions, do you think you could reliably observe for the same behaviors? Explain.

9. Do you think the use and placement of the camera might have influenced students' behavior? Do you think that the results of this study will generalize to other settings where a camera may not be present (i.e., will students in settings without cameras be likely to behave the same)?

10. All students in this study received the independent variable. Thus, this study does not have a traditional

"control group." However, students in different grade levels were given the treatment at different points in time (see Figures 1 and 2). In your opinion, would it be desirable to have a traditional control group under these circumstances? Explain.

11. The researchers studied the interobserver agreement (i.e., reliability). In your opinion, is it adequate? Explain.

12. The differences among the means in Table 1 were not tested for statistical significance. Despite this fact, do you think the differences are sufficiently large to be considered important? Would you characterize the differences as being "dramatic"? Explain.

13. Were you surprised that the independent variable seemingly had no effect on the volleyball skills (i.e., forearm passes and overhead passes)? Explain.

14. The researchers note that they did not interview the students to assess their enjoyment. Do you think it would be a good idea to do so in a future study? Explain.

15. Do you think there is sufficient evidence here to justify tryouts of the independent variable in elementary physical education classes in your community? Why? Why not?

Quality Ratings

Directions: Indicate your level of agreement with each of the following statements by circling a number from 5 for strongly agree (SA) to 1 for strongly disagree (SD). If you believe an item is not applicable to this research article, leave it blank. Be prepared to explain your ratings.

A. The introduction establishes the importance of the study.

SA   5   4   3   2   1   SD

B. The literature review establishes the context for the study.

SA   5   4   3   2   1   SD

C. The research purpose, question, or hypothesis is clearly stated.

SA   5   4   3   2   1   SD

D. The method of sampling is sound.

SA   5   4   3   2   1   SD

E. Relevant demographics (for example, age, gender, and ethnicity) are described.

SA   5   4   3   2   1   SD

F. Measurement procedures are adequate.

SA   5   4   3   2   1   SD

G. All procedures have been described in sufficient detail to permit a replication of the study.

SA   5   4   3   2   1   SD

H. The participants have been adequately protected from potential harm.

SA   5   4   3   2   1   SD

I. The results are clearly described.

SA   5   4   3   2   1   SD

J. The discussion/conclusion is appropriate.

SA   5   4   3   2   1   SD

K. Despite any flaws, the report is worthy of publication.

SA   5   4   3   2   1   SD

Article 24

Drug Use Patterns Among High School Athletes and Nonathletes

ADAM H. NAYLOR
Boston University

DOUG GARDNER
ThinkSport® Consulting Services

LEN ZAICHKOWSKY
Boston University

ABSTRACT. This study examined drug use patterns and perceptions of drug intervention programs among adolescent interscholastic athletes and nonathletes. In particular, it explored the issue of whether participation in high school athletics is related to a healthier lifestyle and decreased use of recreational drugs and ergogenic aids. One thousand five hundred fifteen Massachusetts high school students completed a 150-item survey that assessed illicit and nonillicit substance use. Chi square analyses revealed that athletes were significantly less likely to use cocaine and psychedelics, and were less likely to smoke cigarettes, compared with nonathletes. Conversely, nonathletes were less likely to use creatine than were athletes. There was no difference in the use of anabolic steroids and androstenedione between athletes and nonathletes. Descriptive analyses appear to indicate that drug interventions for athletes are falling short of their objectives. This study suggests that athletes have a healthier lifestyle and that the efficacy of intervention programs must be further examined.

From *Adolescence*, 36, 627–639. Copyright © 2001 by Libra Publishers, Inc. Reprinted with permission.

Drug use by athletes has made newspaper headlines, sport governing body rulebooks, and doctors' waiting rooms on a regular basis. Despite this, the relationship between drug use and participation in athletics is not yet a clear one. On one hand, it has been suggested that participation in athletics leads to a healthier lifestyle and wiser decisions about substance use (Anderson, Albrecht, McKeag, Hough, & McGrew, 1991; Shephard, 2000; Shields, 1995). Conversely, others have suggested that drug use is inherent in sports and its culture (Dyment, 1987; Wadler & Hainline, 1989). In between these two perspectives, one is left wondering if there is any difference in the substance use patterns of athletes and the general public (Adams, 1992; Anshel, 1998).

One way to begin clarifying this issue is to differentiate between recreational substances and ergogenic aids. Recreational substances are typically used for intrinsic motivates, such as to achieve altered affective states. Examples of such drugs are alcohol, tobacco, marijuana, psychedelics, and cocaine. Ergogenic substances are used to augment performance in a given domain. In sports, such drugs are typically used to assist athletes in performing with more speed and strength, and to endure more pain than normal. Examples of ergogenic aids are creatine, androstenedione, anabolic steroids, major pain medication, barbiturates, and amphetamines. The categorization of specific substances is debatable in some cases (Adams, 1992). For instance, although marijuana is traditionally viewed as a recreational substance, it recently has been banned by the International Olympic Committee for its performance-enhancing potential (i.e., lowering of physiological arousal) (H. Davis, personal communication, October 4, 1999). Similarly, amphetamines have been used for recreational purposes. Nevertheless, the attempt to label substances as either recreational or ergogenic assists in clarifying differences between athletes and nonathletes in their drug use patterns.

Recreational Drugs

It has been traditionally believed that participation in athletics leads to a healthier lifestyle and less use of recreational drugs. Increased physical activity not only creates a physically healthier person, but also may lead to changes in overall lifestyle, highlighted by "a prudent diet and abstinence from cigarette smoking" (Shephard, 2000). Some research has supported the popular notion that substance use is negatively correlated with healthful activities. In the university setting, athletes have self-reported less alcohol and drug use than their peers (Anderson et al., 1991), providing further evidence that the high-level physical and mental demands of sports are incompatible with recreational drug use. Shields (1995) indicated that high school athletic directors perceived that students who participated in athletics were less likely to smoke cigarettes, consume alcohol, chew tobacco, and smoke marijuana than were students who did not participate in extracurricular athletic activities. These findings, while encouraging, ought to be verified through confidential self-reports of high school students themselves. Nonetheless, these findings offer support for the notion that participation in sports promotes health and wellness.

Conversely, Wadler and Hainline (1989) have suggested that athletes may be more likely to experiment with recreational and ergogenic aids than individuals not participating in athletics. Physically, athletes might use recreational drugs to cope with the pain of injury rehabilitation. Mentally, stress (arising from the competitive demands of sports) and low self-confidence are issues that might lead athletes to recreational drug use. Furthermore, the "culture" of the particular sport might socialize athletes into drug use (e.g., baseball and smokeless tobacco) (Anshel, 1998). However, there is little evidence to suggest that recreational drug use is higher for athletes than nonathletes.

Ergogenic Aids

70 Unlike recreational substances, use of ergogenic aids is more likely in competitive athletic settings (Dyment, 1987). Wadler and Hainline (1989) have pointed out five instances that might lead athletes to utilize performance-enhancing pharmacological aids: (1) athletes who are at risk for not making a team or achieving the level of performance they 75 desire; (2) athletes who are approaching the end of their career and are striving to continue to compete in their sport; (3) athletes who have weight problems and are seeking a means to increase or decrease weight; (4) athletes who are battling injuries and are trying to find ways to heal quicker; and (5) 80 athletes who feel external pressure, such as from teammates, coaches, and parents, to use performance-enhancing drugs. Little research has contradicted the notion that those participating in sports are more disposed to use ergogenic aids. However, the findings of Anderson and colleagues (1991) 85 did not support the notion that there is an anabolic steroid epidemic in collegiate athletics. Although their study did not examine whether athletes more frequently use anabolic steroids than do nonathletes, Anderson et al. concluded that steroid use by intercollegiate athletes did not increase over a 90 four-year span. However, the prevalence of ergogenic aids a decade later has multiplied, with the advent of over-the-counter supplements (Hendrickson & Burton, 2000).

Educational Interventions

While the relationship between drug use and participation in organized athletics is still unclear, few disagree that 95 early identification of, and education about, drug use is necessary. Andrews and Duncan (1998) have noted that cigarette smoking that begins during adolescence proceeds to more frequent use in the two years following high school. Furthermore, onset of drug use has been found to be a major 100 determinant of adolescent morbidity and failure to perform age-related social roles (Grant & Dawson, 1998). In light of these facts, identification of substance use patterns during the high school years is important for preventing and curbing at-risk behaviors that might arise later in an individual's life.

105 Sports organizations have made it their mission to deter substance use by athletes. In 1986, the National Collegiate Athletic Association implemented a national drug education and drug-testing program for its member institutions (Anderson et al., 1991). Other organizations at various levels of 110 sports have also adopted programs to monitor and police drug use behaviors in athletes (Shields, 1995). The Massachusetts Interscholastic Athletic Association (MIAA) has initiated one such program for high school athletic programs in the state (Massachusetts Interscholastic Athletic Association, 1999). The cornerstone of this intervention is the 115 MIAA Chemical Health Eligibility Rule.

> During the season of practice or play, a student shall not, regardless of the quantity, use or consume, possess, buy/sell or give away any beverage containing alcohol; any tobacco product; marijuana; steroids; or any controlled substance.... The 120 penalty for the first violation is that a student shall lose eligibil-

ity for the next two (2) consecutive interscholastic events or two (2) weeks of a season in which the student is a participant, 125 whichever is greater. If a second or subsequent violation occurs, the student shall lose eligibility for the next twelve (12) consecutive interscholastic events or twelve (12) consecutive weeks, whichever is greater, in which the student is a participant.

It is the desire of the MIAA that this rule will not only be 130 effective during the athletic season, but lead to an overall healthier lifestyle. High school coaches and athletic directors are responsible for implementing this rule and levying punishments as infractions occur. Adams (1992) found that students favored the eligibility rule and would like to see it 135 strictly enforced. Furthermore, student athletes supported the notion of mandatory/random drug testing in high school athletics. Although drug intervention programs have been supported by both administrators and athletes, their efficacy must still be determined.

Purpose of the Present Study

140 The purpose of this study was to examine the incidence of drug use by interscholastic high school athletes, and to see if participation in interscholastic athletics is related to a healthier lifestyle, and specifically decreased use of recreational drugs and ergogenic aids year-round. Exploring possi- 145 ble differences in drug use patterns between athletes and nonathletes was a central element. This study sought to replicate previous high school drug use and abuse surveys conducted in the state of Massachusetts (Adams, 1992; Gardner & Zaichkowsky, 1995).

150 Besides the desire to update the findings on substance use habits since 1991, two other issues motivated this research. First, drug use by athletes has received a great deal of media attention. For example, the supplement androstenedione came to wide public attention during the baseball 155 season in which Mark McGwire broke the home run record. Second, the governing bodies of state high school athletics have instituted wellness programs, drug education, and specific rules to prevent drug use. This study examined descriptive data relating to the effectiveness of these rules and pro- 160 grams.

Method

Participants

One thousand five hundred fifteen students, representing 15 high schools within the state of Massachusetts, were surveyed. Male students represented 51% of the sample ($n = 773$), while female students accounted for 49% ($n = 742$). 165 Thirty-five percent were freshmen, 24.6% were sophomores, 23.4% were juniors, and 17% were in their senior year of high school. Seventy-four percent reported they had participated in one or more formally sanctioned interscholastic sports within the past 12 months.

170 The 150-item questionnaire used in this study was based on previous studies that have examined drug use patterns among high school students and student athletes (Adams, 1992; Anderson & McKeag, 1985; Johnston, O'Malley, & Bachman, 1999; Gardner & Zaichkowsky, 1995; Zaich- 175 kowsky, 1987). It included questions about students' drug

use within the past 12 months, and made "nonuse" as stringent a classification as possible. Consistent with previous studies, both recreational and ergogenic substance use was self-reported. Recreational substances included alcohol, cigarettes, smokeless tobacco, marijuana, cocaine, and psychedelic drugs. Ergogenic aids included major pain medications, anabolic steroids, barbiturates, amphetamines, androstenedione, and creatine. A final section of the questionnaire asked students to address the effectiveness of the Massachusetts Interscholastic Athletic Association's substance use rules and educational interventions.

Table 1
Drug Use Patterns Among High School Athletes and Nonathletes

	Athletes (%)	Nonathletes (%)	Total (%)
Alcohol	68.8	68.4	68.7
Cigarettes**	36.1	44.0	38.4
Smokeless Tobacco	8.0	7.7	7.9
Marijuana	37.5	42.9	39.1
Cocaine**	3.1	7.2	4.3
Psychedelics***	9.8	18.1	12.3
Creatine**	10.4	4.4	8.6
Androstenedione	2.3	2.1	2.2
Anabolic Steroids	2.5	3.4	2.8
Pain Medication	29.3	31.9	30.1
Barbiturates	3.7	6.1	4.4
Amphetamines	6.8	9.6	7.6

**Significant difference between athletes and nonathletes at the .01 level.
***Significant difference between athletes and nonathletes at the .001 level.

Procedure

Permission to conduct the study was obtained from the principals of 15 randomly selected public high schools in Massachusetts. Each principal agreed to allow between 100 and 180 students to participate in the study, and assigned a school athletic director or wellness coordinator to be the primary contact person for the researchers.

Each contact person was asked to select students who were representative of the school's gender, ethnic, and athletic demographics to participate in the study. Students were categorized as athletes if they participated on any state-sanctioned interscholastic athletic team. Upon creating the sample, the principal investigator and each school's contact person selected a class period and date in which to administer the questionnaire.

The principal investigator and two research assistants visited the 15 schools over a period of a month and a half. Students were administered the questionnaire in the school auditorium or cafeteria. They were assured that they would remain anonymous, that their responses would be viewed only by researchers, and that all information would be kept confidential. The questionnaire took approximately 30 minutes to complete.

Data Analysis

The frequencies of all variables were calculated. Descriptive statistics and chi square analyses were conducted using the Statistical Package for the Social Sciences (SPSS).

Results

Athlete/Nonathlete Differences

Chi square analyses indicated statistically significant differences between athletes and nonathletes in reported use of 4 of the 12 substances (see Table 1). In terms of recreational drugs, significantly more nonathletes than interscholastic athletes have smoked cigarettes, $\chi^2(1, N = 520) = 7.455, p < .01$. Nonathletes also reported using cocaine, $\chi^2(1, N = 59) = 11.491, p < .01$, and psychedelics, $\chi^2(1, N = 171) = 18.382, p < .001$, with greater frequency. One ergogenic aid, creatine, was used significantly more by athletes than nonathletes, $\chi^2(1, N = 115) = 7.455, p < .01$. Athletes were less likely to use marijuana, amphetamines, and barbiturates than were nonathletes, although the differences fell just short of being statistically significant.

Interscholastic Drug Intervention Feedback

The Massachusetts Interscholastic Athletic Association's Chemical Health Eligibility Rule seeks to discourage the use of recreational and ergogenic substances by high school athletes. Sixty-eight percent of the student athletes were aware of this rule (see Table 2). Thirty-eight percent reported having violated the rule; only 12% of these student athletes reported having been punished by school officials. Thirteen percent of those caught breaking the rule said they had not been punished. Seventy-one percent believed that some of their teammates had violated the Chemical Health Eligibility Rule.

Table 2
Interscholastic Athletes' Perceptions of Drug Intervention Effectiveness

Topic	Yes	No
Do you know the Chemical Health Eligibility Rule?	68%	32%
Have you violated this rule during the season?	38%	62%
Have you received a penalty if you violated this rule?	12%	88%
Have you been caught and not been penalized?	13%	87%
Have any of your teammates violated this rule?	71%	29%
Does your coach discuss the issue of drugs?	57%	43%
Would you submit to voluntary random drug testing?	48%	52%
Are you interested in drug prevention programs from the athletic department?	31%	69%

Not only does the MIAA set drug use rules for student athletes, but it also seeks to implement intervention programs. Fifty-seven percent of the athletes stated that their coaches further this mission by discussing the issue of drug use and abuse. Thirty-one percent of the athletes expressed interest in drug education programs provided by the athletic department, while 48% stated that they would submit to random drug testing.

Discussion

The results of this study appear to reflect current trends in substance use by high school students when compared with national averages (see Johnson et al., 1999). One encouraging finding was that cigarette smoking in Massachusetts was lower than national averages. Roughly 38% of the students surveyed here reported smoking at least one cigarette as compared with the lowest estimate of 51% of the adolescents surveyed by the National Institute on Drug Abuse (Johnston et al., 1999). Massachusetts has engaged in an aggressive antitobacco campaign over the last decade, which might account for this finding.

Previous research suggests three possible reasons for adolescent drug use: experimentation, social learning, and body image concerns (Anshel, 1998; Collins, 2000). Experimentation with drugs has been associated with boredom and is often supported by adolescents' belief that they are impervious to the harmful side effects of dangerous substances. Social learning theory states that individuals will take their drug use cues from others in the environment. Modeling of parents' and friends' behavior is a prime example of social learning. Last, individuals have been found to use certain drugs to improve their appearance.

Recreational Substances

It has been suggested that recreational drug use does not differ for athletes and nonathletes (Adams, 1992; Anshel, 1998; Dyment, 1987; Wadler & Hainline, 1989). The results of the present study were mixed in regard to student athlete and nonathlete substance use differences. There were no significant differences for three of the six recreational drugs: alcohol, marijuana, and smokeless tobacco.

It is clear that alcohol use is socially accepted (Bailey & Rachal, 1993; Bush & Iannotti, 1992; Reifman et al., 1998), which might explain the high percentage of students who consumed alcohol and the lack of difference in alcohol use between athletes and nonathletes. Further, the media provide opportunities for high school students to model the drinking behaviors of their professional and collegiate counterparts (Collins, 2000). Although the peer group influences the use of most substances, the culture of sports has also promoted alcohol use.

Slightly over 37% of the athletes reported smoking marijuana in the last year as opposed to about 43% of the nonathletes. This is similar to the pattern for cigarette smoking, although the difference between athletes and nonathletes for marijuana was not significant ($p < .052$). Even though marijuana and cigarettes are two different types of drugs, it seems that the athletes were more aware of the negative impact smoking any kind of substance has on athletic performance.

Conversely, the lack of conclusive difference in marijuana use may reflect the availability of marijuana, the rising social acceptability of the drug, and the desire to experiment (Johnston et al., 1999). In addition, athletes might not perceive marijuana as being as harmful as cocaine or psychedelics, and therefore may be more inclined to try the perceived lesser of two evils.

Marijuana has often been labeled a "gateway" drug to more addictive substances (Bush & Iannotti, 1992), yet the present study does not support this contention. Perhaps participation in athletics acts as a barrier to the use of more addictive substances. The significantly lower use of cocaine and psychedelics by athletes can possibly be explained by the commitment necessary to participate in high school athletics. Seasons are year-round for some athletes, and others may be multisports athletes. After-school practices and weekend competitions leave student athletes with less time for drug use/experimentation and less time to recover. Thus, organized athletics might reduce the desire of youth to indulge in more addictive and socially unacceptable drugs.

Ergogenic Aids

There was no significant difference between athletes and nonathletes for most ergogenic aids (anabolic steroids, androstenedione, pain medication, barbiturates, and amphetamines), which is a positive finding. This suggests that the culture of high school athletics in Massachusetts does not encourage widespread use of these illicit substances. However, it should be noted that the lack of differences might reflect body image issues, specifically in regard to nonathletes who take steroids. Steroids increase an individual's muscle mass, thus increasing self-confidence (Anshel, 1998). Additionally, muscle-building substances provide the opportunity for individuals to live up to societal standards for physical appearance. Similarly, amphetamines may be used to lose weight and help an individual achieve the "ideal" figure. These substances may not necessarily be utilized to improve athletic performance, but rather to help students improve their body image (Anshel, 1998).

The lack of differences for most of the ergogenic aids might further be explained by the skill level of the typical high school athlete. Wadler and Hainline (1989) have pointed out that few adolescents compete at "elite" levels. In light of this fact, there is little need for illicit performance-enhancing substances in the average high school athlete's competitive endeavors. As the competitive demands get greater and the opposition tougher, one might expect the usage levels of ergogenic aids to increase (Wadler & Hainline, 1989).

The sole difference in the use of ergogenic aids by athletes and nonathletes was for creatine, a nutritional supplement. High school athletes were more than twice as likely to use creatine than were nonathletes. The legality and availability of creatine are perhaps the greatest reasons for the higher level of use among athletes, who are likely trying to gain a competitive edge (Dyment, 1987).

Intervention

Can the differences in illicit drug use behaviors between student athletes and nonathletes be explained by interscholastic chemical health programs? While it would appear that the eligibility rule has helped in policing the substance use of interscholastic athletes, many are still unaware of this rule

or ignore it. Seventy-one percent of the athletes reported that teammates have violated the Chemical Health Eligibility Rule. Furthermore, almost 40% of the athletes admitted to having broken this rule, with 13% having not been penalized
355 after being caught. These figures bring the effectiveness of the rule and its enforcement into question. Only 57% reported that their coaches addressed the issue of substance use and abuse, which indicates that this is an educational opportunity that needs to be strengthened.

360   Educating this population is not an easy feat. A majority of the students were not interested in any further drug interventions. Over half said they would not submit to voluntary random drug testing, and 69% were not interested in drug prevention programs provided by their athletic departments.
365 These findings indicate a change in student attitudes over the last decade. Adams (1992) found that a majority of student athletes were receptive to the idea of random drug testing and additional substance abuse programming through their athletic departments. One reason for the change might be
370 that students have been saturated with drug education. Alternatively, the fact that athletes generally used fewer illicit substances than nonathletes might suggest that athletes felt they had already acquired healthful behaviors. Furthermore, recent studies have suggested that drug education programming needs to begin early (Faigenbaum, Zaichkowsky,
375 Gardner, & Micheli, 1998), and interventions aimed at high school athletes might be too late for high success rates.

Conclusion

Despite this study's large sample size, one must be cautious regarding generalization of the findings. The high
380 school and sports cultures examined here might only be representative of Massachusetts or the northeastern United States. Because the social circumstances of adolescents and their athletic participation greatly influence their substance use behaviors, more must be done to understand the social
385 climate of high school athletics.

Nevertheless, the present study suggests that participation in athletics is related to a healthier lifestyle. It also reveals that marijuana and alcohol are the two primary substances where more education and intervention are necessary.
390 sary. Furthermore, this study suggests that coaches and administrators must assess the efficacy of their drug prevention programs and their efforts to enforce rules and regulations.

Athletic activities provide many opportunities to promote healthful behaviors. Therefore, sports organizations ought to
395 assess the needs of their athletes and provide effective interventions in a timely manner.

References

Adams, C. L. (1992). *Substance use of Massachusetts high school student athletes.* Unpublished doctoral dissertation, Boston University.
Anderson, W. A., Albrecht, R. R., McKeag, D. B., Hough, D. O., & McGrew, C. A. (1991). A national survey of alcohol and drug use by college athletes. *The Physician and Sportsmedicine, 19,* 91–104.
Anderson, W. A., & McKeag, D. B. (1985). *The substance use and abuse habits of college student athletes* (Report No. 2). Mission, KS: The National Collegiate Athletic Association.
Andrews, J. A., & Duncan, S. C. (1998). The effect of attitude on the development of adolescent cigarette use. *Journal of Substance Abuse, 10,* 1–7.
Anshel, M. H. (1998). Drug abuse in sports: Causes and cures. In J. M. Williams (Ed.), *Applied sport psychology: Personal growth to peak performance* (pp. 372–387). Mountain View, CA: Mayfield Publishing Company.
Bailey, S. L., & Rachal, J. V. (1993). Dimensions of adolescent problem drinking. *Journal of Studies on Alcohol, 54,* 555–565.
Bush, P. J., & Iannotti, R. J. (1992). Elementary schoolchildren's use of alcohol, cigarettes, and marijuana and classmates' attribution of socialization. *Drug and Alcohol Dependence, 30,* 275–287.
Collins, G. B. (2000). Substance abuse and athletes. In D. Begel & R. W. Burton: (Eds.), *Sport psychiatry.* New York: W. W. Norton & Company.
Dyment, P. G. (1987). The adolescent athlete and ergogenic aids. *Journal of Adolescent Health Care, 8,* 68–73.
Faigenbaum, A. D., Zaichkowsky, L. D., Gardner, D. E., & Micheli, L. J. (1998). Anabolic steroid use by male and female middle school students. *Pediatrics, 101,* p. e6.
Gardner, D. E., & Zaichkowsky, L. (1995). *Substance use patterns in Massachusetts high school athletes and nonathletes.* Unpublished manuscript.
Grant, B. F., & Dawson, D. A. (1998). Age of onset of drug use and its association with DSM-IV drug abuse and dependence: Results from the National Longitudinal Alcohol Epidemiologic Survey. *Journal of Substance Abuse, 10,* 163–173.
Hendrickson, T. P., & Burton, R. W. (2000). Athletes' use of performance-enhancing drugs. In D. Begel & R. W. Burton (Eds.), *Sport psychiatry.* New York: W. W. Norton & Company.
Johnston, L. D., O'Malley, P. M., & Bachman, J. G. (1999). *National survey results on drug use from the Monitoring the Future study, 1975–1998: Volume 1. Secondary school students* (NIH Publication No. 99–4660). Rockville, MD: National Institute on Drug Abuse.
Massachusetts Interscholastic Athletic Association. (1999). *Massachusetts Interscholastic Athletic Association wellness manual.* Milford, Massachusetts.
Mayer, R. R., Forster, J. L., Murray, D. M., & Wagenaar, A. C. (1998). Social settings and situations of underage drinking. *Journal of Studies on Alcohol, 59,* 207–215.
Nurco, D. N. (1985). A discussion of validity. In B. A. Rouse, N. J. Kozel, & L. G. Richards (Eds.), *Self-report methods of estimating drug use: Meeting current challenges to validity* (NIDA Research Monograph No. 57, DHHS Publication No. ADM 85–1402). Washington, DC: U.S. Government Printing Office.
Reifman, A., Barnes, G. M., Dintscheff, B. A., Farrell, M. P., & Uhteg, L. (1998). Parental and peer influences on the onset of heavier drinking among adolescents. *Journal of Studies on Alcohol, 59,* 311–317.
Shephard, R. J. (2000). Importance of sport and exercise to quality of life and longevity. In L. Zaichkowsky & D. Mostofsky (Eds.), *Medical and psychological aspects of sport and exercise.* Morgantown, WV: FIT.
Shields, E. W., Jr. (1995). Sociodemographic analysis of drug use among adolescent athletes: Observations–perceptions of athletic directors–coaches. *Adolescence, 30,* 849–861.
Wadler, G. I., & Hainline, B. (1989). *Drugs and the athlete.* Philadelphia: F. A. Davis Company.
Zaichkowsky, L. (1987). *Drug use patterns in Massachusetts high school athletes and nonathletes.* Unpublished manuscript.

Acknowledgments: The researchers would like to thank the Massachusetts Governor's Committee on Physical Fitness and Sports for the grant that supported this study, and Bill Gaine and the Massachusetts Interscholastic Athletic Association for their assistance and support.

Address correspondence to: Adam H. Naylor, School of Education, Boston University, 605 Commonwealth Avenue, Boston, Massachusetts 02215. E-mail: adamnaylor@juno.com

Exercise for Article 24

Factual Questions

1. Barbiturates are classified as
   A. a recreational drug.   B. an ergogenic drug.

2. According to a study reported in the literature review, do student athletes support the notion of mandatory/random drug testing in high school athletics?

3. Male students represented what percentage of the sample?

4. Permission to conduct the study was obtained from whom?

5. What percentage of the athletes reported using cocaine? What percentage of nonathletes reported using cocaine?

6. Was the difference between the two percentages in your answer to question 5 statistically significant? If yes, at what probability level?

7. What percentage of the student athletes reported that their coaches discussed the issue of drugs?

8. Which drug often has been labeled a "gateway" drug?

Questions for Discussion

9. In this study, a relatively large number of schools (15) was represented. To what extent does this increase your confidence in the results? Explain. (See lines 161–163.)

10. The contact person at each school was asked to select students who were representative of the school's gender, ethnic, and athletic demographics to participate in the study. In your opinion, was this a good way to select the sample?

11. The students were asked to report on their drug use during the past 12 months. Do you think that this is an appropriate time interval? Explain. (See lines 175–176.)

12. The students were assured that they would remain anonymous, that their responses would be viewed only by researchers, and that all information would be kept confidential. In your opinion, how important were these assurances? Do you think that some students might still deny their illicit drug use even though they were given these assurances? Explain. (See lines 204–207.)

13. The researchers mention the northeastern United States as an area to which these results "might only be representative." Do you agree? Explain. (See lines 379–382.)

14. The researchers state that "the present study suggests that participation in athletics is related to a healthier lifestyle." Do you agree? Do you also think that this study provides evidence that participation in athletics *causes* a reduction in students' substance use? Explain. (See lines 386–387.)

Quality Ratings

Directions: Indicate your level of agreement with each of the following statements by circling a number from 5 for strongly agree (SA) to 1 for strongly disagree (SD). If you believe an item is not applicable to this research article, leave it blank. Be prepared to explain your ratings.

A. The introduction establishes the importance of the study.

   SA   5   4   3   2   1   SD

B. The literature review establishes the context for the study.

   SA   5   4   3   2   1   SD

C. The research purpose, question, or hypothesis is clearly stated.

   SA   5   4   3   2   1   SD

D. The method of sampling is sound.

   SA   5   4   3   2   1   SD

E. Relevant demographics (for example, age, gender, and ethnicity) are described.

   SA   5   4   3   2   1   SD

F. Measurement procedures are adequate.

   SA   5   4   3   2   1   SD

G. All procedures have been described in sufficient detail to permit a replication of the study.

   SA   5   4   3   2   1   SD

H. The participants have been adequately protected from potential harm.

   SA   5   4   3   2   1   SD

I. The results are clearly described.

   SA   5   4   3   2   1   SD

J. The discussion/conclusion is appropriate.

   SA   5   4   3   2   1   SD

K. Despite any flaws, the report is worthy of publication.

   SA   5   4   3   2   1   SD

Article 25

A Study of Parents of Violent Children

ELLIOTT H. SCHREIBER
Rowan University

KAREN N. SCHREIBER
New Jersey Division of Vocational Rehabilitation

SUMMARY. This study, based on in-depth interviews of 25 parents of violent children and a control group of 25 parents of nonviolent children, concerned the parents' personalities. Parents were between 22 and 48 years of age and were from middle and lower middle socioeconomic backgrounds. Differences in classification by the nonblinded interviewers of parents into the two groups on six behavior characteristics were significant on χ^2 tests. Some recommendations are made for further research.

From *Psychological Reports*, *90*, 101–104. Copyright © 2002 by Psychological Reports. Reprinted with permission.

The present study investigated the personality characteristics of parents of a group of violent children as violence has increasingly involved numerous youth in Western society (Bandura, Ross, & Ross, 1961; Hicks, 1965; Patterson,
5 1986; Schreiber, 1988, 1990; Lewinsohn, Hopps, Roberts, Seeley, & Andrews, 1993; Edelbrock, Rende, Plomin, & Thompson, 1995; Schreiber & Schreiber, 1998).

More work on and knowledge about violence is needed and also on the parents of violent children according to Lane
10 (1997), Widom (1989), and Rutter, MacDonald, LeCouteur, Harrington, Bolton, and Bailey (1990). This was recently supported by continued violence in public schools. The research of Johnson (1972), Loeber (1990), Mussen, Conger, and Kagan (1995), Feshback (1970), Lahey, Loeber, Hart,
15 Frick, Applegate, Zhang, Green, and Russo (1995), and Zimmerman (1994) on violence motivated this study to assess the relation of behavioral characteristics of parents of violent children with their children's behavior. The above references suggested the importance of six personality char-
20 acteristics of parents of violent children who were referred from public schools and compared with those of parents of nonviolent children.

Method

Sample

In the sample were 50 parents from middle and lower-middle socioeconomic classes. All the parents were between
25 22 and 48 years of age ($M = 34$ yr.). The parents gave written consent and were referred from the public schools. There were 25 parents of violent children and 25 parents of nonaggressive (well-functioning) children as controls. The children who were defined as violent had made assaultive acts
30 on people, set fires, and killed animals. Their parents were 13 Euro-American, 8 African American, and 4 Latin American families. The control group of parents included 15 Euro-

American, 7 African American, and 3 Latin American families. For three families of the former and two families of the latter, there was one maternal parent as a result of divorce.
35 One family from each group was excluded because they moved from the area ($N = 25$). The children's ages ranged from 6 to 15 years, with a mean age of 9.5 yr.

Procedure

The parents of the violent children came from five local
40 communities in which the children attended special education classes in New Jersey. These children with violent behavior were diagnosed by the school psychiatrist as having the diagnostic classifications of oppositional defiant disorder ($n = 10$) and conduct disorder ($n = 15$). One notes that eight
45 had a secondary diagnosis of attention deficit disorder. The control group of parents was selected at random from four communities in the same geographical area.

All parents were interviewed for two hours in their homes by the authors on separate visits, separated by 2 mo.
50 Each parent was evaluated on six behavioral characteristics from the literature on violent children and adolescents (Redl & Wineman, 1951; Despert, 1970; Loeber & Schmaling, 1985; Schreiber, 1988). Those personality characteristics most commonly linked to violent behavior in children were
55 abusive behavior (verbal or physical), impulsivity, immaturity, insecurity, emotionally cold, and inconsistent behavior (English & English, 1961). Differential analysis of the responses of these 50 parents was made. None of the parents was aware of the purpose of the study. The decision to clas-
60 sify each parent's responses as yes or no, that is, as indicating each personality characteristic, was made independently by each interviewer. Their decisions were made largely on the basis of predominantly positive or negative responses to single and direct questions about the behavior of the parent
65 as reflecting each personality characteristic (abusive, impulsive, immature, insecure, emotionally cold, and inconsistent behavior). Questions were repeated and explained in a consistent manner to all the parents. Examiners were knowledgeable about these participants and so were not blinded.

Results and Discussion

70 The classifications by the interviewers of the behavioral responses of all parents were tabulated and analyzed by chi square. Since frequencies of several cells were below 5, the Yates correction for continuity was applied. The results by interviewers were not made known until the end of the re-
75 search.

Table 1

Classification of Interview Responses by Parents of Two Groups on Six Personality Characteristics

Interviewer	Personality Characteristic	Parents of Violent Group		Parents of Control Group		χ^2
		Yes	No	Yes	No	
1	Abusive	18	7	4	21	17.60
	Impulsive	20	5	8	17	11.68
	Immature	19	6	7	18	11.60
	Insecure	20	5	6	19	17.10
	Emotionally Cold	19	6	5	20	17.10
	Inconsistent Behavior	20	5	4	21	22.26
2	Abusive	17	8	3	22	18.10
	Impulsive	22	3	4	21	28.98
	Immature	21	4	5	20	22.96
	Insecure	23	2	4	21	32.48
	Emotionally Cold	18	7	5	20	12.90
	Inconsistent Behavior	22	3	2	23	35.78

*$p < .001$.

Table 1 contains classifications of the interview responses, Interviewers 1 and 2, and separates parents by group. The parents' responses were assigned a "Yes" or "No" categorization on six behavioral characteristics. Chi square showed a significant difference in distribution of parents by group on all six personality characteristics ($p < .001$). More parents of the violent group were identified as showing characteristics of personality disturbance than parents of the control group on a two-tailed test.

Analysis by interviewers showed consistency regarding greater presence of disturbed behavioral characteristics in the responses of parents of violent children. The findings encourage further research with larger samples, different age groups, and varying types of population as well as involving interviewers blind to history and related matters. Research on parental discipline, attitudes, and development of violent behavior would be helpful.

References

Bandura, A., Ross, D., & Ross, S. (1961). Transmission of aggression through imitation of aggressive models. *Journal of Abnormal and Social Psychology, 63,* 575–582.

Despert, J. L. (1970). *The emotionally disturbed child.* New York: Doubleday.

Edelbrock, C., Rende, R., Plomin, R., & Thompson, L. A. (1995). A twin study of competence and problem behavior in childhood and adolescence. *Journal of Child Psychology and Psychiatry and Allied Disciplines, 36,* 775–785.

English, H. B., & English, A. C. (1961). *A comprehensive dictionary of psychological and psychoanalytical terms.* New York: Longman & Green.

Feshback, S. (1970). Aggression. In P. H. Mussen (Ed.), *Carmichael's manual of child psychology.* Vol. 2. New York: Wiley, pp. 281–291.

Hicks, D. J. (1965). Imitation and retention of film-mediated aggressive peer and adult models. *Journal of Personality and Social Psychology, 2,* 97–100.

Johnson, R. N. (1972). *Aggression in men and animals.* Philadelphia, PA: Saunders.

Lahey, B. B., Loeber, R., Hart, E. L., Frick, P. J., Applegate, B., Zhang, Q., Green, S. M., Russo, M. R. (1995). Four-year longitudinal study of conduct disorders in boys: Patterns and predictors of persistence. *Journal of Abnormal Psychology, 104,* 89–93.

Lane, R. (1997). *Murder in America.* Columbus, OH: Ohio State Univer. Press.

Lewinsohn, P. M., Hopps, H., Roberts, R. E., Seeley, J. R., & Andrews, J. A. (1993). Adolescent psychopathology: I. Prevalence and incidence of depression and other DSM-III-R disorders in high school students. *Journal of Abnormal Psychology, 102,* 133–144.

Loeber, R. (1990). Development and risk factors of juvenile antisocial behavior and delinquency. *Clinical Psychology Review, 10,* 1–41.

Loeber, R., & Schmaling, K. B. (1985). Empirical evidence of overt and covert patterns of antisocial conduct problems: A meta-analysis. *Journal of Abnormal Child Psychology, 13,* 337–352.

Mussen, P. H., Conger, J. J., & Kagan, J. (1995). Child development and personality. New York: Harper & Row.

Patterson, G. R. (1986). Performance models for antisocial boys. *American Psychologist, 41,* 432–444.

Redl, F., & Wineman, D. (1951). *Children who hate.* New York: Free Press.

Rutter, M., MacDonald, H., LeCouteur, A., Harrington, R., Bolton, P., & Bailey, A. (1990). Genetic factors in child psychiatric disorders: II. Empirical findings. *Journal of Child Psychology and Psychiatry, 31,* 39–83.

Schreiber, E. H. (1988). *Aggression and violence in human behavior.* Lexington, MA: Ginn.

Schreiber, E. H. (1990). *Abnormal behavior.* Lexington, MA: Ginn.

Schreiber, E. H., & Schreiber, D. E. (1998). Use of hypnosis with a case of acquaintance rape. *Australian Journal of Clinical and Experimental Hypnosis, 26,* 72–75.

Widom, C. S. (1989). The cycle of violence. *Science, 244,* 160–166.

Zimmerman, M. (1994). Diagnosing personality disorders: Review of issues and research methods. *Archives of General Psychiatry, 51,* 225–245.

Address correspondence to: Elliott H. Schreiber, Ed.D., 708 Camden Avenue, Moorestown, NJ 08057.

Appendix

Interview Form

1. What types of discipline do you use with your children? Please explain.

2. Do you have a great deal of patience or little patience with your children? For example, do you have a long or short fuse with the children? Elaborate.

3. Describe your personal and social relationships with the family members. Also discuss your responsibilities in the family.

4. How secure do you feel about your role with the children? Describe your feelings about yourself and your role.

5. Describe how you handle affection with your children. Elaborate on some personal experiences.

6. Do you use the same discipline techniques on a daily basis? Describe your feelings on discipline and behavior.

Exercise for Article 25

Factual Questions

1. What suggested the importance of the six personality characteristics that were examined in this study?

2. What was the mean age of the parents?

3. Who interviewed the parents?

4. Were the parents made aware of the purpose of the study?

5. How many of the parents of violent children were classified as abusive by Interviewer 2?

6. There were significant differences between the two groups of parents on how many of the personality characteristics?

Questions for Discussion

7. In lines 30–35, the researchers describe characteristics that suggest the two groups of families were similar demographically. Is it important to know this? Are there other demographics that might have been considered? Explain.

8. The violent children attended special education classes. How important would it be to know whether the control group children also attended special education classes? (See lines 39–47.)

9. The interviewers knew which parents had violent children and which did not (i.e., they were not blinded). Could this affect the validity of the findings? Explain.

10. In your opinion, does this study indicate that the six personality characteristics of parents influence the behavior of their children? Explain.

11. If you were to conduct a study on the same topic, what changes in the research methodology, if any, would you make?

Quality Ratings

Directions: Indicate your level of agreement with each of the following statements by circling a number from 5 for strongly agree (SA) to 1 for strongly disagree (SD). If you believe an item is not applicable to this research article, leave it blank. Be prepared to explain your ratings.

A. The introduction establishes the importance of the study.

SA   5   4   3   2   1   SD

B. The literature review establishes the context for the study.

SA   5   4   3   2   1   SD

C. The research purpose, question, or hypothesis is clearly stated.

SA   5   4   3   2   1   SD

D. The method of sampling is sound.

SA   5   4   3   2   1   SD

E. Relevant demographics (for example, age, gender, and ethnicity) are described.

SA   5   4   3   2   1   SD

F. Measurement procedures are adequate.

SA   5   4   3   2   1   SD

G. All procedures have been described in sufficient detail to permit a replication of the study.

SA   5   4   3   2   1   SD

H. The participants have been adequately protected from potential harm.

SA   5   4   3   2   1   SD

I. The results are clearly described.

SA   5   4   3   2   1   SD

J. The discussion/conclusion is appropriate.

SA   5   4   3   2   1   SD

K. Despite any flaws, the report is worthy of publication.

SA   5   4   3   2   1   SD

Article 26

Comic Book Reading, Reading Enjoyment, and Pleasure Reading Among Middle Class and Chapter I Middle School Students

JOANNE UJIIE
University of Southern California

STEPHEN D. KRASHEN
University of Southern California

ABSTRACT. Seventh-grade boys in two schools, one middle class and one in which 82% of the students were eligible for Chapter I funding, were asked about comic book reading. Those who reported more comic book reading also reported more pleasure reading in general, greater reading enjoyment, and tended to do more book reading. There was no difference in frequency of comic book reading between the two schools.

From *Reading Improvement, 33*, 51-54. Copyright © 1996 by Project Innovation of Mobile. Reprinted with permission.

Contrary to the view of some writers (Wertham, 1954), research shows that comic book reading does not replace other kinds of reading. Comic book readers, in general, read as much as non-comic book readers (Witty, 1941; Heisler,
5 1947; Bailyn, 1959; Swain, 1978) and the results of one study suggest they read more (Blakely, 1958). Krashen (1993) suggests that comic book reading and other kinds of light reading may serve as an important bridge from everyday "conversational" language to what Cummins (1991)
10 terms "academic language." This view is supported by studies showing that comic book texts contain more rare words than ordinary conversation does (Hayes & Ahrens, 1988), as well as case histories of readers who credit comic books with providing them with the linguistic basis for reading
15 more difficult texts (e.g., Mathabane, 1986).

To our knowledge, all previous studies of comic book reading have been done with middle class children. In this paper, we examine comic book reading in two middle schools of different socio-economic class, one middle class
20 and one less affluent, in order to determine the extent to which comic book reading varies with social class. If comics are less available for these children, it may help explain the oft-observed social class differences in literacy development (e.g., Kirsch, Jungeblut, Jenkins, and Kolstad, 1993). A sec-
25 ond goal of the study was to further examine the relationship between comic book reading, book reading, and reading enjoyment.

Method
Sample I (Chapter I): 302 seventh graders (86% of the seventh-grade class) from a middle school in a city near
30 Los Angeles provided information about their comic book

reading. Students filled out a questionnaire in their English class that probed comic book reading, book reading, amount of pleasure reading in general, and reading enjoyment. The school qualified for Chapter I funding; 82.2% of
35 the children were eligible for free or reduced-price meals; 28% of the students were classified as Limited English Proficient.

Sample II (Middle Class): 269 seventh-grade students from a middle school in a suburb of Los Angeles filled out
40 the same questionnaire as the children in Sample I. Only 30.5% of the children in this school were eligible for free or reduced-price meals. Nearly all were native speakers of English; only 3.8% were classified as Limited English Proficient. Included in the sample were 156 students enrolled in
45 a program for gifted students, and 136 "regular" students.

Results
Inspection of the data revealed that in both schools boys were much more involved in comic book reading than girls; in fact, about half the girls in both samples indicated that they never read comic books (Table 1) and very few read
50 them "always." The difference between boys and girls was statistically significant in both samples (Sample I: chi square = 64.171, $df = 2$, $p < .001$; Sample II: chi square = 9.289, $df = 2$, $p < .01$). We thus restricted our analysis to the boys, as the girls' responses would not produce enough variability to
55 reveal relationships between comic book reading and other variables.

Table 1
How often do you read comics?

	Always	Sometimes	Never
Chapter I:			
Boys	25% (35)	57% (81)	18% (25)
Girls	1% (2)	44% (71)	55% (88)
Middle Class:			
Boys	19% (26)	64% (89)	17% (24)
Girls	5% (8)	50% (77)	44% (31)

A recent survey (*Comic Shop News*, 1994) produced similar results. Out of 2,838 replies to a voluntary poll, 93.8% were from males. Readership of *Comic Shop News*
60 and willingness to respond to such a poll are good indicators of strong interest in comic book reading.

There was no significant difference in frequency of comic book reading between the two schools (chi square = 1.711, df = 2).

Comic Book Reading and Reading for Pleasure

65   For boys in both groups, more comic book reading was strongly associated with more pleasure reading (Table 2; for Chapter I, chi square = 14.922, df = 4, p < .01; for Middle Class, chi square = 18.912, df = 4, p < .001).

Table 2
How often do you read for pleasure?

	Daily	Weekly	Monthly/ Never
Chapter I:			
Heavy comic book readers	54% (19)	34% (12)	11% (4)
Occasional comic readers	40% (32)	28% (23)	32% (26)
Non-comic readers	16% (4)	20% (5)	64% (16)
Middle Class:			
Heavy comic book readers	65% (17)	27% (7)	8% (2)
Occasional comic readers	35% (31)	35% (31)	30% (27)
Non-comic readers	33% (8)	17% (4)	50% (12)

Table 3
Do you like to read?

	Yes	Only When I Have Nothing Better to Do	No
Chapter I:			
Heavy comic book readers	34% (12)	54% (19)	11% (4)
Occasional comic readers	31% (25)	54% (44)	15% (12)
Non-comic readers	4% (1)	44% (11)	52% (13)
Middle Class:			
Heavy comic book readers	62% (16)	27% (7)	11% (3)
Occasional comic readers	40% (36)	40% (36)	19% (17)
Non-comic readers	21% (5)	37% (9)	42% (10)

Table 4
Do you read books?

	Yes	No
Chapter I:		
Heavy comic book readers	49% (17)	51% (18)
Occasional comic readers	60% (49)	40% (32)
Non-comic readers	32% (8)	68% (17)
Middle Class:		
Heavy comic book readers	69% (18)	31% (8)
Occasional comic readers	71% (63)	29% (26)
Non-comic readers	46% (11)	54% (13)

Comic Book Reading and Reading Enjoyment

70   For boys in both schools, more comic book reading was significantly associated with more reading enjoyment (Chapter I: chi square = 21.196, df = 4, p < .001; Middle Class: chi square = 12.000, df = 4, p < .025).

Comic Book Reading and Book Reading

For boys in both schools, more comic book reading was associated with more book reading, with the relationship
75   falling just short of statistical significance in the Chapter I

school (chi square = 5.392, df = 2, p < .10) and reaching significance in the middle class school (chi square = 6.505, df = 2, p < .05).

Summary and Conclusions

There was no difference in frequency of comic book
80   reading between a middle class and a less affluent sample of seventh-grade boys. For both groups, those who read more comic books did more pleasure reading, liked to read more, and tended to read more books. These results show that
85   comic book reading certainly does not inhibit other kinds of reading, and is consistent with the hypothesis that comic book reading facilitates heavier reading.

Our results, however, leave us with some questions. Surprisingly, children from the Chapter I school reported just as much comic book reading as more affluent children. Comics
90   are very expensive, typically costing $1.00 to $1.50. Either these children have found a less expensive source, or, despite the cost, they are buying them, which is evidence of the attractiveness of comics.

We did not attempt to determine whether comic book
95   readers are better readers, but there is reason to suspect that they are, given the consistent relationship found in the professional literature between frequency of reading and reading ability (Krashen, 1993), and the finding that comic book readers like reading and read more.

100   We also found that Chapter I boys are not, however, reading as much in general as boys from the middle class school, nor do they enjoy reading as much. One reason this is true, we suspect, is that reading material is not as readily available to the less affluent. Despite this lack of access,
105   however, comic book readers from the Chapter I school still manage to read more than their peers, and even read more than non-comic book readers from the middle class school (e.g., Chapter I heavy comic readers read significantly more than middle class non-comic readers; data from Table 2, chi
110   square = 10.806, df = 2, p < .01). More access to books, we predict, would result in even greater differences between comic and non-comic book readers for less affluent children.

Finally, we did not attempt to determine which comic books were read. There is a large variability in the reading
115   level of comic books. *Archie*, for example, is written at the second-grade level, while some of the superhero comics are written at the fifth- and sixth-grade level (Wright, 1979). It remains to be determined whether different kinds of comic book reading relate to school environment, book reading,
120   and reading ability.

References

Bailyn, L. (1959). Mass media and children: A study of exposure habits and cognitive effects. *Psychological Monographs, 73*, 201-216.

Comic Shop News (1994). Boy, were we surprised! December 14, 1994. Marieta, Georgia.

Hayes, D., & Ahrens, M. (1989). Vocabulary simplification for children: A special case of "motherese"? *Journal of Child Language, 15*, 395-410.

Heisler, F. (1947). A comparison of comic book and noncomic book readers of the elementary school. *Journal of Educational Research, 40*, 458-464.

Kirsch, I., Jungebut, A., Jenkins, L., and Kolstad, A. (1993). *Adult literacy in America.* Washington, D.C.: U.S. Department of Education.

Krashen. S. (1993). *The power of reading.* Englewood, Colorado: Libraries Unlimited.

Mathabane, M. (1986). *Kaffir boy.* New York: Plume.

Swain, E. (1948). Using comic books to teach reading and language arts. *Journal of Reading, 22*, 253-258.

Witty, P. (1941). Reading the comics: A comparative study. *Journal of Experimental Education, 10*, 105-106.

Wright, G. (1979). *The comic book: A forgotten medium in the classroom. Reading Teacher, 33*, 158-161.

Exercise for Article 26

Factual Questions

1. To the best of the researchers' knowledge, what type of children have been used in all previous studies of comic book reading?

2. What percentage of the students in Sample I were eligible for free or reduced-price meals? What is the corresponding percentage for Sample II?

3. In the *Comic Shop News* survey, what percentage of the voluntary responses were from boys?

4. The results in Tables 2, 3, and 4 are for
A. boys only.   B. girls only.   C. both boys and girls.

5. Was the association between comic book reading and reading for pleasure for middle class students in Table 2 statistically significant? If yes, at what probability level?

6. Was the association between comic book reading and reading books for Chapter I students in Table 3 statistically significant? If yes, at what probability level?

7. The researchers characterize which result as surprising?

Questions for Discussion

8. Before reading this article, would you have predicted that boys who report more comic book reading would report more frequent reading for pleasure? Why? Why not?

9. The questions in Tables 1 and 2 ask about the frequency of reading (i.e., they both start with "How often..."). However, the two sets of choices for the items are different (i.e., "Always, Sometimes, and Never" for the question in Table 1, and "Daily, Weekly, Monthly/ Never" for the question in Table 2). In your opinion, is one of these sets of choices better than the other? Explain.

10. What is your opinion of the question and choices in Table 4? Would you have worded it as the researchers did?

11. The researchers point out that they did not attempt to determine whether comic book readers are better read-

ers. Do you think this would be important to determine in future studies? Explain.

12. Do you think it would be interesting to examine whether the two samples differed in the types of comic books they read? Explain. (See lines 113–120.)

13. What changes, if any, would you have made in the research methodology if you had been conducting this study?

14. To what population(s), if any, would you be willing to generalize the results of this study?

Quality Ratings

Directions: Indicate your level of agreement with each of the following statements by circling a number from 5 for strongly agree (SA) to 1 for strongly disagree (SD). If you believe an item is not applicable to this research article, leave it blank. Be prepared to explain your ratings.

A.   The introduction establishes the importance of the study.

SA   5   4   3   2   1   SD

B.   The literature review establishes the context for the study.

SA   5   4   3   2   1   SD

C.   The research purpose, question, or hypothesis is clearly stated.

SA   5   4   3   2   1   SD

D.   The method of sampling is sound.

SA   5   4   3   2   1   SD

E.   Relevant demographics (for example, age, gender, and ethnicity) are described.

SA   5   4   3   2   1   SD

F.   Measurement procedures are adequate.

SA   5   4   3   2   1   SD

G.   All procedures have been described in sufficient detail to permit a replication of the study.

SA   5   4   3   2   1   SD

H.   The participants have been adequately protected from potential harm.

SA   5   4   3   2   1   SD

I.   The results are clearly described.

SA   5   4   3   2   1   SD

J.   The discussion/conclusion is appropriate.

SA   5   4   3   2   1   SD

K.   Despite any flaws, the report is worthy of publication.

SA   5   4   3   2   1   SD

Article 27

Results of a School-to-Careers Preservice Teacher Internship Program

VERNON D. LUFT
University of Nevada, Reno

KIMBERLY VIDONI
University of Nevada, Reno

ABSTRACT. The purpose of this study was to determine the effectiveness of a School-to-Careers teacher education Preservice Teacher Internship Program (PTIP). Specific objectives of the study were to: 1) determine the majors of the students participating in the program, 2) determine the types of businesses in which participating students did their internship, 3) determine if students' self-perceived knowledge of School-to-Careers increased significantly from beginning to the end of the preservice teacher education internship program, 4) determine if students participating in the preservice teacher education internship program significantly increased their perceived level of application of School-to-Careers in their future teaching, 5) determine if participating students would significantly increase their intentions to incorporate key School-to-Career work-based elements into their future teaching, and 6) determine reasons why preservice teacher education students participated in the internship program.

The 12 student interns participating in the program were asked to complete a researcher-developed questionnaire during their first seminar and before any discussion or information was disseminated about School-to-Careers. They were again asked to complete the questionnaire at the completion of their last seminar. A matched-pairs *t* test was used to compare the means of pretest and posttest scores on each item of the questionnaire.

Results from this study indicate that the means increased on all questions on which a *t* test was performed; however, not always significantly. Significant changes to students' knowledge of School-to-Careers occurred in their general understanding of the School-to-Careers system, ways to apply School-to-Careers to their teaching and SCANS skills. Students showed more interest in placing emphasis on business writing in their future teaching as a result of participating in the PTIP. The greatest number of changes occurred in students' intentions to incorporate work-based learning into their future teaching. The main reason students participated in the PTIP was to learn about School-to-Careers so they may integrate key concepts into their future teaching. All of these findings indicate that the PTIP successfully helped students begin to understand the School-to-Careers system and that they intend to incorporate the fundamentals of this system into their future teaching.

From *Education*, *122*, 706–714. Copyright © 2002 by Project Innovation. Reprinted with permission.

The School-to-Work Opportunities Act of 1994 extended federal funding to states for the purpose of developing and implementing systems ensuring all K–12 students smooth transitions into high-quality employment and/or post-secondary education. Educators, both K–12 and post-secondary, play an important role in this system by integrating School-to-Work, also referred to School-to-Careers, ideals into their teaching. To do this, educators should be well informed about the School-to-Work system. Furthermore, preservice teacher education students could benefit from exposure to School-to-Careers during their teacher education program as many will graduate and begin working in schools that espouse and practice School-to-Careers principles.

During the 1999–2000 school year, the Department of Curriculum and Instruction in a mid-sized western university ran a Preservice Teacher Internship Program (PTIP) for students enrolled in teacher education programs in the College of Education. The purpose of this program was to inform prospective teachers of School-to-Careers about key concepts with the hope that they would integrate these concepts into their future teaching. Students were recruited from their teacher education classes and given applications to apply for participation in the program. Candidates were expected to complete their teacher education coursework during the fall 1999 semester and be enrolled in their student teaching internship during the spring 2000 semester. In addition, they were expected to attend a series of three informational seminars, complete a 40-hour internship in a business during the 1999–2000 semester break, and submit lesson plans used in their student teaching that demonstrated how they integrated School-to-Career concepts. Upon completion of all program requirements, students received a $600 scholarship. Fifteen students were initially admitted into the program; however, three dropped out for various reasons. A total of 12 students completed the PTIP.

The first seminar took place in December 1999. Prior to any discussion at the seminar, a survey was distributed to determine the students' existing knowledge of School-to-Careers. Following the survey, a discussion about School-to-Careers took place to help students gain an understanding of its key components. Over the semester break, students worked a minimum of 40 hours in a business and were asked to notice the skills they used at their jobs so that they may incorporate these skills into their future curriculum as teachers. In January 2000, the second seminar was held for the purpose of discussing their internships and how to integrate the knowledge gained from that experience into their student teaching. Students then embarked on their student teaching experiences in which they applied School-to-Careers con-

50 cepts into their teaching. During the final seminar in May 2000, a final survey was taken to determine any changes that may have occurred over their PTIP experience. Students also discussed how they integrated School-to-Careers into their student teaching.

Related Literature

55 A review of the literature revealed a lack of research or practice related to teacher education students working in a business setting in addition to their traditional student teaching as part of their preparation program. Studies have shown, however, that work-related learning experiences help stu-
60 dents gain valuable employment skills prior to graduation by helping students recognize the relationship between work and school. For instance, Greene (2000) investigated gains made by preservice biology teachers enrolled in a Biology Laboratory Internship Program. Van Gyn, Cutt, Loken, and
65 Ricks (1997) conducted a longitudinal study that investigated the gains made by students enrolled in a cooperative educational program. Both of these studies are further discussed later in this article.

A 1998 study surveying administrators at 185 institutions
70 of higher education in 25 different states discovered a "limited awareness, understanding, and acceptance of School-to-Careers concepts among institutions of higher learning" (Keller, Owens, & Clifford, 1998, p. 17). The survey investigated college of education administrators' perceptions of
75 School-to-Careers and the extent to which its concepts are disseminated to preservice educators. Results indicated that preservice teachers were not being exposed to School-to-Careers concepts. Educators are beginning their careers with solid foundations in school-based learning but little ability to
80 teach work-based learning or the connection between school and work to their students (Keller et al., 1998).

Other studies have shown the importance of work-related learning experiences. Van Gyn et al. (1997) investigated the benefits of cooperative education through a 2-year longitu-
85 dinal study examining whether academic progress of students was influenced by participation in cooperative education programs. The study derived its results from surveys taken from over 500 students at 2 different colleges in Canada. Results indicated that students participating in coopera-
90 tive education are better equipped to problem solve and function better socially in work environments than students who do not participate in cooperative education.

Greene (2000) examined the benefits of preservice biology teachers' involvement in a biology laboratory internship
95 program. In an attempt to "help preservice teachers connect their preparation with more actual experience," preservice teacher educators at Southwest Missouri State University implemented the Biology Laboratory Internship Program, which allowed students the opportunity to integrate their lab
100 skills with their teaching skills (p. 109). Results indicated that interns felt their confidence and skills were positively influenced as a result of participating in the internship program.

In addition to these studies, others have indicated that
105 work-related learning experiences have positive academic,

social, and career-related effects on students (Astin, Vogelgesang, Ikeda, & Yee, 2000; Sax & Astin, 1997). The current study aimed to investigate preservice teachers' increased awareness of School-to-Careers concepts through
110 participation in the Preservice Teacher Internship Program.

Purpose and Objectives

The purpose of this study was to determine the effectiveness of a School-to-Careers teacher education preservice teacher internship program. Specific objectives of the study were to:
115 1. Determine the majors of the students participating in the program,
2. Determine the types of businesses in which participating students did their internship,
3. Determine if students' self-perceived knowledge of
120 School-to-Careers increased significantly from beginning to the end of the preservice teacher education internship program,
4. Determine if students participating in the preservice teacher education internship program significantly in-
125 creased their perceived level of application of School-to-Careers in their future teaching,
5. Determine if participating students would significantly increase their intentions to incorporate key School-to-Career work-based elements into their future teaching,
130 and
6. Determine reasons why preservice teacher education students participated in the internship program.

Methods

The target population for this study was the students who participated in the Preservice Teacher Internship Program
135 during the 1999–2000 academic year. Twelve students participated in and completed all requirements of the program. Students participating in the program consisted of majors from elementary education, secondary education, and the dual elementary/special education program.
140 Data for this study were collected by use of a pretest/posttest questionnaire developed by the researchers. The questionnaire asked students to provide information about their major and place of employment during the internship. Parts I, II, and III of the questionnaire asked students to re-
145 spond to questions using a five-point Likert-type scale varying from 1 = strongly disagree to 5 = strongly agree. Part I of the questionnaire consisted of six questions asking students how knowledgeable they considered themselves to be about various aspects of School-to-Careers. Part II asked students
150 to respond to questions about what they planned to do as far as integrating School-to-Careers concepts after they enter their teaching career. Part II also asked students to indicate the extent they planned to incorporate various School-to-Careers activities into their teaching using a Likert-type
155 scale from 1 = never to 5 = very frequently. Part IV of the questionnaire asked students why they participated in the School-to-Careers Preservice Teacher Internship. The items in each part of the questionnaire were developed from School-to-Careers literature and the researcher's experience
160 working in those activities.

Table 1

Comparison of Students' Knowledge of School-to-Careers Before and After the Preservice Teacher Internship

Statement Rated	Before		After			
	M	*SD*	*M*	*SD*	*t* value	*p*
I consider myself knowledgeable about…						
The School-to-Careers System.	2.83	1.19	4.33	1.15	−3.20	.01*
School-based learning.	3.58	1.24	4.33	.89	−1.57	.15
Work-based learning.	3.25	1.36	4.33	1.15	−1.86	.09
Connecting activities.	3.42	1.31	4.25	1.14	−2.06	.06
Ways to apply School-to-Careers to my teaching.	3.17	1.34	4.25	1.14	−2.46	.03*
SCANS skills.	1.67	.89	4.17	.94	−7.97	.01*

Rating Scale: 1 = Strongly Disagree; 2 = Somewhat Disagree; 3 = Neither Agree nor Disagree; 4 = Somewhat Agree; 5 = Strongly Agree.
df = 11
*Indicates significance at the .05 alpha level.

Table 2

Comparison of Students' Perceived Application of School-to-Careers to Future Teaching Before and After the Preservice Teacher Internship

Statement Rated	Before		After			
	M	*SD*	*M*	*SD*	*t* value	*p*
When I begin my teaching career, I plan…						
To place emphasis on business writing.	2.92	1.44	3.92	.79	−2.25	.05*
To include more hands-on activities using real-life examples.	4.58	.67	4.75	.45	−1.00	.34
To use a business approach to class assignments and evaluations.	3.67	.49	4.08	.79	−1.82	.10
To teach the importance of employer–employee relations and social skills.	4.08	1.08	4.25	.87	−.80	.44

Rating Scale: 1 = Strongly Disagree; 2 = Somewhat Disagree; 3 = Neither Agree nor Disagree; 4 = Somewhat Agree; 5 = Strongly Agree.
df = 11
*Indicates significance at the .05 alpha level.

The student interns were asked to complete the questionnaire during their first seminar and before any discussion or information was disseminated about School-to-Careers. They were again asked to complete the questionnaire at the completion of their last seminar. All twelve students completed the questionnaire for a 100% response rate.

Data were analyzed using the Statistical Package for the Social Sciences, Personal Computer version (SPSSxPC). A Chronbach's Alpha statistic was computed for each item of the instrument using a combined pretest and posttest analysis. Reliability ranged from .9085 to .9321. A matched-pairs *t* test was used to compare the means of pretest and posttest scores on each item in the survey.

Results

The 12 students who completed the Preservice Teacher Internship Program came from 6 different areas of study. Five students were dual special education/elementary education majors and 3 were elementary education majors. There were four secondary education students from each of the following areas of study: English, history, math, and physical education. Students interned at nine different business settings. The highest concentrations were in the retail industry (*n* = 4) and the insurance industry (*n* = 2). One student interned in each of the following business settings: banking, computer, hotel/hospitality, restaurant, trucking, and a veterinary hospital.

Table 1 shows a comparison of students' self-reported knowledge of School-to-Careers before and after the Preservice Teacher Internship Program. Significant differences were found at the .05 alpha level in students' knowledge about the School-to-Careers System, ways to apply School-to-Careers to teaching, and the SCANS skills. However, mean scores increased for all items.

Table 2 reports the students' responses to questions regarding their perceived application of School-to-Careers to their future teaching. Although means increased for all questions, only one, to place emphasis on business writing (*p* = .05), showed any significant change at the .05 alpha level.

The *t* test was used to compare mean differences in students' responses to questions regarding their intention to incorporate work-based learning into their teaching (Table 3). All means except one increased at or beyond the .05 alpha level. Those items included career exploration, job shadowing, internships, school-based enterprise, entrepreneurial projects, and apprenticeships.

Means from the first survey taken during the initial seminar were compared to illustrate students' reasons for participating in the PTIP. Results indicated that the main reason was to learn about School-to-Careers so that they could integrate key concepts into their future teaching (*M* = 4.58). They also participated to improve the skills they will

Table 3

Comparison of Students' Intention to Incorporate Key Work-based Learning Elements of School-to-Careers into Their Teaching Before and After the Preservice Teacher Internship

Statement Rated	Before		After		t value	p
	M	SD	M	SD		
Indicate to what extent you plan to incorporate the following elements into your teaching.						
Career exploration	3.33	.89	4.17	.83	−2.42	.03*
Job shadowing	2.42	.79	3.42	.79	−3.32	.01*
Guest speakers	3.92	.72	4.17	.72	−.76	.46
Internships	2.25	.75	3.42	1.16	−4.31	.01*
School-based enterprise	2.64	1.12	3.64	.92	−2.80	.02*
Entrepreneurial projects	2.75	1.36	3.67	.98	−2.56	.03*
Apprenticeships	1.92	.79	3.25	1.14	−4.30	.01*

Rating Scale: 1 = Never; 2 = Rarely; 3 = Sometimes; 4 = Frequently; 5 = Very Frequently.
$df = 11$
*Indicates significance at the .05 alpha level.

teach in their class(es) ($M = 4.42$) and to obtain the scholarship ($M = 3.75$).

Conclusions and Recommendations

Results from this study indicate several important key factors. First, means increased on all questions on which a *t*
215 test was performed; however, not always significantly. Significant changes to students' knowledge of School-to-Careers occurred in their general understanding of the School-to-Careers system, ways to apply School-to-Careers to their teaching and SCANS skills. Students showed more
220 interest in placing emphasis on business writing in their future teaching as a result of participating in the PTIP. The greatest number of changes occurred in students' intentions to incorporate work-based learning into their future teaching. Students indicated an increased willingness to incorporate
225 career exploration, job shadowing, internships, school-based enterprise, entrepreneurial projects and apprenticeships into their teaching, although it may be impossible or inappropriate for one teacher to incorporate all of these elements. However, this showed willingness on the part of the students
230 to experiment with some of these School-to-Careers concepts. Finally, this suggestion was further supported by an indication that the main reason students participated in the PTIP was to learn about School-to-Careers so they may integrate key concepts into their future teaching. Therefore, it
235 appears that when preservice teachers are made aware of School-to-Careers concepts, they are willing to incorporate these concepts into their teaching. All of these findings indicate that the PTIP successfully helped students begin to understand the School-to-Careers system and that they intend
240 to incorporate the fundamentals of this system into their future teaching.

In light of the apparent success of this program, it is recommended that it is continued and its impact continues to be studied. It is also recommended that the students who par-
245 ticipated in the program during this particular year be followed up to determine the extent to which they obtained teaching positions and actually carried out School-to-Careers activities in their teaching situations.

References

Astin, A., Vogelgesang, L., Ikeda, E., & Yee, J. (2000). *Executive summary: How service learning affects students*. Los Angeles, CA: Higher Education Research Institute.

Greene, J. (2000). A Biology laboratory internship program improving preservice teacher education. *The American Biology Teacher, 62*(2), 108–112.

Keller, R., Owens, T., & Clifford, M. (1998). *Teacher preparation and School-to-Work: A 25-state survey of higher education*. Portland, OR: Northwest Regional Educational Laboratory.

Sax, L., & Astin, A. (1997). The benefit of service: Evidence from undergraduates. *The Educational Record, 78*(3–4), 25–32.

Van Gyn, G., Cutt, J., Loken, M., & Ricks, F. (1997). Investigating the educational benefits of cooperative education: A longitudinal study. *Journal of Cooperative Education, 32*(2), 70–85.

About the authors: Vernon D. Luft, Ph.D., associate dean and professor of occupational education, College of Education, University of Nevada, Reno, and Kimberly Vidoni, graduate assistant, University of Nevada, Reno.

Exercise for Article 27

Factual Questions

1. The letters PTIP stand for what words?

2. What was the minimum number of hours that the students worked in a business?

3. What is the name of the statistical test that was used to compare the means of pretest and posttest scores on each item in the survey?

4. The students responded to the statement "I consider myself knowledgeable about work-based learning" before and after their internship. Was the difference between the two means statistically significant?

5. In Table 2, how many of the differences are statistically significant at the .05 level?

6. What was the mean for intending to incorporate guest speakers into their teaching before participating in the program?

7. Was the difference between the means for intending to incorporate apprenticeships into their teaching statistically significant?

Questions for Discussion

8. The students reported that one of the main reasons they participated was to obtain the scholarship. In your opinion, could this affect the generalizability of the results to instructional situations where no scholarships are offered? Explain.

9. Do you think the questions were clearly worded and appropriate for evaluating the PTIP program? Explain. (See the questions in the three tables.)

10. In lines 237–239, the researchers indicate that they think the program was successful in helping students begin to understand the School-to-Careers system. Overall, to what extent do you think that it was successful based on the results of the evaluation reported in this article?

11. In the last paragraph, the researchers recommend a follow-up to determine the extent to which the students actually carry out School-to-Careers activities once they become teachers. Do you agree? Explain.

12. The researchers did not include a control group. If you were conducting a similar study, would you attempt to include one? Why? Why not?

Quality Ratings

Directions: Indicate your level of agreement with each of the following statements by circling a number from 5 for strongly agree (SA) to 1 for strongly disagree (SD). If you believe an item is not applicable to this research article, leave it blank. Be prepared to explain your ratings.

A. The introduction establishes the importance of the study.

SA   5   4   3   2   1   SD

B. The literature review establishes the context for the study.

SA   5   4   3   2   1   SD

C. The research purpose, question, or hypothesis is clearly stated.

SA   5   4   3   2   1   SD

D. The method of sampling is sound.

SA   5   4   3   2   1   SD

E. Relevant demographics (for example, age, gender, and ethnicity) are described.

SA   5   4   3   2   1   SD

F. Measurement procedures are adequate.

SA   5   4   3   2   1   SD

G. All procedures have been described in sufficient detail to permit a replication of the study.

SA   5   4   3   2   1   SD

H. The participants have been adequately protected from potential harm.

SA   5   4   3   2   1   SD

I. The results are clearly described.

SA   5   4   3   2   1   SD

J. The discussion/conclusion is appropriate.

SA   5   4   3   2   1   SD

K. Despite any flaws, the report is worthy of publication.

SA   5   4   3   2   1   SD

Article 28

Does D.A.R.E. Work?
An Evaluation in Rural Tennessee

MATTHEW J. ZAGUMNY
Tennessee Technological University

MICHAEL K. THOMPSON
Tennessee Technological University

ABSTRACT. The current evaluation examined the effectiveness of the D.A.R.E. program in a rural Tennessee school system using self-report data on alcohol/drug use. The evaluation was longitudinal in nature with data from the first sample of controls (non-D.A.RE. participants) collected in 1991, data from the second sample of controls collected in 1996, and data from the experimental group (D.A.R.E. participants) collected in 1996. Analysis of the self-administered survey response showed that significant differences existed only between the 1991 sample (n = 253) and the entire 1996 sample for the frequency of both alcohol ($p < .0001$) and drug use ($p < .001$). Comparisons between 1996 controls (n = 93) and 1996 experimentals (n = 49) proved nonsignificant, as did all other comparisons among the three groups. Results suggest that the factor of time between 1991 and 1996 may be the causal element in the observed differences.

From *Journal of Alcohol and Drug Education*, 42, 32–41. Copyright © 1997 by the American Alcohol and Drug Information Foundation. Reprinted with permission.

Introduction

Understanding and preventing use and abuse of alcohol and drugs by American youth has become a top priority in the United States. Two different approaches have been developed in an attempt to combat this problem. Incarceration
5 and sometimes court-ordered drug treatment represents one approach, which is aimed at reducing alcohol/drug abuse by means of punishment for the offense. The second approach relies on early intervention and education concerning the negative aspects of alcohol/drug abuse. Neither approach has
10 proved one-hundred percent effective in addressing this problem. A multifaceted approach may be necessary in order to realize real reduction of alcohol/drug related problems. This is true for both adults and children. Regardless of the philosophical paradigm employed to combat the problem, it
15 can be stated with certainty that research and evaluation of policy and programs is necessary to determine effectiveness.

United States drug abuse violations have been on a steady increase from 647,411 arrests in 1985 to 1,040,351 in 1994 (U.S. Department of Justice, 1995). The increase of
20 drug abuse violations among America's youth from 73,446 in 1985 to 121,951 in 1994 (U.S. Department of Justice, 1995) have also led to questions concerning the effectiveness of alcohol/drug abuse education programs. Researchers continue to investigate this rise and the effectiveness of in-
25 tervention programs (Carlson, 1994; Snow, Tebes, Arthur, & Tapasak, 1992; Smart, Adlaf, & Walsh, 1993). However, these dramatic increases have led to a large variety of alcohol/drug intervention programs, most of which have not received scientific evaluation. Therefore, while more programs
30 are being developed to combat the rise in alcohol/drug abuse violations, evaluation research of these programs has not kept pace.

The 1990 national education summit established six goals, one of which was drug free schools by the year 2000.
35 Many school systems have incorporated drug awareness programs into their curricula. Many programs have been developed and evaluated with mixed results. One such program is the Adolescent Decision-Making (ADM) program used during the sixth grade, which is based on a social-
40 cognitive model. Snow et al. (1992) conducted a two-year follow-up study of the ADM program. The investigators used a self-administered drug survey to assess the levels of drug use by program participants. The researchers found a significant reduction in tobacco use but did not find similar
45 significant effects on the use of alcohol, marijuana, or "hard" drugs (i.e., LSD, amphetamines, barbiturates, heroin, and cocaine). "Here's Looking at You, Two" is a program which focuses on comprehensive alcohol and drug education taught at the K–12 levels. Two major components of the program
50 are a comprehensive school curriculum, which is experienced throughout students' primary and secondary education, as well as an extensive thirty-hour training program for teachers involved in the program. Green and Kelly (1989) evaluated the program using data from the Educational
55 Quality Assessment (EQA). The researchers found that the program had a positive effect on knowledge of drug and alcohol abuse but had little to no effect on decision making, self-esteem, and coping skills, all potentially key elements to long-term reduction of alcohol/drug abuse.
60 One program that did have a positive effect on drug and alcohol use was the drug education programs used by Ontario schools. In a longitudinal study, data were gathered from 1979 to 1991 using a self-administered questionnaire in the Ontario school systems. Results of the trend analysis
65 showed a strong correlation between amount of alcohol/drug education experienced and a decline in self-reported use of alcohol, tobacco, and marijuana (Smart, Adlaf, & Walsh,

1993). The most significant reduction was observed in seventh graders who had received the most alcohol/drug abuse education.

Drug Abuse Resistance Education (D.A.R.E.) is an intervention program designed to prevent violence and the use of tobacco, alcohol, marijuana, inhalants (e.g., paints, glue, markers, etc.) by America's youth. The program was developed in 1983 by educators for the Unified School District of Los Angeles, California, in collaboration with the Los Angeles Police Department, which was the first law enforcement organization to implement the program in schools. A main tenet of the D.A.R.E. program is that the solution to the alcohol/drug abuse problem is prevention beginning at an early age.

Research on the effectiveness of the D.A.R.E. program has been mixed (Dept. of Justice and Risk Administration, 1990; Ennett, Tobler, Ringwalt, & Flewelling, 1994; Evaluation and Training Institute, 1990; Kochis, 1995). While this may be due in part to differences in the scientific rigor of individual studies, the specific issue of extraneous variables must be considered. It is difficult at best, and impossible at worst, to control these variables when finding suitable comparison groups. Media, schools, churches, and homes are all potential sources of anti-drug/alcohol information. Thus, while it is possible to examine differences between students who have experienced the D.A.R.E. program and those who have not, it is difficult to determine if the D.A.R.E. program itself is the causal agent of any observed differences.

Wysong, Aniskiewicz, and Wright (1994) conducted a longitudinal evaluation of attitudes toward drugs and coping skills employing a nonequivalent control group approach. The authors found no significant differences between D.A.R.E. participants measured in the 12th grade and the nonequivalent seniors on self-esteem, coping, skills, and drug attitudes. A 1995 study on the effectiveness of the D.A.R.E. program implemented in a southern New Jersey township found virtually no differences between students who experienced the D.A.R.E. program and non-D.A.R.E. students (Kochis, 1995). The only significant difference between the two groups [significance level not reported by author] was the number of criminal offenses that were officially recorded. However, out of 12 reported criminal offenses, 11 were perpetrated by the D.A.R.E. students, which may suggest that the D.A.R.E. program actually increased criminal behavior. Of course, these results must be interpreted cautiously since a random sample of 50 experimental (D.A.R.E.) students and 50 control (non-D.A.R.E.) students was selected for the study. The sampling procedure [not reported by author] may have resulted in noncomparable samples.

Ennett, Tobler, Ringwalt, & Flewelling (1994) recently examined the D.A.R.E. program in a meta-analysis, which included eight of the approximately 20 evaluation studies conducted to date. Effect sizes were calculated for knowledge of drugs, alcohol, and tobacco (.42), anti-drug attitude (.11), positive attitude toward police (.13), self-esteem (.06), social-skills to resist (.19), and self-reported drug use (.06). These effect sizes suggest that D.A.R.E. may be marginally effective at improving knowledge and attitudes but may need development to increase positive change in behaviors.

Program and Evaluation Design

To add to the current literature of D.A.R.E. evaluations, the current study examined the long-term effectiveness of the D.A.R.E. program in a rural Tennessee community. The D.A.R.E. program was first introduced to the rural Tennessee school system in 1991 by the Tennessee Highway Patrol. Specially trained Highway Patrol officers served as instructors for the program, which was required of all sixth-grade students. In 1993, the administration of the D.A.R.E. program in this school system was transferred from the Tennessee Highway Patrol to the county police. During this program administration transfer, the D.A.R.E. program was not offered for one year that resulted in a cohort of students who did not receive the program. When surveyed in 1996 for this study, this cohort of students was in the ninth grade. Those high school students questioned in 1996 who did receive the program were sophomores and juniors. Seniors from the 1996 survey had not been offered the D.A.R.E. program because it had not yet been developed by the Highway Patrol.

For this D.A.R.E. program, instructors are county police officers who have completed two weeks of training to prepare for the D.A.R.E. program. This program is implemented at the sixth-grade level and is taught one day a week, one hour a day for 17 weeks. Students are required to complete a D.A.R.E. book addressing the issues and methods of alcohol/drug resistance presented during the D.A.R.E. program. Topics of the one-hour session include the types of peer pressure commonly experienced by adolescents and ways to resist that pressure, eight ways to say "no," approaches to developing positive self-esteem, and ways to deal with stress. An important element of this D.A.R.E. program is the introduction of high school role models to the sixth graders. The program utilizes role models and role playing as the primary methods to accomplish its goals.

Original data for the current investigation were collected in 1991 from freshmen, sophomores, juniors, and seniors of a rural Tennessee high school. None of the students surveyed in 1991 had received formal alcohol/drug education. The current research, designed to assess the effectiveness of this D.A.R.E. program as well as assess current drug and alcohol use trends, compared the 1996 sample of students who had received the D.A.R.E. program with participants who had not received the program.

Method

Participants

Two hundred fifty-three high school students (22.5% freshman, 31.6% sophomore, 22.9% junior, and 22.9% senior) were surveyed in 1991; 55.3% were male and 44.7% were female. The average age of participants was 15.89 (SD = 1.88). None of the 253 students surveyed in 1991 had participated in an alcohol and drug prevention program. One hundred forty-two students were surveyed in 1996 with 31.0% freshman, 16.2% sophomore, 18.3% junior, and 34.5% senior; 45.1% were male and 54.9% were female.

180 The average age of the participants was 16.25 (*SD* = 1.42). The 1996 sophomore and junior classes received the D.A.R.E. program in the sixth grade. All students were asked to participate in the study, however, participation was

185 voluntary. No students refused to participate. The current study required students and their parents to sign an informed consent before participating. The consent form was distributed to students via their homeroom teachers two days prior to the study. Use of the homeroom classroom assured that no students were measured more than once during both the

190 1991 and 1996 surveys. Students were treated in accordance with the ethical guidelines of the American Psychological Association (1995).

Materials

An anonymous survey of attitudes and use of alcohol and drugs was conducted in the 1991 study. The 1996 survey

195 included the same items assessed in the 1991 study (see Appendix). Results of a reliability analysis showed a coefficient alpha of .78 for the scale measuring frequency of alcohol/drug use and .77 for the scale measuring the age of alcohol/drug use.

Procedure

200 Homeroom teachers administered the study survey to all students who returned a signed consent form. This same procedure was followed in the 1991 study. The informed consent forms were collected on the same day but prior to administering the surveys. Homeroom teachers allowed stu-

205 dents 10 to 15 minutes to complete the surveys. Students were instructed to place their completed surveys on the desk at the front of the classroom.

Results

The research design allowed for two comparison groups and one experimental group. Comparisons were made be-

210 tween 1996 D.A.R.E. participants (*n* = 49), 1996 non-D.A.R.E. students (*n* = 93), and 1991 non-D.A.R.E. students (*n* = 253). Alcohol and drug usage are reported in Table 1. Data on parent use of alcohol and drugs are reported in Table 2. Two hundred ninety-one students (73.7%) reported no

215 use of alcohol or drugs, 79 (20%) reported they had used marijuana, 8 (2%) reported the use of cocaine, 4 (1%) reported using barbiturates, 12 (3%) reported the use of amphetamines, and 1 student (.3%) reported the use of inhalants. Fifty-three of the 395 students surveyed from 1991

220 and 1996 reported that they used both alcohol and drugs. When asked if their parent(s) used drugs, 9 (2.3%) answered in the affirmative, while 165 (41.8%) reported that their parent(s) used alcohol.

To examine differences among the three groups in this

225 study (1991 controls, 1996 controls, and 1996 experimentals) one-way analyses of variance (ANOVA) were conducted employing Tukey's Honestly Significant Difference (HSD) test for pairwise comparisons, when appropriate. ANOVA results of differences on the self-reported fre-

230 quency of alcohol used revealed significant differences among the three groups [$F(2,392) = 9.32$, $p = .0001$]. Tukey's HSD test revealed that the 1991 non-D.A.R.E. par-

ticipants (*M* = 1.62) reported significantly more frequent alcohol use than either 1996 non-D.A.R.E. participants (*M* =

235 1.38) or 1996 D.A.R.E. participants (*M* = 1.19) (*p* < .0001). Similarly, significant differences were found for the frequency of drug use with the 1991 non-D.A.R.E. participants (*M* = 1.23) reporting more frequent use than either 1996 non-D.A.R.E. participants (*M* = 1.06) or 1996 D.A.R.E. par-

240 ticipants (*M* = 1.00) [$F(2,392) = 6.79$, $p = .001$]. Comparisons among the three groups for both the age of first alcohol consumption ($F(2,294) = 3.25$, $p > .01$) and age of first drug use [$F(2,295) = 1.87$, $p > .01$] proved to be nonsignificant.

Table 1
Number (and Percentage) of Students Reporting Alcohol/Drug Use

| | How often do you drink alcohol? | | | | |
	Never	Seldom	Some-times	Often	Regularly
1991 Non-D.A.R.E.	144 (57%)	62 (24%)	47 (19%)	0	0
1996 Non-D.A.R.E.	67 (72%)	17 (18%)	9 (10%)	0	0
1996 D.A.R.E.	42 (86%)	5 (10%)	2 (4%)	0	0

| | How often do you do drugs? | | | | |
	Never	Seldom	Some-times	Often	Regularly
1991 Non-D.A.R.E.	214 (85%)	21 (8%)	18 (7%)	0	0
1996 Non-D.A.R.E.	80 (86%)	5 (5%)	8 (9%)	0	0
1996 D.A.R.E.	42 (86%)	3 (6%)	4 (8%)	0	0

245 In order to examine differences among the three study groups on reported use of both drugs and alcohol, parent(s) use of alcohol, and parent(s) use of drugs, Kruskal-Wallis nonparametric one-way ANOVAs were conducted. All three chi square statistics proved to be nonsignificant (*p* > .01 [χ^2 (2) = 1.33; χ^2 (2) = 5.95; χ^2 (2) = 1.33, respectively]).

Table 2
Parents' Alcohol/Drug Use As Reported by Student

| | Do your parents drink alcohol? | |
	No	Yes
1991 Non-D.A.R.E.	156 (62%)	97 (38%)
1996 Non-D.A.R.E.	49 (53%)	44 (47%)
1996 D.A.R.E.	30 (61%)	19 (39%)

| | Do your parents use illegal drugs? | |
	No	Yes
1991 Non-D.A.R.E.	247 (98%)	6 (2%)
1996 Non-D.A.R.E.	92 (99%)	1 (1%)
1996 D.A.R.E.	47 (96%)	2 (4%)

Discussion

250 These results suggest that time, rather than D.A.R.E. participation, produced lower frequencies of alcohol and drug use. This is evident in the significant differences between 1991 participants and 1996 participants. An effective D.A.R.E. program would have resulted in significant differ-

255 ences between 1996 D.A.R.E. participants and both 1991 and 1996 non-D.A.R.E. participants. These differences were not found. Widespread anti-alcohol and anti-drug informa-

tion may be the main causal element in the reduction of alcohol/drug use among high school students. As further evidence of the limited utility of the D.A.R.E. program in this rural school system, the D.A.R.E. program did not result in significantly older ages of first time use of alcohol or drugs. This indicates that the D.A.R.E. program did not delay the use of alcohol or drugs by adolescents in this study.

Since the current data was collected by self-report surveys, which had only moderate reliability, the results must be evaluated cautiously. Future evaluations of the D.A.R.E. program could include multiple measurement methods including self-report and behavioral based data. Methods could include checking juvenile arrests prior to the commencement of a prevention program as well as after program completion. A related measurement issue is the limited number of items used to assess alcohol/drug use. An expanded survey could not be used in this study because of similar limitations in the original 1991 data. Future evaluations must also include larger D.A.R.E. participant cohorts and ideally employ random assignment of students to D.A.R.E. programs in order to achieve true control groups.

In order to determine if alcohol and drug prevention programs effectively achieve their goals, programs must be constantly evaluated. Society as a whole may need to place a greater emphasis on the secondary schools' alcohol/drug problem. The first step is a thorough assessment of the alcohol/drug problems currently experienced in specific locations. Following this systematic assessment, well planned and implemented prevention programs are necessary throughout primary and secondary school systems.

References

American Psychological Association (1995). *Publication Manual* (4th ed.). Washington, DC: American Psychological Association.

Carlson, K.A. (1994). Identifying the outcomes of prevention: Results of a longitudinal study in a small city school district. *Journal of Drug Education, 24,* 193–206.

Department of Justice and Risk Administration (1990). *Volume II: 1989 Impact Assessment of Drug Abuse Resistance Education in the Commonwealth of Virginia.* Virginia: Virginia Commonwealth University, Institution for Research in Justice and Risk Administration.

Ennett, S.T., Tobler, N.S., Ringwalt, C.L., & Flewelling, R. (1994). How effective is Drug Abuse Resistance Education? A meta-analysis of Project DARE outcome evaluations. *American Journal of Public Health, 84,* 1394–1401.

Evaluation and Training Institute (1990). *DARE Evaluation Report for 1985–1989.* Los Angeles, CA.

Green, J., & Kelley, J. (1989). Evaluating the effectiveness of a school drug and alcohol prevention curriculum: A new look at *Here's looking at you, two. Journal of Drug Education, 19,* 117–132.

Kochis, D.S. (1995). The effectiveness of project DARE: Does it work? *Journal of Alcohol and Drug Education 40*(2), 40–47.

Smart, R.G., Adlaf, E.M., & Walsh, G.W. (1993). Declining drug use in relation to increased drug education: A trend study 1979–1991. *Journal of Drug Education, 23,* 125–132.

Snow, D.L., Tebes, J.K., Arthur, M.W., & Tapasak, R.C. (1992). Two-year follow-up of a social-cognitive intervention to prevent substance use. *Journal of Drug Education, 22,* 101–114.

U.S. Department of Justice (1995). *Crime in the United States 1994: Uniform Crime Reports.* Washington, D.C.: Federal Bureau of Investigation.

Wysong, E., Aniskiewicz, R., & Wright, D. (1994). Truth and DARE: Tracking drug education to graduation and as symbolic politics. *Social Problems, 41,* 448–472.

Send all correspondence to first author at: Department of Psychology, Box 5031, Cookeville, TN 38501, (615) 372-6255, MJZ5495@tntech.edu

Appendix

Please circle or check the answer that best describes you.

1. How often do you drink alcohol?
   Never   Seldom   Sometimes   Often   Regularly
2. How old were you when you tried alcohol? _____
3. How much do you drink at once? _____
4. Have you ever tried an illegal drug? Yes ____ No ____
5. If yes, check all drugs you have tried:
   ____ Marijuana
   ____ Cocaine
   ____ Barbiturates
   ____ Amphetamines
   ____ Other (Specify) _____
6. How often do you do drugs?
   Never   Seldom   Sometimes   Often   Regularly
7. How old were you when you tried drugs? _____
8. Do you mix alcohol and drugs? Yes ____ No ____
9. Do you think you can stop? Yes ____ No ____
10. What is your gender? Male ____ Female ____
11. What grade are you in? _____
12. How old are you? _____
13. Do your parents drink alcohol?
    Never   Seldom   Sometimes   Often   Regularly
14. Do your parents use illegal drugs?
    Never   Seldom   Sometimes   Often   Regularly
15. What is your race? _____
16. Have you participated in the D.A.R.E. program?
    Yes ____ No ____

Exercise for Article 28

Factual Questions

1. According to the evaluators, what do the data collected by Kochis in 1995 suggest about the relationship between D.A.R.E. and criminal behavior?

2. In the meta-analysis (a statistical way of combining results from various studies) cited by the researchers, which two outcomes had the smallest effect sizes?

3. In 1996, freshmen, sophomores, juniors, and seniors were surveyed for this evaluation. Which two of these groups had *not* previously received the D.A.R.E. program?

4. Participation was voluntary. Did any students refuse to participate?

5. Which group reported significantly more alcohol and drug use than the 1996 D.A.R.E. participants?

6. Were there statistically significant differences among the groups on age of first alcohol consumption?

7. Why did the evaluators decide not to use an expanded survey with more questions in their 1996 evaluation?

8. The evaluators recommend what type of assignment in future evaluations of this program?

Questions for Discussion

9. Speculate on what the evaluators mean by "nonequivalent control group" as used in the evaluation by Wysong et al. (See lines 96–98.) Were nonequivalent control groups also used in the present evaluation? Explain.

10. The evaluators state that there have been about 20 evaluations of D.A.R.E. to date. Yet, they provide details on only a small number of them in their review of literature. Given that journal articles need to be relatively brief, what criteria would you use when selecting a few evaluations to discuss in such a literature review?

11. The evaluators had the homeroom teachers administer the questionnaires. Do you think this was a good idea? In your opinion, might some students be afraid that the teacher could link them with their responses even though the questionnaires were anonymous? Explain.

12. Do you agree with this statement from the article: "An effective D.A.R.E. program would have resulted in significant differences between 1996 D.A.R.E. participants and *both* 1991 and 1996 non-D.A.R.E. participants"? Explain.

13. The evaluators mention that the results should be evaluated cautiously, in part because of the use of students' self-reports. (See lines 265–272.) Do you agree? Why? Why not?

14. The evaluators conclude that society, as a whole, may need to place greater emphasis on the secondary schools' alcohol/drug problems. In your opinion, do the data from this evaluation support their conclusion? Explain.

15. In your opinion, is the D.A.R.E. program described in sufficient detail? Would you feel confident in implementing a D.A.R.E. program in your local schools using the description? Explain.

16. If you were on the school board in this rural Tennessee community, would you vote for permanent continued funding for D.A.R.E. given the results of this study? Would you vote for temporary continuation of funding pending additional studies? Would you vote to terminate funding? Justify your choice.

Quality Ratings

Directions: Indicate your level of agreement with each of the following statements by circling a number from 5 for strongly agree (SA) to 1 for strongly disagree (SD). If you believe an item is not applicable to this research article, leave it blank. Be prepared to explain your ratings.

A. The introduction establishes the importance of the study.

SA   5   4   3   2   1   SD

B. The literature review establishes the context for the study.

SA   5   4   3   2   1   SD

C. The research purpose, question, or hypothesis is clearly stated.

SA   5   4   3   2   1   SD

D. The method of sampling is sound.

SA   5   4   3   2   1   SD

E. Relevant demographics (for example, age, gender, and ethnicity) are described.

SA   5   4   3   2   1   SD

F. Measurement procedures are adequate.

SA   5   4   3   2   1   SD

G. All procedures have been described in sufficient detail to permit a replication of the study.

SA   5   4   3   2   1   SD

H. The participants have been adequately protected from potential harm.

SA   5   4   3   2   1   SD

I. The results are clearly described.

SA   5   4   3   2   1   SD

J. The discussion/conclusion is appropriate.

SA   5   4   3   2   1   SD

K. Despite any flaws, the report is worthy of publication.

SA   5   4   3   2   1   SD

Article 29

The Other Side of the Story: Student Narratives on the California Drug, Alcohol, and Tobacco Education Programs

MARIANNE D'EMIDIO-CASTON
University of California, Santa Barbara

JOEL H. BROWN
Center for Educational Research and Development

ABSTRACT. Within the context of a large-scale, comprehensive evaluation of the California Drug Alcohol Tobacco Education (DATE) program, this study sought to extend knowledge of student perceptions of prevention education using a naturalistic approach. The constant comparative method was used to analyze 40 focus group interviews of risk and thriving groups conducted in 11 high, middle, and elementary school districts. This article presents three assertions generated solely from 490 "narrative stories" found in the data set. "At-risk" and "thriving" students at all three levels of schooling (a) use "story" to make sense of prevention education, and (b) distinguish use from abuse. High school students of both groups (c) believe that hearing only one side of the substance use/abuse story and strict expulsion policies further alienate students most in need of help. Implications for the use of story as an assessment tool are discussed, as are implications for substance use prevention policy.

From *Evaluation Review*, 22, 95–117. Copyright © 1998 by Sage Publications, Inc. Reprinted with permission of Sage Publications, Inc.

When social problems capture public imagination, public schools often become the vehicle for social change (Sarason, 1982). With the focus of public attention, efforts are made by politicians to "do something" to solve the problem. The "something" often results in a mandate to public schools. Directly tied to and intricately connected with state and federal government through funding, schools are readily available settings for delivery of the mandated solution. In the last decade, public schools have increasingly been held accountable to teach young people about the dangers of drugs, alcohol and tobacco, AIDS, gangs, and violence. Each of these issues now claims time in the curriculum delivered to students alongside a basic program of academic study. Beginning in the 1980s, "Just Say No!" became the slogan for an ongoing social change effort known as the War on Drugs, aimed at the target of a drug-, alcohol-, and tobacco-free society.

In 1991, the California Drug, Alcohol, and Tobacco Education (DATE) Program was initiated in an effort to consolidate programs to prevent substance use and abuse by children and adolescents. School districts were mandated to provide comprehensive drug, alcohol, and tobacco education for students K through 12th grade. A large-scale evaluation of DATE by the Southwest Regional Laboratory (SWRL) suggests that "at a minimum California schools spent $83.78 per student in 1992–93 to provide students with prevention education curricula, and positive alternative activities, provide personnel with staff development and Alcohol Tobacco or Other Drugs (ATOD) training in curricula, identification and referral services" (Romero et al., 1994, p. 38). Since 1991, the cost of DATE has been estimated at $1.6 billion (Brown, D'Emidio-Caston, & Pollard, 1997). Such public focus and fiscal priority on a perceived social problem requires comprehensive evaluation and public accountability.

From 1991 to 1994, an evaluation was conducted along three quantitative dimensions: cost, program implementation, and self-reported student substance use knowledge, attitudes, beliefs, and behaviors (Romero et al., 1993, 1994). Another study, using the same school districts included in the Romero evaluation, looked at the social processes of DATE program implementation (Brown et al., 1993, 1995). These two studies present findings that are often contradictory. Romero, for example, leaves the reader with a positive impression of the effects of DATE. Brown and colleagues are not so convinced of the benefits in relation to students who are labeled most at risk for substance abuse. Although both studies are valuable, an explanation for the discrepancy in findings may be that the voices of students are more clearly heard in the Brown et al. study.

DATE programs have been designed and implemented from a "risk orientation" toward prevention (Brown et al., 1993). A risk orientation includes three characteristics. First, the terms substance use and substance abuse are interchangeable. Second, a risk orientation assumes that a majority of children fall into the "at-risk" category. Thus, "at-risk" is not differentiated from "high-risk." Third, with a risk orientation, there is an absence of focus on resilience as a prevention strategy. As it applies to prevention, the risk orientation is an operational definition of a deficit model, where young people are seen as problems to be fixed rather than resources who make contributions to their families, schools, and communities (Blue-Swadener, 1995; Benard, 1993).

There are serious problems associated with the risk-orientation. Using it to inform the solution of one or another perceived social problems masks the underlying social, economic, or environmental conditions that contribute to alienation and hopelessness. Another problem with the risk orien-

tation we argue is that by using broadly defined categories (Hawkins et al., 1987), risk-oriented programs cannot be
70 sufficiently targeted to students most in need of help. Given these limitations, we contend that the risk orientation limits practices in such prevention programs to those that are primarily symbolic (Brown et al., 1997). The appearance of a uniformed officer in classrooms, as in the widely imple-
75 mented D.A.R.E. (Drug Abuse Resistance Education) program or Red Ribbons tied around trees during Red Ribbon Week are public displays of something being done about the drug problem. The risk orientation makes it easier to believe that such symbolic public displays are effective programs
80 (Brown & D'Emidio-Caston, 1995; Brown et al., 1997).

It is time to sort out the symbolic from the actual effects of DATE services. The story of DATE from the students' point of view is essential to the comprehensive assessment of DATE. If the alienation and hopelessness that young peo-
85 ple feel leads to drug or other substance abuse, it is crucial to know whether the risk orientation that guides program development contributes to reducing the alienation and hopelessness. The primary focus of this article is to illuminate the influence DATE services have on students, through analysis
90 of the unsolicited stories students told.

Results of the 1992–1993 qualitative evaluation are reported in Brown et al. (1993). Student perspectives were not included in the first-year results. The second year (1993–1994) qualitative study recognizes the centrality of the
95 learner in prevention education. What meanings do students make of the programs in which they participate? This article posits that the voices of students can be heard through their narrative attempts to make meaning of prevention education. From the story data, we have a better understanding of the
100 answer to the question, Do students perceive that prevention education makes a positive difference in their lives, or are the effects of these programs primarily symbolic?

Theoretical Framework

"Narrative" is becoming more widely accepted as "a way of knowing" in educational research (Schubert & Ayers,
105 1992; Witherell & Noddings, 1991; Connelly & Clandinin, 1990; Polkinghorne, 1988; Rosen, 1985; Mitchell, 1980). Mitchell's *On Narrative* brought the study of the role of narrative "out of the realm of the aesthetic into the realm of social and psychological formations," particularly in struc-
110 tures of value and cognition. The study of narrative "has now become a positive source of insight for all the branches of human and natural science" (Mitchell, 1980, ix). Cognitive psychologists have been interested in the study of the general structure and function of narrative (Chomsky, 1966;
115 Rosen, 1985) and the acquisition of narrative skills by children (Bruner, 1990; Kemper, 1984). The role of narrative in curriculum studies has influenced a reconceptualization of curriculum at the macro and micro levels. Curriculum developed from one perspective has been reconceptualized as the
120 collective story made of multiple perspectives. In "narrative inquiry" (Connelly & Clandinin, 1990), researchers seek to understand the ways in which curriculum is constituted in the subjectivity of teachers and other curriculum workers by

privileging individual storytelling.

125 Nevertheless, the role of narrative in evaluation research is in its infancy. Researchers could uncover no work in which narrative as an evaluation tool was applied to substance use and abuse prevention. Researchers did, however, uncover one scientifically sound and germane narrative
130 evaluation. In the *Voices from the Inside* Report (Poplin & Weeres, 1992), a "bottom up" narrative approach was taken to examine the state of public schools. Here, they used context-dependent units to produce an infrastructure that, when compared with the primary target population, explains pro-
135 gram effects (Patton, 1990; Manning & Cullum-Swan, 1994). *Voices from the Inside* established the narrative of the target population (presumably the "bottom" in a bottom-up evaluation) in comparison with a given context as an important way to determine program effectiveness. In the Clare-
140 mont *Voices* study, Poplin and Weeres interviewed teachers, custodians, parents, day-care workers, security guards, cafeteria workers, nurses, and administrators to create a contextual infrastructure for "multiethnic student voices," who formed the centerpiece of their evaluation. By contrasting
145 these contextual voices with the students' voices, they determined that "heretofore identified problems of schooling (lowered achievement, high dropout rates, and problems in the teaching profession) are rather consequences of much deeper and more fundamental problems" (p. 11). In both
150 methodology and findings, the *Voices* evaluation represents an important advance in evaluation research.

In conjunction with other methods, in the DATE evaluation, researchers also use the bottom-up narrative evaluation format to help determine program effectiveness. By inter-
155 viewing nearly 400 educators, administrators, and community members, the Brown and D'Emidio-Caston (1995) publication described the contextual infrastructure of DATE, contrasting it with the student voices. This research showed that 42.5% of 40 student focus groups (Grades 5–12) re-
160 ported receiving health/science courses delivered by teachers and 95% of student focus groups reported receiving prevention education from specialists such as D.A.R.E. officers. It was also reported that in delivering prevention, the risk orientation as described above was the dominant context. In
165 this article, with primary focus on prevention-related stories, students are once again the evaluation centerpiece.

Because drug, alcohol, and tobacco education is primarily an effort to influence the knowledge, value orientation, and behavior of students, attention to the construction of
170 meanings revealed through narrative "story" is an exciting and valuable approach. Through the methods of narrative inquiry, our data reveal the construction of students' understanding of DATE. In effect, what they tell us is their side of the story of the War on Drugs.

Evaluation Questions

175 Our evaluation research questions focus on qualitative process and outcome examinations as described by Donabedian (1980), who viewed process as the set of activities that go on within and between practitioners (and in this case service recipients) and the outcome as a change in a service

180 recipient's current and future status that can be attributed to antecedent practices.

This article is based on the assumption that if school programs are effective, such effects will be borne out in extensive student interview data regarding program process
185 (how children construct understanding of the effects of substance use) and outcomes (how students feel these understandings have affected their current status as related to prevention programs).

These specific questions focus attention on the process
190 and product of students' meaning making:

- Process: In the context of focus groups, how do students at different school levels (elementary, middle, high school) share their understanding of the effects of substance use?
195 - Outcome: How do students perceive the effects of substance use prevention programs?

Methods

Data Collection

The 11 of 12 California districts represented in the second-year follow-up evaluation study of DATE were purposely chosen based on the 1992 evaluation of 50 California
200 districts (Brown et al. 1993; Brown, D'Emidio-Caston, & Pollard, 1997). A balance was sought among districts with respect to socioeconomic status (SES), demographics, and average daily attendance (ADA). Of these, 7 were from Southern and Central California, 2 were from the Bay Area,
205 and 2 were from extreme Northern California. One of the state's largest districts was purposefully selected, corresponding to the Romero et al. (1994) study. Two schools from each district were randomly assigned by computer selection. In the largest district only, three were selected. Be-
210 cause a detailed description of the methods used to determine participation in this study has already been presented elsewhere (Brown, D'Emidio-Caston, & Pollard, 1997), methods are presented here in only as much detail as necessary to provide the reader with an understanding of the ana-
215 lyzed data subset.

From 23 randomly selected schools, two focus groups of students from each school were interviewed. The two groups were chosen by their principal or other delegated authority on the basis of perceived characteristics of "at risk for sub-
220 stance abuse" or "thriving." Criteria for selection for each group were found to be consistent with expectations. For example, inclusion criteria for the perceived at-risk students were the risk factors of low academic achievement and low commitment to school. Criteria for inclusion in the perceived
225 thriving group were characterized by leadership in the school community. The sampling process yielded 40 useable focus group interviews: 20 elementary school interviews, 9 middle school interviews, and 11 high school interviews, representing approximately 240 students. This process gen-
230 erated 18 complete pairs (thriving and at-risk), three mixed groups, and 1 unpaired thriving and 1 blank interview due to audio tape malfunction. The three mixed interviews, from the largest school district, offered a means of comparing

mixed groups with the risk versus thriving groups. The data
235 presented here are representative of the entire sample of thriving and at-risk student groups ($N = 40$). The student focus groups allowed researchers to evaluate DATE programs from the student point of view.

Students were interviewed by four trained interviewers in
240 focus groups using a semistructured, open-ended interview schedule (Brown et al., 1995). Interviews were subsequently transcribed for analysis.

Data Analysis

Using the grounded theoretical approach (Strauss & Corbin, 1990), conceptual categories were developed induc-
245 tively from the data and systematically related to one another. Among the categories emerging from the data set were a surprising number of unsolicited stories students used to explain or elaborate their ideas, to give examples of what they meant, or to demonstrate their immediate engagement
250 with the content of the interview question. Stories are distinctive from other interview data in that they illuminate the connections students make of the stimulus topic to what they know in an authentic and recognizable discourse form. Restricting the data analysis to the stories students told in-
255 creased the internal validity of the data (Goetz & LeCompte, 1984).

What "counted" as story? Stein and Policastro (1984) in their studies of what counts as "story" found that no one single structural definition can account for the wide range of
260 compositions people accept as stories. Their work showed that "segments must include at least an animate protagonist and some type of causal sequence before they will be considered a story" (Polkinghorne, 1988, p. 111). Susan Kemper described the simplest form of story as a dyadic event where
265 something happens and the protagonist responds. A more complete definition of the prototypical story identifies a protagonist and a predicament and attempts to resolve the predicament, the outcomes of such attempts, the reactions of the protagonists to the situation, and the causal relationships
270 among each of the elements in the story (Polkinghorne, 1988). Many student stories fit Polkinghorne's prototypical story, including all of the required elements. In our analysis, a student statement was considered a story if it had at least one of these characteristics:

275 1. The statement included at least the elements of a subject and an action related to the use or abuse of substances. For example, R (Respondent): My grandmother is not very old, she's in her 50s and she drinks one beer a day.

280 2. It was an expression of personal experience or a tale that had been told and passed along to the speaker. For example, R: Deputy J. told us that this one lady sold her baby for crack.

3. The story had a subject who had performed some action or been involved in some event. For example,
285

R: A lot of people who get drunk and stuff and they go out and do something like usually they'll get in accidents or what happened was I had an uncle, I don't remember his name, but—no Uncle Jack, I think his name was Jack. He was

290   drunk and he went fishing and he was fooling around with the fishing and so he got the hook caught in his leg [several voices: ugh] and so he got gangrene.

R: He got what?

R: Gangrene and died.

295   Well-formed stories (Burke, in Bruner, 1990, 50) include the following five elements: actor, action, goal, scene, instrument. Bruner asserts that when there is a disunity between any of the five elements (trouble), the narrative agent uses the pattern of discourse known as narrative to make
300   sense of the trouble. The addition of "trouble," or what Bruner refers to as a "deviation from canonical culture," provides the stimulus for the telling of the tale. Using Burke's dramatism model, the fishing story is the student's attempt to illustrate his statement that "a lot of people who
305   get drunk go out and get in accidents" (deviation from the canonical culture): Uncle Jack (actor), was drunk (trouble), went fishing (scene), was fooling around (action), got the hook stuck in his leg (instrument), got gangrene and died (goal). This exemplar has all of the required elements of a
310   well-formed story. It is, for the student, a schema for making meaning of the concept "getting drunk." An important caveat for those who find little credibility in the story told above is that the veracity of the story is not as important as the student's use of narrative as a form of communicating
315   his understanding of the concept of getting drunk. Regardless of the truth of the story, it is a recognizable discourse unit that we believe illuminates how this student thinks about the concept.

When encountered in the evaluation of substance use
320   prevention education, the students' stories become an authentic assessment tool to illuminate what young people know, believe, and hope. It is through their stories that students tell us how they connect with their world, how they see themselves as members of school communities, and how
325   they see themselves in relation to the use of substances.

Findings

The results of analysis show that in 40 interviews, there were a total of 494 stories told by students. The stories weave together numerous topics including how students understand the no-use message of DATE, the difference
330   between what they hear in school and what they see at home, their understanding of addiction and of harmful consequences to their health, their understanding of what happens if they get caught using a substance at school, their fears for friends who have substance-related problems, who they
335   think are helping them and who they think are not, and what they think would make a difference. The findings presented in this article, stated as assertions, illuminate the relationships of the various topics, the process of making sense of prevention education, and the outcomes. The findings are
340   organized in the following manner: First, evidence is presented to support the assertion that students at all three levels of schooling use personal narrative to make sense of the information they receive in substance prevention programs. This assertion corresponds to the evaluation question fo-
345   cused on the process of students' meaning making. Second,

building on the evidence presented to support the first assertion, evidence is presented to support the related assertion that by connecting and contrasting the information they learn in school about substance use/abuse with their own experi-
350   ence, students at all three levels in contrast to prevention education programs distinguish use from abuse. This assertion corresponds to both the process and outcome questions. Finally, story evidence is presented to support the assertion that the application of sanctions (detention, suspension, and
355   expulsion) provokes further alienation and disconnection of those students who already see themselves on the periphery of the school community. This assertion corresponds to the outcome question guiding this study. The excerpts provided in all cases represent the predominant point of view found
360   throughout the story data. The excerpts chosen are the most articulate exemplars.

Process

In the context of focus groups, how do students at different school levels share their understanding of what they know about the effects of substance use? Students at all
365   three levels of schooling use personal narrative to make sense of the information they receive in drug prevention education. In the following excerpt, a high school student tells his own story about experimentation with marijuana. He contrasts what he has heard in school with his own experi-
370   ence.

Personal Experience in Narrative Form

R: People say you use it once you're gonna get addicted! I don't see that! But, there, I don't even see, some people say that the drug is addictive, like with a little pressure that you could do anything to keep on using it! Any drug is addic-
375   tive! And I mean, I, myself, I have smoked marijuana before and I believe it's all in the way you look at it.

I: Uh huh.

R: I tried it and it wasn't nothing, there wasn't anything there for me! People say oh, it makes you feel better and all this
380   stuff, I didn't, there was nothing there for me! And I made my choice to say there's what I thought to myself, what compels people to do this? Because there was nothing there for me, and I was thinking what is there for them? (0211, ST.S 593, p. 19)

385   The preceding excerpt is an example of personal experience in the form of narrative story. It offers insights to the meaning the student makes of the prevention education he received. He has clearly not been convinced to forgo experimentation with marijuana. Rather, the information he
390   received conflicts with what others have said, causing disequilibrium, which in turn has prompted personal experimentation. He is struggling to understand the different choices people make. In the next excerpt during a discussion of the various effects of alcohol on people the students
395   knew, two elementary students were moved to tell their own stories:

R: [first] Like, see my uncle, he can drink and he won't get drunk and then my other uncle he can drink a couple of beers and he will get drunk and get into stuff.

400 R: [second] Like my dad he can drink like three or four beers and he doesn't really get drunk, he gets kind of weird [said with a kind of laugh], but he doesn't get drunk and if my mom if she drinks anything alcoholic she gets really sick, because he, I mean, my dad used to drink more than he does

405 now. I mean, lately he has maybe one beer a month and my mom doesn't drink. So, it just kind of depends on the attitude of the person they drink, too, because if they're already violent then if they drink they might get even more violent and then if it doesn't bother them, you know.

410 I: Does the D.A.R.E. officer teach you those things?

R: [third] No, not really.

R: [different respondent] I don't think so.

I: So how did you come to know that? Just by watching?

R: [second] You just kind of know it. [short laugh] [second re-

415 spondent says "Yes" in the background] You know just by observing your surroundings and you can tell how people act. I mean, all families have different examples of stuff but you can just about get in any family somebody that drinks. (0027, ST.E 567, p. 6–7)

420   The stories told by these elementary students are typical of both risk and thriving groups. They are aware that alcohol has a negative effect on the behavior of some people. They are also aware that others who drink do not have a problem and can use alcohol occasionally. Most important, the

425 D.A.R.E. officer has not given them this message. As the high school excerpt also illuminated, they have constructed it from their own personal observations and experiences. Through the stories about uncles' and parents' alcohol use, they reveal the understanding they have of use ("he can

430 drink and won't get drunk") and abuse ("he can drink a couple of beers and he will get drunk and get into stuff").

    In the following middle school excerpt, during a discussion of what the students think should be in the curriculum they receive, the researcher asked a question that prompted

435 the student to talk about her parents' enjoyment of wine.

I: Well then, what would you guys like to see in the classes that you don't get now?

R: Two sides of the story.

R: Yeah, we…

440 I: Wait. Can you explain to me what you mean by two sides to the story?

R: Because they give one side, telling you how bad it is, and then they should have another side saying, cause well, they always tell us drinking it really bad and don't drink cause

445 you get drunk and you end up killing people and yourself. But, that's not true cause they tell you that one glass of wine could do that! But, I think they all had another side. That it's okay if you have a little, but not get drunk.

R: Yeah, because everybody is going to drink when they get

450 older! Maybe just, I mean my parents enjoy a glass of wine with dinner and that's just the way it goes! [laughs] It's not like we can stop them from having a…

I: Well, would you want to stop them from having a glass of wine with dinner?

455 R: No, because I think they enjoy it. They don't get drunk on one glass of wine! [laughs] I think they enjoy having a glass of wine once in a while. They go up to Napa and get some nice aged wine and have some nice wine with dinner or at a

party. I wouldn't want to stop them from doing something

460 that they enjoy! (0005, ST.M 507, p. 19)

    One of California's largest industries is wine making, as many California students are aware. By telling the story of her parents' trip to Napa, this student demonstrates an awareness of the culture that enjoys wine with dinner. She

465 believes that everyone will drink when they get older. She is also able to distinguish use (enjoy a glass of wine with dinner) from abuse (it's OK if you have a little but not get drunk), and she is outspoken in her desire to hear both sides of the story from those who deliver substance use prevention

470 education. More significant, she says clearly that what she has heard in school is not true.

    The excerpts presented above are representative of 38 of 40 interviews. In each case, the student uses his or her own personal experience or a significant other's experience with

475 a substance to make a connection with the information he or she has received in school. It is apparent from the above excerpts that the students use narrative to not only link their personal experience to what they have learned in school but also to contrast it.

480   Close examination of the three excerpts above reveals that in each case, what students learned in their substance abuse prevention education is not consistent with other life experiences. In the elementary school excerpt, two students present stories. The first story is about an uncle who is

485 harmed by using alcohol and an uncle who is not. The second student describes the different reactions of his mother and father to the use of alcohol. These students are aware that different people have different reactions to the use of alcohol. The D.A.R.E. officer has not given them this infor-

490 mation; they have constructed it from their observations of people in their lives. In the middle school story, the student contrasts her parents' enjoyment of wine with the no-use message she has heard at school. The distinction is not present in the education she receives, and she is clearly aware

495 of the difference, labeling the prevention message "untrue." In the high school excerpt, the student contrasts his own experience of using marijuana with the two different ideas he has heard about the use of the substance. He has been taught that "if you use substances you will get addicted."

500 Others in his experience have told him it "will make you feel better." His personal experimentation has not confirmed either of the two predictions. Bruner's (1990) assertion that stories are stimulated by the mismatch of an event and the "canonical" would certainly seem to be operating here.

505   All of the preceding leads to a more developed version of the process assertion. Through the narrative form, students in our study relate the experiences they have in their personal lives to the information they receive at school. By linking and contrasting the two experiences, they construct their

510 own understanding of the effect of using drugs, alcohol, and tobacco.

Outcomes

    How do students perceive the effects of substance use prevention programs? In the next section, we will make more explicit the contrasts between prevention education

515 and the students' constructed understandings. When students contrast their experiences with what they are taught, a common theme emerges. The theme corresponds to the outcome question guiding this evaluation. Students perceive the effects of prevention education as having little influence on

520 their decision making. We have presented evidence throughout the article to support the assertion that students construct their own understandings of the effects of the use of substances. When students' understandings are different enough from the message they receive in DATE, the credibility of

525 the information they receive and in some cases the students' trust in those who offer the information may be called into question. The following example illustrates a student's blatant distrust of the information he has received.

Student Constructed Understandings

530 R: No, I don't believe that stuff about one cigarette! No! My mom smokes to calm her, my mom is a really hyper person and she smokes to calm her nerves. She's allowed to do it, she works, she pays her bills, so she's allowed to do it! (0005, ST.M 507, p. 23)

535 The middle school student is certain about his mother's right to smoke when she wants to calm her nerves. He appreciates the fact that she is a responsible adult and can make her own decisions.

Students at all three school levels are able to distinguish use from abuse. The following representative excerpts at

540 each of the three school levels constitute evidence that students distinguish between use and abuse. The stories students told distinguishing use from abuse often included their personal experiences. Although elementary students are legally prohibited from drinking, it must be acknowledged that

545 many of the elementary students have tried alcohol in one form or another under various conditions.

Distinction of Use and Abuse

R: But if you drink like too much alcohol at one time, too fast, it happened to me once, it was an occasion and I had a little shot of wine and I was thirsty and I drank it all at once be-

550 cause I was really thirsty and five minutes later I was sort of snoring.

I: [laughs] Right, right.

R: I'm in the seat going [makes snoring noises].

I: So you were out, huh?

555 R: Yes. I'm not going to do that again. (0072, ST.EH 533, p. 8)

Students at the elementary level are aware that drinking "too much" "too fast" is abuse. The story illustrates the power of personal experience to teach and reinforce lessons that adults would like students to learn. The middle school

560 students in the following excerpt use story to support their conclusion that not everyone who tries alcohol or drugs "has a problem."

R: I have a friend in high school and she used to do alcohol and she quit. She used to do drugs, but she quit. It's very easy to

565 quit! If you put your mind to it.

R: Some people it's easy for, some people it ain't.

I: So, you don't think that everybody that tries it has a problem?

R: Right. No. (0005, ST.MH 508, p. 8)

570 Stories told throughout the data illuminate students' understanding of what constitutes a "problem" or "abuse" of a substance. "Being able to stop" is one way students identify who does and who does not have a problem. In the next excerpt, a story of a person who "can't stop" offers an ex-

575 ample of what the high school student sees as the road to alcoholism.

R: My friend's girl has 3 or 4 beers and she'll get real buzzed and she has to keep drinking more and more! She can't just enjoy it, she has to get loaded. She can't stop! I can just

580 walk away from it anytime, or drink several and have a buzz and be alright. And I see her, I don't like people who drink to get drunk! You know, just to drink?

R: Yeah!

R: People like that are turning into alcoholics! You can see it

585 coming! (0185, ST.SH 545, p. 14)

The stories selected to support the notion that students distinguish between use and abuse are, again, typical of those found in the majority of interviews. The importance of this assertion is understood in the context of the clear mes-

590 sage presented to the students at all grade levels that use of substances equals abuse. Students typically understand that all use of alcohol is not abuse, and they clearly identify what is abuse. The disparity between what they are taught and what they present as story demonstrates that the no-use mes-

595 sage is not being "taken up" (Bruner, 1990, p. 63).

From the excerpt presented above, an extension of the disparity between what is taught in school and what is understood by students is uncovered. Many students not only differentiate use from abuse, they believe that a person has

600 to want to stop abusing substances for counseling or sanctions to have an effect. The idea that it is easy to quit for some people and more difficult for others is linked to a story about a high school friend who was successful when she "put her mind to it." This story illuminates an important is-

605 sue for students at all grade levels but most notably at the high school level when young people are most likely to start using substances. Students believe that it is up to the person to want to stop. Neither counseling nor sanctions levied against students who are caught using have much preventive

610 influence.

R: Um, no. I don't think that counseling can really, it can help you, but I don't think it's gonna change your mind. You have to be willing to change your mind! To not to do it, or to not want to do it. If you go to counseling and they tell you

615 it's all bad, but you still think it's good, then you're gonna do it! (0005, ST.SH, p.12)

This extension of the assertion will also be discussed.

Inconsistent Message of Home and School

If what is taught in school is not being accepted by students, is it because what they learn in school is different

620 from what their parents say and do? As in several of the prior story examples, dissonance occurs when students witness their parents' use of substances. They are forced to deny what they learn in school, "I don't believe them…" or

make a judgment about their parents, "she had a right to smoke…" The following elementary excerpt is presented in order to make explicit the lack of consistency between what parents are telling their children and what the school is telling them.

I: OK, but what I'm asking you guys—this is a very personal question—what I'm asking you guys is how do you decide that a little bit is OK and a lot is too much? Did someone tell you that?

R: Yes.

I: Or did you just make up your mind on your own?

R: My dad when he was—I don't remember how old—he told me that he was with his friends at a party and they told him to try a beer and so he said OK and so he drank one and then drank another and he started getting sick and he threw up so since he's only drank like a half a beer or something so he doesn't get sick any more.

I: So did most of you get that idea—is he right and most of you got that idea from your parents?

R: Yes. [several voices] (0072, ST.E 532, p. 19)

The notion that students use narrative story to construct meaning of their diverse experiences with substance use and abuse is very powerful. When there is a mismatch between home and school, the student is forced to resolve the dissonance she or he experiences by making sense of the two worlds. In effect, the students are being asked to make choices between two authorities, both of whom lose credibility in the students' eyes in too many cases. Often, the dissonance results in undermining the students' trust in adults in general.

Undermining of Students' Trust in Adults

Analysis of the stories found in the high school data revealed a general outcome related to the lack of trust, but having even more serious consequences in the "high risk" population (Hawkins et al., 1987) the very student prevention programs were originally intended to help. The following excerpt is typical of students who see themselves outside the school community.

R: I mean they always do it like we're all bad people here.

R: I don't think the schools are for like helping it's just for getting the bad kids out and it's just…

R: Yeah.

R: Well, maybe if you could get them to care more then they would do that [a different respondent than the others above].

R: If they suspect you of smoking or having drugs on you or whatever, if they see a kid like that in their school then, instead of suspending them and getting them out of school, why don't they help them? (0072, ST.SH 531, p. 13)

These at-risk students, according to the "risk factor model" (Hawkins et al., 1987), are the most likely to become dropouts, drug addicts, homeless, or criminals. Yet, all too often these young people feel hopeless and disheartened and see no future for themselves in the school or society. Another excerpt gives further insight to the minimal effects of prevention education.

R: It's pretty sad if society puts you in a position where you can't be happy unless you use drugs. I mean if you got school and you got the wrong problem, not a drug user, but about the way society treats kids. (0072, ST.SH 531, p. 10)

These students believe the treatment (prevention education) is for the wrong problem. They see themselves as victims of social pressures, and they are concerned about the lack of care and support they receive from school personnel to cope with these perceived pressures.

If only the voices of at-risk students were raised urging those in authority to help, they would probably not be heard. However, they are not the only voices urging a change in the way students are treated when they have a problem. School personnel recognize the failure of the school system to help these students as well. "We still get rid of too many kids… those are the kids that the state of California and the United States of America have identified as their target population…. The kids that are at risk the most, are the kids that are exited from the system and they do not have access to the resources…. The kids that we need to help in and provide resources to are the kids that we exit from the system" (0027, GF 558, p. 18).

Given the previous data, we come to the final assertion generated in this study: The application of sanctions (detention, suspension, and expulsion) provokes further alienation and disconnection of those students who already see themselves on the periphery of the school community.

The next section of the article will discuss the implications of the preceding assertions.

Discussion

Returning to the first of the two questions that guided this evaluation, it is apparent from the evidence supporting the assertions that the students of both groups, at all three levels of school, use narrative story to display their understandings of substance use and abuse. The ubiquity of this form of discourse in the student data adequately supports the proposition that story provides a way of sorting out our thoughts about the world. The student stories also support Bruner's (1990) idea that narrative mediates between the canonical world of culture and the idiosyncratic world of beliefs, desires, and hopes. If stories are the medium by which human beings construct meaning, we argue that the student stories found in the interviews are a key to understanding how students are making sense of the programs they receive. Unsolicited stories were woven throughout all but two of the interviews. Curiously, these two interviews were conducted by the same interviewer whose style of interaction with the students included interrupting them while they were speaking and making references to time during the interview. This interview style undoubtedly contributed to the lack of stories. Excerpts from the interviews have adequately shown how the students, stimulated by the conversation, voluntarily share the stories they associate with the stimulus. This primary assertion supports Polkinghorne's (1988) notion that "experience is constructed when a person assimilates the stimuli and matches them with his or her existing structural representations of events which are judged to be similar to the input given" (p. 108). During the interviews, questions were asked that stimulated the mental representations of similar events (stories) that, in the student's mind, matched the stimuli.

In analyzing the data, we did not view the stories of students uncritically. The DATE evaluation used multiple methods to assess program effectiveness, and narrative story was one of them. Narrative stories were not anticipated in our data collection process. It was the overwhelming number of stories that the students told that focused our attention on the value of narrative. Our primary concern is not the factual basis of these stories. As we have shown, whereas many stories may represent facts, others represent misconceptions or partial truths regarding substances like alcohol. We see, through students' stories, as in the construction of understanding of other types of knowledge, the logic the student uses to make sense of the world. The importance of narrative as an evaluation tool is twofold. It features the voices of the target population at the center of the evaluation of programs, and it helps evaluators gain insight to the construction of meaning students are making. In this study, when students told their stories, we gained insight to what they have learned and how they make sense of prevention education. Viewing these findings critically, we feel reassured by the triangulation of other results from different data sources in the DATE evaluation (Brown, D'Emidio-Caston, & Pollard, 1997; Brown & D'Emidio-Caston, 1995).

Regarding the outcomes of prevention education and what we now understand as the mismatch between prevention education and personal experience, we can begin to sort out the effects. In some cases, the stories told were simple accounts of someone's use of a substance. In other cases, they are elaborate, well-formed stories that illustrate the students' confusion, disequilibrium, or dissatisfaction with the lack of consistency between their personal experience and what the school authorities tell them. Students' ability to distinguish between the use and abuse of substances is an indicator of such lack of consistency. The narrative evidence revealed how the students interpret and connect what they learn in school with what they experience out of school in the popular culture and home environment. When a student's home life includes drinking wine with dinner, for example, or one parent's capacity to drink and another not, there is a problem with telling that student that all drinking is unhealthy or bad. They must resolve their disequilibrium, and often do, at the expense of not believing the information or the person who delivers the inconsistent message. When that person is a teacher or a police officer in the D.A.R.E. program, the unfortunate result is a loss of credibility in those who represent social authority.

For many students, particularly those who are active, thriving members of the school community, the loss of credible authority in the form of teachers and police officers is not alienating. These students see themselves as members of the school community. They perceive that the reason behind the inconsistent message is good will and "caring" for their well-being. The unfortunate antithesis of this is true for those who are already on the periphery of the school community. For the students who have "low commitment for school," the loss of credible adult authority pushes them further toward the periphery.

Clearly, the hard line policies called for by the DATE application are successful in reducing the number of students with drug-related problems in the schools. Equally as clear is the unfortunate way this outcome is enacted. The schools do not seem to have the capacity to help or heal. They have only the capacity to punish and expel. Those students who perceive themselves as "bad" have no incentive whatever to comply with the no-use policies (Napier & Gershenfeld, 1993). For them, detention, suspension, and expulsion confirm their perceived non-member status. These implications undermine the position that a risk orientation is a valuable tool to change patterns of substance use or abuse in young people. We argue here that it would seem appropriate and propitious to change the assumptions guiding the substances use prevention programs in California public schools.

Others, too, have urged a different approach. Benard (1993) and Brown and Horowitz (1993) have clearly stated a different orientation to working with students who see themselves as alienated from the school community. Benard urges schools to become places characterized by caring, participation, and high expectations for all students. Her argument is that when students feel connected to the school community, they feel cared for, and they have better resiliency and healthy responses to challenges. Brown and Horowitz urge a "harm-reduction" model that reduces the actual damage a person might experience from secondary causes related to use of substances. Designated driver programs are one example of a harm-reduction strategy.

What do students say? It is fitting to end this article with some final excerpts from students who have a great deal more knowledge than we often credit them. When asked what the goal of a drug education program should be, this high school student replied:

> To know what your limitations are, to make yourself aware enough so that you know—personally, I've never felt very worried that I would ever become a substance abuser. When I was like elementary school it was crammed down my throat, Just Say No, it's the most awful thing in the world, and so when it first came, like in ninth grade, I remember this girl was trying to get me to do pot I'm like, "No, that's evil." It was that kind of a thing, but I think the goal of education should be you're going to be in the situation, you're going to see this, that and the other thing, it's not evil if you've got a good enough sense of self-worth, if you know what your boundaries are, if you know what you feel comfortable with and if you know what it's going to do to you and you know what the consequences may be. (0072, ST.S 530 p. 15)

Her recommendation that students need to have a good sense of self-worth and know what their boundaries are resounds the wisdom of the adults cited above. If the school creates a climate where all students experience success and a sense of accomplishment, they will be more resilient when faced with the givens of conflicting authorities or economic hardship. Another student had this recommendation:

I just want to say that I guess the best education would be the education that would allow you to evaluate yourself and allow you to evaluate your own personal beliefs and your morals and your values and take a strong look at what you're feeling and if you might have the possibility to be a substance abuser. (0072, ST.S 530, p. 31)

The figure attached to the DATE Program during the years of this evaluation in the state of California is estimated at more than $1.5 billion. Public accountability for this large an expenditure is appropriate. Our research has shown that risk-oriented policies and programs like D.A.R.E., Red Ribbon Week, and anti-drug assemblies are highly implemented. Their primary program components are some form of scare tactics, offering a reward in exchange for not using substances and enhancing self-esteem through refusal skills. Policies widely in place are intended to enforce the social and legal consequences of substance use (Brown et al., 1997; Brown & D'Emidio-Caston, 1995). The stories presented in this article are representative of hundreds of stories the students in the DATE evaluation told. It is clear that they do not believe what they are being told and instead construct their own version of the consequences of substance use. The DATE evidence stands with other evidence in suggesting a high level of program implementation and low level of effectiveness (Klitzner, 1987; Moskowitz, 1989; Tobler, 1992; Ennett et al., 1994). We have presented an argument here that demonstrates that prevention programs designed with the risk orientation have a potentially more insidious effect, that of reinforcing the perception of alienated young people that adult authorities are not credible or caring. We suggest we listen to their voices as they tell us we are treating the wrong problem. In examining and observing programs and program records, performing interviews, doing surveys, and performing meta-analyses of other study results, we are left with few alternative explanations in our inability to show positive program effects.

The War on Drugs has had many casualties. Our results indicate that students who demonstrate the need for the most support may be unintended victims of that war; not from the use of substances themselves but from the process of substance use prevention education and the policies in place in school districts, which exclude them. Those students who are thriving, although they may experiment, have good reason for not abusing substances. They see themselves in the future, and they have legitimate, school-sanctioned support networks. Those who abuse substances are often those with little vision of themselves in the future. Without a legitimate, sanctioned support system, they may seek in gangs the affiliation and recognition society has withheld. Without condoning the use of substances by young people, a more authentic and realistic orientation to working with students who have problems must be found. Emphasis on resiliency and harm reduction are two possibilities. With each day, as our jails take up more and more of the available resources, an ever greater need is apparent. For prevention programs to be effective, they must support those most at risk to be able to see a future when they close their eyes and dream.

References

Benard, B. (1993). *Turning the corner risk to resiliency*. San Francisco: Western Regional Center.

Blue-Swadner, B., & Lubeck, S. (1995). *Children and families at promise: Reconstructing the discourse of risk*. New York: SUNY Press.

Brown, J. H., & D'Emidio-Caston, M. (1995). On becoming at risk through drug education: How symbolic policies and their practices affect students. *Evaluation Review, 19* (4), 451–492.

Brown, J. H., D'Emidio-Caston, M., Goldsworthy-Hanner, T., & Alioto, M. (1993). *Technical report of 1992 qualitative findings for the drug, alcohol, and tobacco education program evaluation*. Los Alamitos, CA: South West Regional Laboratory.

Brown, J. H., D'Emidio-Caston, M., Kaufman, K., Goldsworthy-Hanner, T., & Alioto, M. (1995). *In their own voices: Students and educators evaluate school based drug, alcohol, and tobacco education programs*. Prepared for the California Department of Education by Pacific Institute for Research and Evaluation.

Brown, J. H., D'Emidio-Caston, M., & Pollard, J. A. (1997). Students and substances: Social power in drug education. *Educational Evaluation and Policy Analysis, 19* (1), 65–82.

Brown, J. H., & Horowitz, J. E. (1993). Deviance and deviants: Why adolescent substance use prevention programs do not work. *Evaluation Review, 17* (5), 529–555.

Bruner, J. (1990). *Acts of meaning*. Cambridge, MA: Harvard University Press.

Chomsky, N. (1966). *Cartesian linguistics: A chapter in the history of rationalist thought*. New York: Harper and Row.

Connelly, F. M., & Clandinin, D. J. (1990). Stories of experience and narrative inquiry. *Educational Researcher, 19* (5), 2–14.

Donabedian, A. (1980). *Explorations in quality assessment and monitoring: Vol. 1. The definition of quality and approaches to its assessment*. Ann Arbor, MI: Health Administration Press.

Ennett, S. T., Tobler, N.S., Ringwalt, C. L., & Flewelling, R. L. (1994). How effective is drug abuse resistance education? A meta-analysis of project D.A.R.E. outcome evaluations. *American Journal of Public Health, 84* (9), 1394–1401.

Goetz, J. P., & LeCompte, M. (1984). *Ethnography and qualitative design in educational research*. Orlando, FL: Academic Press.

Hawkins, J. D., Kuagbwen, J. M., Jenson, J. M., & Catalano, R. F. (1987). Delinquents and drugs: What the evidence suggests about prevention and treatment programming. In B. S. Brown & A. R. Mills (Eds.), *Youth at high risk for substance abuse* (DHHS Publication No. ADM 87-1537; reprinted 1990 as ADM 90-1537), (pp. 81–131). Washington, DC: U.S. Government Printing Office.

Kemper, S. (1984). The development of narrative skills: Explanations and entertainments. In S. A. Kuczaj (Ed.) *Discourse development: Progress in cognitive development research* (pp. 99–124). New York: Springer-Verlag.

Klitzner, M. D. (1987). *Part 2: An assessment of the research on school-based prevention programs*. Report to Congress and the White House on the nature and effectiveness of federal, state, and local drug prevention/education programs. Washington, DC: U.S. Department of Education.

Manning, P. K., & Cullum-Swan, B. (1994). Narrative, content, and semiotic analysis. In N. K. Denzin & Y. S. Lincoln (Eds.), *Handbook of qualitative research*. Newbury Park, CA: Sage.

Mitchell, W. J. T. (Ed.) (1980). *On narrative*. Chicago: University of Chicago Press.

Moskowitz, J. M. (1989). The primary prevention of alcohol problems: A critical review of the research literature. *Journal of Studies on Alcohol, 50*, 54–88.

Napier, R. W., & Gershenfeld, M. K. (1993). *Groups theory and practice*. Boston: Houghton Mifflin.

Patton, M. Q. (1990). *Qualitative evaluation and research methods* (2d ed). Newbury Park, CA: Sage.

Polkinghorne, D. E. (1988). *Narrative knowing and the human services*. New York: State University of New York Press.

Poplin, M., & Weeres, J. (1992). *Voices from the inside: A report on school from inside the classroom*. Claremont, CA: The Institute for Education in Transformation at The Claremont Graduate School.

Romero, F., Bailey, J., Carr, C., Flaherty, J., Fleming, T., Gaynor, J. R., Houle, D., Karam, R., Lark, M., Martino, T., & Thomas, C. (1994). *1992–93 California programs to prevent and reduce drug, alcohol, and tobacco use among in-school youth: Annual evaluation report*. Prepared for the California Department of Education by Southwest Regional Laboratory. Los Alamitos, NM: The Southwest Regional Laboratory.

Romero, F., Carr, C., Pollard, J., Houle, D., Brown, J., Gaynor, J. R., Fleming, T., Flaherty, J., Martino, T., & Karam, R. (1993). *Drug, alcohol, and tobacco education evaluation: Second year interim evaluation report*. Prepared for the California Department of Education by Southwest Regional Library. Los Alamitos, NM: The Southwest Regional Laboratory.

Rosen, H. (1985). The importance of story. *Language Arts, 63* (3), 226–237.

Sarason, S. B. (1982). *The culture of the school and the problem of change* (2d ed). Boston: Allyn & Bacon.

Schubert, W. H., & Ayers, W. C. (Eds.). (1992). *Teacher lore, learning from our own experience*. New York: Longman.

Stein, N. L., & Policastro, M. (1984). The concept of story: A comparison between children's and teacher's viewpoints. In H. Mandl, N. L. Stein, & T. Trabasso (Eds.), *Learning and comprehension of text* (pp. 113–155). Hillsdale, NJ: Lawrence Erlbaum.

Strauss, A., & Corbin, J. (1990). *Basics for qualitative research: Grounded theory procedures and techniques*. Newbury Park, CA: Sage.

Tobler, N. S. (1992). Drug prevention programs can work: Research findings. *Journal of Addictive Diseases, 11* (3), 1–26.

Witherell, C., & Noddings, N. (Eds.) (1991). *Stories lives tell.* New York: Teachers College Press.

About the Authors: Marianne D'Emidio-Caston is presently the coordinator of the Elementary Teacher Education Program and Lecturer in the Graduate School of Education, University of California at Santa Barbara. She has more than 20 years of field experience as a teacher and administrator and has published articles on the development of practical theory in beginning teachers and the use of the affective domain to enhance teaching and learning. Joel H. Brown is an educational consultant. Currently, he directs the Center for Educational Research and Development (CERD), a Berkeley-based educational evaluation, research, and policy development organization focusing on the development and well-being of youth. Among many other studies, he was the principal investigator of the nationally recognized research entitled "In Their Own Voices: Students and Educators Evaluate California School-Based Drug, Alcohol, and Tobacco Education (DATE) Programs." His areas of expertise, all within social welfare, public health, and psychological contexts, include the study of adolescent development, organizational change, school evaluation program/policy development, and the integration of qualitative with quantitative research methods.

Authors' Note: This research was supported by the California State Department of Education, Contract No. 3279. It was originally presented at the Annual Meeting of the American Educational Research Association (AERA), April 1995. The views expressed herein are those of the authors and do not necessarily represent those of the California State Department of Education.

Exercise for Article 29

Factual Questions

1. The acronym "DATE" stands for what words?

2. Did the evaluations of the program by Romero et al. and by Brown et al. provide consistent findings?

3. What was the specific "outcome" question for this evaluation?

4. When selecting school districts for this evaluation, the evaluators sought a balance in terms of which school district characteristics?

5. How many students participated in the interviews?

6. When reporting on the interviews, the evaluators use the letter "R" before many of the quotations. For what does this letter stand?

7. In the 40 group interviews, how many stories were told by the students?

8. Unsolicited stories were woven throughout how many of the group interviews?

9. Did the evaluators anticipate that they would hear narrative stories during data collection?

Questions for Discussion

10. At two points in their report, the evaluators discuss the costs of the program. In your opinion, should costs be an important consideration in a program evaluation? Why? Why not?

11. In the introduction to their article, the evaluators argue that there are serious problems with risk-oriented programs. In your opinion, is it appropriate for evaluators to state their own beliefs and orientations in an introduction? Would it be better to let the results speak for themselves? Explain.

12. Within each school, the evaluators had the principal or other delegated authority choose students who were at-risk and students who were thriving. Do you think it was a good idea to have principals do this? If no, how would you have selected the students?

13. The evaluators state that they used "semistructured, open-ended questions." What is your understanding of the meaning of this phrase? Would you have used questions of this type if you were conducting the evaluation? Explain.

14. The evaluators state that they chose excerpts (i.e., quotations) that "are the most articulate exemplars." Do you think that this was a good decision? Would you be interested in seeing excerpts from less articulate students? Explain.

15. The evaluators reported their results in terms of themes and trends with quotations from the students as supporting evidence. An evaluator with a quantitative orientation would be more likely to report statistics such as "such and such a percentage of the students reported that…" Which type of reporting is more convincing to you? Are they both equally valid? Explain.

16. Do you agree with the assertion that the validity or factual truthfulness of the stories is not relevant (that is, the stories provide valid insights even if they are not true)? Explain.

17. Are you willing to generalize the results of this study to all public school students in California? Explain.

18. The researchers mention that the stories were unsolicited. Is this important? Would it also be interesting to conduct an evaluation in which students were solicited to tell stories about alcohol, drugs, and tobacco? Explain.

19. Based on this evaluation, do you think it is advisable for California to continue funding DATE? Would you

want more information before making a decision? If yes, what types of information would you like to have?

20. Do you think that the last paragraph of the article provides a strong "close" to the article? Do you think that the statements in this paragraph are supported by the results of this evaluation? Explain.

Quality Ratings

Directions: Indicate your level of agreement with each of the following statements by circling a number from 5 for strongly agree (SA) to 1 for strongly disagree (SD). If you believe an item is not applicable to this research article, leave it blank. Be prepared to explain your ratings.

A. The introduction establishes the importance of the study.

    SA   5   4   3   2   1   SD

B. The literature review establishes the context for the study.

    SA   5   4   3   2   1   SD

C. The research purpose, question, or hypothesis is clearly stated.

    SA   5   4   3   2   1   SD

D. The method of sampling is sound.

    SA   5   4   3   2   1   SD

E. Relevant demographics (for example, age, gender, and ethnicity) are described.

    SA   5   4   3   2   1   SD

F. Measurement procedures are adequate.

    SA   5   4   3   2   1   SD

G. All procedures have been described in sufficient detail to permit a replication of the study.

    SA   5   4   3   2   1   SD

H. The participants have been adequately protected from potential harm.

    SA   5   4   3   2   1   SD

I. The results are clearly described.

    SA   5   4   3   2   1   SD

J. The discussion/conclusion is appropriate.

    SA   5   4   3   2   1   SD

K. Despite any flaws, the report is worthy of publication.

    SA   5   4   3   2   1   SD

Article 30

The "Stay Alive From Education" (SAFE) Program: Description and Preliminary Pilot Testing*

TAMARA TUCKER WILKINS
Minnesota State University

ABSTRACT. Traffic accidents are the leading cause of death among young people in the United States. Nearly half of these accidents involve the consumption of alcohol and/or drugs, and seat belts are not worn in over 85% of all motor vehicle accidents. SAFE is a one-hour behavior modification program that informs students of the dangers associated with driving under the influence of drugs and/or alcohol and not wearing seat belts. Pretests and posttests were offered to 60 students to determine preliminary efficacy of the program. Quantitative data and open-ended comments seem to suggest that students may change their driving behaviors due to the influence of this presentation.

From *Journal of Alcohol and Drug Education*, *45*, 1–11. Copyright © 2002 by American Alcohol and Drug Information Foundation. Reprinted with permission.

Introduction

According to the National Highway Traffic Safety Administration (1996), traffic accidents are the leading cause of death among young people in the United States. Approximately 15 youths between the ages of 16 and 20 die every
5 day from injuries incurred during a traffic crash. This rate is twice that of the general population. A vehicular accident claims the life of one teenager every 90 minutes. Nearly half these wrecks involve the consumption of alcohol and/or drugs. Seat belts are not worn in 85% to 90% of all motor
10 vehicle accidents (National Highway Traffic Safety Administration, 1996).

Figures for Florida, the location of the current study, are even more disturbing. Florida ranks third in the nation in terms of traffic fatalities. One out of every 15 teenage driv-
15 ers has a traffic accident every year, and teenage drivers are more likely to die in wrecks than any other age group. Almost two-thirds of the 2,806 traffic fatalities in 1996 involved occupants not wearing seat belts. Alcohol is a factor in one out of every three traffic fatalities (Florida Depart-
20 ment of Highway Safety and Motor Vehicles, 1997). While teenage drivers between the ages of 15 and 17 constitute 2.2% of the state's motor vehicle operators, they appear in 5% of all vehicle crashes and represent 4% of the driver fatalities.

25 The budgetary outlays associated with the medical care of trauma victims are staggering. The average cost for dispatching paramedics and their equipment to an accident scene exceeds the $1,700 mark. The typical traffic fatality commands a price tag that hovers around $425,000 (U.S.
30 Department of Transportation, 1996). Because these numbers are likely to continue their upward spiral, policy makers have a keen interest in promoting intervention programs aimed at reducing this highway carnage.

The "Stay Alive From Education" (SAFE) program was
35 initiated by two paramedics from the Metro Dade (Miami) Fire Rescue in 1990 and was first presented in South Florida area high schools. Response was favorable, and some observers mentioned they would like to see the program take place throughout the state. As a result, various chapters of
40 SAFE were formed throughout Florida. A "chapter" is simply a location where local emergency medical service personnel have been trained and certified to present SAFE. The Tallahassee Chapter is the first unit to include the local police department. Traffic homicide investigators and certified
45 paramedics present a one-hour program to high school students about the dangers of driving under the influence of alcohol or drugs, not wearing seat belts, and the trauma associated with these dangers. The purpose of this manuscript is to describe the SAFE program, its goals, and report pre-
50 liminary results from a pilot testing of high school students.

The SAFE program presentation consists of three phases. Introductions start the first phase. Presenters quickly move into a casual, informal discussion of the goals of the program, definitions of traumatic injury and death, and what
55 constitutes a medical versus trauma call. Graphic photographs of traffic victims who are roughly the same age as those in the audience are passed around while various props are being set up for later use. Descriptive accounts of "what happened" in various photos are offered. Students learn that
60 seat belts were not worn, that alcohol and/or other drugs were involved in all the accidents depicted, and that all of the victims they just saw in the photos died as a result of their injuries.

The second phase is essentially a demonstration of phys-
65 ics. By placing an egg in a jar and shaking it, the laws of physics are obvious when the jar is abruptly stopped. The egg is broken, and students appear to realize that the same thing often happens to a person's brain during a traffic crash. The presenter asks for a show of hands of those who don't

---

* For more information on the SAFE program, contact Vince Easevoili (305-852-2651) or Ralph Jimenez (305-375-9543).

use their seat belt all the time, no matter where they sit in the vehicle, and the reasons why. Some common responses are, "I don't think about it," "I'm too lazy," "I'm going somewhere close by—right around the corner," "Seat belts are uncomfortable," "It wrinkles my clothes," "I have air bags and an automatic seat belt," or "I'm in the back seat!" The SAFE presenter, upon hearing the excuse of being in the back seat, says, "See this picture? See these two guys in the back seat? They weren't wearing their seat belts. The two in the front were. The two in the back became the objects in motion, like the egg in the jar, until the movement was stopped by the heads of the two people in the front seat. When the rescue team arrived at the scene, all four were dead from massive head injuries. They found the teeth of the guys in the back seat embedded in the back of the heads of the guys in the front seat."

The third phase involves the recruitment of a student volunteer who will play the part of an injured "crash victim." Paramedics demonstrate and decipher the medical consequences associated with driving while under the influence of alcohol and/or drugs. They inform students that all intoxicated persons are likely not to receive pain relievers due to the high risks associated with combining drugs and/or alcohol with pain relievers and anesthesia. Likewise, they graphically depict what happens when a car accident victim does not wear a seat belt. This role playing is done in a realistic fashion by strapping a student volunteer to a backboard. Students see their fellow classmate role play a crash victim who is strapped down and perforated with various tubes for blood and medication disbursement. The hope, of course, is that students will empathetically relate the experience of trauma to their own lives. Because hands-on techniques are employed rather than lectures, students gain insight of what paramedics and traffic homicide officers encounter when they respond to a traumatic traffic accident. Paramedics show students how trauma victims are treated in the field on a step-by-step basis, and traffic homicide officers share their experiences of telling family members about the death of their loved ones.

The primary goal of SAFE is to change, modify, or "recondition" the behavior of students who participate in irresponsible driving behaviors so they become more responsible drivers and riders. Behavior modification involves at least four stages. The four stages include identifying the target behavior(s), gathering baseline data, developing techniques of punishment and reinforcement, and execution and evaluation (Weiten, 1994; Watson & Tharp, 1989).

The target behaviors entail wearing a seat belt and driving "drug/alcohol" free. Paramedics and traffic homicide officers offer statistics and graphic details from their personal experiences to paint a picture of real-life tragedies that stem from irresponsible driving. The "egg in the jar" demonstrates the consequences or punishments of irresponsible driving behaviors. Furthermore, the discomfort experienced by the student volunteer who is strapped to a wooden backboard for approximately 15 minutes amplifies the message. While paramedics assure the volunteer and the audience that

these feelings are minor, had a real accident occurred, the pain would be intense and last significantly longer. The final stage involves encouraging observers to adopt safe driving habits. The targeted goals are to convince students to wear seat belts, require those who ride with them to wear seat belts, and refuse to drive or ride with someone who is under the influence of alcohol and/or drugs.

The tactics employed by SAFE place it within the genre of a "shock" program. It is similar to "Scared Straight," where juveniles are shocked into the realities associated with incarceration. At the conclusion of the "Scared Straight" program, teens who took part in this Juvenile Awareness Project recall their experiences of the program, the time with prisoners, and the prison location or scene. Deemed successful by audiences, "Scared Straight" was made into an Oscar-winning TV documentary and filmed at Rahway State Prison in New Jersey. Reasons for the program's success were perceived to be the growing crime problem (i.e., at the time), a reduction in support for rehabilitation, and a "dramatic promise of a new, synthetic solution for delinquency" (Heeren & Shichor, 1984).

While there is little conclusive evidence that shock incarceration programs have a positive effect on offender behavior over time, analyses of these programs suggest that intense supervision efforts via "shock" programs play a critical role in limiting some irresponsible behaviors (MacKenzie & Brame, 1995). Several community-based intervention programs are similar in the implementation of strong "shock" techniques. Antipregnancy programs attempt to show the realities of being a full-time parent, and some AIDS prevention programs use similar "shock" format approaches. In an evaluative study of AIDS prevention programs, Ostrow (1989) offers four determinants of behavioral change as crucial elements of effective education. He claims "effective education" to be the behavior-changing mechanism of choice. Determinants of behavioral change include: (1) general factual knowledge of the problem, (2) perceived susceptibility or risk, (3) perceived severity, and (4) perceived benefits and costs. These programs share a similar feature with the SAFE project. Each presentation is very dramatic, and presenters seek to jolt kids (and others) into a picture of reality where enormous adverse consequences derive from irresponsible behavior.

Other preventive literature centers around the need to get entire communities involved in traffic safety education programs. Designated driver programs are one such effort. These community-based programs are intended to offer intoxicated persons an alternative to getting behind the wheel and driving. A designated driver is one person in a group of two or more drinkers who agrees not to drink alcoholic beverages and to transport the members of the group home safely. Many communities who participate in this type of program offer safe travel in the form of a free or subsidized taxicab ride if a designated driver is not available (National Highway Traffic Safety Administration, 1994). Other educational program efforts include Maryland's "Kids in Safety Seats" Program, which targets child passenger safety; Cali-

Table 1
Self-Report Participant Scores Prior to and One Month After Exposure to the SAFE Presentation

$n = 60$ Statement		Always	Most of the time	Sometimes	Never	Mean	sd	t
How often do you...								
wear your seat belt while riding in	Pretest	32	21	6	1	1.60	0.74	5.56**
the front seat?	Posttest	52	8	–	–	1.13	0.34	
wear your seat belt while riding in	Pretest	7	24	16	13	2.58	0.96	3.77**
the back seat?	Posttest	28	21	10	1	1.87	1.52	
ride in a car where the driver wears	Pretest	23	27	9	1	1.80	0.75	2.66**
a seat belt?	Posttest	31	25	4	–	1.55	0.62	
ride in a car where all passengers	Pretest	5	19	29	7	2.63	0.80	3.36*
wear seat belts?	Posttest	10	29	19	2	2.22	0.76	
ride in a car where driver has used	Pretest	1	1	28	30	3.45	0.62	– 4.46**
alcohol or drugs?	Posttest	–	1	8	51	3.83	0.42	
see other students driving in an	Pretest	11	10	38	1	2.48	0.81	5.71**
unsafe manner?	Posttest	18	27	15	–	1.95	0.75	

* Denotes significance at .01 level of analysis, two-tailed.
** Denotes significance at .001 level of analysis, two-tailed.

fornia's Contra Costa County Prevention Program, which
advocates helmet usage by motorcyclists and bicyclists, and
Rhode Island's Community Traffic Safety Program, which
focuses on issues related to pedestrian safety (National
Highway Traffic Safety Administration, 1993).

The founders of SAFE have good intentions of rousing
community support and participation. In some cities, presentations of SAFE have been offered to the general public.
While some individuals and groups take advantage of this
opportunity, SAFE presenters are mainly concerned with the
program's effectiveness on young, more risk-taking attendees. The program has not yet received any independent
empirical attention to determine whether it is effective. The
evaluation model employed in this research project is often
referred to as an "outcome model" (Adams, 1975). An outcome model seeks to ascertain how effective or efficient an
agency or program is in attaining goals. Determining the
impact of SAFE on *stated* attitudinal and participant *reported* behavioral changes is the primary goal of this descriptive and evaluative research project.

Procedure

Several local high school classes participated in the
SAFE program during the spring of 1998. Quantitative data
and open-ended questionnaires were obtained using self-administered surveys. The data set for this study is made up
of two participating classes, for a total of 60 students. Regular attendees of two high school classes were selected based
upon convenience to the SAFE presenters. It was not necessary to gain parental consent in order to distribute questionnaires to students. The information was collected both before
the program presentation and 30 days later. This pretest/posttest design is a common tool in evaluating intervention strategies.

Upon arrival for the program, students completed a pretest or pre-program survey. Demographics were asked in an
attempt to ascertain identifiable characteristics. That is, participants' date of birth, sex, and race/ethnicity were asked in
order to match the anonymous questionnaires. One month

after the SAFE program was presented, the same participants
were offered a post-program survey. The follow-up questionnaire was designed exactly like the pre-program questionnaire with one exception: Students were asked whether
they thought the SAFE program should be repeated for new
students and the reasons behind their feelings. Sixty pre-program surveys were matched by demographic information
with post-program surveys and serve as the study group.

Results

The study group participants were 52% male ($n = 31$)
and 48% female ($n = 29$). Concerning race and/or ethnicity,
60% stated they were white, 37% marked black, and 3%
chose Hispanic. As of April 1, 1998, all participants were of
legal driving age in Florida. One person was 18 years of age,
18 students were 17 years old, and 41 were 16 years old.

Table 1 presents the results of a paired-samples t test,
which compares the means for responses offered in the pretest and the posttest. Average scores concerning how often
students claim to wear a seat belt while riding in the front
seat drop from the original mean score of 1.60 to 1.13 during
the posttest period. Because wearing a seat belt while riding
in the front seat is required by state law, many students
probably already engage in such behavior on a regular basis.
For those who profess to use a seat belt less often, it appears
that statistically significant changes were indicated. In other
words, a month later, SAFE participants reported a higher
level of seat-belt usage while riding in the front seat. Students specify they are more likely to use a seat belt while in
the back seat as well ($t = 3.77$, $p = .01$). Thus, it would appear that the SAFE program satisfied its desired goal of altering stated seat belt use.

While students have little or no control over what another driver does concerning the use of safety belts, there is
a significant difference between the first and second time-frames under evaluation ($t = 2.66$, $p = .01$). It may be that
the SAFE presentation made students more adept at noticing
when a driver was or was not wearing a seat belt. Two students even offered comments to the fact that they will now

say something or put pressure on their friends and family members to "always" fasten their seat belts.

260   The fourth question under evaluation deals with the frequency of riding in a motor vehicle when all passengers are wearing seat belts. The difference from Phase I to Phase II was also statistically significant. This finding may also reflect the assumption that persons of this age group have little or no control over what others do, but at least they may ask others to buckle up.

Perhaps the most risky of driving behaviors involves the driver's use of alcohol and/or drugs. Both before and after the SAFE presentation, students know driving under the influence of alcohol and/or drugs is dangerous. Statistically significant differences were found from Time 1 to Time 2. Prior to the SAFE presentation, 30 students said that they would sometimes (or more frequently) ride with a driver they knew was intoxicated, and 30 students said they would "never" ride with an intoxicated driver. After the presentation, 51 of the 60 students under evaluation declared they would "never" ride with a driver who had been drinking alcohol and/or using drugs. Subjects were also asked how often they see other students driving in an unsafe manner. Statistically significant differences are detected, with more students seeing unsafe driving occurring more frequently ($t = 5.71$, $p = .01$). While not entirely conclusive, it is quite possible that the differences may be due to an increased level of awareness by participants as dramatically stressed by the SAFE program presenters.

Students were asked if the SAFE program should be repeated next year for new students and why. Of the 60 responses, all but one student said the program should be made available. Once again, the written comments about the SAFE presentation were overwhelmingly positive:

"Yes, definitely! It gives us a huge reality check of what could happen when [driving and] using drugs/alcohol and not wearing a seat belt."

"The SAFE program reviewed a lot of things I already knew, but it taught me a lot of new things too."

"It opened my eyes to what can really happen when you get into a wreck."

"The students who come here next year need to learn this stuff the same as us. It helps."

"Those pictures scared us. They made us think. Others need to learn to think too."

"It changed my views about driving in an unsafe manner."

"If I wouldn't have seen those pictures, a seat belt would never cross my mind."

"It put that lasting thought about not wearing seat belts in my mind."

Finally, it is important to mention that neither sex nor racial background played a role in how the program was perceived, as indicated by an analysis of variance (i.e., ANOVA) or test comparison of Phase I to Phase II. In other words, no systematic differences or effects were found to be statistically relevant based on the demographic characteristics of participants. This may be evidence the program generates a fairly uniform picture for all students regardless of social category.

Limitations of the Study

There are, at minimum, four major limitations to the present study. First, this study only describes the SAFE program and reports on stated behavioral changes. Any actual changes in driving behavior cannot be calculated. This preliminary study was undertaken to simply describe the program and to ask students if they thought the program was effective. It was not in the scope of this project to physically observe any behavioral changes.

Second, there was no control group involved. Students who participated in the SAFE presentation were not compared to students who were absent, dropped out of high school, or who did not attend a SAFE demonstration. This makes the significance of any outcome measure dubious and uncertain.

Third, only short-term self-reported effects are included in the evaluation. Whether or not any long-term effects or lasting impacts result in behavioral changes simply cannot be determined. In order to conclude any long-term or ultimate effects, the same sample of students would have to complete another questionnaire at some point in the future. Because high school drivers serve as the primary SAFE presentation population, it is unlikely a follow-up, long-term study will be tackled. Locating the same participating subjects after an extended period of time (e.g., after graduation) would require both time and money.

Fourth, the sample was selected out of convenience to those collecting the data and is relatively small in number ($n = 60$). Thus, any conclusions drawn from this study may be exaggerated and empirically limited. In a future study, a systematic sampling frame should be developed and sample size increased. These two steps would help increase inference or the ability to generalize results to an overall population.

Discussion

The purpose of this study was to describe and evaluate the "Scared Straight" driving behavior-modification program known as SAFE. The evidence shows that this program does change or modify responses regarding irresponsible driving in the short-term. However, it is not known whether it generates any behavior or long-term educational effects. Knowing that the program has short-term benefits, school and police administrators may want to manipulate student behavior by presenting SAFE just prior to those "special occasions" that are marked by high traffic fatality rates. For example, some thought might go into conducting a SAFE campaign one week prior to homecoming, the senior prom, graduation, or another event that has the potential to be marred by traffic accidents and their aftermath. Additionally, a "booster" presentation may be helpful as one might anticipate the program would experience a decaying effect with the passage of time. Until a longitudinal design is implemented, it is difficult to say just what degree of decay exists.

High school students are the primary targets of the current SAFE project. However, college students, and even the public at large, may be appropriate participants in the SAFE program should funding for such be available. If the changes are as dramatic as the high school student participants openly state, the current figures may indicate a potentially downward trend in the rate of traffic fatalities. If increased awareness occurs and responsible driving behaviors replace irresponsible ones, for whatever length of time, the result may be health instead of harm and/or life rather than death.

Last, the demand for evaluative research has surged in recent years. Because of budgetary constraints and limitations, studying the process and effectiveness of particular programs is necessary (Williamson, Karp, Dalphin, & Gray, 1992). Economic costs are involved in programs like this one, but these costs are incomparable to that of the human suffering and loss of life, which, all too often, accompany irresponsible driving behaviors. While limited by the time period under evaluation, this research project indicates the SAFE program is well received by participants and is a potentially relevant and beneficial behavior modification program.

References

Adams, S. (1975). *Evaluative research in corrections: A practical guide.* Washington, D.C.: U.S. Department of Justice.

Florida Department of Highway Safety and Motor Vehicles. (1997). *Publication of annual statistics.* Tallahassee, FL: State of Florida.

Heeren, J., & Shichor, D. (1984). Mass media and delinquency prevention: The case of Scared Straight. *Deviant Behavior, 5*(1–4), 375–386.

MacKenzie, D., & Brame, R. (1995). Shock incarceration and positive adjustment during community supervision. *Journal of Quantitative Criminology, 11*(2), 111–142.

National Highway Traffic Safety Administration. (1996). *Annual publication.* Washington, D.C.: Government Printing Office.

National Highway Traffic Safety Administration. (1994). *A guide to developing a community-based designated driver program.* Washington, D.C.: Government Printing Office.

National Highway Traffic Safety Administration. (1993). *Commitment, communication, cooperation: Traffic safety and public health working together to prevent traffic injury.* Washington, D.C.: Government Printing Office.

Ostrow, D. G. (1989). AIDS prevention through effective education (Living with AIDS: Part II). *Daedalus, 118*(3): 229.

United States Department of Transportation. (1996). *Annual report.* Washington, D.C.: Government Printing Office.

Watson, D., & Tharp, R. (1989). *Self-directed behavior: Self-modification for personal adjustment.* Pacific Grove, CA: Brooks and Cole Publishing Co.

Weiten, W. (1994). *Psychology: Themes and variations* (2nd ed.). Pacific Grove, CA.

Williamson, J., Karp, D., Dalphin, J., & Gray, P. (1992). *The research craft: An introduction to social research methods.* Glenview, IL: Scott, Foresman and Company.

Address correspondence to: Tamara Tucker Wilkins, 109 Morris Hall—Dept. of Law Enforcement, Minnesota State University, Mankato, MN 56001-8400. Phone: (507) 389-1118 or 389-2721. E-mail: tamara.willkins@mankato.msus.edu

Exercise for Article 30

Factual Questions

1. In Florida, teenage drivers between the ages of 15 and 17 constitute 2.2% of the state's motor vehicle operators. They appear in what percentage of all vehicle crashes?

2. In "Scared Straight," juveniles are shocked into the realities associated with what?

3. On the pretest, how many students reported always wearing seat belts while riding in the back seat? How many students reported always doing this on the post-test?

4. Was the difference between the two means for riding in a car where the driver has used alcohol or drugs statistically significant? If yes, at what probability level was it significant?

5. In response to the question regarding whether the SAFE program should be repeated next year for new students, how many answered in the affirmative?

6. The researcher discusses four limitations of this evaluation. What is the third limitation?

Questions for Discussion

7. In your opinion, are the three phases of the program described in sufficient detail? Explain. (See lines 51–108.)

8. To calculate the means in Table 1, a score of 1 was assigned to "Always," a score of 2 to "Most of the time," a score of 3 to "Sometimes," and a score of 4 to "Never." Hence, for wearing your seat belt while riding in the front seat, the *decrease* in the mean from 1.60 to 1.13 indicates a change of behavior in the desired direction (i.e., more students wearing seat belts). Would you have scored the questions in this way? If not, would you have given a score of 4 to "Always," a score of 3 to "Most of the time," and so on? Explain.

9. The Results section includes both quantitative and qualitative information. (See lines 287–307 for qualitative results.) In your opinion, are both types of information equally important? If not, which do you think is more important? Explain.

10. The researcher notes that this evaluation is limited because it reports on only "stated behavioral changes." In other words, it depends on self-reports. In your opinion, is this an important limitation? Explain. (See lines 317–319.)

11. The researcher notes that there was no control group. In your opinion, is this an important limitation? Explain. (See lines 325–330.)

12. If you were a member of a school board, would you be inclined to vote to fund the SAFE program based on the information in this study? Would you request that

the program be evaluated again (if it were funded in your school district)? Explain. (See lines 379–385.)

Quality Ratings

Directions: Indicate your level of agreement with each of the following statements by circling a number from 5 for strongly agree (SA) to 1 for strongly disagree (SD). If you believe an item is not applicable to this research article, leave it blank. Be prepared to explain your ratings.

A. The introduction establishes the importance of the study.

      SA   5   4   3   2   1   SD

B. The literature review establishes the context for the study.

      SA   5   4   3   2   1   SD

C. The research purpose, question, or hypothesis is clearly stated.

      SA   5   4   3   2   1   SD

D. The method of sampling is sound.

      SA   5   4   3   2   1   SD

E. Relevant demographics (for example, age, gender, and ethnicity) are described.

      SA   5   4   3   2   1   SD

F. Measurement procedures are adequate.

      SA   5   4   3   2   1   SD

G. All procedures have been described in sufficient detail to permit a replication of the study.

      SA   5   4   3   2   1   SD

H. The participants have been adequately protected from potential harm.

      SA   5   4   3   2   1   SD

I. The results are clearly described.

      SA   5   4   3   2   1   SD

J. The discussion/conclusion is appropriate.

      SA   5   4   3   2   1   SD

K. Despite any flaws, the report is worthy of publication.

      SA   5   4   3   2   1   SD

Appendix A

Criteria for the Evaluation of Educational Research

Suggested Scale:

5—Excellent (A model of good practice.)
4—Good (A few minor defects.)
3—Mediocre (Not good, not bad.)
2—Poor (Some serious defects.)
1—Completely incompetent (A horrible example.)

Title

1. Title is well related to content of article.

Problem

2. Problem is clearly stated.

3. Hypotheses are clearly stated.

4. Problem is significant.

5. Assumptions are clearly stated.

6. Limitations of the study are stated.

7. Important terms are defined.

Review of Literature

8. Coverage of the literature is adequate.

9. Review of literature is well organized.

10. Studies are examined critically.

11. Source of important findings is noted.

12. Relationship of the problem to previous research is made clear.

Procedures

13. Research design is described fully.

14. Research design is appropriate to solution of the problem.

15. Research design is free of specific weaknesses.

16. Population and sample are described.

17. Method of sampling is appropriate.

18. Data-gathering methods or procedures are described.

19. Data-gathering methods or procedures are appropriate to the solution of the problem.

20. Data-gathering methods or procedures are used correctly.

21. Validity and reliability of data-gathering procedures are established.

Data Analysis

22. Appropriate methods are selected to analyze data.

23. Methods used in analyzing the data are applied correctly.

24. Results of the analysis are presented clearly.

25. Tables and figures are effectively used.

Summary and Conclusions

26. Conclusions are clearly stated.

27. Conclusions are substantiated by the evidence presented.

28. Conclusions are relevant to the problem.

29. Conclusions are significant.

30. Generalizations are confined to the population from which the sample was drawn.

Form and Style

31. Report is clearly written.

32. Report is logically organized.

33. Tone of the report displays an unbiased, impartial, scientific attitude.

Appendix B

Examining the Validity Structure of
Qualitative Research

R. BURKE JOHNSON
University of South Alabama

ABSTRACT. Three types of validity in qualitative research are discussed. First, descriptive validity refers to the factual accuracy of the account as reported by the qualitative researcher. Second, interpretive validity is obtained to the degree that the participants' viewpoints, thoughts, intentions, and experiences are accurately understood and reported by the qualitative researcher. Third, theoretical validity is obtained to the degree that a theory or theoretical explanation developed from a research study fits the data and is, therefore, credible and defensible. The two types of validity that are typical of quantitative research, internal and external validity, are also discussed for qualitative research. Twelve strategies used to promote research validity in qualitative research are discussed.

From *Education, 118,* 282–292. Copyright © 1997 by Project Innovation. Reprinted with permission of the publisher and author.

Discussions of the term "validity" have traditionally been attached to the quantitative research tradition. Not surprisingly, reactions by qualitative researchers have been mixed regarding whether or not this concept should be applied to qualitative research. At the extreme, some qualitative researchers have suggested that the traditional quantitative criteria of reliability and validity are not relevant to qualitative research (e.g., Smith, 1984). Smith contends that the basic epistemological and ontological assumptions of quantitative and qualitative research are incompatible, and, therefore, the concepts of reliability and validity should be abandoned. Most qualitative researchers, however, probably hold a more moderate viewpoint. Most qualitative researchers argue that some qualitative research studies are better than others, and they frequently use the term validity to refer to this difference. When qualitative researchers speak of research validity, they are usually referring to qualitative research that is plausible, credible, trustworthy, and, therefore, defensible. We believe it is important to think about the issue of validity in qualitative research and to examine some strategies that have been developed to maximize validity (Kirk & Miller, 1986; LeCompte & Preissle, 1993; Lincoln & Guba, 1985; Maxwell, 1996). A list of these strategies is provided in Table 1.

One potential threat to validity that researchers must be careful to watch out for is called *researcher bias.* This problem is summed up in a statement a colleague of mine once made to me. She said, "The problem with qualitative research is that the researchers find what they want to find, and then they write up their results." It is true that the problem of researcher bias is frequently an issue because qualitative research is open-ended and less structured than quantitative research. This is because qualitative research tends to be exploratory. (One would be remiss, however, to think that researcher bias is never a problem in quantitative research!) Researcher bias tends to result from selective observation and selective recording of information, and also from allowing one's personal views and perspectives to affect how data are interpreted and how the research is conducted.

The key strategy used to understand researcher bias is called *reflexivity,* which means that the researcher actively engages in critical self-reflection about his or her potential biases and predispositions (Table 1). Through reflexivity, researchers become more self-aware, and they monitor and attempt to control their biases. Many qualitative researchers include a distinct section in their research proposals titled Researcher Bias. In this section, they discuss their personal background, how it may affect their research, and what strategies they will use to address the potential problem. Another strategy that qualitative researchers use to reduce the effect of researcher bias is called *negative case sampling* (Table 1). This means that they attempt carefully and purposively to search for examples that disconfirm their expectations and explanations about what they are studying. If you use this approach, you will find it more difficult to ignore important information, and you will come up with more credible and defensible results.

We will now examine some types of validity that are important in qualitative research. We will start with three types of validity that are especially relevant to qualitative research (Maxwell, 1992, 1996). These types are called descriptive validity, interpretive validity, and theoretical validity. They are important to qualitative research because description of what is observed and interpretation of participants' thoughts are two primary qualitative research activities. For example, ethnography produces descriptions and accounts of the lives and experiences of groups of people with a focus on cultural characteristics (Fetterman, 1998; LeCompte & Preissle, 1993). Ethnographers also attempt to understand groups of people from the insider's perspective (i.e., from the viewpoints of the people in the group; called the *emic* perspective). Developing a theoretical explanation of the behavior of group members is also of interest to qualitative researchers,

Table 1
Strategies Used to Promote Qualitative Research Validity

Strategy	Description
Researcher as "detective"	A metaphor characterizing the qualitative researcher as he or she searches for evidence about causes and effects. The researcher develops an understanding of the data through careful consideration of potential causes and effects and by systematically eliminating "rival" explanations or hypotheses until the final "case" is made "beyond a reasonable doubt." The "detective" can utilize any of the strategies listed here.
Extended fieldwork	When possible, qualitative researchers should collect data in the field over an extended period of time.
Low inference descriptors	The use of description phrased very close to the participants' accounts and researchers' field notes. Verbatims (i.e., direct quotations) are a commonly used type of low inference descriptors.
Triangulation	"Cross-checking" information and conclusions through the use of multiple procedures or sources. When the different procedures or sources are in agreement, you have "corroboration."
Data triangulation	The use of multiple data sources to help understand a phenomenon.
Methods triangulation	The use of multiple research methods to study a phenomenon.
Investigator triangulation	The use of multiple investigators (i.e., multiple researchers) in collecting and interpreting the data.
Theory triangulation	The use of multiple theories and perspectives to help interpret and explain the data.
Participant feedback	The feedback and discussion of the researcher's interpretations and conclusions with the actual participants and other members of the participant community for verification and insight.
Peer review	Discussion of the researcher's interpretations and conclusions with other people. This includes discussion with a "disinterested peer" (e.g., with another researcher not directly involved). This peer should be skeptical and play the "devil's advocate," challenging the researcher to provide solid evidence for any interpretations or conclusions. Discussion with peers who are familiar with the research can also help provide useful challenges and insights.
Negative case sampling	Locating and examining cases that disconfirm the researcher's expectations and tentative explanation.
Reflexivity	This involves self-awareness and "critical self-reflection" by the researcher on his or her potential biases and predispositions as these may affect the research process and conclusions.
Pattern matching	Predicting a series of results that form a "pattern" and then determining the degree to which the actual results fit the predicted pattern.

especially qualitative researchers using the grounded theory
75　perspective (Glaser & Strauss, 1967; Strauss and Corbin, 1990). After discussing these three forms of validity, the traditional types of validity used in quantitative research, internal and external validity, are discussed. Internal validity is relevant when qualitative researchers explore cause and
80　effect relationships. External validity is relevant when qualitative researchers generalize beyond their research studies.

Descriptive Validity

The first type of validity in qualitative research is called *descriptive validity*. Descriptive validity refers to the factual accuracy of the account as reported by the researchers. The
85　key questions addressed in descriptive validity are: Did what was reported as taking place in the group being studied actually happen? and Did the researchers accurately report what they saw and heard? In other words, descriptive validity refers to accuracy in reporting descriptive information (e.g.,
90　description of events, objects, behaviors, people, settings, times, and places). This form of validity is important because description is a major objective in nearly all qualitative research.

One effective strategy used to obtain descriptive validity
95　is called *investigator triangulation*. In the case of descriptive validity, investigator triangulation involves the use of multiple observers to record and describe the research participants' behavior and the context in which they were located. The use of multiple observers allows cross-checking of ob-

100　servations to make sure the investigators agree about what took place. When corroboration (i.e., agreement) of observations across multiple investigators is obtained, it is less likely that outside reviewers of the research will question whether something occurred. As a result, the research will be
105　more credible and defensible.

Interpretive Validity

While descriptive validity refers to accuracy in reporting the facts, interpretive validity requires developing a window into the minds of the people being studied. *Interpretive validity* refers to accurately portraying the *meaning* attached by
110　participants to what is being studied by the researcher. More specifically, it refers to the degree to which the research participants' viewpoints, thoughts, feelings, intentions, and experiences are accurately understood by the qualitative researcher and portrayed in the research report. An important
115　part of qualitative research is understanding research participants' inner worlds (i.e., their phenomenological worlds), and interpretive validity refers to the degree of accuracy in presenting these inner worlds. Accurate interpretive validity requires that the researcher get inside the heads of the par-
120　ticipants, look through the participants' eyes, and see and feel what they see and feel. In this way, the qualitative researcher can understand things from the participants' perspectives and provide a valid account of these perspectives.

Some strategies for achieving interpretive validity are provided in Table 1. *Participant feedback* is perhaps the most important strategy (Table 1). This strategy has also been called "member checking" (Lincoln & Guba, 1985). By sharing your interpretations of participants' viewpoints with the participants and other members of the group, you may clear up areas of miscommunication. Do the people being studied agree with what you have said about them? While this strategy is not perfect, because some participants may attempt to put on a good face, useful information is frequently obtained and inaccuracies are often identified.

When writing the research report, using many low inference descriptors is also helpful so that the reader can experience the participants' actual language, dialect, and personal meanings (Table 1). A verbatim is the lowest inference descriptor of all because the participants' exact words are provided in direct quotations. Here is an example of a verbatim from a high school dropout who was part of an ethnographic study of high school dropouts:

> I wouldn't do the work. I didn't like the teacher and I didn't like my mom and dad. So, even if I did my work, I wouldn't turn it in. I completed it. I just didn't want to turn it in. I was angry with my mom and dad because they were talking about moving out of state at the time (Okey & Cusick, 1995: p. 257).

This verbatim provides some description (i.e., what the participant did) but it also provides some information about the participant's interpretations and personal meanings (which is the topic of interpretive validity). The participant expresses his frustration and anger toward his parents and teacher, and shares with us what homework meant to him at the time and why he acted as he did. By reading verbatims like this one, readers of a report can experience for themselves the participants' perspectives. Again, getting into the minds of research participants is a common goal in qualitative research, and Maxwell calls our accuracy in portraying this inner content interpretive validity.

Theoretical Validity

The third type of validity in qualitative research is called *theoretical validity*. You have theoretical validity to the degree that a theoretical explanation developed from a research study fits the data and, therefore, is credible and defensible. Theory usually refers to discussions of *how* a phenomenon operates and *why* it operates as it does. Theory is usually more abstract and less concrete than description and interpretation. Theory development moves beyond just the facts and provides an explanation of the phenomenon. In the words of Joseph Maxwell (1992):

> ...one could label the student's throwing of the eraser as an act of resistance, and connect this act to the repressive behavior or values of the teacher, the social structure of the school, and class relationships in U.S. society. The identification of the throwing as resistance constitutes the application of a theoretical construct...the connection of this to other aspects of the participants, the school, or the community constitutes the postulation of theoretical relationships among these constructs (p. 291).

In the above example, the theoretical construct called "resistance" is used to explain the student's behavior. Maxwell points out that the construct of resistance may also be related to other theoretical constructs or variables. In fact, theories are often developed by relating theoretical constructs.

A strategy for promoting theoretical validity is *extended fieldwork* (Table 1). This means that you should spend a sufficient amount of time studying your research participants and their setting so that you can have confidence that the patterns of relationships you believe are operating are stable and so that you can understand why these relationships occur. As you spend more time in the field collecting data and generating and testing your inductive hypotheses, your theoretical explanation may become more detailed and intricate. You may also decide to use the strategy called *theory triangulation* (Table 1; Denzin, 1989). This means that you would examine how the phenomenon being studied would be explained by different theories. The various theories might provide you with insights and help you develop a more cogent explanation. In a related way, you might also use investigator triangulation and consider the ideas and explanations generated by additional researchers studying the research participants.

As you develop your theoretical explanation, you should make some predictions based on the theory and test the accuracy of those predictions. When doing this, you can use the *pattern matching* strategy (Table 1). In pattern matching, the strategy is to make several predictions at once; then, if all of the predictions occur as predicted (i.e., if the pattern is found), you have evidence supporting your explanation. As you develop your theoretical explanation, you should also use the negative case sampling strategy mentioned earlier (Table 1). That is, you must always search for cases or examples that do not fit your explanation so that you do not simply find the data that support your developing theory. As a general rule, your final explanation should accurately reflect the majority of the people in your research study. Another useful strategy for promoting theoretical validity is called *peer review* (Table 1). This means that you should try to spend some time discussing your explanation with your colleagues so that they can search for problems with it. Each problem must then be resolved. In some cases, you will find that you will need to go back to the field and collect additional data. Finally, when developing a theoretical explanation, you must also think about the issues of internal validity and external validity to which we now turn.

Internal Validity

Internal validity is the fourth type of validity in qualitative research of interest to us. Internal validity refers to the degree to which a researcher is justified in concluding that an observed relationship is causal (Cook & Campbell, 1979). Often, qualitative researchers are not interested in cause and effect relationships. Sometimes, however, qualitative researchers are interested in identifying potential causes and effects. In fact, qualitative research can be very helpful in describing how phenomena operate (i.e., studying process) and in developing and testing preliminary causal hypotheses and theories (Campbell, 1979; Johnson, 1994; LeCompte & Preissle, 1993; Strauss, 1995; 1994).

When qualitative researchers identify potential cause and effect relationships, they must think about many of the same issues that quantitative researchers must consider. They should also think about the strategies used for obtaining theoretical validity discussed earlier. The qualitative researcher takes on the role of the detective searching for the true cause(s) of a phenomenon, examining each possible clue, and attempting to rule out each rival explanation generated (see *researcher as "detective"* in Table 1). When trying to identify a causal relationship, the researcher makes mental comparisons. The comparison might be to a hypothetical control group. Although a control group is rarely used in qualitative research, the researcher can think about what would have happened if the causal factor had not occurred. The researcher can sometimes rely on his or her expert opinion, as well as published research studies when available, in deciding what would have happened. Furthermore, if the event is something that occurs again, the researcher can determine if the causal factor precedes the outcome. In other words, when the causal factor occurs again, does the effect follow?

When a researcher believes that an observed relationship is causal, he or she must also attempt to make sure that the observed change in the dependent variable is due to the independent variable and not to something else (e.g., a confounding extraneous variable). The successful researcher will always make a list of rival explanations or rival hypotheses, which are possible or plausible reasons for the relationship other than the originally suspected cause. Be creative and think of as many rival explanations as you can. One way to get started is to be a skeptic and think of reasons why the relationship should not be causal. Each rival explanation must be examined after the list has been developed. Sometimes you will be able to check a rival explanation with the data you have already collected through additional data analysis. At other times you will need to collect additional data. One strategy would be to observe the relationship you believe to be causal under conditions where the confounding variable is not present and compare this outcome with the original outcome. For example, if you concluded that a teacher effectively maintained classroom discipline on a given day but a critic maintained that it was the result of a parent visiting the classroom on that day, then you should try to observe the teacher again when the parent is not present. If the teacher is still successful, you have some evidence that the original finding was not because of the presence of the parent in the classroom.

All of the strategies shown in Table 1 are used to improve the internal validity of qualitative research. Now we will explain the only two strategies not yet discussed (i.e., methods triangulation and data triangulation). When using *methods triangulation*, the researcher uses more than one method of research in a single research study. The word methods should be used broadly here, and it refers to different methods of research (e.g., ethnography, survey, experimental, etc.) as well as to different types of data collection procedures (e.g., interviews, questionnaires, and observations). You can intermix any of these (e.g., ethnography and survey research methods, or interviews and observations, or experimental research and interviews). The logic is to combine different methods that have "nonoverlapping weaknesses and strengths" (Brewer & Hunter, 1989). The weaknesses (and strengths) of one method will tend to be different from those of a different method, which means that when you combine two or more methods you will have better evidence! In other words, the "whole" is better than its "parts."

Here is an example of methods triangulation: Perhaps you are interested in why students in an elementary classroom stigmatize a certain student named Brian. A stigmatized student would be an individual that is not well liked, has a lower status, and is seen as different from the normal students. Perhaps Brian has a different haircut from the other students, is dressed differently, or doesn't act like the other students. In this case, you might decide to observe how students treat Brian in various situations. In addition to observing the students, you will probably decide to interview Brian and the other students to understand their beliefs and feelings about Brian. A strength of observational data is that you can actually see the students' behaviors. A weakness of interviews is that what the students say and what they actually do may be different. However, using interviews you can delve into the students' thinking and reasoning, whereas you cannot do this using observational data. Therefore, the whole will likely be better than the parts.

When using *data triangulation*, the researcher uses multiple data sources in a single research study. "Data sources" does not mean using different methods. Data triangulation refers to the use of multiple data sources using a single method. For example, the use of multiple interviews would provide multiple data sources while using a single method (i.e., the interview method). Likewise, the use of multiple observations would be another example of data triangulation; multiple data sources would be provided while using a single method (i.e., the observational method). Another important part of data triangulation involves collecting data at different times, at different places, and with different people.

Here is an example of data triangulation: Perhaps a researcher is interested in studying why certain students are apathetic. It would make sense to get the perspectives of several different kinds of people. The researcher might interview teachers, interview students identified by the teachers as being apathetic, and interview peers of apathetic students. Then the researcher could check to see if the information obtained from these different data sources was in agreement. Each data source may provide additional reasons as well as a different perspective on the question of student apathy, resulting in a more complete understanding of the phenomenon. The researcher should also interview apathetic students at different class periods during the day and in different types of classes (e.g., math and social studies). Through the rich information gathered (e.g., from different people, at different times, and at different places), the researcher can develop a better understanding of why students are apathetic than if only one data source is used.

External Validity

External validity is important when you want to generalize from a set of research findings to other people, settings, and times (Cook & Campbell, 1979). Typically, generalizability is not the major purpose of qualitative research. There are at least two reasons for this. First, the people and settings examined in qualitative research are rarely randomly selected, and, as you know, random selection is the best way to generalize from a sample to a population. As a result, qualitative research is virtually always weak in the form of population validity focused on "generalizing to populations" (i.e., generalizing from a sample to a population).

Second, some qualitative researchers are more interested in documenting particularistic findings than universalistic findings. In other words, in certain forms of qualitative research the goal is to show what is unique about a certain group of people, or a certain event, rather than generate findings that are broadly applicable. At a fundamental level, many qualitative researchers do not believe in the presence of general laws or universal laws. General laws are things that apply to many people, and universal laws are things that apply to everyone. As a result, qualitative research is frequently considered weak on the "generalizing across populations" form of population validity (i.e., generalizing to different kinds of people), and on ecological validity (i.e., generalizing across settings) and temporal validity (i.e., generalizing across times).

Other experts argue that rough generalizations can be made from qualitative research. Perhaps the most reasonable stance toward the issue of generalizing is that we can generalize to other people, settings, and times to the degree that they are similar to the people, settings, and times in the original study. Stake (1990) uses the term *naturalistic generalization*[1] to refer to this process of generalizing based on similarity. The bottom line is this: The more similar the people and circumstances in a particular research study are to the ones that you want to generalize to, the more defensible your generalization will be and the more readily you should make such a generalization.

To help readers of a research report know when they can generalize, qualitative researchers should provide the following kinds of information: the number and kinds of people in the study, how they were selected to be in the study, contextual information, the nature of the researcher's relationship with the participants, information about any informants who provided information, the methods of data collection used, and the data analysis techniques used. This information is usually reported in the Methodology section of the final research report. Using the information included in a well-written methodology section, readers will be able to make informed decisions about to whom the results may be generalized. They will also have the information they will need if they decide to replicate the research study with new participants.

Some experts show another way to generalize from qualitative research (e.g., Yin, 1994). Qualitative researchers can sometimes use *replication logic,* just like the replication logic that is commonly used by experimental researchers when they generalize beyond the people in their studies, even when they do not have random samples. According to replication logic, the more times a research finding is shown to be true with different sets of people, the more confidence we can place in the finding and in the conclusion that the finding generalizes beyond the people in the original research study (Cook & Campbell, 1979). In other words, if the finding is replicated with different kinds of people and in different places, then the evidence may suggest that the finding applies very broadly. Yin's key point is that there is no reason why replication logic cannot be applied to certain kinds of qualitative research.[2]

Here is an example: Over the years you may observe a certain pattern of relations between boys and girls in your third-grade classroom. Now assume that you decided to conduct a qualitative research study and you find that the pattern of relation occurred in your classroom and in two other third-grade classrooms you studied. Because your research is interesting, you decide to publish it. Then other researchers replicate your study with other people and they find that the same relationship holds in the third-grade classrooms they studied. According to replication logic, the more times a theory or a research finding is replicated with other people, the greater the support for the theory or research finding. Now assume further that other researchers find that the relationship holds in classrooms at several other grade levels (e.g., first grade, second grade, fourth grade, and fifth grade). If this happens, the evidence suggests that the finding generalizes to students in other grade levels, adding additional generality to the finding.

We want to make one more comment before concluding. If generalizing through replication and theoretical validity (discussed above) sound similar, that is because they are. Basically, generalizing (i.e., external validity) is frequently part of theoretical validity. In other words, when researchers develop theoretical explanations, they often want to generalize beyond their original research study. Likewise, internal validity is also important for theoretical validity if cause and effect statements are made.

References

Brewer, J., & Hunter, A. (1989). *Multimethod research: A synthesis of styles.* Newbury Park, CA: Sage.

Campbell, D.T. (1979). Degrees of freedom and the case study. In T.D. Cook & C.S. Reichardt (Eds.), *Qualitative and quantitative methods in evaluation research* (pp. 49–67). Beverly Hills, CA: Sage Publications.

Campbell, D.T. (1986). Relabeling internal and external validity for applied social scientists. In W. Trochim (Ed.), Advances in quasi-experimental design and analysis: *New Directions for Program Evaluation,* 31, San Francisco: Jossey-Bass.

Cook, T.D., & Campbell, D.T. (1979). *Quasi-experimentation: Design and analysis*

---

[1] Donald Campbell (1986) makes a similar point, and he uses the term *proximal similarity* to refer to the degree of similarity between the people and circumstances in the original research study and the people and circumstances to which you wish to apply the findings. Using Campbell's term, your goal is to check for proximal similarity.

---

[2] The late Donald Campbell, perhaps the most important quantitative research methodologist over the past 50 years, approved of Yin's (1994) book. See, for example, his introduction to that book.

issues for field settings. Chicago: Rand McNally.

Denzin, N.K. (1989). *The research act: Theoretical introduction to sociological methods.* Englewood Cliffs, NJ: Prentice Hall.

Fetterman, D.M. (1998). Ethnography. In *Handbook of Applied Social Research Methods* by L. Bickman & D.J. Rog (Eds.). Thousand Oaks, CA: Sage.

Glaser, B.G., & Strauss, A.L. (1967). *The discovery of grounded theory: Strategies for qualitative research.* New York: Aldine de Gruyter.

Kirk, J., & Miller, M.L. (1986). *Reliability and validity in qualitative research.* Newbury Park, CA: Sage.

Johnson, R.B. (1994). Qualitative research in education. *SRATE Journal, 4*(1), 3–7.

LeCompte, M.D., & Preissle, J. (1993). *Ethnography and qualitative design in educational research.* San Diego, CA: Academic Press.

Lincoln, Y.S., & Guba, E.G. (1985). *Naturalistic inquiry.* Beverly Hills, CA: Sage.

Maxwell, J.A. (1992). Understanding and validity in qualitative research. *Harvard Educational Review, 62*(3), 279–299.

Maxwell, J.A. (1996). *Qualitative research design.* Newbury Park, CA: Sage.

Okey, T.N., & Cusick, P.A. (1995). Dropping out: Another side of the story. *Educational Administration Quarterly, 31*(2), 244–267.

Smith, J.K. (1984). The problem of criteria for judging interpretive inquiry. *Educational Evaluation and Policy Analysis, 6,* 379–391.

Smith, J.K. (1986). Closing down the conversation: The end of the quantitative-qualitative debate among educational inquirers. *Educational Researcher, 15,* 12–32.

Stake, R.E. (1990). Situational context as influence on evaluation design and use. *Studies in Educational Evaluation, 16,* 231–246.

Strauss, A. (1995). Notes on the nature and development of general theories. *Qualitative Inquiry 1*(1), 7–18.

Strauss, A., & Corbin, J. (1990). *Basics of qualitative research: Grounded theory procedures and techniques.* Newbury Park, CA: Sage.

Yin, R.K. (1994). *Case study research: Design and methods.* Newbury Park: Sage.

Notes

Notes